# THE ENGLISH CLERGY
## AND THEIR ORGANIZATION IN
## THE LATER MIDDLE AGES

# THE ENGLISH CLERGY
## AND THEIR ORGANIZATION IN THE LATER MIDDLE AGES

### THE FORD LECTURES
#### FOR 1933

BY

A. HAMILTON THOMPSON

OXFORD
AT THE CLARENDON PRESS

*Oxford University Press, Ely House, London W. 1*

GLASGOW NEW YORK TORONTO MELBOURNE WELLINGTON
CAPE TOWN SALISBURY IBADAN NAIROBI LUSAKA ADDIS ABABA
BOMBAY CALCUTTA MADRAS KARACHI LAHORE DACCA
KUALA LUMPUR HONG KONG

FIRST PUBLISHED 1947
REPRINTED LITHOGRAPHICALLY IN GREAT BRITAIN
AT THE UNIVERSITY PRESS, OXFORD
BY VIVIAN RIDLER
PRINTER TO THE UNIVERSITY
1966

# PREFACE

THE long delay in publication which has followed the delivery of these lectures has been due to a variety of work crowded into a busy life, and constantly interfering with the completion of the illustrative material collected in the notes and appendixes. The author's thanks are specially due to those who have for many years given him access to the records in their custody, and enabled him to make use of the documents published or quoted in these pages, and chiefly to the librarians of Lambeth Palace and the Dean and Chapter Library at Durham, and to the officials in charge of the diocesan registries at York, Lincoln, and other cathedral cities. Last, but not least, there is one who must be specially remembered:

CONIVGI DILECTISSIMAE

IN TERRAM VIVENTIVM INGRESSAE

V ID. AVG. A.D. MCMXLV

ISTAS DEDICAT PRAELECTIONES

GRATISSIMVS NVNQVAM IMMEMOR.

A. H. T.

7 BEAUFORT MANSIONS, S.W. 3
*February* 1946

# CONTENTS

# BIBLIOGRAPHY

IN this list are included only those books to which reference is made by abbreviated titles or simply by the author's or editor's surname in the footnotes to the text and in the appendixes. In other instances the titles of books and articles are given in full.

| | |
|---|---|
| *A.A.S.R.P.* | *Associated Architectural Societies' Reports and Papers.* |
| *A.J.* | *Archaeological Journal.* |
| Alcock, R. | Register of John Alcock, Bishop of Worcester, 1476–86. (MS.) |
| *Antiq. Warw.* | Dugdale, Sir W. *The Antiquities of Warwickshire illustrated*, 2nd ed., ed. Thomas, W. 2 vols., 1730. |
| *Arch.* | *Archaeologia* (Soc. Antiquaries, London). |
| Arundel, R. | Register of Thomas Arundel, Archbishop of Canterbury, 1396–1414. (MS.) |
| Assh., R. | Register of Richard Assheton and William Ramsey, Abbots of Peterborough, 1438–71 and 1471–96. (MS.) |
| | |
| *B. & G.A.S.* | *Transactions of the Bristol and Gloucestershire Archaeological Society.* |
| Bain., R. | Register of Christopher Bainbridge, Archbishop of York, 1508–14. (MS.) |
| Bath & Wells, Episcopal Registers, *see Bek., Bub., Drok.* | |
| *Beauchamp, R.* | *Register of Richard Beauchamp, Bishop of Hereford 1449–50*, ed. Bannister, A. T. (Cantelupe and Cant. & York Soc.) 1919. |
| Bek, R. | Register of Thomas Bek, Bishop of Lincoln, 1342–7. (Lincoln Epis. Reg. vi, MS.) |
| *Bek., R.* | *Register of Thomas Bekynton, Bishop of Bath and Wells 1443–65*, ed. Maxwell-Lyte, Sir H. C., and Dawes, M. C. B. (Somerset Record Soc.) 2 vols., 1934–5. |
| *Bev. Ch. A.* | *Memorials of Beverley Minster: the Chapter Act Book of the Collegiate Church of St. John of Beverley*, A.D. *1286–1347* (&c.), ed. Leach, A. F. (Surtees Soc.) 2 vols., 1898, 1903. |
| Blomefield, F., and Parkin. | *An Essay towards a Topographical History of the County of Norfolk.* 11 vols., 1805–10. |
| *Bothe, C., R.* | *Register of Charles Bothe, Bishop of Hereford 1516–35*, ed. Bannister, A. T. (Cantelupe and Cant. & York Soc.) 1921. |
| Bothe, W., R. | Register of William Bothe, Archbishop of York, 1452–64. (MS.) |

Boulers, R.  *Register of Reynold Boulers, Bishop of Hereford 1451–3,* ed. Bannister, A. T. (Cantelupe and Cant. & York Soc.) 1919.

Bowet, R.  Register of Henry Bowet, Archbishop of York, 1407–23. 2 vols. (MS.) *See also Surt. Misc.*

Bradshaw, H., and  *Statutes of Lincoln Cathedral.* 2 vols. in 3. Cambridge,
Wordsworth, Chr.  1892–7.

Brant., R.  *Register of Thomas Brantyngham, Bishop of Exeter 1370–94,* ed. Hingeston-Randolph, F. C. 1 vol. in 2, 1901–6.

Brian, R.  Register of Reynold Brian, Bishop of Worcester, 1352–61. 2 vols. (MS.)

Bridges.  *The History and Antiquities of Northamptonshire compiled from the MS. Collections of the late Learned Antiquary John Bridges, esq.,* by the Rev. Peter Whalley. 2 vols., 1791.

Brones., R.  *Register of Walter Bronescombe, Bishop of Exeter 1257–80,* &c., ed. Hingeston-Randolph, F. C., 1889.

Bub., R.  *Register of Nicholas Bubwith, Bishop of Bath and Wells 1407–24,* ed. Holmes, T. S. (Som. Record Soc.) 2 vols.

Buck., R.  Register of John Buckingham, Bishop of Lincoln, 1363–98. (Lincoln Epis. Reg. x–xii, MS.)

Burg., R.  Register of Henry Burghersh, Bishop of Lincoln, 1320–40. (Lincoln Epis. Reg. iv, v, MS.)

C.C.R.  *Calendar of Close Rolls.*
C.P.L.  *Calendar of Papal Registers: Papal Letters,* vols. i–xi.
C.P.P.  *Calendar of Papal Registers: Papal Petitions,* vol. i.
C.P.R.  *Calendar of Patent Rolls, 1232–1509,* 54 vols.

Canterbury, Archiepiscopal Registers (at Lambeth), *see* Arundel, *Chich.,* Court., Langham, Morton, *Peckham,* Warham.

Carp., R.  Register of John Carpenter, Bishop of Worcester, 1444–76. (MS.)

Charl., L., R.  *Register of Lewis Charlton, Bishop of Hereford 1361–70,* ed. Parry, J. H. (Cantelupe and Cant. & York Soc.) 1914.

Ched., R.  Register of John Chedworth, Bishop of Lincoln, 1452–74. (Lincoln Epis. Reg. xx, MS.)

Chich., R.  *Register of Henry Chichele, Archbishop of Canterbury 1414–43,* ed. Jacob, E. F. Vols. i–iii. Oxford, 1943–5.

Chichester Episcopal Registers: *see* Praty, Rede.

Chr. Ang.  *Chronicon Angliae 1328–88,* ed. Thompson, E. Maunde. ˎ(Rolls Ser.) 1874.

Chr. Lan.  *Chronicon de Lanercost 1201–1346,* ed. Stevenson, J. (Bannatyne Club) Edinburgh, 1839.

Churchill, Irene J.  *Canterbury Administration.* 2 vols., 1933.

Cobham, R.  *Register of Thomas Cobham, Bishop of Worcester 1317–27,* ed. Pearce, E. H. (Worces. Histor. Soc.) 1930.

| | |
|---|---|
| *Cor., R.* | *Register of Thomas Corbridge, Archbishop of York 1300–5,* ed. Brown, W., and Thompson, A. Hamilton. (Surtees Soc.) 2 vols., 1925, 1928. |
| *Corr. Bek.* | *Official Correspondence of Thomas Bekynton, secretary to Henry VI,* ed. Williams, G. (Rolls Ser.) 2 vols., 1872. |
| *Court., R. (Her.)* | *Register of William Courtenay, Bishop of Hereford 1370–5,* ed. Capes, W. W. (Cantelupe and Cant. & York Soc.) 1914. |
| Court., R. (Cant.) | Register of William Courtenay, Archbishop of Canterbury, 1381–96, 2 vols. (MS.) |

| | |
|---|---|
| *D.B.* | *Domesday Book.* (Record Comm.) 2 vols., 1783. |
| *D.U.J.* | *Durham University Journal.* |
| *D. & C. Wells.* | *Calendar of the MSS. of the Dean and Chapter of Wells.* (Hist. MSS. Comm.) 2 vols., 1907, 1914. |
| Dald., R. | Register of John Dalderby, Bishop of Lincoln 1300–20. (Lincoln Epis. Reg., iii, iv, MS.) |
| *Drok., R.* | *Calendar of the Register of John de Drokensford, Bishop of Bath and Wells 1309–29,* ed. Hobhouse (Som. Rec. Soc.) 1887. |
| Durham Episcopal Registers: *see* Fox, Hat., Langley. | |
| *Dur. Stat.* | *The Statutes of the Cathedral Church of Durham,* &c., ed. Thompson, A. Hamilton. (Surtees Soc.) 1929. |

| | |
|---|---|
| *E.H.R.* | *The English Historical Review.* |
| *E.Y.C.* | *Early Yorkshire Charters,* vols. i–iii, ed. Farrer, W.; index to vols. i–iii, and vols. iv–vi, ed. Clay, C. T., 1914–42. |
| *Eccl. Proc. Barnes.* | *The Injunctions and other Ecclesiastical Proceedings of Richard Barnes, Bishop of Durham from 1575 to 1587,* ed. Raine, J. (Surtees Soc.) 1850. |
| Ecton, John. | *Thesaurus rerum ecclesiasticarum,* 2nd ed. by Willis, Browne, 1754. |
| Exeter, Episcopal Registers: *see* Brant., Brones., Grand., *Lacy (Ex.)*, Oldham, *Stap.* | |
| *Extra.* | *Gregorii papae noni Decretalium libri v,* ap. *Corpus juris canonici,* ed. Richter and Friedberg, vol. ii. |
| *Extrav. comm.* | *Extravagantes communes,* ap. *Corpus juris canonici,* u.s. |
| Eyton, R. W. | *Antiquities of Shropshire.* 12 vols., 1854–60. |

| | |
|---|---|
| *Fast. Ebor.* | *Fasti Eboracenses: Lives of the Archbishops of York,* by Dixon, W. H., ed. Raine, J., jun. Vol. i, 1863. |
| *Fast. Paroch.* | *Fasti parochiales* (deanery of Doncaster), ed. Thompson, A. Hamilton, and Clay, C. T. (Yorks. Record Ser.) 2 vols., 1933–43. |
| Flem., R. | Register of Richard Flemyng, Bishop of Lincoln, 1420–31. (MS.) *See also Linc. Vis.* |
| *Fox. R.* | *Register of Richard Fox, Bishop of Durham 1494–1501,* ed. Howden, M. P. (Surtees Soc.) 1932. |

Gibson, Edmund.   *Codex juris ecclesiastici Anglicani*, 1713. 2nd ed. 2 vols. Oxford, 1761.

*Giff., G., R.*   *Register of Godfrey Giffard, Bishop of Worcester 1268–1301*, ed. Bund, J. W. Willis. (Worces. Histor. Soc.) 1902.

*Giff., W., R.*   *Register of Walter Giffard, Archbishop of York 1266–79*, ed. Brown, W. (Surtees Soc.) 1904.

Gigl., J., R.   Register of Giovanni de' Gigli, Bishop of Worcester, 1497–8. (MS.)

Gigl., S., R.   Register of Silvestro de' Gigli, Bishop of Worcester, 1498–1521. (MS.)

*Gilbert, R.*   *Register of John Gilbert, Bishop of Hereford 1375–89*, ed. Parry, J. H. (Cantelupe and Cant. & York Soc.) 1914.

*Grand., R.*   *Register of John Grandisson, Bishop of Exeter 1327–69.* 1 vol. in 3, 1894–9.

*Graves., R.*   *Register (Rolls) of Richard Gravesend, Bishop of Lincoln 1258–80*, ed. Davis, F. N., Foster, C. W., and Thompson, A. Hamilton. (Cant. & York Soc.) 1925.

*Gray, Walt., R.*   *Register (Rolls) of Walter Gray, Archbishop of York 1215–55*, ed. Raine, J. [jun.] (Surtees Soc.) 1870 [1872].

Gray, Will., R.   Register of William Gray, Bishop of Lincoln, 1431–6. (MS.) *See also Linc. Vis.*

*Green., R.*   *Register of William Greenfield, Archbishop of York 1306–15*, ed. Brown, W., and Thompson, A. Hamilton. (Surtees Soc.) 5 vols., 1931–8 [1940].

*Greg. VII, R.*   *Register of Pope Gregory VII* (Migne, *P. L.* cxlviii).

*Grosse., R.*   *Register (Rolls) of Robert Grosseteste, Bishop of Lincoln 1235–53*, ed. Davis, F. N. (Cant. & York Soc.) 1913.

Gyne., R.   Register of John Gynewell, Bishop of Lincoln, 1347–62. (MS.)

*H.C.Y.*   *Historians of the Church of York*, ed. Raine, J. [jun.] (Rolls Ser.) 3 vols., 1879–94.

Hat., R.   Register of Thomas Hatfield, Bishop of Durham, 1345–81. (MS.)

Heimbucher, Max.   *Die Orden u. Kongregationen der katholischen Kirche*, 3rd ed. revised, 2 vols. Paderborn, 1943–4.

Hennessy, G.   *Novum repertorium parochiale Londinense*, 1898.

Hereford Episcopal Registers: *see Beauchamp, Bothe, C., Boulers, Charl., L., Court. (Her.), Gilbert, Lacy (Her.), Mascall, May., Myll., Spoff., Stan., Tref., Trill.*

Hol., R.   Register of Robert Holgate, Archbishop of York, 1545–54. (MS.)

Janauschek, P. L.   *Originum Cisterciensium* tom. i. Vienna, 1877.

Jones, W. H. Rich.   *Fasti ecclesie Sarisberiensis*, 1879.

Kempe, R.              Register of John Kempe, Archbishop of York, 1425–52.
                       (MS.)   *See also Surt. Misc.*
Knowles, Dom D.   *The Religious Houses of Medieval England*, 1940.

*L. & P. H. VIII.*    *Letters and Papers, Henry VIII*, ed. Brewer, J. S., and
                       Gairdner, J., &c.   Vols. i–xxi (ii).
*Lacy (Ex.), R.*      *Register of Edmund Lacy, Bishop of Exeter 1420–55*, ed.
                       Hingeston-Randolph, F. C., Browne, C., and
                       Reichel, O. J.   Vol. i, 1909; vol. ii, 1915.
*Lacy (Her.), R.*     *Register of Edmund Lacy, Bishop of Hereford 1417–20*, ed.
                       Parry, J. H.   (Cantelupe and Cant. & York Soc.)
                       1918.
Langham, R.           Register of Simon Langham, Archbishop of Canter-
                       bury, 1366–8.   (MS.)
Langley, R.           Register of Thomas Langley, Bishop of Durham, 1406–
                       37.   (MS.)
Lawton, G.            *Collectio rerum ecclesiasticarum in diocesi Eboracensi: Col-
                       lections relative to churches and chapels within the dioceses
                       of York and Ripon.*   2nd ed. 1842.
Lee, R.               Register of Edward Lee, Archbishop of York, 1531–44.
                       (MS.)
*Leices. Arch. Soc.*  *Transactions of the Leicestershire Archaeological Society.*
Le Neve, J.           *Fasti ecclesiae Anglicanae*, ed. Hardy, T. D.   3 vols.,
                       1854.
*Liber Antiquus de ordinationibus vicariarum tempore Hugonis Welles Lincolniensis
                       episcopi 1209–35*, ed. Gibbons, A.   1888.
Lichfield, Episcopal Registers: *see Stretton.*
Lincoln, Episcopal Registers: *see* Bek, Buck., Burg., Dald., Flem., *Graves.*,
                       Gray, Will., *Grosse.*, Gyne., *Welles. See also Linc.
                       Dioc. Vis., Linc. Vis.*
Lincoln, Registers of Dean and Chapter, vols. i–vii (MS.) and *Chapter Acts
                       1526–59*, ed. Cole, R. E. G.   (Lincoln Record Soc.)
                       3 vols., 1915–20.
*Linc. Dioc. Vis.*    *Visitations in the Diocese of Lincoln 1517–1531*, ed.
                       Thompson, A. Hamilton.   (Lincoln Record Soc.)
                       vol. i, 1940; vol. ii, 1944.
*Linc. Vis.*          *Visitations of Religious Houses in the Diocese of Lincoln*
                       (1420–49), ed. Thompson, A. Hamilton.   (Lincoln
                       Record and Cant. & York Soc.)   2 vols. in 3,
                       1915–27.
*Loc. L. V.*          *Loci e Libro Veritatum, passages selected from Gascoigne's
                       theological dictionary*, ed. Rogers, J. E. Thorold.
                       Oxford, 1881.
London, Episcopal Registers: *see Sud.*
Lyndwood, W.          *Provinciale*, &c.   Oxford, 1679.

*Magnum Reg. Album.  The Great Register of Lichfield Cathedral known as M.R.A.*
                       ed. Savage, H. E.   (Will. Salt Archaeol. Soc.) 1924.

Mascall, R.            Register of Robert Mascall, Bishop of Hereford 1404–16,
                       ed. Parry, J. H.  (Cantelupe and Cant. & York
                       Soc.) 1917.
May., R.               Register of Richard Mayew, Bishop of Hereford 1504–16,
                       ed. Bannister, A. T.  (Cantelupe and Cant. & York
                       Soc.) 1921.
Melton, R.             Register of William Melton, Archbishop of York, 1317–
                       40.  (MS.)
Mem. Bury.             Memorials of St. Edmund's Abbey, ed. Arnold, T.   (Rolls
                       Ser.)  3 vols., 1890–6.
Mem. Ripon.            Memorials of the Church of SS. Peter and Wilfrid, Ripon, ed.
                       Fowler, J. T.  (Surtees Soc.)  4 vols., 1882–1908.
Migne, P. L.           Patrologia Latina, ed. Migne, J. P.
Mon.                   Monasticon Anglicanum, ed. Dugdale, Sir W.; new ed.,
                       by Caley, J., Ellis, H., and Bandinel, B.  6 vols.
                       in 8, 1817–30.
Morton, J., R.         Register of John Morton, Archbishop of Canterbury,
                       1486–1500.  (MS.)
Morton, R., R.         Register of Robert Morton, Bishop of Worcester,
                       1487–97.  (MS.)
Myll., R.              Register of Thomas Myllyng, Bishop of Hereford 1474–92,
                       ed. Bannister, A. T.  (Cantelupe and Cant. & York
                       Soc.) 1920.

Nash, T. R.            Collections for the History of Worcestershire.  2 vols.,
                       1781–99.
Neville, A., R.        Register of Alexander Neville, Archbishop of York,
                       1373–88, 2 vols.  (MS.)
Neville, G., R.        Register of George Neville, Archbishop of York, 1464–
                       76, 2 vols.  (MS.)
Newcourt, R.           Repertorium ecclesiasticum parochiale Londinense.  2 vols.,
                       1708–10.
Nichols, John.         The History and Antiquities of the County of Leicester.
                       4 vols. in 8, 1795–1815.
Nicolas, [Sir] N. H.  Testamenta Vetusta.  2 vols., 1826.
Nom. Cist.             Nomasticon Cisterciense.  Solesmes, 1892.
Norf. & Norw.          Norfolk Archaeology: Miscellaneous Tracts of the Norfolk
  Arch. Soc.           and Norwich Archaeol. Soc.

O.E.D.                 Oxford English Dictionary.
Oldham, R.             Register of Hugh Oldham, Bishop of Exeter, 1505–19.
                       (MS.)
Oliver, G.             Monasticon dioecesis Exoniensis, 1846.
Ormerod, G.            The History of the County Palatine and City of Chester, 2nd
                       ed. by Helsby, T.  3 vols., [1875]–82.

P.C.C.                 Registers of Wills proved in the Prerogative Court of Canter-
                       bury.  Vol. i (1383–1558), ed. Smith, J. C. C.
                       (British Record Soc.) 1893.

Peckham, R.     *Register of John Peckham, Archbishop of Canterbury 1279–94*, parts i, ii.   (Cant. & York Soc.)

Pet. Bles.     Petrus Blesensis, *Epistolae*.   See Migne, *P. L.* ccvii.

Peterborough, Abbey Registers.   *See* Assh.

Pol. P. & S.     *Political Poems and Songs relating to English History from the Accession of Edward III to that of Richard III*, ed. Wright, T. (Rolls Ser.) 2 vols., 1859–61.

Pont., R.     *Register of John of Pontoise (de Pontissara), Bishop of Winchester 1282–1304*, ed. Deedes, C.   (Cant. & York Soc.) 1 vol. in 2, 1915–24.

Praty, R.     *Register of Richard Praty, Bishop of Chichester 1438–45* (extracts from), ed. Deedes, C.   (Sussex Record Soc.) 1905.

R.P.     *Rotuli parliamentorum*.   6 vols., n.d., and index vol., 1832.

R.S.A.     *Registrum sacrum Anglicanum*, ed. Stubbs, W.   2nd ed. Oxford, 1897.

Rede, R.     *Register of Robert Rede, Bishop of Chichester 1397–1415*, ed. Deedes, C.   (Sussex Record Soc.) 2 pts., 1908–10.

Reg. Antiq. Linc.     *The Registrum Antiquissimum of the Cathedral Church of Lincoln*, ed. Foster, C. W., and Major, K.   (Lincoln Record Soc.) vols. i–v, 1931–40.

Reg. Joh. Whet.     *Registra Johannis Whethamstede, &c., abbatum monasterii S. Albani*, ed. Riley, H. T.   (Rolls Ser.) 2 vols., 1872–3.

Rom., R.     *Registers of John le Romeyn, and Henry of Newark, Archbishops of York 1286–96, 1296–9*, ed. Brown, W. (Surtees Soc.) 2 vols., 1913, 1916.

Rot. Litt. Pat.     *Rotuli litterarum patentium, 1201–6*, ed. Hardy, T. D. (Record Comm.) 1835.

Roth. R.     Register of Thomas Rotherham, Archbishop of York, 1480–1500, 2 vols.   (MS.)

Rymer.     *Foedera, conventiones*, &c., ed. T. Rymer.   20 vols., 1704–35.

S.R.     *Statutes of the Realm* (Record Comm.), vols. i, ii, 1810.

Salop Arch. Soc.     *Transactions of the Shropshire Archaeological Society.*

Sav., R.     Register of Thomas Savage, Archbishop of York, 1501–7.   (MS.)

Scr. Tres     *Historiae Dunelmensis Scriptores Tres*, ed. Raine, J. (Surtees Soc.) 1839.

Scrope, R.     Register of Richard Scrope, Archbishop of York, 1398–1405.   (MS.)

Sext.     *Liber sextus decretalium* (ap. *Corpus juris canonici*, ed. Richter & Friedberg, vol. ii.).

Spoff., R.     *Register of Thomas Spofford, Bishop of Hereford 1422–48*, ed. Bannister, A. T.   (Cantelupe and Cant. & York Soc.) 1919.

*Stan., R.*      *Register of John Stanbury, Bishop of Hereford 1453–74,* ed. Parry, J. H., and Bannister, A. T. (Cantelupe and Cant. & York Soc.) 1919.

*Stap., R.*      *Register of Walter Stapeldon, Bishop of Exeter 1307–26,* ed. Hingeston-Randolph, F. C., 1892.

*Stat. Y. C.*      *The Statutes, &c., of the Cathedral Church of York.* 2nd ed. Leeds, 1900.

*Stretton, R.*      *Register of Robert Stretton, Bishop of Coventry and Lichfield 1358–85,* abstract of, ed. Wilson, R. A. (Will. Salt Soc., new ser.) 2 vols., 1905, 1907.

*Sud., R.*      *Register of Simon Sudbury, Bishop of London 1362–75,* ed. Fowler, R. C., and others. (Cant. & York Soc.) 2 vols., 1927, 1938.

*Surt. Misc.*      *Miscellanea,* vol. ii, containing Documents relating to Diocesan and Provincial Visitations from the Registers of Henry Bowet . . . and John Kempe, ed. Thompson, A. Hamilton. (Surtees Soc. cxxvii. 131–302) 1916.

*Tax. Eccl.*      *Taxatio ecclesiastica Angliae et Walliae auctoritate Nicolai IV.* (Record Comm.) 1802.

*Test. Ebor.*      *Testamenta Eboracensia.* (Surtees Soc.) 6 vols., 1836–1902.

*Thor. Soc.*      *Transactions of the Thoroton Society.*

Thores., R.      Register of John Thoresby, Archbishop of York, 1352–73. (MS.)

*Tout, T. F.*      *Chapters in Medieval Administrative History.* 6 vols. Manchester, 1920–33.

*Trans. R. Hist. Soc.*      *Transactions of the Royal Historical Society.*

*Tref., R.*      *Register of John Trefnant, Bishop of Hereford 1389–1404,* ed. Capes, W. W. (Cantelupe and Cant. & York Soc.) 1916.

*Trill., R.*      *Register of John Trillek, Bishop of Hereford 1344–61,* ed. Parry, J. H. (Cantelupe and Cant. & York Soc.) 1912.

*V.C.H.*      *Victoria County Histories.*

*V.E.*      *Valor ecclesiasticus.* (Record Comm.) 6 vols., 1810–34.

*Vis. & Mem. Southwell.*      *Visitations and Memorials of Southwell Minster,* ed. Leach, A. F. (Camden Soc.) 1891.

Wake., R.      Register of Henry Wakefield, Bishop of Worcester, 1375–95. (MS.)

Wals. *H. A.*      Walsingham, T., *Historia Anglicana,* ed. Riley, H. T. (Rolls Ser.) 2 vols., 1863–4.

Warham, R.      Register of William Warham, Archbishop of Canterbury, 1503–32. (MS.)

Weaver, F. W.      *Somerset incumbents.* Bristol, 1889.

*Welles. Rot. Hug.*    *Register (Rolls) of Hugh Welles, Bishop of Lincoln 1209–35,* ed. Phillimore, W. P. W., and Davis, F. N. (Cant. & York Soc.) 3 vols., 1907–9.

Wharton, H.    *Anglia sacra, sive collectio historiarum de archiepiscopis et episcopis Angliae ad annum 1540.* 2 vols., 1691.

Whitaker, T. D.    *History and Antiquities of the Deanery of Craven, 1805,* 3rd ed. 1878.

*Wick., R.*    *Register of William Wickwane, Archbishop of York 1279–85,* ed. Brown, W. (Surtees Soc.) 1907.

Wilkins, D.    *Concilia Magnae Britanniae et Hiberniae, A.D. 446–1718.* 4 vols., 1737.

Will. Malmes, *G. P.* William of Malmesbury, *De gestis pontificum,* ed. Hamilton, N. E. S. A. (Rolls Ser.) 1870.

Winchester Episcopal Registers. *See Pont., Wyke.*

Wolsey, Reg.    Register of Thomas Wolsey, Archbishop of York, 1514–30. (MS.)

Worcester, Episcopal Registers. *See* Alcock, Brian, Carp., *Cobham, Giff.,* G., Gigl., J., Gigl., S., Morton, R., Wake.

Workman, H. B.    *John Wyclif, a Study of the English Medieval Church,* 2 vols. Oxford, 1926.

*Wyggeston Hosp. Rec.* A *Calendar of Charters and other Documents belonging to the Hospital of William Wyggeston at Leicester,* by Thompson, A. Hamilton. Leicester, 1933.

*Wyke., R.*    *Register of William Wykeham, Bishop of Winchester 1367–1404,* ed. Kirby, T. F. (Hants Record Soc.) 2 vols., 1896, 1899.

*Y.A.J.*    *Yorkshire Archaeological Journal.*

York, Archiepiscopal Registers: *see* Bain., Bothe, W., Bowet, *Cor., Giff., W., Gray, Walt., Green.,* Hol., Kempe, Lee, Melton, Neville, A., Neville, G., *Rom.,* Roth., Sav., Scrope, Thores., *Wick.,* Wolsey, Zouche.

Zouche, R.    Register of William Zouche, Archbishop of York, 1342–52. (MS.)

# I

## THE EPISCOPATE

THE purpose of these lectures is to give some account of the condition of ecclesiastical institutions in fifteenth-century England. In so doing, however, it is difficult to confine oneself to any very strict limit of date. Every student of ecclesiastical history realizes that during the period under discussion such institutions wore a settled form which had been achieved at an earlier date. Though liable to local disturbance, they preserved that form with very little alteration into the next century. Local disputes, such as the famous quarrel between the dean of Lincoln and his chapter, prolonged for nearly forty years, ended, in spite of efforts after a settlement which should embody principles of reform, in a tacit acceptance of the *status quo ante* by the weary combatants. Constitutional problems which had arisen repeatedly during the twelfth and the thirteenth centuries had gradually worked their way to solution, and the common forms by which the Church, like every department of medieval life, was governed, had been devised by mutual accommodation between its rulers and their subjects.

The history of the diocese and province of York offers a conspicuous example of this process. Among English medieval dioceses York was pre-eminent for the importance of the spiritual republics within its borders which claimed exemption from the ordinary jurisdiction of the diocesan; while in addition it included certain outlying districts in which the archbishop's authority was open to challenge from other prelates. The rights of the archbishop within his province were strictly limited. The bishops of the small diocese of Carlisle owned his authority; but from the middle of the twelfth century his claim to metropolitan jurisdiction over the Scottish sees was acknowledged only by the bishops of Galloway, and the last consecration of a bishop of Galloway by an archbishop of York took place in 1294, though the formal profession of obedience was maintained till a later date.[1] The efforts of Archbishop Romeyn

[1] The consecration of Thomas of Kirkcudbright or Dalton was performed by Archbishop Romeyn at Gedling, near Nottingham, 10 Oct. 1294. See the collection

and his successors to bring the proud spirit of Antony Bek into subjection had been signally defeated; for Bek and the chapter of Durham, though at war among themselves, were of one mind when their metropolitan proposed to assert himself in their midst.[1] Even the right of the archbishop to hold visitations of the church and diocese of Durham in vacancies of the see long remained unexercised after Wickwane's attempt, at the peril of his life, to visit the prior and convent in 1283.[2] Nearly a hundred years later, on the death of Bishop Hatfield in 1381, Alexander Neville issued mandates and made all arrangements for a visitation; but the time chosen for such a proceeding, in the disturbed state of the realm, was inauspicious, and a royal writ forbade its execution.[3] This, however, was merely a measure of expediency, and, in 1438, after the death of Langley, and again after the translation of Fox to Winchester in 1501, visitations of the church and diocese by archbishops' commissaries met with no opposition;[4] but, while a bishop of Durham was on his throne, no intrusion of the metropolitan was permitted,[5] and in convocations of the province of York formal protests were registered by the bishops' proctors against the prerogative of the archbishop to command the attendance of his powerful suffragan.[6]

of documents relating to it and to the administration of the diocese by the primate *sede vacante, R. Rom.* ii. 114–33.

[1] See ibid. xxv–xxxi. 90, 95–104, 106–8, 110–14.

[2] *R. Wick.* viii–xi; *Scr. Tres.* 65–9 and app. nos. lxxii, lxxiii; *Chr. Lan.* 120.

[3] R. A. Nev. i, ff. 113b–114b.

[4] For the 1438 visitation see *Surt. Misc.* 221–8. The details of the 1501 visitation are printed from R. Sav., in *Eccl. Proc. Barnes,* app. i–xl.

[5] Alexander Neville, with characteristic lack of tact, proposed to visit the diocese in 1376, while Bishop Hatfield was alive. A royal writ, dated 17 July 1376 and prohibiting Neville from pursuing his intention, is entered R. Hat., fo. 90, as is a confirmation of the same by Richard II, 27 Dec. 1377 (ibid., fo. 129b). Pointing hands and *Nota contra archiep. Ebor.* accompany these in the margin.

[6] The text of such a protestation was read by Hatfield's chancellor in Convocation at York, 12 Feb. 1359–60 (ibid., fo. 39b). 'In dei nomine amen. Cum nos Thomas permissione diuina Dunelm. episcopus ex priuilegio sedis apostolice nobis indulto simus ab obediencia et subieccione omnimodis domini archiepiscopi Ebor. et successorum ac ecclesie Ebor. exempti et totaliter absoluti protestamur palam et publice quod non intendimus per comparicionem nostram presentem nec per aliqua per nos seu nostro nomine dicenda proponenda seu quouis modo exercenda priuilegio et exempcioni nostris predictis quomodolibet preiudicare sed si qua per nos aut nostro nomine dici fieri aut aliqualiter proponi contigerit que in lesionem priuilegii et exempcionis predictorum tendere poterunt volumus quod pro non dictis non factis et non propositis habeantur omnino.' In 1379–80 Neville's

THE EPISCOPATE 3

Thus relations between the archbishop and his province had reached a definite understanding by the opening of the fifteenth century.  Similarly, in the course of the previous century, the outstanding difficulties of the archbishops in their diocese had been settled.  As regards their outlying jurisdictions, the bishops of Durham, jealous of any infringement of their own liberties, made no systematic attempt to interfere with the rule of the archbishops in Hexhamshire, and it may be noted that neither the bishop nor the prior and convent of Durham questioned the archbishops' ordinary powers in the churches of their Yorkshire property round Northallerton and Howden.[1]  In the priory of St. Oswald at Gloucester, however, and its dependent parishes, the spirituality of Churchdown, the exclusive jurisdiction of the archbishops was assailed towards the close of the thirteenth century by the bishops of Worcester and the archbishop of Canterbury.[2]  Here the standing quarrel between the two primates, not settled until the compromise between Islip and Thoresby in 1353[3] allayed its bitterness, gave added zest to the dispute, which reached its height in 1301.  Then the combined onslaught of Archbishop Winchelsey and Godfrey Giffard upon Archbishop Corbridge was repelled by the intervention of Edward I, on the ground that St. Oswald's was a royal free chapel which, with its possessions, had been long before given by the Crown to the see of York; and this remained a recognized fact until 1545, when Archbishop Holgate surrendered his

summons to Convocation was directed to the bishop as his suffragan, and a similar protest was embodied in Hatfield's mandate directing his commissaries to appear on his behalf (ibid., ff. 171b, 172). See also the instrument in R. Fox, 158–62, appointing proctors for the Convocation of 1501. Hatfield's claim to complete independence of the see of York rested upon the indult granted to him by Clement VI, 22 Sept. 1348 (C.P.L. iii. 283: cf. C.P.P. i. 137–8). But it was represented to Urban V in 1363 that the bishop had no university degree, that the remoteness of his diocese, in a province with only two suffragans (or only one, if Hatfield's claim to autonomy was allowed), made it possible for him to do much as he liked, and that he led a dissolute life. Consequently, the archbishop of Canterbury was ordered to examine the case and, if the statements were accurate, to revoke the indult granted in 1348 (C.P.P. i. 472).

[1] In 1291, however, Archbishop Romeyn took occasion to summon the prior and convent to make answer concerning their infringement of his jurisdiction in Allertonshire and Howdenshire (R. Rom. ii. 97, 98).

[2] See the summary account of the dispute by the present writer, 'The Jurisdiction of the Archbishop of York in Gloucestershire' (B. & G.A.S. xliii. 85–180.

[3] Wilkins, iii. 31–2.

Gloucestershire possessions to Henry VIII in exchange for other property.[1]

Jurisdictions nearer home needed careful handling. The cathedral chapter of York and the three collegiate chapters of Beverley, Ripon, and Southwell, all in the archbishop's patronage, nevertheless were the ordinaries of a large number of prebendal and other parochial churches which, in the cases of York and Beverley, were scattered over a wide area.[2] Within the great archdeaconry of Richmond the archdeacon exercised all ordinary jurisdiction in virtue of privileges which he seems to have acquired before the middle of the twelfth century.[3] The archbishop's right to include the archdeaconry in his primary visitation was not disputed, and during vacancies caused by the death or resignation of archdeacons, ordinary jurisdiction naturally lapsed to him.[4] With the chapters of Ripon and Southwell he was habitually on good terms. York and Beverley, however, regarded his interference with their affairs with singular jealousy and strove to protect themselves by elaborate safeguards against him as visitor of both churches. As regards the dean and chapter of York, a *modus vivendi* was arranged with Archbishop Romeyn in 1290, by which archiepiscopal visitations were limited by careful precautions to little more than mere formalities, and a final and more restricted form was given to this by a composition with Archbishop Melton in 1328.[5] Melton, a wise ruler under whose administration the government of the diocese acquired its fixed and permanent character, was also responsible for the agreement by which the privileges of the archdeacon of Richmond were defined and confirmed

[1] See *L. & P. H. VIII*, xx (1), 214 (no. 465/39), 14 Mar. 1544–5.

[2] For peculiar jurisdictions in Yorkshire see Lawton *passim* and lists in *V.C.H. Yorks*. iii. 80 sqq. For the jurisdiction of Southwell see the list ap. Ecton, 559, 560.

[3] See *Y.A.J.* xxv. 129–39 and references there given.

[4] The York archiepiscopal registers of the first half of the fourteenth century contain important sections relating to this exempt archdeaconry, owing to long vacancies consequent upon the deaths of foreigners whose tenure was not undisputed. Information from later registers is comparatively scanty. The registers of the archdeacons with one exception (John Rylands MS. Latin 333) have disappeared: an abstract of an earlier volume made by Matthew Hutton of Aynhoe is in B.M. MS. Harl. 6978. This and a full calendar of the later register have been edited by the present writer in *Y.A.J.* xxv. 129–268, xxx. 1–132, and xxxiii. 111–45.

[5] The composition of 1290 is printed in *H.C.Y.* iii. 216–20; that of 1328 in *Surt. Misc.* 280–90. It is curious that the second of these, which revised and superseded the first, is left unprinted and unnoticed in *Stat. Y.C.*

in 1331.[1] From that time, with one exception, the active conflict of jurisdictions within the diocese came to an end. The exception occurred in the time of Alexander Neville, who, with characteristic tactlessness, endeavoured to override the privileges of York and Beverley in 1381. In both places his action added fuel to the fire of serious local dissensions. At York it produced strong opposition and resentment; but his endeavour to force an ordinary visitation upon the canons of Beverley, in defiance of their cherished privileges, was met by a flat refusal to recognize his authority and by the temporary retirement from the church of its resident clergy.[2] The storm thus raised was finally settled by his successor Arundel, who issued new statutes for the church in 1388.[3]

From other dioceses come striking instances of the settlement of constitutional points of a similar kind before the opening of the fifteenth century. It may definitely be said that these, so hotly debated at a previous epoch, no longer played an engrossing part in ecclesiastical affairs. Bishops had long ceased to regard their archdeacons as competitors for their place in the the sun;[4] their relations with the chapters of cathedral churches were as a rule amicable and cautiously paternal. They still, from time to time, tried to break down the vexatious exemptions enjoyed by religious houses.[5] But diocesan business was carried on smoothly with the aid and largely by the energy of experienced clerks trained in the routine work of ecclesiastical administration and practised in the complicated procedure of the ecclesiastical courts. From a wider point of view than that of purely diocesan activities and internal discipline, the English Church was faced with problems of a new and pressing kind. In its relations with the State the opening of the century nearly coincided with the accession to the throne of a new dynasty pledged to political reform. In the events which led to that

[1] *H.C.Y.* iii. 248–50.
[2] See *Bev. Ch. A.* i, pp. lxxiv–lxxxi; ii. 202–65; Leach, 'A Clerical Strike at Beverley Minster' (*Arch.* lv. 1–20).
[3] Printed in *Bev. Ch. A.* ii. 265–78; also in *Mon.* vi (iii), 1308. See also *Y.A.J.* xxiv. 226–31.
[4] There does not seem to be satisfactory evidence that England was affected by this form of competition.
[5] For Bishop Bateman's attack upon the liberties of the abbey of St. Edmund in, 1345, see *Mem. Bury*, iii, pp. xi–xv, 56–71; for Alnwick's similar endeavour a century later, *Mon.* iii. 136.

change a leading part had been played by the primate, Arundel, whose staunch conservatism guided the ecclesiastical policy of the new reign. The repression of heresy, with its double menace to political and religious orthodoxy, assumed an increasing importance in the duties of the episcopate. While uniformity of religious doctrine and practice was threatened at home, the unity of the whole Church was disturbed by the Great Schism. As time went on, the established order of things maintained itself securely; the sheer weight of custom resisted all demands for the internal reform of the Church. If heretical opinions gained ground quietly, it was without organized propaganda, and their open manifestations in isolated places were easily checked by episcopal vigilance. On England the effects of the schism fell lightly; apart from the divines and diplomatists who were called upon to take part in general councils, the ordinary churchman looked upon the schism as a foreign affair which occupied his attention rather remotely. And when, after the schism had been healed and the restored papacy, victorious over its conciliar opponents, employed its recovered supremacy in the work of maintaining and extending its temporal power in Italy, the Church in England continued to pursue its old paths, an unchangeable and apparently impregnable institution, mechanical no doubt in its processes, restrained from beneficial innovations by the prevailing spirit of legalism, but presenting a calm and unruffled front to the political chaos and social change which accompanied the struggle between the houses of Lancaster and York.

Records of the period, in their composition and the character of the documents which they contain, reflect the smooth and placid immobility of the ecclesiastical system. Not that the life with which it had to deal was undisturbed by quarrels or free from offences. It had been built up largely as a system of correction and prevention. The highest officers of the Church exercised powers which were pre-eminently judicial: their pastoral care was discharged, not in evangelical exhortation and pious encouragement, but in bringing their subjects to book for defaults against the spiritual code, and even their acts of grace were executed with a strictly legal propriety. In the eyes of those subjects they were first and foremost judges ordinary, the ordinaries whose tribunals were held in virtue of their office. They might, and habitually did, perform that office by delegation or deputy, but their powers in any case were corrective and were enforced by pains and penalties.

This is the system whose workings in their greatest variety can be studied in the registers of diocesan bishops, the most important series of ecclesiastical records which we possess. Numerous though they are, they are by no means complete. In some diocesan series there are large gaps, and even where a series is apparently continuous, some of the volumes fail to account for certain years of a bishop's rule, whether owing to the dilatoriness of a registrar or to the disappearance of some separate record of which all trace has been lost. The series which is of especial interest to Oxford, a series which also is practically unbroken until the middle of the sixteenth century, is that of the registers of the bishops of Lincoln. From the first quarter of the thirteenth century until 1290 these registers exist in the form of rolls recording institutions to benefices, with supplementary entries, chiefly letters of institution, on the dorse of each roll. Ordinations of vicarages also occur among the institutions with increasing fullness of detail.[1] In 1290 the practice, already adopted in some other dioceses—the earliest examples which we possess are the registers of Walter Giffard at York, and his brother Godfrey Giffard at Worcester[2]—of registering institutions and miscellaneous letters and memoranda on folio quires of parchment, subsequently bound into books, came into use at Lincoln. Here, however, institutions and ordinations of vicarages and various religious foundations, instead of being mixed up with miscellaneous material, were recorded on separate quires for the cathedral chapter (*Collaciones prebendarum*) and the several archdeaconries of the diocese; while other letters and memoranda were entered apart without local distinction. This practice continued until 1547, though in some of the later registers institutions were entered without division among archdeaconries.

It is the memoranda which chiefly concern us. These at first are so numerous that throughout the fourteenth century each

---

[1] The existing rolls to 1280 have been printed in five volumes by Cant. & York Soc. So also two rolls of Archbishop Walter Gray of York with other documents form *Surt. Soc.* vol. lvi (1870).

[2] For printed editions and calendars of these see Bibliography, *R. G. Giff., R. W. Giff.*

register is divided into two volumes, one of which contains the
institution quires and the other the memoranda.[1] This copious-
ness was due to two reasons, the first of which was the obvious
one that certain documents from a bishop's correspondence
were of sufficient intrinsic importance to be put on permanent
record. But there was also the necessity of keeping letters and
mandates as precedents for official correspondence, by reference to which the style of the episcopal chancery was regulated
and stereotyped. The register was not kept for the benefit of the
historian in the future, nor was it wholly a record of episcopal
acts: it was also a repertory of common forms. Another set of
registers, those of the bishops of Worcester, show this very
clearly; for, from the beginning of the fourteenth century, the
marginal description of each entry, apart from institutions,
frequently gives only its general character without reference to
the places or persons which it concerns.[2]

Individual registrars no doubt used their own judgement in
selection and rejection of the large material from their store.
But by the middle of the fourteenth century the contents of the
registers furnished precedents for all but exceptional occasions,
and though at Lincoln memoranda occupy one of the three
huge volumes of Bishop Buckingham's register, their variety is
less interesting than that of earlier books. The long and formal
document, encumbered by legal verbiage, had been developed
from its briefer and more direct predecessors, though official
prolixity had still to attain its full stature. From the beginning
of Beaufort's episcopate in 1398, the Lincoln memoranda show
a gradual falling-off in number and interest, and from this date
until 1496, with one exception, the register of each bishop is a
single volume, in which the memoranda section is comparatively
short and scanty. But it may be noted that the documents which
are registered, where they are not purely formal, are of a
character for which precedents are extremely hard to find in

---

[1] R. Buck. consists of three large volumes, covering the thirty-five years of
Buckingham's episcopate: two of these are devoted to institutions, the third to
memoranda. In this last a considerable portion of the text is duplicated.

[2] See, e.g., R. Cobham, in which examples constantly occur. R. Brian ii. is a
book of precedents in which the documents in vol. i. of the register are duplicated
with initials in place of names of places and persons. York, R. A. Nev. ii. is
largely a precedent-book in which entries from various sources are made in similar
fashion.

the mass of material contained in the earlier registers, and often concern particular cases for which precedents were wanting.[1]

There are of course exceptions, and the interest of the great collection of registers at Lambeth, covering a far wider area than the affairs of a single diocese, is fully maintained throughout the fifteenth century. Compared with them, the contemporary series at York, in ponderous volumes which show much industry on the part of successive registrars, is concerned almost entirely with diocesan business, and that business largely formal and rehearsed at great length with endless repetitions. The diocesan machinery ran smoothly in well-worn grooves, and such matters as were thought worthy of permanent record were merely those which involved such cases as would inevitably call for future reference, for renewal, confirmation, or revision.

Abundance of material, however, remains in these repertories, to say nothing of other official sources of information which supplement their contents and to which reference will be made, for an estimate of the working of ecclesiastical institutions in England during this period. Each collection of diocesan records bears a strong family likeness to the rest. Each diocese, in its internal government, in the problems with which its rulers had to contend, was as it were a microcosm of the English Church as a whole: the church of York, the church of Lichfield, within their local limits, were compendious illustrations of the *ecclesia Anglicana* of which they formed integral parts. Retaining local customs, jealous of external interference with their jurisdictions, they pursued existences which at first sight appear to be highly parochial and self-contained. Seldom during the century was their peace disturbed by contact with outward affairs: the relations between diocesan bishops were marked as a rule by formal courtesy, while the old hostility which bishops had shown to encroachments on the part of their metropolitans, even the obstinate resistance of the see of Durham to the obedience demanded by the see of York, had given place to a recognition of the rights of the metropolitan during vacancies of bishoprics.

Here it may be said that the relation of these local churches to the provinces of the English Church was simply on a smaller

[1] A conspicuous instance of this kind occurs in R. *Mascall*, 74, 75, where the bishop prohibits the superstitious use of a holy well.

scale the relation of the English Church to the Western Church
as a whole. Fortified by individual privileges, left much to
themselves in matters of internal discipline, they were nevertheless neither autonomous nor self-sufficient. Few people to-day
cling to the old theory that the medieval English Church was a
distinctively Anglican body, in communion with Rome, imbued
with respect for the Holy See, but claiming a right to independence of action where its interests collided with the wishes of the
papacy.[1] It is true, of course, that throughout the fourteenth
century, and earlier still, the growth of national sentiment was
accompanied by an increasing sensitiveness to the demands of
the popes upon the complete obedience of the English Church.
Their uncontrolled disposal of its benefices by acts of reservation
and provision was resented. As early as the last quarter of the
thirteenth century we find an enunciation of the theory, embodied afterwards in the preamble of the Statute of Provisors,
that the English Church as a whole had been founded and
endowed by the kings of England and other of Christ's faithful
people for the spread of the orthodox faith, for the remission of
their sins, for the increase of divine worship, for the keeping of
hospitality, the distribution of alms to the poor, and the supply
of suitable and resident ministers to individual churches. These
expressions did not come from a layman: they formed part of
a protest addressed by Archbishop Romeyn of York, a prelate
of Italian descent, to one of the cardinals against the design of
Nicholas IV to annex a prebend in the cathedral church of
York to a hospital in Rome. They were probably written, as
the date of the letter indicates, with the personal encouragement of Edward I; but they are put so clearly and decidedly
that it can hardly be doubted that the archbishop had some
earlier formula in mind and that he was putting into words a
theory which already had taken a clear-cut shape in his mind.[2]

---

[1] F. W. Maitland's *Roman Canon Law in the Church of England*, 1898, was a
damaging criticism of the theory summed up in the words 'But the canon law of
Rome, although always regarded as of great authority in England, was not held
to be binding on the courts' (*Report of the Eccl. Courts Commission*, 1883). Of later
works in which Maitland's point of view receives support in detail, see especially
Z. N. Brooke, *The English Church and the Papacy from the Conquest to the Reign of John*,
1931.

[2] Printed in *Fast. Ebor.* 342–4; some corrections of the text are in *R. Rom.* ii. 29n.
The relevant passage is as follows: 'Verumtamen non hec fuit pia intentio ac
devota clare memorie catholicorum regum Anglie et aliorum Christi fidelium qui

On the other hand, if such ideas as these were advanced, from time to time, against the papal claim to be universal ordinary, and if they became officially formulated in acts of parliament, the fact remained that the objection which they contained was aimed at papal encroachments upon the temporalities of the Church and its endowments. No one doubted the spiritual supremacy of the pope or the validity of his legislative powers for the Church at large. The catastrophe of Boniface VIII was caused, not by his exercise of authority over the Church, but by his attempt to domineer over kings. In spite, however, of the decisive check given to his ambitions and in spite of the subsequent captivity of the papacy, the Avignonese popes for half a century did what they would with English benefices: the reservation of bishoprics, dignities in cathedral churches, and well-endowed livings was practised almost as a matter of course, and every bishop with canonries and prebends in cathedral chapters at his disposal was faced with a long waiting list of candidates furnished with papal provisions. So far as the flooding of the best benefices in the Church with foreign cardinals and officers of the papal court was concerned, the anti-papal legislation of the middle of the fourteenth century marks a turning-point. The practice did not cease, but it was sensibly diminished, and after the beginning of the fifteenth century the promotion of foreigners in England became rare.[1] But, if the

---

nedum prefatas nostras ecclesias sed et totam ecclesiam Anglicanam ad dilatationem fidei orthodoxe fundantes eas temporalium bonorum largitionibus dotaverunt amplissimis et libertatum immunitatibus munierunt sed ea nimirum consideratione constat sic eos eisdem ecclesiis fuisse munificos ut cum delictorum expiatione consequerentur per hoc salubre remedium animarum cultus divini nominis augeretur servaretur hospitalitas elemosine darentur pauperibus et per ministros idoneos ad quos pro tempore ex eisdem bonis ecclesiastica stipendia devenirent servire prefatis ecclesiis personaliter tenerentur.' Cf. this with the preamble to the Statute of Provisors (*S.R.* i. 316), which is an expansion of that to the Statute of Carlisle (1306–7: ibid. 150): 'come seinte eglise Dengletere estoit founde en estat de prelacie, deins le Roialme Dengleterre, par le dit Ael & ses progenitours, & Countes Barons et Nobles de son Roialme & lour ancestres, pur eux & le poeple enfourmer de la lei Dieu, & pur faire hospitalites aumoignes & auters oeveres de charite es lieux ou les eglises feurent fondes pur les almes de foundours & de lour heirs & de touz Cristiens.'

[1] The lists in Le Neve, though greatly in need of revision, may be used to illustrate the decline in this practice. Late in the fourteenth century, however, reservations and provisions to foreigners were frequent. On the death of Jacopo Orsini, cardinal of St. George's in Velabro in 1379, Urban VI provided another member of the family of Orsini to the vacant deanery of Salisbury. Meanwhile the chapter

statutes of 1351 and 1353 and their re-enactment fifty years later set up a barrier against the uncontrolled action of the papacy, they could not touch the spiritual powers of the head of the Church. If the pope found himself limited in the matter of providing bishops to vacant sees *motu proprio*, he could at any rate use his power of loosing a bishop from the tie that bound him in spiritual marriage to one see and translating him to another spouse, and thus create and fill vacancies at his will. Further, his prerogative of granting dispensations for plurality enabled him to exercise an influence over appointments to ecclesiastical benefices the patronage of which he could no longer override with freedom.

More will be said of this in the sequel, and here it need be said only that, in an age when the income of clerks in the service of the king or in episcopal and other noble households were largely furnished by the benefices given them or obtained for them by their patrons, pluralism was an obvious consequence, and the days of indiscriminate pluralism, unregulated by a strict system of papal dispensations, were past.[1] The practical working of this system, the frequency of personal petitions by clerks desiring to hold an extra cure of souls, or of petitions by patrons on behalf of their protégés, the constant issue of indults accompanied by minutely defined conditions of tenure of the desired benefices, may be studied in detail in the volumes of the *Calendar of Papal Registers*. While questions relating to presentations to livings had long been in England matters for decision at common law, the dispensing power of the pope in cases of plurality, and the spiritual pains and penalties incurred by unlicensed pluralists, could not be disregarded with impunity

elected Robert Braybroke, and when in 1382 Braybroke became bishop of London, they elected Thomas Mountagu to succeed him. Nevertheless, the Orsini cardinal remained titular dean of Salisbury, and on his death in 1390 Boniface IX provided Angelo Acciajuoli, the cardinal of Florence, to the deanery. Angelo, however, resigned it, and on 30 July 1391 Thomas Mountagu, the actual occupant, was granted letters of provision which put papal and local interests at rest for the time being. See *C.P.L.* iv. 401.

[1] Such irregularities as made the career of Bogo de Clare (see an account of his benefices in *A.A.S.R.P.* xxxiii. 19–22) possible, and gave rise to the legend that John Mansel acquired 300 benefices (see ibid. 16), flourished in spite of the constitution *De Multa* of the fourth Lateran Council, and it was not until John XXII's constitution *Execrabilis* that they were effectively checked. See the present writer's 'Pluralism in the Medieval Church' (*A.A.S.R.P.* xxxiii. 35–73; xxxiv. 1–26; xxxv. 87–108, 199–244; xxxvi. 1–41).

by patrons or presentees, or by the diocesan bishops with whom lay the institution to benefices.[1]

Deferring further consideration of this topic, we may confine ourselves at present to the appointment of bishops. Translation, as has been said, from one see to another was an expedient of which popes, curbed in their freedom of provision, readily availed themselves; and with translation went the right of providing an incumbent to the see thus vacated. During the first half of the fourteenth century, out of seventy appointments to sees, only nine were made by translation; but, under changed conditions, from 1351 to 1400, out of eighty-six appointments there were thirty-one translations, while, in consequence of translations, thirteen sees were filled by papal provision. The retirement of Archbishop Langham as a cardinal to Avignon in 1368[2] gave Urban V the opportunity of a series of translations. William Whittlesey passed from Worcester to Canterbury, William Lynn from Chichester to Worcester, and the see of Chichester was filled by the consecration of William Reade at Avignon in 1369.[3] The political revolution of 1388 was

---

[1] Professor G. Barraclough, in his learned treatise on *Papal Provisions*, 1935, traces the growth of the system, laying stress upon its legality and the recourse made to it by petitioners. His treatment of the influence of the lay aristocracy in their own interest upon ecclesiastical affairs, and of the continued existence of the Germanic *Eigenkirchenwesen* in opposition to papal efforts, is a valuable corrective to a wholesale condemnation of provisions. But the complaints against provisions were not audible only in preambles to parliamentary statutes, and, in view of facts, it is most difficult to accept a theory which would lay the main blame for ecclesiastical abuses upon the particularist tendencies of an Erastianly minded laity. Whatever may be said for the popes in this matter, and even if the provision of foreigners to English dignities and benefices may argue a weakness of the papacy in face of demands by cardinals and other members of the Curia, it is going very far to praise the papal system of procedure in spiritual cases, not merely as 'as impartial and well-balanced as human ingenuity could contrive', but as 'a great achievement, and probably an achievement which only a jurisprudence exercised with a consciousness of the nearness of God and of eternity could have produced' (p. 81). But can this be meant to be taken seriously?

[2] Langham retained and acquired certain English benefices after his retirement, including parish churches. On 14 Sept. 1368 he, as cardinal priest of St. Sixtus, received collation of the church of Wearmouth from Bishop Hatfield. The deed of collation, saluting the cardinal with the phrase *promptum complacendi spiritum cum salute*, continues *De vestris supportacione patrocinio et benevolencia in nostris et ecclesie nostre agendis negociis non modicum confidentes*, &c. (R. Hat., fo. 67b). In August 1372 Langham exchanged Wearmouth for the church of Somersham, Hunts (ibid., fo. 77). The exchange in itself was not profitable, for Somersham was taxed at £33. 6s. 8d., and Wearmouth at £52. 13s. 4d. (*Tax. Eccl.*, pp. 35, 379).

[3] See Rymer, vi. 596–7, for the text of the letter from Urban V to Edward III,

followed by another series. The condemnation of Alexander Neville, with his mock translation to St. Andrews, brought Thomas Arundel from Ely to York; John Fordham was translated from Durham to Ely, Walter Skirlaw from Bath and Wells to Durham; Ralph Erghum from Salisbury to Bath and Wells, while John Waltham was provided to Salisbury,[1] and the translation of the king's confessor, Thomas Rushook, from Chichester to the Irish see of Kilmore left Chichester vacant for more than a year until in 1390 it was filled by the provision of Richard Metford.[2] Another batch of translations followed the removal of Arundel from York to Canterbury in 1396.[3] Although in the fifteenth century there are no such extensive instances of translation, yet the proportion of translations to the ordinary method of appointment remained at much the same level as in the preceding half-century.

Employed though it was with apparent freedom, the process of translation was guided by political considerations. The translation of Alexander Neville to the schismatic see of St. Andrews by Urban VI and the consequent shuffling of bishoprics was the work of the government which for the time being held the king in control. The removal of Fordham, deprived of the privy seal, from Durham to the wealthy, but less important see of Ely, made room at Durham for an adherent of the lords appellant. His successor in the privy seal was promoted to Salisbury. On the other hand, the vacancy at Chichester, a see with small revenues, lasted long enough to allow Richard II, after he had shaken off the yoke of his adversaries, to press upon Boniface IX a candidate who had fallen under the displeasure of the parliament of 1388. Bishops were too important a factor in the State to be left entirely to the nomination of the pope: it was a useful expedient to throw upon the pope the responsibility for their appointment, but the nominations were none the less those of the government in power, and, amid the difficulties

announcing the translation of Lynn to Worcester and referring to that of Whittlesey to Canterbury, dated Viterbo, 11 Oct.

[1] See Rymer, vii. 573–7, papal letters dated Perugia, 2 Apr. The mandates for restitution of temporalities were issued 13 Sept. following (ibid. 605–7: cf. *C.P.R.* 1385–9, p. 504), except in the case of Fordham, whose mandate bears date 27 Sept. (*C.P.R.* 1385–9, p. 510).

[2] Mandate for restitution, 10 Mar. 1389–90 (Rymer, vii. 664; *C.P.R.* 1388–92, p. 170).

[3] See Rymer, vii. 842–4, letters dated Rome, 5 Oct.

of the Great Schism, the popes were compliant. The preamble of the statute of Praemunire in 1393 complained of translations by which prelates were removed from the realm by the pope and the State deprived of their assistance.[1] Officially the pope bore the blame, but the reproach was actually levelled against the political leaders who had proscribed and banished the king's episcopal friends five years before; and this objection to the practice of translation, which served a special opportunity, was entirely disregarded by the king himself, when in 1397, imitating the dealings of his enemies with Archbishop Neville, he procured the translation of the exiled Arundel from Canterbury to the see of St. Andrews.[2]

No appointment of a bishop, at any rate to the more important sees, was made without respect to his possible services to the government. The influence of the Church in parliament, the fact that the Crown sought for and found its most competent ministers among the bishops and clergy, the position of the king as founder and patron of episcopal sees, into whose hands their temporalities passed during vacancies, necessarily gave him a powerful voice in nominations of bishops. Consequently, when a vacancy occurred in a see, the practice was for the king to transmit his wishes to the pope with the recommendation of a suitable nominee. This of course was no new custom, but from the twelfth century onwards the acceptance of the king's candidate by the pope was by no means certain. After the middle of the fourteenth century, however, the king's hand was strengthened by parliamentary hostility to the provisory authority of the

---

[1] *S.R.* ii. 85: 'Et auxint dit est & comune clamour yad qe le dit seint piere le Pape ad ordeigne et purpose de translater aucuns prelates de mesme le Roialme, ascuns hors du Roialme & aucuns de un Eveschee a autre deing mesme le Roialme, saunz assent & conisance & saunz assent du prelat qi ainsi serroit translate, queux prelatz sont moult profitables & necessaires a nostre dit seignur le Roi & tout son Roialme; par queux translacions sils fusent sufertz les estatutz du Roiaume serront defaitz & anientez, & ses sages lieges de son conseill sanz son assent & encountre sa voluntee subtrez & esloignez hors de son Roiaume, & lavoir & tresore du Roiaume serroit emporte, & ensi mesme le Roiaume destitut sibien de counseill come davoir a final destruccion de mesme le Roialme; & ensy la Corone Dengleterre qad este si frank de tout temps qele nad hieu nulle terrien soveraigne, mes immediate subgit a Dieu en toutes choses tuchantz la regalie de mesme la Corone & a nulle autre, serroit submuys a Pape & les leys et estatutz du Roialme par luy defaitz & anientez a sa volente, en perpetuele destruccion de la soveraynte nostre seignur le Roy, sa Corone & sa regalie & tout son Roialme, que Dieu defende.'

[2] See Rymer, viii. 31.

pope. The success of his application was by no means a fore-
gone conclusion; but in most instances the royal candidate
was accepted, or, where the pope showed opposition, a compromise was arranged. Even where, as in the cases of translation and provision already mentioned, the pope appeared to act
*motu proprio*, it was at the suggestion of the government for the
time being. But in any case the dignity of the pope was saved
by the bull of provision which marked his formal acquiescence
in the appointment and gave it final validity.

Thus anti-papal legislation did not render such provisions
obsolete, nor did it check direct access to the papal tribunal for
the confirmation of appointments. The claim of the Holy See
to take part in such proceedings and to stamp them with the
seal of its authority had been recognized too long to be neglected
or rejected. The act of provision to English sees was in fact
regularized and to some extent formalized by the understanding that, if the pope offered no opposition to the royal nominee,
no exception would be taken to the bull of provision, save in so
far as the bishop, on doing homage for his temporalities, was
bound to renounce the clauses in it which were prejudicial to
the authority of the Crown. Thus, during the last century and a
half of the Middle Ages in England, appointments to bishoprics
were invariably made by provision under these conditions, and
became a matter of mutual agreement between the Crown and
the papacy.

In this agreement two elements which formerly had been regarded as a necessary part of the procedure in the appointment
of bishops were virtually set aside, the election of the diocesan
by his chapter and its confirmation by his metropolitan. The
freedom of elections from royal control had been prominent in
the mind which framed the first clause of the Great Charter,
when the outstanding example of violation of the liberties of the
English Church had been John's obstinate resistance to the
wishes of the chapter of Canterbury. Elections of abbots in
monasteries in the patronage of the Crown were allowed to
proceed freely, at any rate as a general rule;[1] but the close

---

[1] A noteworthy example of the intrusion of a provisor into an abbey was the
appointment of Edmund Brounfeld (Bromfield) as abbot of Bury in 1379, which
hindered the candidate elected by the convent and approved by the Crown from
obtaining possession till four years later (*C.P.R.* 1377–81, pp. 317, 418, 420, 494;
1381–5, p. 300; Wals. *H.A.* i. 414, &c.). Some years after this interregnum, with

connexion of bishops with public affairs brought royal influence constantly to bear upon their election. In fact, the familiar procedure by which the *congé d'élire* is accompanied by letters missive, naming the candidate acceptable to the king, has a very much earlier origin than modern objectors to its unreality suppose. Ordinarily speaking, the election was followed by the king's signification of assent, conveyed in letters patent with the order to the metropolitan to give his confirmation, and, after the election had been confirmed by the metropolitan, he did homage for temporalities and mandates for their restitution were issued. The course of this procedure had been modified by papal reservations and provisions. Thus when Bishop Edington died in October 1366 the see of Winchester had already been reserved by Urban V. The see was designed by the king for William of Wykeham, who almost at once was put in custody of its temporalities and was readily elected by the prior and convent of St. Swithun's.[1] His consecration was delayed, however, for nearly a year by the formalities consequent upon the papal reservation of the see, the pope in the meanwhile appointing him administrator of its spiritual and temporal affairs.[2] Here the chapter played its regular part; but the act of election was simply an act of consent to the king's choice, and the appointment actually lay between the king and the pope, whose bull of

its disastrous consequences, Richard II obtained a papal indult by which it was conceded that the election of an abbot should imply *ipso facto* apostolic confirmation (*C.P.R.* 1422–9, p. 528). The royal assent to the election of William Cratfeld in 1388–9 was signified to the pope (*C.P.R.* 1388–92, p. 4): after that date none is recorded, and in all subsequent cases the shortness of the interval between the election of an abbot and the restitution of the temporalities bears witness to the lasting effect of the indult. As regards other exempt houses, a similar indult had been granted to Evesham before 1367 (*C.P.R.* 1364–7, p. 420), while in the case of St. Albans the last signification of assent addressed to the pope is recorded in 1336, though here the indult was obtained about the same time as that for Bury at the petition of Richard II (see Rymer, xi. 538). Waltham also appears to have received an indult between 1389 and 1400. On the other hand, in the cases of Westminster and St. Augustine's, Canterbury, the old procedure was observed until the reign of Henry VII. The royal assent to the elections of heads of non-exempt houses was regularly conveyed to the local diocesan, and such significations are entered with fair regularity upon the patent rolls throughout the fifteenth century as in earlier times.
[1] *Congé d'élire* dated 13 Oct. 1366; signification of assent to election, 24 Oct. (*C.P.R.* 1364–7, pp. 311, 324).
[2] The bull, dated at Avignon 11 Dec. 1366, is printed in *R. Wyke.* i. 2, 3. For the provision and licence for consecration (Viterbo, 14 July 1367) and for Wykeham's consecration at St. Paul's on 10 Oct. see ibid. 8–10. The temporalities were restored two days after the consecration (Rymer, vi. 574–5; *C.P.R.* 1367–70, p. 15).

provision was the necessary preliminary to Wykeham's consecration. While the provision was made in accordance with the
king's wishes, the procedure which gave it the appearance of an
act performed by the pope without external pressure was carefully observed; and the pope had this advantage, that if he
chose to be dilatory or obstructive, the see could be left destitute
of the solace of a pastor for an indefinite period.

After the accession of Henry IV, however, the popes made
more than one endeavour to control episcopal appointments,
in the hope, no doubt, that a government rooted in orthodoxy
and determined to put down heresy would prove compliant.
In the spring of 1400 the see of Bath and Wells fell vacant and
Boniface IX provided Richard Clifford, dean of York and
archdeacon of Canterbury.[1] This came to nothing; the king
refused the temporalities to Clifford, and in the following year
the matter was settled by a compromise. Henry Bowet, the
candidate of the Crown, went to Bath and Wells and Clifford
obtained the see of Worcester after canonical election by the
cathedral chapter. Although Clifford was not consecrated till
October 1401, the bull by which Bowet was appointed to Bath
and Wells declared that the see was vacant by the translation
of Clifford to Worcester.[2] While the pope had been obliged
to yield to the king's wishes, the bull by which Clifford had been
provided to Bath and Wells was not formally withdrawn.

On two occasions during the fifteenth century appointments
to the see of York were seriously delayed by collisions between
the wills of pope and king. After the execution of Archbishop
Scrope on 8 June 1405, the chapter elected their dean, Thomas
Langley, a candidate probably acceptable to the king and certainly to themselves. The king gave his assent,[3] but the affront
given to the Church by his summary treatment of Scrope was
met by the papal provision of the famous jurist Robert Hallum,
then archdeacon of Canterbury; while in the meantime Langley

[1] Bull dated 12 May 1400 (*C.P.L.* v. 287).
[2] Bowet was given custody of the temporalities of Bath and Wells 20 Apr. 1401.
The see of Worcester fell vacant 13 June following by the death of Tideman of
Winchcombe; the *congé d'élire* was issued 20 June and the temporalities were given
in custody to Clifford 2 July. Clifford was consecrated 9 Oct., Bowet not until
20 Nov. Both, however, received their temporalities 21 Sept. (*C.P.R.* 1399–1401,
pp. 470–1, 505, 529, 547). For dates of consecration see *R.S.A.*
[3] 8 Aug. 1405 (Rymer, viii. 406–7; *C.P.R.* 1405–8, p. 48).

was got out of the way by his provision to Durham.[1] In the end
the pope consented to translate Hallum, as yet unconsecrated,
from York to Salisbury, and the matter was settled by the
translation of Henry Bowet from Bath and Wells to York, more
than two years after Scrope's death.[2] Bowet's death in 1423 was
followed by a similar deadlock. In the first case the difficulty
had arisen from the infringement of ecclesiastical liberties by
Henry IV, a point which Gregory XII, in spite of the loyalty
of the English Crown to the Roman pope throughout the
schism, could not pass over. But in the interim the schism had
been healed, and Martin V was bent on asserting the independence of the papacy, and had been encouraged in his efforts by
the orthodoxy of Henry V.[3] During the minority of Henry VI,
disturbed as it was by growing factions among the king's
counsellors, he translated Richard Flemyng from Lincoln to
York, in spite of the assent given by the council to the election
of Philip Morgan, then bishop of Worcester.[4] The council,
however, refused to accept the translation, and Flemyng was
threatened with the penalties of Praemunire if it was persisted
in.[5] Nevertheless, the candidature of Morgan was dropped;
the council put forward, under the influence of Beaufort, a
candidate of its own, John Kempe, bishop of London, and in
July 1425 Flemyng was retranslated to Lincoln and Kempe
translated to York.[6] In both these instances we see nominees

[1] Hallum was provided 14 May 1406 (*C.P.L.* vi. 82–3). The provision to
Langley bears the same date (ibid. 83).

[2] The temporalities of York were restored to Bowet and those of Salisbury to
Hallum, 1 Dec. 1407 (Rymer, viii. 503–4; *C.P.R.* 1405–8, pp. 384, 391).

[3] See the letter from Eugenius IV to Henry VI, announcing his reluctant provision of Thomas Bourchier to the see of Worcester. After complaining of the
imperfect obedience of the realm of England, alone among Christian realms, to the
pope, he urges the king to follow in the footsteps of his father, whose decision to
give Martin V full liberty to collate benefices was cut short only by his death
(*C.P.L.* viii. 216–18).

[4] Bull dated 15 Feb. 1423–4 (*C.P.L.* vii. 345–6). The signification of assent to
Morgan's election bears date 25 Jan. previously (*C.P.R.* 1422–9, p. 169).

[5] The translation of Flemyng may be regarded as a *ballon d'essai* by which the
pope hoped to create a precedent for future action. Its failure was soon followed
by his demand for the repeal of the obnoxious statute and his endeavour to cow
Archbishop Chichele into obedience to the Holy See.

[6] Bulls dated 20 July 1425, as noted in R. Flem. See *Surt. Misc.* 136, for a difficulty involved in the date of Kempe's bull as noted in his register. Neither prelate
recovered his temporalities till the following year, Kempe on 22 Apr., Flemyng
on 3 Aug. 1426 (*C.P.R.* 1422–9, pp. 330, 351).

backed by the chapter of York; for, in the first, if the Crown favoured Langley, it was at a time when Henry IV was anxious to conciliate the chapter, and in the second Morgan was undoubtedly the chapter's candidate. But, in the final arrangement of a compromise between king and pope, the wishes of the chapter were put on one side and the principle of free election was disregarded.

Once again before the death of Martin V an election was thwarted, and this time successfully, by the pope. In 1429 Thomas Brouns, a well-known jurist in the service of Chichele,[1] was elected bishop of Chichester with the royal assent.[2] The pope succeeded in providing Simon Sydenham, dean of Salisbury, in his place,[3] and Brouns had to be content with Sydenham's deanery. During the next few years he played a prominent part at the Council of Basel, and, when the see of Worcester fell vacant in 1433, Eugenius IV lost no time in providing Brouns, relying upon the fact that the death of the bishop of Worcester at Basel had placed the see at his disposal, and not without confidence that Brouns would be acceptable to the king and council.[4] His hopes, however, were premature. The provision was disregarded: seven weeks after it had been made a *congé d'élire* was issued to the chapter of Worcester, who elected the nominee of the Crown, Thomas Bourchier.[5] It must be owned that the pope had some reason for feeling annoyed. He had exercised his canonical right of providing to a benefice that had fallen vacant at the Curia, and in so doing had flattered himself upon his diplomatic choice of an eligible person. He was now confronted by a rival candidate, in point of birth eminently eligible,[6] but a young man under canonical age and without experience. He wrote to the king and Chichele in anger thinly veiled by sorrow, protesting his disappointment and commenting with surprise upon the contumacy of the realm of England.[7]

[1] Brouns was Chichele's chancellor and auditor of causes *c.* 1425-9 (Churchill, i. 487; ii. 243, 245). For his various preferments see *Linc. Vis.* i. 16, 201-2.
[2] Signification of assent 3 Aug. 1429 (*C.P.R.* 1422-9, p. 544).
[3] Bull dated 14 Oct. 1429 (*C.P.L.* viii. 114).
[4] Bull dated 24 Sept. 1433 (ibid. 213).
[5] *Congé d'élire* 16 Nov. 1433 (*C.P.R.* 1431-6, p. 326).
[6] Bourchier's mother, the daughter of Thomas, duke of Gloucester, was first cousin to Henry IV and his niece by marriage.
[7] *C.P.L.* viii. 212-19. See p. 19 above, note 3. The last letter of the series is a letter of paternal advice to Bourchier.

But, although he long delayed his consent, the widening breach between the pope and the fathers of Basel and the growing disposition of national governments to limit papal jurisdiction in spiritual matters made opposition dangerous. Early in 1435 a see was at last found for the deserving Brouns, who was provided to Rochester and translated to a higher manger at Norwich in the following year; and, as Worcester was thus left open, Bourchier received his bull of provision without further controversy.[1]

This series of events, however, had a sequel. Bourchier was consecrated to Worcester on 13 May 1435: the ceremony took place at Blackfriars, with Cardinal Beaufort as chief consecrator, assisted by Archbishop Kempe and three other bishops.[2] Between five and six months later the see of Ely was vacant by the death of Philip Morgan. The *congé d'élire* was issued in a very short time and Robert Fitzhugh, bishop of London, was elected.[3] But Fitzhugh died before anything had been done towards the completion of his translation.[4] The king now pressed Thomas Rudborne, bishop of St. Davids, upon the chapter and endeavoured to secure a bull of provision for him. The prior and convent of Ely, however, rejected Rudborne and elected the young bishop of Worcester. Thus for the second time Bourchier became a bone of contention between king and pope, but this time Eugenius was on his side. He translated him from Worcester to Ely and endeavoured to satisfy the king by translating Rudborne from St. David's to Worcester.[5] The whole business was complicated by the rivalry of political factions, and it seems probable that, in his support of Rudborne's candidature for Ely, Henry VI was influenced by Beaufort, with whom Rudborne was associated as one of the plenipotentiaries at the Congress of Arras in 1435.[6] In the end, neither candidate obtained the disputed see. Henry put for-

---

[1] The provision of Brouns to Rochester was made 21 Feb. and that of Bourchier to Worcester 9 Mar. 1434-5 (*C.P.L.* viii. 213, 498). Bourchier recovered his temporalities 15 Apr., and Brouns his 12 May 1435 (*C.P.R.* 1429-36, pp. 458, 460). The letter from the king to the pope, requesting the promotion of Bourchier to Worcester (Rymer, x. 640) is out of place where it stands, for the date, 10 May, must belong to 1434, not to 1436.     [2] *R.S.A.* 88.

[3] Morgan died 25 Oct. 1435 (ibid. 86), and the *congé d'élire* went out on the 30th of the same month (*C.P.R.* 1429-36, p. 491).

[4] Fitzhugh died 15 Jan. 1435-6 (*R.S.A.* 88).

[5] See *C.P.L.* viii. 260-1.     [6] Rymer, x. 611.

ward a new name, that of Louis of Luxemburg, archbishop of Rouen, and an arrangement was made by which Eugenius consented to the appointment of Louis as administrator of the revenues of the see of Ely. In September 1437 a papal bull granted him the see of Ely to be held *in commendam* with that of Rouen.[1] When Louis died in 1443 Bourchier was elected and translated to Ely without competition[2] and eleven years later succeeded Kempe as archbishop of Canterbury.

Details of appointments to bishoprics in the second half of the fifteenth century are somewhat obscure and the particulars and even the dates of several consecrations of bishops are wanting. The record of the *congé d'élire* on the patent rolls is fitful, while that of the royal signification of assent ceases.[3] Election in fact had become a formality to which little attention was paid. The king, through his agents at the Roman court, postulated his candidates for provision. The papal provision was accepted as a personal act of grace and the mention of it as such formed part of the royal mandate for restitution of temporalities; but for such restitution the renunciation by the bishop-designate of all clauses and phrases in the bull which might be deemed prejudicial to the royal authority was necessary.[4] This indeed was

[1] See *Corr. Bek.* i. 4–8, for the king's letter, 22 June 1437, asking the pope's consent to the appointment of Louis and excusing himself for his change of mind. The bull annulling the translation of Bourchier was issued 27 Sept. (*C.P.L.* viii. 252). For Chichele's opposition to the appointment see Wilkins, iii. 526, and cf. *C.P.L.* viii. 254. The temporalities of Ely were delivered to Louis 3 Apr. 1438 (Rymer, x. 697; *C.P.R.* 1436–41, p. 154).

[2] *Congé d'élire* 4 Oct. 1443 (Rymer, xi. 44; *C.P.R.* 1441–6, p. 225). Bourchier was translated to Ely 20 Dec. 1443 and recovered his temporalities 27 Feb. following (Rymer, xi. 52; *C.P.R.* 1441–6, p. 251).

[3] This applies only to bishoprics. The case of religious houses is different: see p. 16 above, note 1.

[4] The habitual form of the mandate for delivery of temporalities, for which see Rymer, *passim*, is as follows, after the direction to the escheator: 'Cum dominus summus pontifex, nuper vacante ecclesia cathedrali de A. per mortem (seu resignationem, &c.) venerabilis patris B nuper episcopi loci illius eidem ecclesiae praedilectum clericum nostrum C. providerit ipsumque in episcopum loci illius praefecerit et pastorem sicut per litteras ipsius domini summi pontificis nobis inde directas nobis constat, Nos pro eo quod idem episcopus omnibus et singulis verbis nobis et coronae nostrae prejudicialibus in dictis litteris bullatis contentis coram nobis renunciavit et gratiae nostrae humiliter se submisit volentes cum eo agere gratiose cepimus fidelitatem eiusdem episcopi et temporalia episcopatus illius una cum exitibus inde a tempore vacationis eiusdem provenientibus restituimus eidem. Et ideo tibi precipimus quod eidem episcopo temporalia praedicta cum pertinentiis in balliva tua una cum exitibus inde a tempore praedicto, liberes in forma praedicta.'

no new thing: since the middle of the fourteenth century it had been invariable, but its formal character had increased with years. The king, it is true, might occasionally sue in vain. The letters collected in the series known as the *Official Correspondence of Thomas Bekynton* throw much light on the tediousness of the negotiations of Henry VI's agents with popes and cardinals. Efforts to obtain the bishopric of Coutances for one of these agents, Andrew Holes, failed altogether.[1] One candidate occasionally had to be substituted for another, or, as in the case of Bekynton himself, another see was substituted for that for which he had previously been designed.[2] The king postulated Thomas Kempe, nephew of the cardinal archbishop of York, for the next provision to the see of London;[3] but when in 1448 London fell vacant, he put forward, whether by accident or design, another name. Nicholas V refused to gratify this change of mind and insisted upon providing Kempe.[4] During the period covered by most of the correspondence Eugenius IV, in his struggle with and his eventual victory over the Council of Basel, maintained to the king and his council an attitude open to persuasion but deaf to coercion. In this respect he adhered closely to the example of his predecessor Martin V, whose opposition to the independent spirit of the king's council during the early years of Henry VI's reign had gone to the length of suspending the legatine powers of Archbishop Chichele and threatening England with an interdict.[5] But under the successors of Eugenius IV the principle of mutual agreement

[1] *Corr. Bek.* i. 26, &c. This was in 1440: at an earlier date Holes had been provided by Eugenius IV to the archdeaconry of Northampton; but Bishop Gray of Lincoln had taken the opportunity of the vacancy to appoint another person, his young kinsman William Gray, afterwards bishop of Ely (ibid. ii. 251; R. Will. Gray, fo. 84*b*).

[2] On 23 May 1443 Angelo Gattola informed Bekynton of his appointment to the see of Salisbury (*Corr. Bek.* i. 162). This appointment, however, was contingent upon the possible acceptance of Bath and Wells, then vacant by the translation of Bishop Stafford to Canterbury, by the bishop of Salisbury (William Ayscough), and, as Ayscough declined translation, Henry VI postulated Bekynton for Bath and Wells (ibid. ii. 76, 77).

[3] Ibid. i. 155–9. The king's second candidate for London, Marmaduke Lumley, bishop of Carlisle, was also put forward by the duke of Suffolk. The pope, while recognizing his merits, refused to accept him but promised to promote him in the future. This was fulfilled by his translation from Carlisle to Lincoln in 1450.

[4] *C.P.L.* x. 387–8.

[5] See the series of letters printed by Wilkins, iii. 471–86, for the chronology of which see E. F. Jacob in *Trans. R. Hist. S.* xv. 111–19.

between king and pope worked smoothly; and this concurrence, which eliminated the chapters from any active part in the process, prevailed regularly through the reign of Henry VII.[1]

The habitual collusion between the Crown and the papacy in the matter of provisions was one of the favourite themes of that severe critic of the Church of his day, Thomas Gascoigne. 'Of late years', he says, writing in the sixties of the fifteenth century, 'I have known disgraceful promotions of men in England who had licence from King Henry VI to sue out and accept provisions from the pope; and so in my days by provisions granted at Rome many bishops, abbots and deans have been appointed without any election whatever but the election of the pope which is called provision.'[2] As regards abbots and deans, the accusation is overdrawn: on provisions to abbeys Gascoigne was judiciously vague, while his stock instance of a provision to a deanery is the intrusion of Richard Andrew at York in 1452, in face of the election of John Bermyngham by the majority of the chapter.[3] Of bishoprics, however, his words are substantially true. 'There are three things to-day that make a bishop in England, the will of the king, the will of the pope or of the court of Rome, and the money paid in large quantities to that court; for thousands of pounds of English money are paid here in England to Lombards for exchange to the impoverishment of the realm.'[4]

[1] Such is the conclusion derived from the entries in patent rolls, most of which are reproduced at length by Rymer, xi, xii.

[2] *Loc. L. V.*, p. 26: 'Novi enim nuper in Anglia homines pessime promotos qui habuerunt licenciam a rege Henrico sexto ut laborarent papae Romano pro provisione, et quod illam acceptarent, et sic per provisionem factam Romae in diebus meis facti sunt plures episcopi et abbates et decani sine electione quacunque, excepta electione papae, quae vocatur provisio.' Cf. ibid., p. 47.

[3] Ibid., pp. 37, 47, 193, 203.

[4] Ibid., p. 52: 'Tria ista faciunt hominem iam esse episcopum in Anglia—voluntas regis Angliae, voluntas papae vel curiae Romanae, et pecuniae in habundancia solutae curiae Romanae, scilicet diversa milia librarum Anglicanae monetae solutae hic in Anglia Lumbardis pro cambio, quod depauperat regnum.' Cf. ibid., p. 202. For the system of payments to the apostolic camera and the part of foreign bankers in it see A. I. Cameron, *The Apostolic Camera and Scottish Benefices 1418–1488*, 1934. Such points are well illustrated at a much earlier date by the *Intrinseca de camera* (sc. archiepiscopali) in R. Melton, in which further the necessity of prompt and punctual payment is stressed by the urgency of the archbishop's orders to his financial agents to make no delay in obtaining the best exchange for money furnished them by his receivers, e.g. 'et hoc non omittatis aliqualiter nostris precibus et amore' (fo. 26*b*).

There is no reason for supposing that the formalities of election were actually dispensed with in any particular instance, but it is certain that its part in the procedure and influence upon the result were insignificant. The letters sent by the king to the pope on these occasions may, from those which remain, be gathered to have taken two forms, a formal signification of the king's assent to the election, requesting the pope to deign favourably to perform what further appertained to him, and letters commendatory in favour of the elect. We may suspect, however, that letters commendatory usually preceded any announcement of the election. In 1457 there was a repetition of the incident, already mentioned, which had occurred when Thomas Kempe was provided to the see of London, and with a like result. On 1 August a *congé d'élire* was issued to the prior and convent of Durham, deprived of their pastor by the death of Robert Neville.[1] Only three weeks later Calixtus III announced to the king that he had provided Lawrence Booth, dean of St. Paul's, to the vacant see. Booth, brother of the archbishop of York,[2] had been recommended by letters from the king, Margaret of Anjou, and some of the chief magnates of the realm. But later another letter had come from the king, recommending his doctor, John Arundel. Calixtus preferred the first candidate and promised to take future notice of Arundel, who some eighteen months later was provided to Chichester. It is perfectly clear that, as the *congé d'élire* for Durham went out, as has been said, only on 1 August, the time between the election at Durham and the provision at Rome is narrowed down to little more than a fortnight, so that, if any news of the election reached Rome by 21 August, the recommendation of Booth must at any rate have preceded it.[3]

[1] Rymer, xi. 402; *C.P.R.* 1452–61, p. 361.

[2] Gascoigne, who hated the Booths, describes him as *in adulterio genitum* (*Loc. L. V.*, p. 194). Lawrence, however, is more credibly reckoned to have been the son of Sir John Booth of Dunham Massey by his first wife Maud Savage, while William was a son of Sir John's second wife, Joan Trafford. On the table-tomb of William's younger brother Roger in Sawley Church, co. Derby, where he obtained a three-life lease of the prebend of Sawley annexed to the treasurership of Lichfield, the inscription, now partly destroyed, described him as brother of William and Lawrence. Twelve years after the death of William (1464), Lawrence in his turn became archbishop of York and died in 1480. For the chantries founded by both archbishops at Southwell see *Thor. Soc.* xv. 75–80.

[3] The pope's letter, containing the details referred to above, is printed in Rymer, xi. 404–5.

It is also likely that those licences to accept provisions which are occasionally recorded were granted without regard to capitular elections. There is no indication that such grants were habitual, for the acceptance of the provision was sufficiently covered by the subsequent renunciation of the prejudicial clauses contained in the bull. Their object was rather to enable their holder to go to Rome and take his chance of securing a vacant see. An interesting example is the licence granted in 1468 to Dr. James Goldwell, the king's proctor at the Curia, to accept a provision to any vacant bishopric, with certain specified exceptions.[1] After some delay Goldwell obtained his bishopric in 1472–3, when he was elected and provided to the see of Norwich.[2] His memory is recalled to us there by the presence of his rebus, the golden well, repeated over and over again, on the bosses of the presbytery vault in his cathedral church. In connexion with Goldwell's preferment, it is worth while remarking that the provision by Alexander VI of two Italians to the see of Worcester, Giovanni de' Gigli in 1497 and Silvestro de' Gigli in 1499, can hardly be regarded as a Borgian stratagem to Italianize the English Church, but was actually a recognition of their services as Henry VII's agents at Rome.[3] The preferment of Italians to more than one English see at the beginning of the sixteenth century was of no spiritual advantage to their flocks, whom in truth it affected but little. The diocesan machinery went on as usual, and the episcopal registers of Giovanni and Silvestro show a creditable record of business conducted by their vicars-general. At no time probably was the intrusion of foreigners into English benefices less fraught with danger than under the early Tudors. If Hadrian di Castello held the sees of Hereford and of Bath and Wells, if the

[1] Rymer, xi. 638–9; C.P.R. 1467–77, pp. 125, 126.

[2] Restitution of temporalities 25 Feb. 1472–3 (Rymer, xi. 768–9; C.P.R. 1467–77, p. 373). He had already been consecrated at Rome 4 Oct. 1472 (R.S.A., p. 92).

[3] Giovanni, 'king's proctor at the court of Rome', had custody of temporalities 18 July and restitution 5 Dec. 1497 (C.P.R. 1494–1509, p. 139). He died 25 Aug. 1498, and Silvestro was provided 24 Dec., having already had custody of the temporalities 1 Dec., when he is described as archpriest of Lucca and 'solicitor of the king's causes in the court of Rome'. The mandates for restitution bear date 17 March 1498–9 (ibid., pp. 154, 172). The date of the consecration of neither Giovanni nor Silvestro is known, but it obviously took place between the grants of custody and restitution in both instances. See R.S.A., p. 95; Rymer, xii. 657–8, 666, 670, 704–5, 710.

future pope Clement VII was for a while bishop of Worcester, and Campeggio bishop of Salisbury, these were concessions to a foreign prince which the Crown could complacently afford and could recall at will.[1]

Not only were cathedral chapters left in the cold, but the rights of the metropolitan were also overlooked. Theoretically, the election of a bishop by a chapter required confirmation by the archbishop of the province: confirmation was necessary before the elect could be consecrated. The authority of the papacy had grown at the expense of metropolitans. The False Decretals on which so much of its claims depended—and the False Decretals, like so many 'forgeries' in the Middle Ages, were statements intended to confirm and regularize recognized custom—were the work of prelates who, restive under the demands of metropolitans, chose, by exalting the Holy See, to acknowledge the superiority of a distant power to an obedience required by their next-door neighbours. As papal authority increased in the west and the pope became the supreme source alike of spiritual blessings and ecclesiastical law, the intermediate position of the metropolitan between pope and bishops almost vanished. The title *legatus natus*, habitually borne by the archbishops of Canterbury and York from the middle of the fourteenth century, implied that their metropolitan dignity was an office delegated to them by the pope. But the popes never encouraged the theory that such a delegation was permanent. It could be overridden by the bestowal of legatine authority upon some other person, as when Martin V suspended Chichele's legation and appointed Beaufort as his legate.[2] An act of this kind, it is true, might lead to threats of calling the statute of Praemunire into operation; but these were merely threats and their fulfilment was avoided with apprehension of the grave consequences which it might involve.[3] The papal attitude to metropolitans, however, was that of a superior power to officers invested with a limited authority, commissaries for special purposes rather than delegates with full power of action. In this light the confirmation of a bishop-elect by his archbishop

[1] With regard to such appointments see the well-known essay by Creighton, 'The Italian Bishops of Worcester', in his posthumous *Historical Essays and Reviews*, 1902, pp. 202–34. [2] The bull of suspension is printed in Wilkins, iii. 484–5.
[3] On the history of this statute see W. T. Waugh, 'The Great Statute of Praemunire' (*E.H.R.* xxxvii. 173–205).

fell into the background and confirmation by the pope himself took its place. The pope was the universal ordinary claiming direct jurisdiction over all churches: the bull of provision was a necessary step to a bishopric and every bishop took an oath of personal obedience to the pope in terms which admitted of no doubt as regarded his direct subservience to the Holy See.[1] Moreover, the profession of obedience, reverence, and subjection which he made to his metropolitan at the time of his consecration was couched in brief and general terms, and his promise was qualified by the words 'according to the decrees of the Roman pontiffs' and a clause saving his order.[2]

In the first quarter of the fifteenth century the end of the Great Schism and the interval between the deposition of John XXIII and the election of Martin V gave the metropolitan the opportunity of recovering the right of confirmation. In view of the inconvenience of leaving sees void for lack of papal confirmation, the parliament of March 1416 enacted that, so long as the papacy remained vacant, the custom which was being followed in more than one foreign see should obtain in England and that, on receipt of a royal writ, the elect should go for confirmation to his metropolitan.[3] In pursuance of this

[1] See the oath taken by Chichele on the receipt of the pallium (*R. Chich.* i. 17) and that taken by Benet Nicolls on his translation from Bangor to St. David's (ibid. i. 42). Examples of this common form are abundant. For later versions with additions see the oaths taken by Ruthall in 1509 and Wolsey in 1513–14 as bishops respectively of Durham and Lincoln (Rymer, xiii. 268, 393).

[2] For examples of the profession of obedience to the metropolitan see *R. Chich.* i. 14, &c.

[3] *R.P.* iv. 71: 'Nostre Seignur le Roy, aiant consideration a la longe voidance de la see Apostolique, pur la dampnable seisme qe ja longement ad endure en Seinte Esglise, et l'em ne sciet unqore cumbien s'endurera, et coment certeins Esglises Cathedrales deinz son Roialme, que sount de la fundation de ses nobles Progenitours et de son patronage, ont este ja piecea, et sont uncore destitutz de pastorele governaunce, a cause qe les persones qi sont esluz a ycelles, ne purrount estre confermez ez parties de dela, pur defaute d'Appostoill, combien qe nostre dit Seignur le Roy sur ceo ait ottroie son royal assent, en graunt diminition de divine service es dites Esglises, subtraction d'ospitalitees, tres graundz peril des almes de plusours, devastacion et destruction des Seigneuries et possessions d'icelles, et empoverissement des eslitz des ditz Esglises, et coment par possibilitee en tiel manere puissent voidier toutz les Esglises Cathedrales de son dit Roialme, et issint estre destitutz de governaille et le Roy et son Roialme, du Conseil, Comfort, et Aide, qu'il deusse avoir de la Prelacie, et considerant auxint coment en plusours parties de dela, depuis la voidance du dite see, diverses confirmacions ount este faitez, et ceo font de jour en autere, par les Metropolitans des lieux, sicome creablement il est enforme, et vuillant pur tant pur ouster les ditz meschiefs purvoier, come appent, de remedie, de plein et deliberat avis et assent des Seignurs et Com-

measure Chichele in April 1416 confirmed the election of John
Wakering as bishop of Norwich, and, eleven months later,
that of Edmund Lacy as bishop of Hereford. Similarly on
7 December 1417 he confirmed John Chaundeler in the see of
Salisbury.[1] But a month earlier the election of Martin V had
taken place, and the new pope, crowned on 21 November,
took advantage of the general satisfaction at the ending of the
schism to reserve to himself appointments to all vacant sees.
The bull notifying this to Chichele was dated at Constance
14 February 1417–18 and contained the news that the pope
had translated Benet Nicolls from Bangor to St. David's and
had provided William Barowe to Bangor. These acts had
actually been effected in the previous December. Technically
therefore the see of Salisbury, which had fallen vacant by the
death of Robert Hallum at the Council of Constance on
4 September 1417, lay at the pope's disposal, and the confirmation of Chaundeler, having taken place after the accession of
the pope, was invalid. It seems impossible that the fact of the
papal election was wholly unknown to Chichele when he
confirmed the election to Salisbury; but, whether the act was
performed in ignorance or with the deliberate intention of
creating a precedent for the future, it is certain that application
was made to Martin V for a confirmation of its validity. The
pope answered from Geneva on 21 July 1418, naturally admitting the metropolitan rights of Canterbury over Salisbury, but
treating the election, confirmation, and consecration of the
bishop, not indeed as null and void, but as in need of apostolic
authority, and confirming them retrospectively. From that
time forward, however, the archiepiscopal confirmation, thus
temporarily asserted, fell again into disuse.

munes de son Roialme esteantz en cest present Parlement, voet et ordeigne, qe les
persones issint eslitz et a eslirz, deinz son Roialme, durante la voidance du dite see
Apostoliqe, soient confermez par les Metropolitans des lieux, saunz excusation ou
outre tarier en cele partie a faire, et qe les briefs du Roy, s'il besoigne, soient adres-
sez as ditz Metropolitans, lour estroitement enchargeantz de faire les ditz confirmations, et tout ceo qe a lour office en appent; et auxintz as ditz eslitz, q'ils
devers eux effectuelment pursuyent lour ditz confirmacions, issint q'en defaute des
ditz Metropolitans, ou eslitz, damage ou prejudice n'aviegne a nostre dit Seignur
le Roy, et a son Roialme, et a lez ditz Esglises, pur l'enchesons dessus ditz, que
Dieu ne voille.'
  [1] For the full series of documents relating to these appointments see *R. Chich.*
i. 26–40, followed by those relating to the provisions to St. David's and Bangor.

The appointment of bishops is the test question by which the relations between the English Church and the Apostolic See in the fifteenth century can be put to the proof, and it has there- fore been examined at some length. If it was guided by con- siderations of state, if bishops were habitually royal nominees accepted by the pope, if the pope could not hope to thrust a candidate of his own into an English bishopric unchallenged, yet his acts of confirmation and provision were essential to the recognition of the canonical tenure of a see. At the same time, the position of the king in such matters was greatly strengthened by his hold over the temporalities of a see during its vacancy. It is significant that while, as has been said already, the *congé d'élire* is recorded irregularly, and even rarely, upon the patent rolls, and the signification of the royal assent vanishes altogether —although in the case of religious houses both were still habitual[1]—the mandates for restitution of temporalities are almost invariably entered. Further, in the later part of the century, when the papal consent to the king's request came to be taken for granted, it became customary for the Crown to bestow the temporalities upon its candidate at pleasure, with- out waiting for his confirmation or translation. This indeed was no new thing, for examples of the practice occur in the fourteenth century.[2] Several instances occur early in the reign of Henry IV—Richard Young, bishop of Bangor, William Strickland, of Carlisle, Richard Clifford, of Worcester, and Henry Bowet, of Bath and Wells.[3] In one at least of these the provision had been made in the previous reign, but nothing had come of it. It was obviously at this date to the king's advantage, while his throne was still insecure, to put his candi- dates in charge of the possessions of their sees as early as possible. There are a few instances in the reign of Henry V: Kempe, for example, received a grant from the temporalities of Chichester before his bull of translation can have reached England, but full restitution was not granted till nearly six months later.[4] Under Henry VI instances increased. In 1453

---

[1] See p. 16 above, note 1.

[2] Thus William of Wykeham, who had been placed in full administration of the see of Winchester by Urban V, 11 Dec. 1366, had restitution of temporalities 12 July 1367 and was not consecrated till 10 Oct. (*R. Wyke.* i. 2, 3; *C.P.R.* 1367–70, p. 15; *R.S.A.*, p. 79).          [3] *C.P.R.* 1399–1401, pp. 31, 198, 448, 470.

[4] The grant of 650 marks bears date 3 Mar. 1420–1; the bull of translation was

Reynold Boulers, bishop of Hereford, was given custody of the temporalities of Coventry and Lichfield before his translation to that see. In this case the grant appears to have been made when he was already bishop elect.[1] But in September 1464 George Neville, then bishop of Exeter, had a similar grant of the temporalities of York eleven days before any *congé d'élire* was granted,[2] and, on the vacancy caused at York by the death of Lawrence Booth in 1480, the grant of custody to Thomas Rotherham, bishop of Lincoln, preceded the *congé d'élire* by nearly three weeks.[3] Six years later John Morton held the temporalities of Canterbury for nearly three months before the pope translated him from Ely.[4] The practice, though by no means invariable, was common in the reign of Henry VII, and both the Gigli received grants of custody of the temporalities of Worcester before either obtained the see, and the grant was made to Giovanni nine days before the date of the licence which empowered the chapter to elect their bishop.[5]

The fifteenth century, then, it may be said, marks a steady growth in the influence of the Crown over the choice of spiritual rulers of the Church. It is extremely interesting to trace this in the records of a single diocese whose episcopal registers are in print. The registers of the bishops of Hereford are not as a whole first-rate examples of such collections, but for the present purpose they are of exceptional value. From 1344 onwards the registrars, as a rule, followed the custom of prefixing to their work careful notes of the initial stages of each episcopate, naming the acts by which each bishop entered into possession of his see. These, it may be concluded, constituted in their view a sufficient title to jurisdiction. In the register of Bishop John Trillek there are two such entries. The first, heading a preliminary section, records his canonical election in February

issued 28 Feb., and the temporalities restored 21 Aug. 1421 (*C.P.R.* 1416–22, pp. 317, 396; *C.P.L.* vii. 191).

[1] The date is 15 Jan. The translation followed 7 Feb., and temporalities were restored 26 Mar. (*C.P.R.* 1452–61, pp. 33, 49; *C.P.L.* x. 600).

[2] The grant was made 16 Sept., and the *congé d'élire* was issued on the 27th (*C.P.R.* 1461–7, pp. 327, 329).

[3] Grant of custody 24 May; *congé d'élire* 12 June (*C.P.R.* 1476–85, pp. 202, 206).

[4] Grant of custody 13 July 1486 (Rymer, xii. 302–3; *C.P.R.* 1485–94, p. 119). The bull of translation is dated 6 Oct.

[5] Custody granted 18 July; *congé d'élire* 27 July (*C.P.R.* 1496–1509, pp. 111, 113). For the Gigli see also p. 26 above, note 3.

1343-4, his confirmation by Archbishop Stratford, and the restitution of temporalities by the Crown on 29 March, which took place three months before his consecration. The second records his consecration at Waverley Abbey on 29 June 1344 and his subsequent enthronization at Hereford on 24 October.[1] Of the bull of provision, actually issued between his election and confirmation,[2] nothing is said, nor is it mentioned in Stratford's letters of confirmation.[3]

Lewis Charlton, who succeeded Trillek in 1361, was provided by Innocent VI and was consecrated at Avignon. The bull of provision, though duly registered, is omitted from the printed edition of the register.[4] The heading of the volume records merely the limiting dates of the episcopate from 25 October 1361, when Charlton had arrived in London and appointed his vicars-general, to his death on 23 May 1369:[5] there is no mention of election and confirmation and from the patent rolls we know only that, when the temporalities were restored on 14 November 1361, he renounced the prejudicial clauses of the bull.[6] It seems that this was a case of papal provision *motu proprio* after previous reservation of the see; but the details which we possess are insufficient. Before Charlton's death, however, Urban V had reserved the next appointment and in 1369 provided William Courtenay, canon of York. This is recorded in the register, together with the dispensation granted to Courtenay, who was under episcopal age, and there are subsequent details of his enthronement on 15 September 1370.[7] It may be noted, however, that, while the register lays stress only upon the provision, it was not made until after Courtenay had been elected, and that he was consecrated at Lambeth in March 1370.[8] In the selection of Courtenay for promotion the pope, although professing to act upon his own responsibility with the advice of the cardinals, was probably meeting the wishes of the king; and Courtenay, the son of a great magnate,

[1] *R. Trill.* i. 21. The *congé d'élire* was granted 27 Jan. and the royal assent signified 5 Mar. 1343-4 (*C.P.R.* 1343-5, pp. 189, 216). The grant of restitution as above is on pp. 222-3).

[2] 15 Mar. 1343-4 (*C.P.L.* iii. 95).    [3] *R. Trill.*, p. 1.

[4] R. L. Charl. int., p. ii, notes it as recorded on fo. 26.

[5] Ibid., p. 1.    [6] *C.P.R.* 1361-4, p. 106.

[7] *R. Court.* (Her.), pp. 1-5.

[8] *Congé d'élire* 8 July 1369 (*C.P.R.* 1367-70, p. 282): the date of the bull of provision, as recorded in the register, is 17 Aug. in that year.

was obviously a person in whose eligibility both pope and king would concur.

Courtenay was translated to London in 1375 and was succeeded by the Dominican John Gilbert, translated from Bangor. All that the register notes is his translation,[1] but we know from the contemporary Winchester register that he made his profession of obedience to the pope, required of every prelate, before William of Wykeham at Farnham.[2] As a diplomatist and as treasurer of the exchequer he plays some part in the history of his day and continued to be active after his translation from Hereford to St. David's in 1379. His successor at Hereford was John Trefnant, canon of St. Asaph, a lawyer practising at the Curia, who was provided by Urban VI to a see which, being vacant by translation, was at his entire disposal. This appointment appears to have proceeded entirely from Rome. Trefnant was consecrated in one of the chapels of St. Peter's by the archbishop of Bologna and two other prelates, as is set forth in the heading of his extremely interesting register, together with a note of his admission to his temporalities by Richard II on 16 October 1389. It is perhaps worth noting that in the mandate for their restitution Trefnant is referred to as bishop-elect, although he had been consecrated on 20 June.[3] From the point of view of the Crown, the acts which admitted a bishop to free exercise of his jurisdiction were homage for his temporalities and the renunciation of the compromising conditions of his provision.

The next register, that of the Carmelite Robert Mascall, merely notes the beginning of his episcopate without details. The *congé d'élire* is on the patent rolls, and was followed by his provision and consecration at Rome.[4] He was succeeded in 1417 by Edmund Lacy, dean of the chapel royal. Lacy was one of the three bishops who, as already noted, were appointed during the vacancy of the Holy See before the election of Martin V, and whose elections were confirmed by Archbishop Chichele. The relevant documents are in Chichele's register;[5]

[1] *R. Gilbert*, p. 1.
[2] *R. Wyke.* i. 74–5.
[3] *R. Tref.*, p. 1; Rymer, vii. 646; *C.P.R.* 1388–92, p. 121.
[4] Rymer, viii. 372–3; *C.P.R.* 1401–5, p. 421. The date of consecration (*R.S.A.* 84) was 6 July.
[5] *R. Chich.* i. 33–6.

but the heading of the Hereford register, with its assertion of the legality of the proceedings, is worth full quotation.

'The Register of the reverend father in Christ and lord, the lord Edmund, by the grace of God bishop of Hereford, who, with the unanimous and universal election of his brethren, and then with lawful confirmation by the ordinary, the apostolic see being at that time without a pastor, was duly and lawfully consecrated to the title of the same church by the most reverend father in Christ and lord, the lord Henry, by the grace of God archbishop of Canterbury, primate of all England and legate of the apostolic see, with the assistance of the right reverend fathers in Christ and lords, the lords Thomas and Stephen, by the same grace bishops of Worcester and St. David's, in the lower chapel of the king's castle of Windsor, and in the presence there and then of the most dread and most Christian prince in Christ and our lord, the lord Henry, by the grace of God the illustrious king of England and France and lord of Ireland, with other noblemen and magnates of his realm, on the eighteenth day of April in the year of our Lord 1417.'[1]

Lacy was translated to Exeter in 1420, when Thomas Polton, a papal notary and dean of York, was provided to Hereford by Martin V and consecrated at Florence.[2] His register has a merely general heading. In 1422 Polton, absolved by the pope, with the counsel of his brethren and in the plenitude of his apostolic power, from the chain wherein he was bound to the church of Hereford, departed—in the spirit perhaps rather than in the flesh, for he was usually to be found at the Curia—to Chichester, and Thomas Spofford, bishop-elect of Rochester and abbot of St. Mary's at York, took his place.[3] Spofford's register is headed by an account of his previous career as a monk professed for thirteen years, for sixteen years and five months abbot of St. Mary's, then called and provided by apostolic authority to be bishop of Rochester, and finally translated to Hereford.[4] As he had never obtained the see of Rochester,

[1] R. Lacy, 1: 'Registrum [etc.] qui ad ipsius ecclesie titulum unanimi et universali cum eleccione fraternali et deinde ordinarii confirmacione legitima sede apostolica ad tunc pastore carente per reverendissimum [etc.] assidentibus ei reverendissimis [etc.] in inferiori capella castri regii de Wyndesore metuendissimo et Christianissimo in Christo principe et domino nostro [etc.] cum ceteris nobilibus et proceribus regni sui tunc ibidem presentibus xviii° die Aprilis anno Domini m° cccc° xvij° rite et legitime fuit consecratus.'

[2] C.P.L. vii. 214; R.S.A., p. 86.

[3] Bull of translation from Rochester 17 Nov. 1421 (C.P.L. vii. 214; R. Spoff. 2–4).

[4] Ibid. 1.

he was not consecrated until 24 May 1422, and received his temporalities on the following day from Humphrey, duke of Gloucester, then Henry V's lieutenant in England.[1]

Spofford resigned in 1448. The register of his successor, Richard Beauchamp, is headed by the record of his consecration at Lambeth by Archbishop Stafford and seven other bishops on 9 February 1448–9.[2] He had received a bull of provision from Nicholas V, mentioned in the course of an appeal made by him to the pope for the protection of the Holy See and the court of Canterbury against unspecified impugners of his title.[3] Ten days before his consecration he had been granted, first, custody, and then restitution of the temporalities.[4] In about eighteen months he was translated to Salisbury, and in September 1450 the vacant see was filled by the provision of Reynold Boulers, abbot of Gloucester. The bull of provision is entered in his register, and its date is given in the heading as that of his promotion, followed by his admission to the temporalities and his subsequent consecration by Bishop Low of Rochester.[5]

Boulers's translation to Coventry and Lichfield in 1452 was followed by the translation of John Stanbury, a Carmelite, from Bangor. As in the previous register, the date of the bull of translation is given in the heading, and is followed by that of the restitution of temporalities, 26 March 1453.[6] It will be noticed that in these headings, while the part of the pope in the appointments is merely implied in dates, the effective action of the Crown in the disposal of temporalities is heavily stressed. This is also the case in the heading of the register of Thomas Myllyng, abbot of Westminster, Stanbury's successor in 1474. In the printed edition of this register some words are wanting; but the essential facts recorded are the restitution of temporalities by Edward IV on 13 May and the bishop's subsequent consecration in the Lady Chapel at Westminster on 21 August.[7]

The registers of Edmund Audley, translated from Rochester

---

[1] *R.S.A.*, p. 86; *C.P.R.* 1416–22, pp. 436–7.
[2] *R. Beauchamp*, 3.                              [3] Ibid. 4, 5.
[4] 31 Jan. 1448–9 (*C.P.R.* 1446–52, p. 223; Rymer, xi. 222–3).
[5] *R. Boulers*, 1.                                [6] *R. Stan.* 1.
[7] *R. Myll.* 1. The temporalities, however, were actually not restored till 15 Aug. (Rymer, xi. 817; *C.P.R.* 1467–76, p. 467). The date in the register may be that of a grant of custody.

in 1492 and to Salisbury in 1502, and of Cardinal Hadrian di Castello are wanting. But the wording of the headings of the two remaining registers departs from previous forms. The first is:

'The register of the reverend father in Christ and lord, the lord Richard Mayhew, professor of sacred theology, by divine compassion bishop of Hereford, of all and sundry the acts or deeds given and granted by him and by his vicars-general while he was on business in distant parts, in the year of his consecration, which was on the 27th day of October in the year of our Lord 1504, and in the first, second and third years of the same consecration; who previously, having been created and appointed president of Magdalen college, Oxford, ruled the same college for 27 years and more, and was at the same time archdeacon of Oxford and elected chancellor of the same benign university and for very many years almoner and councillor of the most illustrious lord king Henry VII; and then, by apostolic authority and by nomination of the abovesaid most illustrious king Henry, was called, after he had completed the 64th year of his age, to the church of Hereford, [void] by the translation of the reverend father in Christ the lord Adrian, cardinal priest of the title of San Crisogono, to the church of Bath and Wells, as appears by the letters apostolic of the lord Julius the second, by divine providence pope, which follow shortly after and are inserted in the second leaf with the oath annexed in manner accustomed.'[1]

The second is as follows:

'The register of the reverend father in Christ and lord, the lord Charles Bothe, by divine permission bishop of Hereford, doctor of laws of Bologna, who being first an advocate in the benign court of Canterbury, and then treasurer of the cathedral church of Lichfield and prebendary of Sallow[2] in the same, afterwards chancellor of the reverend father, etc., William Smythe, bishop of Lincoln, and vicar-general in spirituals depute of the same when on business outside his diocese, and created archdeacon of Buckingham, and thereafter chancellor of the most illustrious prince in Christ and lord Henry VIII, king of England and France and prince of Wales, in the principality and marches of Wales, finally on the 22nd day of the month of April in the year of our Lord 1516, being nominated

---

[1] *R. May.* 1. The essential phrases are: 'deinde auctoritate apostolica et nominacione supradicti illustrissimi regis [etc.] vocatus erat ad Herefordensem ecclesiam per translacionem [etc.] ut patet per litteras apostolicas [etc.].' The papal bulls with the usual form of oath follow on pp. 3–5.

[2] i.e. Sawley, co. Derby.

by the said most illustrious prince to the church and bishopric of Hereford, void by the death of the lord Richard Mayowe of honest memory, bishop of Hereford, obtained custody of the temporalities of the said bishopric of the king's grant by his letters drawn up to that end. And on the last day of the month of November next following, which then happened on the first Sunday of the Advent of our Lord, he was consecrated bishop of Hereford by the most reverend father, etc., William, archbishop of Canterbury, in the chapel within his manor of Otford, with the assistance of the reverend fathers, etc., Richard and Richard, bishops of Winchester and Norwich.'[1]

Now Charles Booth was actually provided by Leo X in the ordinary way, and, when he finally received the temporalities, of which he had had custody for some ten months, on 19 February 1516–17, he made the usual renunciation.[2] While the grant of custody is fully entered in the register, the bull of provision, which had been inserted in the register of his predecessor, is omitted without any reference to the pope's action in the matter. In a certain sense the preamble of Mayew's register is the most papalist of the series: it alone, of all those which have been discussed, definitely calls attention to the existence of a bull of provision and names the pope who granted it. At the same time, the mention of the royal nomination is a novelty which places the appointment in a new light. In point of fact, Mayew's appointment followed what had become the customary course; but hitherto no registrar had laid emphasis upon the initiative of the Crown. Twelve years later the action of the Crown alone is noted.

Such preambles occur in other registers, but the Hereford series is of peculiar value for the preciseness of its detail. It would be a mistake to read too much into such passages or to imagine that the insistence upon the delivery of temporalities and the introduction of the word 'nomination' indicate a desire on the part of diocesan officials to make light of the papal share in the transaction. It might be argued, of course, that, in the largely biographical headings of Mayew's and Booth's registers, the registrar was merely providing a preface to the opening

[1] *R. C. Bothe*, 1. The essential phrases are: 'per memoratum illustrissimum principem nominatus custodiam temporalium dicti episcopatus ex concessione regia per suas litteras inde confectas . . . obtinuit.'

[2] He had custody 17 May 1516 (*R. C. Bothe*, 1–3; *L. & P. H. VIII*, ii (1), 550 (no. 1903). He was promoted in consistory 21 July following (ibid. 670, no. 2199).

documents of each and so bringing events up to date. Nevertheless, the object of such prefaces, taking the series as a whole, is to show how the bishop came to his see and thereby to give some account of his title to it; thus to the official mind the king's action is obviously a matter of prime importance which it is necessary to put on record. This, it becomes clear, is the motive force of the whole proceeding. Nothing was further from the conservative mind of the ecclesiastical lawyer, trained in ancient formulas, than to depreciate the spiritual authority of the papacy to provide and translate bishops to the.sees of its obedience; but its complacency with the royal will in such matters had become a recognized fact, and its part in the proceeding, though productive of delay and expense, was largely mechanical. The royal power in fact loomed so prominently in dealings where king and pope were jointly concerned that Henry VIII's task in severing the ties which bound the English Church to Rome was materially lightened by the passive attitude into which the Holy See had fallen where the will of the Crown was in question. And such passages as have been noted show that the mental tendency with regard to such matters at the beginning of the sixteenth century had reached a point from which no very violent transition was necessary to lead it to acknowledgment of the royal supremacy in matters spiritual.

In conclusion, it may be remarked that the bishops of Hereford to whom reference has been made, while, with one or two exceptions, somewhat inconspicuous among their brethren, illustrate excellently the variety of types of person from which the bishops of the later Middle Ages were selected. The great prizes of the Church still fell, as they had done throughout the fourteenth century, to secular clerks of the ministerial class. The fifteenth-century archbishops of Canterbury and York were all drawn from the *sublimes* and *litterati* who had won preferment and amassed pluralities in the service of the Crown. Younger sons of noble houses, such as Arundel, Stafford, Bourchier, and George Neville, had no monopoly of the high offices for which their personal ability was an important qualification. Chichele, Kempe, Morton, the Booths, Rotherham, and in the next century Warham and Wolsey were sons of franklins, yeomen, or traders. At Winchester the magnificent series of chantry-chapels reminds us of a succession of ministerial prelates, Beaufort and Peter Courteney alone of noble birth, Wykeham, Waynflete, Thomas Langton, and Fox all of various degrees of less exalted origin. Members of religious orders were almost excluded from the greater sees: the Austin canon Henry Dean, archbishop of Canterbury for a brief period, and the Benedictine abbot William Sever, for a few years bishop of Durham, were rare exceptions. At Hereford, however, and in the less important sees generally, a wider type of selection is shown. For noble clerks, William Courtenay, Richard Beauchamp, and Edmund Audley, Hereford was a stepping-stone to richer sees. It formed a convenient resting-place for diplomatists and jurists, the curialist lawyers Trefnant and Polton, Mayew and Booth, servants of the Crown. But three of its bishops, Gilbert, Mascall, and Stanbury, were friars; three, Boulers, Spofford, and Myllyng, abbots of famous Benedictine monasteries; and of these religious Gilbert alone was conspicuous in affairs of state. Other dioceses may show more illustrious names, few a more interesting variety.

The aspect of ecclesiastical affairs which has been discussed has led us naturally to the crisis which befell the English Church in the reign of Henry VIII. The history of the relations between the Crown and the papacy, illustrated by their influence upon the episcopal government of the Church, during the period preceding the Reformation, is of fundamental interest to the survey of that period; and in later lectures the subject will recur in other contexts. But the trial of strength between the spiritual and temporal powers is not the only aspect, though it is a very important aspect, of the prelude to the Reformation. The internal condition of the English Church, the state of things with which the diocesan administrator had to deal, demands detailed investigation, and this will form the basis of the next and subsequent lectures.

# II

## THE ORGANIZATION AND ADMINISTRATION
## OF THE DIOCESE

FOR four centuries the number of English dioceses remained unchanged. During the last quarter of the eleventh century sees of bishops had suffered some local alteration, and disputes with regard to territorial claims had, generally speaking, been settled; but after the Conquest no addition was made to the existing number of bishoprics until in 1109 that of Ely was formed. In 1133 the diocese of Carlisle came into being, though its continuous existence cannot be said to begin until the thirteenth century.[1] But after that period no new diocese was created until the reign of Henry VIII. Further, during this long interval the territorial divisions of the seventeen English and four Welsh dioceses remained in a fixed condition. The period in which the sees of Ely and Carlisle were founded is the period in which the subdivision of dioceses into archdeaconries appears to have assumed a more or less final form, and about the same time, though more gradually, it is possible to distinguish rural deaneries corresponding to the clearly marked areas which were certainly well established at the beginning of the thirteenth century.

Something has been said already of the medieval conception of the episcopal office. The benignant idea of a father in God and a shepherd of souls, with the tenderness and patience which it implies, no doubt existed in theory. But the prevailing aspect of the bishop's paternity was its severity, and in the attitude of the pastor to his flock the spirit of correction was more prominent than that of compassion. In the language of the episcopal chancery the charge which he bore was the duty of moral

---

[1] The reason for the foundation of the diocese of Ely, *quia Lincoliensis episcopatus diocesis nimium protendebatur*, is given by Will. Malmes. *G. P.* (Rolls ser.), 325. *Hist. Eliensis* ap. Wharton i. 613–14 asserts the previous exemption of the monastery from diocesan authority and the endeavour of the bishop of Lincoln *sibi assiduis accusationibus subiicere*. The diocese of Carlisle was formed by Henry I out of the district annexed to the English Crown by Rufus's seizure of Carlisle in 1092. Its early history and relation to surrounding dioceses are summed up by Hill, *The English Dioceses*, 1900, 279–96.

reformation among the people and clergy subject to his jurisdiction, of planting virtues and plucking and rooting out vices
with the hoe of his ordinary power of correction.[1] He was the
*judex ordinarius*, the normal judicial authority within his own
diocese, from whose sentences there was within that area no
higher court of appeal for the spiritual offender. When he went
upon his ordinary visitation, he sat judicially as a tribunal.[2]
The texts of the sermons preached on such occasions contained
notes of warning rather than encouragement. 'This is the city
of visitation' implied a prospect of judgement to come: 'I will
search out Jerusalem with candles' was not the preface to a
message of mercy.[3] It is perhaps unfortunate that we see
medieval bishops so entirely through the medium of documents
and records which are official and impersonal that we have
little opportunity of becoming acquainted with individual traits
of character. In this respect we know more of the twelfth
century than we do of the fifteenth: Anselm and Turstin,
Becket and St. Hugh are living figures, but of Beaufort and
Kemp, Bourchier and Rotherham, in spite of their prominence
in the State, we have only faint outlines.

At all times, it is needless to say, the higher clergy had been
indispensable to the government of the realm, and the episcopate was largely recruited from the ministerial class. It may be
stated as a general fact that bishops were habitually appointed
on the ground of their ability without distinction of rank.[4] If
younger sons of noble families, such as Archbishop Courtenay
or Cardinal Beaufort, obtained bishoprics, it was not merely
because kings called them cousin—though such relationship
was an asset—but because their talent marked them out for
preferment, even at an early age. The path to high preferment

---

[1] See Bishop Gray's injunctions to Burnham and Wellow Abbeys (*Linc. Vis.* i.
22, 126): 'Ad reformandum subditorum nostrorum excessus attenciori cura pro-
spicimus, vt que a religionis tramite exorbitant et sanctimonie fructibus sunt nociua
visitacionis nostre ordinarie sarculo euellantur, et extirpatis vicijs virtutum plan-
taria ipsorum subditorum nostrorum mentibus inserantur.' Cf. ibid. i. 46 (Gray
to Dunstable). Also ibid. ii. 199 (Alnwick to New College, Leicester): 'Cure
nobis est mores in populo et clero nobis subditis reformare, virtutes plantare et
vicia sarculo correccionis ordinarie euellere et extirpare; propter que visitacio
ordinaria noscitur instituta.'

[2] See ibid. ii. 36, &c.: 'sedente dicto reverendo patre iudicialiter pro tribunali.'

[3] The first text (Jer. vi. 6) occurs ibid. ii. 54, 184.

[4] See also p. 39 above, with regard to the bishops of Hereford.

was equally open to men of lower social standing who had approved themselves in government offices or in positions about the court. Of the archbishops of Canterbury during the fifteenth century, Arundel, Stafford, and Bourchier were of noble birth, belonging to some of the highest families in the kingdom and connected more or less closely with the royal house; but Chichele sprang from a well-to-do family of the middle class in Northamptonshire, Kempe was the son of a petty squire with an estate in Kent, Morton and Dean, and their sixteenth-century successors, Warham and Cranmer, were all of the class which sent its sons, if not engaged in trade or farming, to make their way in the clerical profession.[1] In all sees of importance the same disregard of discrimination in the matter of rank may be noticed. The family of Booth, which between 1454 and 1516 supplied four prelates to six sees, belonged to the small country gentry: it was seated on the borders of Lancashire and Cheshire, at Barton-on-Irwell and Dunham Massey, and acquired further means by obtaining a lease for three lives of the prebend of Sawley in Derbyshire, annexed to the treasurership of Lichfield.[2] Such families produced competent men of business, versed in politics and civil and ecclesiastical law, who took advantage of their profession—we can perhaps hardly call it a vocation—to obtain its highest prizes.

The association of bishops with politics, however, became more constant in the fifteenth century than before. Earlier prelates, however necessary their counsels might be to the Crown, were nevertheless able to devote a large part of their time to their dioceses. Greenfield and Melton, who were archbishops of York in succession from 1306 to 1340, were typical *ministeriales*, both of whom had been chancellors of England before their elevation to the episcopate; but their administration of their diocese was exemplary, and, considering the part which of necessity they had to take in affairs of state, it is sur-

---

[1] Dean was an Austin canon, who was prior of Llanthony Secunda before his quick progress to Canterbury by way of the sees of Bangor and Salisbury.

[2] See p. 25 above, note 2, and Ormerod, i. 523–35; iii. 597, 598. The relationship of the clerical members of the family has often been misstated. John Booth, bishop of Exeter 1465–78, was nephew of the brothers (or half-brothers) William and Lawrence Booth, both archbishops of York, and Charles Booth, bishop of Hereford 1516–35, was their grand-nephew and second cousin to John. William was bishop of Coventry and Lichfield 1447–52 and archbishop of York 1452–64; Lawrence was bishop of Durham 1457–76 and archbishop of York 1476–80.

prising to notice how much time in each year they were able to give to diocesan duties, supervising the business of the diocese from the numerous manor-houses of the see, from one to another of which they changed their residence at short intervals.[1] But towards the end of the century the absence of bishops from their dioceses became more common, and their residence in London more permanent. There were bishops who, like Alnwick at Norwich and Lincoln, found diocesan administration highly congenial and soon withdrew almost entirely from public life to pursue it. On the other hand, Kempe, who passed quickly through the sees of Rochester, Chichester, and London to York, and thence, after a quarter of a century during which he obtained a cardinalate, to Canterbury, spent all his life closely involved in politics and made his habitual residence in London. Gascoigne, extreme to mark the sins of the bishops of his day, says that, during his long tenure of the see of York, Kempe stayed in his diocese only for two or three weeks at a time at intervals of ten or twelve years.[2] Gascoigne was by no means infallible, but the evidence of Kempe's register shows that, while this may be an exaggeration, there is some excuse for it. It may be remembered to Kempe's credit, however, that he did attempt a primary visitation of the diocese of York, though, hindered by much business, he delayed any part of it until the third year of his translation, and then accomplished but little.[3] In the late summer of 1428 he set out to visit its

[1] See itinerary in *R. Green.* v. 299–328. Melton's itinerary (unpublished) is very similar for a much longer period. In the next century detailed itineraries are less satisfactory, but such a register as that of Langley shows that, while the absences of bishops in London were longer than before, they also found time for personal administration of their dioceses.

[2] *Loc. L. V.* 36, 37: 'per xxviij fere annos in quibus stetit archiepiscopus Eboracensis fuit totaliter absens a sua diocesi, manens Londoniis vel in Cancia, vel in aliis locis in Anglia remotis a sua diocesi Eboracensi, excepto quod aliquando semel in decem vel in duodecim annis mansit in sua diocesi Eboracensi per duas vel tres septimanas, paucis diebus vel nullis mansit in Eboraco, et in tempore suo palacium archiepiscopi Eboracensis defecit et fere ad solum ruebat, et ipsum palacium ipso existente archiepiscopo reparatum non fuit', &c.

[3] *Surt. Misc.* 202. His mandate for the visitation of the archdeaconry of Richmond bears date 22 June 1428. The visitation began on 24 Aug. and was abandoned on the 26th. From that time onwards, apart from a visitation of the vacant see of Durham, delegated to a commissary, in 1437–8 and 1438–9 (ibid. 226–38), public business hindered him from doing anything more until Sept. 1440, when he seems to have visited the cathedral church and city of York in person (ibid. 238–44). Subsequently he obtained a papal indult (9 Nov. 1440) to visit the rest of the

most remote portion, the great archdeaconry of Richmond, to whose farthest regions in north Lancashire, Cumberland, and Westmorland no archbishop seems to have penetrated for a century and a half.[1] But visitations, however kindly meant, were not an unmixed blessing to those who had to endure them, and the edifying sight of an archbishop, at the head of a large retinue of clerks, notaries, servants, and minions of the law such as Chaucer drew in the Sompnour, was impaired by the thought of the expense which it involved in entertainments, fees, and gratuities. At any rate, when the archbishop had entered the dales which lead into the heart of the Pennines, he was met in the church of Wensley by the abbots of Jervaulx and Coverham, the archdeacon, his predecessor's favourite nephew, and some of the local incumbents, who informed him on behalf of the clergy of the archdeaconry that the country-side was too greatly impoverished by failure of crops, murrain, and other disasters incidental to medieval country life to bear the heavy cost of such a visit, and begged him to accept a fee by way of composition. Kempe acceded to the petition and returned to York and shortly afterwards, without completing his visitation elsewhere, entered upon a career of practically permanent absenteeism.[2]

Nothing of course is easier than to condemn a course of conduct so inconsistent with a strict view of the pastoral office, and the political bishop who was at the beck and call of the government of his day was fair game for the satirist.[3] Absentee prelates, when called to deal directly with some diocesan matter, might treat it lightly and negligently, or might use their powers so irresponsibly that their actions deserved grave censure. If Gascoigne was not merely repeating gossip about his favourite objects of attack, they were occasionally guilty of transactions for which no excuse can be found.[4] Taken as a whole the

diocese by commission, and this visitation, according to the programme, was carried out in 1441 and 1442 (ibid. 244–80).

[1] Archbishop Wickwane certainly visited the whole of the archdeaconry in April–June 1281 (*R. Wick.* 345). Greenfield, though on several occasions he was in Cumberland at Lanercost and Rose Castle, was there upon affairs of state and seems never to have visited the portion of the archdeaconry which was in that county. [2] *Surt. Misc.* 218–20.

[3] See the stanzas on the death of the duke of Suffolk (3 May 1450) printed in *Pol. P. & S.* ii. 232–4.

[4] See the remarkable story of John Delabere, bishop of St. David's, *Loc. L. V.* 35, 36.

English bishops of the fifteenth century were not a strong body of men: the period of the loss of France and the Wars of the Roses produced many clerical politicians, but no great clerical statesman. But custom had decreed that these liege sages of his council were very profitable and necessary to our lord the king and to all his realm,[1] and from that point of view, at a disturbed epoch in which the position of the king was insecure and the future of the realm critical, it was inevitable that the relation which many of them bore to their dioceses should be little more than nominal. And, when we take into account that highly formal conception of their diocesan activities to which reference has been made, so totally different from our modern ideas of the episcopal office, we may question whether their presence or absence mattered so greatly to their dioceses.

At best, outside the centres of administration, the cathedral city and the episcopal manor-houses, the bishop was not a familiar figure to his subjects. His primary visitation after his enthronement took the form of a progress through the diocese, according to a programme by which the clergy and parochial lay representatives were summoned from large areas to convenient central places.[2] Where the diocese was large, the visitation invariably was spread over a considerable period, and, although it was sometimes followed after some years' interval by a second visitation, this seem to have been incomplete, and I know of no instance, even at earlier periods when it is possible to follow a bishop's movements from day to day, in which the rule of triennial visitations was strictly observed.[3] Normally, while in his diocese, the bishop resided, not in his

[1] See *S. R.* ii. 85, quoted p. 15 above, note 1.

[2] See *Surt. Misc.* u.s. Visitation programmes are not regularly recorded in episcopal registers, but are often found, e.g. in the registers at Worcester. For late fifteenth- and early sixteenth-century examples see R. Carp., ff. 168b–169b, R. Alcock, fo. 99b, R. R. Morton, fo. 32, R. J. Gigl., fo. 9, R. S. Gigl., ff. 94, 123. Notices of visitations are commonly entered in the earlier fourteenth-century registers at York: see, e.g. *R. Green.* i, 8; ii. 25, &c. There is a good programme for the archdeaconry of Durham in 1355 in R. Hat., ff. 21b–22b. For Lincoln see introd. to *Linc. Vis.* ii: the progress and conduct of later visitations may be studied at length in *Linc. Dioc. Vis.* i, ii. See also the very detailed documents relating to visitations of dioceses *sede vacante* by archbishops' commissaries in R. J. Morton and R. Warham.

[3] Between 1317 and 1340 archbishop Melton held three visitations of the diocese of York, or parts of it. Alnwick visited portions of the diocese of Lincoln twice, but his second visitation was incomplete.

palace in the cathedral city, where his presence was not a source of content to the cathedral authorities, but in one of his country houses. In these places he maintained, as is said of Archbishop Melton, a large household and splendid hospitality;[1] eighty casks of red wine were not sufficient to stock Archbishop Bowet's cellars for a year;[2] and although a century later Archbishop Savage saved the cost of the banquets and festivities accompanying an enthronement by never being enthroned at all, he looked after the repairs of his houses and kept a household remarkable for its tall servants.[3] Such a household, indeed, must have caused some anxiety to guests with moderate means, for clerks of the chapel, gentlemen, yeomen, grooms, and scullions all expected douceurs on a fixed scale for each class from every parting guest.[4] To these houses came presentees to benefices for institution, offenders whose cases were reserved to the bishop from every part of the diocese, petitioners who sought confirmation for the foundation of chantries and hospitals, or renewal of licences for non-residence and private oratories. The bishop or his chancellor and clerks were always accessible on their own ground, but outside that area he was seldom seen.

For all ordinary purposes his work could be well done by deputy. At places where he was in residence his tribunal was held, not by himself personally, but by his household chancellor or one of his clerks.[5] By the beginning of the fifteenth century the greater part of his work, in view of his constant absences, was delegated to his vicar-general. In the first instance the vicar-general was the deputy who, for all acts for which episcopal orders were not necessary to the agent, was appointed by the bishop when he left his diocese for a short period. On his return the appointment was cancelled, to be renewed or bestowed upon someone else on the next similar occasion. As late as the middle of the fourteenth century a famous bishop, William Bateman of Norwich, a diplomatist frequently engaged as an ambassador to the pope or the French king, appointed

---

[1] *H.C.Y.* ii. 417.          [2] Ibid. 434.          [3] Ibid. 442.

[4] See an account of the expenses incurred by Abbot Assheton of Peterborough on his visit to the bishop of Lincoln for the confirmation of his election, printed *A.A.S.R.P.* xxxiv. 277–9.

[5] This is exemplified by the entries in the fragment of Alnwick's Court-book referred to below.

temporary vicars-general whose powers came to an end on his return to the diocese.[1] The permanent vicar-general, however, gradually superseded these temporary officers: usually chosen from the members of the cathedral chapter, he received his commission at the beginning of an episcopate, and, though removable at the bishop's pleasure, he continued to hold his office until his commission was withdrawn.[2] In any case, it was terminable with the bishop's death or resignation, but it was frequently continued during vacancies of the see by mandate from the chapter, and renewed by the next bishop.[3]

The vicar-general exercised the bishop's gracious jurisdiction as a deputy of his master. His commission usually specified his duties. He was empowered to receive the oath of obedience from the incumbents of benefices whom he instituted, to issue dispensations for non-residence and letters dimissory for orders, to summon and hold diocesan synods, to collect and receive Peter's pence and all sums of money due to the bishop in virtue of his church, to absolve and reconcile persons excommunicated in cases reserved to the bishop, to examine, discuss, and terminate elections of heads of religious houses, and to confirm such elections and provide for the installation of persons elected, or if necessary to annul them; to collect and receive fruits of vacant benefices, to arrange for ordinations and commit their celebration to suitable bishops, to examine presentations to benefices

---

[1] See *Norf. and Norw. Arch. Soc.* xxv. 126–7.　　　　[2] See App. I.

[3] Practice, however, varied in this respect. R. Flem. shows that, in the vacancy of the see of Lincoln after the resignation of Bishop Repyngdon (10 Oct. 1419), the administration of spiritualities in the diocese was committed to John Southam, archdeacon of Oxford. After Flemyng's arrival in the diocese Robert Leek, to whom he gave a prebend in Lincoln minster in Nov. 1420, became his vicar-general, acting in that capacity during his absences from the diocese. During Chichele's metropolitical visitation in 1424–5 Leek, who was also official principal, acted as vicar-general under commission from the archbishop. But, in the temporary vacancy caused by the abortive translation of Flemyng to York in 1425, the vicar-general was Richard Hethe, one of the senior members of the chapter, and it is evident that the dean and chapter preferred to entrust the spiritualities of the see to old and experienced colleagues than to a clerk who had been introduced to the diocese in the interest of the bishop. In 1406 Langley, after his consecration as bishop of Durham, appointed the prior and the archdeacon of Durham his vicars-general before his arrival in the diocese. In 1409, when about to start for the council of Pisa, he issued a commission to two canons of Darlington. His vicars-general were habitually chosen from the members of the collegiate churches of his diocese, and those the register of whose acts occupies ff. 258–304 of his register, covering considerable periods of his episcopate, were Thomas Lyes or Leys, dean of Auckland, and John Hunteman, dean of Lanchester.

and institute presentees, to deprive incumbents or usurpers of benefices, to admit the purgation of the bishop's prisoners and deliver them from jail, and to execute and return royal writs. The bishop reserved all collations of benefices in his gift to himself, as well as his ordinary right of visitation: these the vicar-general could not exercise, unless under a commission *ad hoc.*[1] With these duties were sometimes combined others which properly belonged to the bishop's official, such as the correction and punishment of offences and the proof of wills. It became usual in the course of the fifteenth century to unite the offices of vicar-general and official, and in any case the line between their respective provinces was rather thin; but actually the two offices were distinct.[2]

The vicar-general in fact, while the bishop was present in his diocese, was frequently in request for the execution of business which the bishop was hindered from directing in person. During the bishop's absence he supplied his place, as has been said already in the performance of all those acts for which episcopal orders were not necessary. For those which required episcopal orders, ordinations, confirmations, consecrations of chapels and churchyards, reconciliations of consecrated sites polluted by bloodshed, benedictions of heads of religious houses, the consecration of the holy oil and chrism on Maundy Thursday, the blessing of numerous objects for sacred use, the services of a suffragan were called in.[3] From the early part of the fourteenth century the employment of a suffragan for such purposes became fairly common; and as time went on it became very usual, so usual that large additions may be made to the list of such prelates in Stubbs's *Registrum Sacrum.*[4] There were many

[1] In the later York registers, which are largely those of vicars-general, the sections entitled *Collationes* are records of acts performed by the archbishops in person.

[2] See App. I. Gibson, in his introductory discourse to the *Codex*, discusses these offices at length with regard to their union in the office of the bishop's chancellor. 'But this mixture of the Powers', he says, 'did not at all alter the nature of the powers themselves; which, tho' held by the same person, were conveyed, as well as held, under the same conditions and limitations, as before they were in their separate State.'

[3] See App. II.

[4] The suffragans acting in the diocese of Hereford during the period after 1400 were as follows: Nicholas, bishop of Dunkeld (1404–7); Matthew, bishop of Hebron (1415); John, bishop of Annaghdown (1420–1); Richard, bishop of Achonry (1425–40); Geoffrey, bishop of Kildare (1448–51 and 1455–9); Thomas, bishop of Cloyne (1477); Richard, bishop of Down and Connor (1479); Richard

such bishops available, for the most part friars who had been provided to titular sees *in partibus infidelium* or to the equally unproductive dignity of an Irish see to which effective access was impossible. In either case the intention was that they should give help to diocesan bishops, and, where their assistance was wanted, there was always a bishop of Philippopolis or Sidon, Annaghdown or Cloyne, ready to accept an offer of temporary work. Their appointment was made by commission for a limited period and renewed from year to year: it implied no settled tenure of office, for the suffragan could be dismissed by the diocesan at will. The commission emanated from the diocesan himself in most instances, but it could proceed from the vicar-general, from whom, in the absence of the diocesan, came those special commissions by which the suffragan celebrated ordinations.[1] Thus it is obvious that the suffragan was quite subordinate to the bishop's regular deputy, the vicar-general. He had no place in diocesan administration, his indispensability was a matter of certain acts and rites which a vicar-general could not perform. There were exceptions, rare instances in which a member of a secular cathedral chapter received consecration for suffragan work: in the latest part of the fifteenth and the beginning of the next century, Thomas Cornish, bishop of Tenos, was a remarkably active dignitary of the church of Wells,[2] John Hatton, bishop of Negropont, was

'episcopus Olonensis' (1482–92); Ralph, bishop of Ascalon (1505); Thomas, 'Lachorensis episcopus' (1505–19); John, bishop of Syene (1525). All but two of these are noted by Stubbs, but not all in connexion with Hereford; and, where Hereford is mentioned, his dates need correction. At Durham, Langley, throughout his episcopate, employed suffragans, Oswald, bishop of Whithorn, appointed in 1406, John, bishop of Annaghdown in 1414, Robert Foston, bishop of Elphin, in 1419–20, and Thomas Ratclyf, bishop of Dromore, in 1435. The bishop of Elphin resigned his see in 1430, but continued to act until Dec. 1434 as bishop *in universali ecclesia.*

[1] Thomas 'episcopus Lachorensis' celebrated two ordinations in Hereford cathedral in 1506 by licence of the vicar-general (*R. May.* 246, 247). In York R. Bowet there are two sets of ordinations, one of which, extending from 1408 to 1416, consists of notices of ordinations by suffragans held by licence of the vicar-general. Bowet's suffragans were William 'Pharensis episcopus' (1408–11), John 'Soltoniensis' (1411–20), John, bishop of Annaghdown (1416–20), Nicholas 'Loniciensis' (1419), Nicholas, bishop of Dromore (1421–3). One of Langley's suffragans, John, bishop of Annaghdown, received his commission under the seal of the vicar-general (R. Langley, fo. 287).

[2] To be distinguished from John Valens, bishop of Tenos, appointed as Bekynton's suffragan 17 Oct. 1459 (*R. Bek.* i. 329–30), whom Stubbs (*R.S.A.* 200) states to have been an Austin canon, and who was succeeded in his titular bishopric

also archdeacon of Nottingham in the church of York.[1] But the customary friar-suffragan enjoyed no exalted status: he was a general utility man who did what he was told and had no jurisdiction of his own outside his nominal sees. His business was not heavy, and he sometimes exercised his functions in more than one diocese at a time. The distinction of his office from that of the diocesan, and his entire dissociation from any part in the diocesan's jurisdiction, are illustrated by the fact that, when he celebrated orders, it was only in very rare instances at the high altar in the cathedral church, where his presence might be taken as a precedent for a claim to represent the bishop in the fullness of his authority.[2] Himself generally a member of an exempt religious order, he was often employed to give episcopal benediction to abbots and priors of exempt houses, to whom benediction by the diocesan implied a risk of submitting to his jurisdiction and loss of exemption in the future. His services were paid, not by a fixed stipend, but by the bestowal upon him of benefices in the bishop's gift, rectories of parish churches, masterships of hospitals, occasionally a prebend in a collegiate church. Thus an early-sixteenth-century suffragan, the Dominican William Hogeson, bishop of Dara, who acted as suffragan for Fox at Winchester and Wolsey at York, was rector of Burghclere and Chilbolton in Hampshire, a canon of Beverley Minster, and master of a hospital near Beverley.[3] As a friar his canonical right to hold these benefices might well be questioned, but his consecration brought at any rate an implied dispensation from observing the precepts of his order and from rejecting the sources of income necessary to maintain his suffraganship in some degree of modest dignity.[4]

by Thomas Cornish about 1486. Thomas, rector of Axbridge in 1489, exchanged his church for the prebend of Cudworth in Wells 1494, became chancellor of Wells 1499, prebendary of Compton Dundon 1501, and precentor 1502. He died in 1513 and is buried in Wells Cathedral (see Le Neve, Weaver, D. & C. Wells).

[1] See *R.S.A.* 201. He was succeeded as suffragan at York by another bishop of Negropont, Richard Wilson, not noted by Stubbs, who occurs in R. Wolsey.

[2] See App. II.

[3] See *Y.A.J.* xxiv. 236–57. He is buried in the south aisle of the choir at Beverley.

[4] Of the Hereford suffragans in the fifteenth century, Richard, bishop of Achonry, was rector of Eastnor (*R. Spoff.* 356), Geoffrey, bishop of Kildare, rector of Pembridge and Mitcheldean (*R. Stan.* 186, 192, 193), Richard, 'episcopus Olonensis', was rector of Donnington and warden of St. Katherine's Hospital, Ledbury (*R. Myll.* 193, 197), and Thomas, 'Lachorensis episcopus', was vicar of Bosbury and subsequently prior of Monmouth (*R. May.* 274, 275).

Although the vicar-general held so important a position in the diocese, the jurisdiction which he exercised was merely delegated. It was ordinary jurisdiction which belonged *pleno jure* to the bishop himself and was inseparable from his office. When the bishop was at home and was unable or unwilling to act in person in any contingency, he issued commissions, not as a matter of course to the vicar-general, but to any person whom it might be convenient to appoint for the purpose; and similarly the vicar-general, when left in charge of the diocese, appointed commissaries *ad hoc* at his pleasure. But, as has already been said, the jurisdiction delegated to the vicar-general was of the type known as gracious in which the ordinary, either on petition or of his own free will, confers such benefits as lie within his power or initiates the procedure of certain acts which form part of his diocesan routine, synods, visitations, and miscellaneous inquiries. That portion of the ordinary jurisdiction described as contentious, which included *cognitio causarum*, the judgement of suits within the competence of the ecclesiastical court, whether instituted by the bishop against spiritual offenders, or brought before him by plaintiffs, was delegated to the official principal. The growth of the powers of the official in French dioceses has been traced in a well-known treatise by M. Paul Fournier;[1] and the evidence which he has collected produces results which are applicable also to England. The appointment of diocesan officials with cognizance of ecclesiastical causes, holding permanent courts in the capital of the diocese, was already habitual while that of vicars-general was merely temporary. The official, however, was entrusted merely with the hearing of causes and with the pronouncement of sentence. Preliminary inquiries and the correction and punishment of offenders lay outside his competence, to be instituted and executed by order of the bishop or the vicar-general. Thus he had no control over the deprivation of incumbents of benefices: on the other hand, the proof and administration of last wills and testaments, with the disputes involved in their execution, were matters for the court of the official.[2]

This court was known as the consistory court, in which the official executed the *officium domini*, the bishop's office. In virtue of his delegation, his court was identical with a court personally

---

[1] Fournier, *Les Officialités au moyen âge*, 1880.     [2] See App. I.

presided over by the diocesan, and from its judgement there was no appeal to the bishop. This of course continues in our own day, when the diocesan chancellor, identical with the official principal, is still the bishop's *alter ego*, speaking with his voice and delivering decisions which are final. The title of official for the judge of the court was subject to variation: the official who presided over the provincial court of Canterbury was the archbishop's official principal, while his diocesan official was and is still appointed with the title of commissary-general.[1] It may be noted that, while Lyndwood, whose experience in the court of Arches gave his opinion exceptional weight, denied the power of correction and punishment *ex officio* to officials,[2] nevertheless such powers were sometimes included in their commissions. The commissary-general, for example, appointed by Archbishop Courtenay in January 1382 was empowered, not only to terminate cases which came before the consistory court,

[1] For the provincial court of Canterbury see Churchill, i, ch. x; for the commissary-general ibid. 54–60. Originally the dean of Arches, the dean of the archbishop's peculiar jurisdiction in London, acted as the official's commissary-general in the court of Canterbury, which, sitting in the church of St. Mary-le-Bow (*Sancta Maria de Arcubus*), became known as the court of Arches. Though earlier instances occur, the combination of the offices of official principal and dean of Arches in one person did not become habitual until the beginning of the sixteenth century. At Hereford the bishop's commissary-general, appointed with powers very similar to those of an official principal (*R. Mascall*, 2, 3), was actually an assessor to the official, as appears ibid. 73. Bishop Mascall's official, John Cateby, was also his vicar-general. Lacy's official, John Berewe, was also commissary-general and was usually addressed by that title (*R. Lacy*, 9, 34, &c.). He was commissary to Bishop Spofford, who in 1423 appointed Edmund Ruyhall as official (*R. Spoff.* 39), but appears again as official in 1434 (ibid. 174). In 1440 Richard Reed became official, and in the following year John Dylew (Dilwyn) appears as commissary-general (ibid. 240, 242). John Assheby was appointed commissary-general by Bishop Stanbury in 1453 (*R. Stan.* 3, 4) and filled that office in 1460 (ibid. 54); but in 1459 and 1460 Richard Pede was 'official of the consistory of Hereford' (ibid. 50, 53). From 1462 to 1466 John Greneway was commissary-general (ibid. 70, &c.). In 1476 John Bayly was appointed official principal and vicar-general (*R. Myll.* 27, 28), and there is a similar appointment of Richard Jaquessone in 1482–3 (ibid. 87–9). No such appointments are recorded in *R. May.* but on 1 Sept. 1516 Charles Booth made William Burghill his official and vicar-general and on 6 Dec. following appointed him commissary-general and principal sequestrator (*R. C. Bothe*, 13–15), and the three offices were again combined by Humphrey Ogle, appointed in 1526 (ibid. 184). Lyndwood, tit. *De sequest.* c. *Frequens*, ver. *Officiales* (p. 105), says that not all *deputati ad universitatem causarum* are officials, but several of them are called commissaries-general.

[2] Lyndwood, ibid. 'Cessat tamen eorum potestas in criminum correctione, excessuum punitione, et a beneficiis vel administrationibus amotione: nec etiam possunt conferre beneficia absque commissione speciali.'

but to make the consequent corrections, punishments, and reforms, and further to inflict canonical penalties for crimes and transgressions committed throughout the diocese of Canterbury.[1] From this and other instances it seems that in the following century Lyndwood, in defining the limitations of the official's powers, was enunciating a theory which was actually contra- dicted in practice.

In the earlier registers of the archbishops of York a special section is devoted to the correspondence of the archbishops with the officiality, including mandates by which proceedings were initiated in the consistory court.[2] It is obvious that there were certain points at which the jurisdictions committed respectively to the official and the vicar-general coincided or at any rate admitted of very slight distinction. Lyndwood noted that the powers whose exercise he denied to the official could be employed by the vicar-general.[3] At the date at which he wrote —he died in 1447—the commission of both offices to one man had become usual, so that we may assume that in his view the official who terminated the causes within his cognizance pro- ceeded to acts of correction and reformation *qua* vicar-general. Commissions, however, which confer both the offices upon one man make no specific distinction between their several pro- vinces, and in that issued by Fox, as bishop of Durham, in 1495 to Richard Nykke, afterwards bishop of Norwich, the duties of both are blended without discrimination.[4] It may be said that, as a matter of convenience, the vicar-general absorbed the specialized functions of the official into the wide field of his jurisdiction. Neither office was held as a permanency by its

---

[1] R. Court. (Cant.), fo. 3*b*, printed by Churchill, ii. 15, 16. In the appointment of William Burghill as official and vicar-general of Hereford in 1516 (see p. 52, note 1 above), although full power is given to terminate causes coming before the bishop's court of audience and the consistory, nothing is said of corrections; but in his appointment as commissary-general he receives full power of correction, even in reserved cases. Probate of wills is also included in this second appointment.

[2] This section disappears from the registers after 1352 (*T.A.J.* xxxii. 253).

[3] Lyndwood, u.s., ad ver. *Vicarios Generales*: 'Officiales dicuntur, quibus causarum cognitio generaliter per habentes jurisdictionem ecclesiasticam com- mittitur. Et in tales transfunditur cognitio causarum totius dioeceseos, non tamen inquisitio, nec correctio, sive punitio criminum . . . nec possunt aliquos amovere a beneficiis, nec conferre beneficia, nisi specialiter fuerint talia eis commissa. Sed vicarii generales omnia praedicta facere possunt virtute officii, excepta collatione beneficiorum.'

[4] R. *Fox*, 3–6.

occupant. It was subject to revocation at any time and it ceased with the death or resignation of the prelate on whose behalf it was exercised. In practice, the occupant generally continued in office during the vacancy of a see, but under a new commission from the keepers of the spiritualities, and was reappointed or superseded upon the accession of a new bishop.[1]

It should be understood, however, that the delegation of ordinary jurisdiction to vicars-general and officials did not admit them to an automatic exercise of power independent of episcopal supervision. It is true that, where a bishop was an habitual absentee, the vicar-general in the nature of things was left to his own devices: all that the bishop in such cases reserved to himself was the personal collation of benefices in his own gift. The register of an absentee bishop, such as that of Wolsey at York or Silvestro de' Gigli at Worcester, was kept in the name of his vicar-general, who acted upon his own responsibility and in the strength of his general commission. The general commission given to the official, however, was subject to special mandates by which causes were taken into his court: his procedure, that is, came into operation at the motion either of the bishop or the vicar-general. Further, the court of the official, while there was no appeal from its judgements to the bishop,[2] did not supersede the episcopal court. It was not the only consistory, for a number of cases were reserved by the bishop for his own judgement or were submitted to him directly. The official's court, working in a fixed centre was, so to speak, the Common Bench of the diocese: but there was also the court held *coram episcopo* by his household chancellor and clerks, changing its site with his changes of residence.[3] Here the *officium domini* was *officium merum*, exercised against serious offenders. A large

---

[1] 'Et nota, quod potestas horum officialium non solum per revocationem, sed etiam per mortem deputantis cessat. . . . Mortuo tamen episcopo transfertur de jure communi jurisdictio in capitulum sede vacante, vel in alium prout de consuetudine praescripta fuerit observatum' (Lyndwood, u.s., p. 105).

[2] 'Nec ab eis appellatur ad episcopos, sed ad eos, ad quos appellaretur ab ipsis episcopis' (Lyndwood, u.s.). He goes on to explain that this applies only to officials principal, 'ab aliis vero bene potest appellari ad ipsum episcopum'. In fact 'hi officiales sunt ordinarii, alii vero sunt delegati'.

[3] For the archbishop of Canterbury's court of audience see Churchill, i, pt. ii, c. xi. It may be noted that the commission granted by Bishop Booth of Hereford to his official includes cognizance of causes in his court of audience, 'ad nos et nostram audienciam vel ad nostrum consistorium spectantibus' (*R. C. Bothe*, 14).

fragment remains of the court-book kept by the clerks of Bishop Alnwick of Lincoln, which throws considerable light upon the social disorders of his large diocese in the middle of the fifteenth century.[1] A Huntingdonshire squire, for example, instigates his serving-men to attack the rector of his parish church, whom they chase into the fields of a neighbouring village and beat and wound. A number of Hertfordshire villagers pay similar attentions to an apparitor of the bishop and compel him to eat the writ which he is sent to serve upon a local defaulter. A woman of Belton in Lincolnshire, at variance with the rector, who is evidently not 'loth to cursen for his tythes', flings a chicken at his head while he is celebrating mass, and, summoned on this ground, brings a counter-charge against his moral character. Fraudulent executors, sorcerers, suspected Lollards, incumbents guilty of dilapidation, parishioners absenting themselves from divine service, are only some of the persons with whom this tribunal had to deal. It travelled with the bishop, and the offender who failed to obey its summons to one particular place was often compelled to appear before it in some distant part of the diocese or follow it as it moved with the bishop during a diocesan visitation.[2] Records of such proceedings are rare, and it may be presumed that, when a bishop was busy with public engagements and seldom in his diocese, the court was held by his vicar-general and the absolution of the guilty was imparted by his penitentiary. But, although the powers given to the penitentiary were wide and were sometimes extended to cases specially reserved to the bishop, there were certain general types of offence excepted for his personal treatment—perjury in matrimonial causes or in the civil courts where bloodshed or disherison were concerned, wilful murder, usury, sins against

[1] For the instances cited below see App. III.

[2] A good example of such mobility occurs in *R. Green.* v. 205–6, where the prior of the alien priory of Ecclesfield, on 21 June 1308, was cited at Mappleton Church in the East Riding, he being there present, to exhibit his title to his office at Kirkleatham in Cleveland on 12 July. The case was adjourned to the archbishop's manor of Scrooby in Nottinghamshire early in Oct., thence to Cawood on 12 Nov., thence on 18 Jan. 1308–9 to Bishop Wilton in the East Riding, and thence to Brotherton on 7 Apr. Thence to York, where it was heard by the official and master Peter Dene on 28 Apr. The prior's final appearance was at Scrooby, 23 June, when the case was dismissed *sine die*. But, on the question of the ordination of a vicarage in the church of Ecclesfield, he had to return on 4 Nov. to the archbishop, who was then north of Leeds, and the vicarage was not ordained until 7 Dec.

maidens and nuns, assaults on clerks in holy or, if serious damage were done, in minor orders, breaches of sanctuary, breaches of the episcopal parks and warrens, wilful hindrance of the bishop's officers in pursuit of their calling, conspiracies and other offences against the rights and liberties of the see.[1] Such cases might come before the bishop at the house in London where much of his time outside his diocese was usually spent, but it is probable that they often had to be held over until he came within his own borders.[2]

Reference already has been made to the visitations of the diocese in which the bishop gave a general exhibition of his powers as ordinary. While they lasted, all other local jurisdictions were suspended, except those which by custom were exempt from his authority. With these he seldom interfered, and, if he did so, it was with little chance of success. The

---

[1] This list of reserved cases occurs in R. Court. (Cant.), i, fo. 7*b*, in a commission of the office of penitentiary, dated 20 Feb. 1381–2. 'Willelmus, permissione divina electus confirmatus Cantuar. dilecto in Christo filio domino Willelmo Fodderynghey capellano parochiali ecclesie de Haddeleygh nostre iurisdiccionis inmediate salutem graciam et benediccionem. Animarum saluti que in confessionibus audiendis et penitenciis iniungendis potissime procuratur prospicere cupientes, ut confessiones quorumcumque parochianorum dicte ecclesie tibi confiteri volencium licite audire valeas et eis penitentibus pro peccatis que tibi confitebuntur penitencias iniungere salutares et absolucionis beneficium impertiri eciam in casibus nobis specialiter reservatis tibi de cuius fidelitate et industria plene confidimus committimus vices nostras, periurii in causis matrimonialibus vel in assisis et indictacionibus ubi vertitur causa sanguinis vel exheredacio alicuius, voluntarii homicidii, usure manifeste, oppressionis virginum, corrupcionis sanctimonialium, inieccionis manuum violentarum in clericos in sacris constitutos vel in minoribus si lesio sit enormis, abstraccionis fugitivorum ad ecclesiam causa immunitatis habende vel impedicionis quominus eis necessaria ministrentur, fraccionis et invasionis parcorum warennarum et aliorum locorum nostrorum, conspiracionis contra ecclesiam nostram Cantuar., impedicionis manifeste et maliciose ministrorum nostrorum in execucione ecclesiastice iurisdiccionis, violacionis maliciose iurium et libertatum ecclesie nostre Cantuar. casibus dumtaxat exceptis; presentibus usque ad octabas Pasche prox. futuras tantummodo duraturis. Dat. sub sigillo nostro privato in manerio nostro de Lamheth xx die mensis et anni predictorum.' In view of these offences the distinction drawn by Lyndwood between *peccatum, delictum,* and *crimen* may be noted (tit. *De foro competenti,* c. *Contingit,* ver. *Delicto,* ed. 1679, p. 93): 'Est enim peccatum idem quod malus actus, delictum vero boni desertio, i.e. derelictum. Crimen autem est grave peccatum, accusatione et damnacione dignissimum . . . vel dic quod delictum est genus generalissimum, sive veniat ex animo sive non. Crimen vero est genus subalternum, et continet sub se furtum, et adulterium, et alia quae ex animo proveniunt, et ex conscientia.'

[2] Some of the longer cases given in App. III illustrate the mobility of the bishop's court in such circumstances. The bishop of Lincoln's London lodging, like that of several other bishops, was in the Old Temple.

repeated attacks of the bishops of Norwich upon the liberties of the abbey of St. Edmunds,[1] the attempt of Bishop Alnwick to visit the priories of St. Albans at Binham and Wymondham, met with signal failure.[2] The liberties of cathedral chapters, conceded by earlier bishops and securely established by long custom, were usually let alone, and attempts to override them became extremely rare. As for the exempt religious orders, the diocesan had a right to claim hospitality from each of their houses for a night, when he came in person on his primary visitation, but merely as a guest.[3] In exempt areas, though he might be acknowledged as local diocesan, his ordinary jurisdiction ceased.

The term 'ordinary' is somewhat general and vague, and it is necessary to remember that the full phrase is judge ordinary, *judex ordinarius*. By the fifteenth century, outside the exempt jurisdictions to which I have referred, its simple use without qualification was understood to imply the diocesan bishop. The chief manifestation of his *jus ordinarium* was his right to institute and deprive incumbents of benefices. Only when the metropolitan, as ordinary of the province, came on visitation did the ordinary right of the bishop lapse, just as it lapsed to the metropolitan during vacancies of the sees in his province.

Subject to the diocesan, however, there were local authorities with a certain degree of ordinary jurisdiction, and the phrase *ordinarii locorum* includes the bishops' chief ministers in the parochial administration of dioceses, the archdeacons.[4] Of them

---

[1] This was a standing quarrel in which successive bishops attempted to break down the exemption of the abbot and convent.

[2] See *Reg. Joh. Whet.* i. 300–67, and *Linc. Vis.* ii, p. xx.

[3] For the form of notice issued to an exempt house by a bishop *ratione primi adventus sui* see *Surt. Misc.*, 165 (Archbishop Bowet to the abbot and convent of Kirkstall).

[4] Lyndwood has much to say of ordinaries, e.g. the long notes, pp. 16, 17. Ibid., p. 148: Bishops 'sunt perpetui et naturales [sc. ordinarii] respectu legatorum sedis apostolicae, qui non sunt perpetui, sed temporales . . . et etiam respectu aliorum, qui licet ordinarii dicantur, tamen principales ordinarii non sunt, sed episcopo subsunt, nisi privilegio speciali ab eo eximantur.' The provincial constitution *Excussis* (ibid., p. 58) refers to 'quidam episcoporum, archidiaconorum, et aliorum ordinariorum officiales'. Deans of cathedral churches (*decani*, as distinct from *decani rurales*) are coupled with archdeacons in this context, as in the constitutions *Exhorrenda* and *Ut clericalis* (ibid., pp. 76, 117), and had ordinary jurisdiction within their churches and the liberties attached to them: Lyndwood says (ibid., p. 96): 'Inferior vero judex ordinarius, utputa Decanus, archidiaconus, et alii hujusmodi.' Where the ordinary right of an archdeacon lay is sufficiently

and the areas subject to their control the present writer has given some account elsewhere,[1] and it would be possible to say more of this wide and difficult subject than can be said here. By the time of the Norman Conquest the subdivision of dioceses into archdeaconries was not a new thing, but its origin is somewhat obscure and its progress was gradual. In England such progress advanced during the first half of the twelfth century, but is difficult to trace with certainty, and signs of the use of territorial designations are extremely rare during this period. The archdeacon attached to the cathedral church was an officer of old standing: his importance in this connexion as the chief member of the episcopal *familia* long survived in many continental chapters of which he was the head. In England, however, at any rate after the Conquest, his association with the cathedral church became much less intimate: he was a canon and prebendary with his stall in choir and voice in chapter, he frequently held one or more parish churches appropriated to his office or *personatus*, but his main duty was the supervision under the bishop of the churches of the diocese. In large dioceses, including, like those of Bath and Wells or Chichester, one widespreading county area, or as, in most other cases, a collection of counties, such oversight could not be exercised effectually by a single man. Only in four small dioceses, Canterbury, Rochester, Ely, and Carlisle, was one archdeacon sufficient. Elsewhere the office was divided according to geographical convenience, from the two archdeaconries in Chichester, Durham, Hereford, Winchester, and Worcester, to the eight archdeaconries in Lincoln. The archdeacon who took his title from the cathedral church was *archidiaconus major*, the *grand archidiacre*, but his duties, like those of the archdeacon of York, known also as archdeacon of West Riding, were limited to a recognized area and his superiority to his brother archdeacons was merely one of precedence.

The multiplication of archdeacons began early, but it is difficult to be sure how far special territories were assigned to them in the first instance, and Le Neve's lists of early arch-

---

indicated in the constitutions included by Lyndwood under the title *De officio archidiaconi* (ibid., pp. 49–54).

[1] 'Diocesan Organization in the Middle Ages: Archdeacons and Rural Deans' (Raleigh Lecture, 1943; *Proc. Brit. Acad.* xxix).

deacons needs much revision in this and in other respects. The most careful attempts to establish a succession of individual occupants of archdeaconries for the first half of the twelfth century involve a certain amount of conjecture. This is illustrated by the notes on the early archdeacons who appear as witnesses in Farrer's collection of *Early Yorkshire Charters*[1] and the tentative list of the earliest archdeacons of Richmond in Mr. Clay's continuation of that work.[2] The five archdeaconries of the diocese of York in the Middle Ages were the archdeaconry of York, known also as that of St. Peter's or of the West Riding, that of the East Riding, which was at first attached to the treasurership of the cathedral church,[3] and those of Richmond, Cleveland, and Nottingham. The names of four archdeacons, including the treasurer, are found in a charter of which the date lies between 1125 and 1135,[4] but without indication of the areas which they served, and more than one instance occurs of the application of the title *Eboracensis ecclesiae archidiaconus* to more than one archdeacon in charters to which they were fellow witnesses. But, though it may be doubted whether at first the limits of their separate jurisdictions were clearly defined, the treasurer's archdeaconry appears by 1133,[5] the archdeaconry of Nottingham is mentioned in a charter before the death of Archbishop Turstin in 1140,[6] and the archdeaconry of 'Westrithing' is definitely named in a charter of which the earliest date is about 1160.[7] It is certainly not until after 1160 that the archdeacons of the church of York began to describe themselves by territorial titles: it is somewhere between 1164 and 1172 that Ralph is described as archdeacon of Cleveland and John as archdeacon of Nottingham.[8] Dr. Farrer's conclusion that two archdeacons shared the archdeaconry of York about 1140 seems to be merely a misunderstanding of the use of the general title *Eboracensis ecclesiae archidiaconus* for any of the archdeacons with-

[1] *E.T.C.* i. 133, 410.
[2] Ibid. iv, pp. xxiv–xxvi. Since the publication of this volume Mr. Clay has continued his researches into the succession of early archdeacons in the church of York with fruitful results.
[3] See ibid. ii. 445, in a charter relating to Bridlington dated *c.* 1125–33. 'Willelmus thesaurarius in cuius archidiaconatu est ipsa ecclesia.'
[4] Ibid. i. 278.
[5] See note 3 above.
[6] *E.T.C.* i. 127.      [7] Ibid. i. 128.
[8] For Ralph see ibid. ii. 307; for John, ibid. i. 48, 56, &c.

out respect to his area of jurisdiction.[1] It is at least likely that
the assignment of individual members of the body of archdeacons to each of the five divisions into which the diocese
naturally fell was subsequent to the recognition of those areas
and not simultaneous with it.

In England there is no conspicuous example of the conflict
between bishops and archdeacons which in the twelfth and
thirteenth centuries disturbed the peace of continental dioceses.[2]
The only English archdeacon who achieved complete exemption
from episcopal authority was the archdeacon of Richmond; and
he, though he was ordinary within his own archdeaconry,
instituting to its benefices and enjoying all the powers which
could be delegated to a vicar-general, admitted the visitation
of the archbishop of York by an amicable agreement.[3] Other
archdeacons possessed small peculiar jurisdictions of their own
in parishes whose incumbency was annexed to their office.[4]
Their ordinary right, however, consisted in the duty of holding
yearly visitations in their archdeaconries for purposes already
noted as defined in provincial constitutions, and these were in
theory superseded every third year by episcopal visitations.
Archdeacons were never popular and, as they themselves well
knew, their methods of dealing with their subjects were hard
and grasping. In his last will, master William Doune, archdeacon of Leicester and official principal of the bishop of
Worcester, who died in 1361, prayed God's forgiveness for
exactions and extortions in which, however, he was careful to

[1] Dr. Farrer's statement in *E.Y.C.* i. 133 seems to be derived from the prominent
position given to Ralph as *archidiaconus Eboracensis* among the witnesses to a charter,
ibid. iii. 442, at a time when Osbert of Bayeux was without doubt *archidiaconus
major* of the church; but this is no safe ground for any positive conclusion of so
unlikely a character. A papal document of 1154 refers to R. and B. *archidiaconis
Laudunensibus*, i.e. archdeacons in the church of Laon, doubtless the *archidiaconus
major* and the archdeacon of Thiérache (Jaffé, ii. 99).

[2] It is possible that the appointment of vice-archdeacons, found in the twelfth
century, may mark an attempt on the part of archdeacons to provide themselves
with deputies corresponding to the vicars-general of diocesan bishops; but the
term soon disappears. See below, p. 65, note 3.

[3] The agreement is printed in *H.C.Y.* iii. 248–50: its points are summarized in
the introduction to the first part of 'The Registers of the Archdeacons of Richmond' (*Y.A.J.* xxv. 129–268). See p. 4 above, note 4.

[4] Thus the peculiar of the archdeacon of York consisted of the church of
Mexborough and its original chapel of Ravenfield, Yorks, W.R., while that of the
archdeacon of East Riding consisted of the church of Mappleton in Holderness
(Lawton, pp. 2, 3).

point out that he merely followed the example of his brethren.[1]
Complaints of the extravagance and expense of archidiaconal
visitations came in the thirteenth century from clergy who
suffered by them.[2] Archdeacons like William Doune were first
and foremost acute ecclesiastical lawyers: was not one of the
standard glossators of the texts of Canon Law, the authority of
whose commentary was not far, if at all, inferior to that of his
text, the archdeacon *par excellence*?[3] Their study was but little
on the Bible: for their earthly profit they betook themselves to
pore upon the Decretals and fill their margins with comments.[4]
The spiritual comfort of their subjects, which indeed formed no
necessary part of their eminently practical calling, meant much
less to them than the fees due to them from each parish in lieu
of hospitality to them and their attendants. We have seen how
ready the clergy and people of the archdeaconry of Richmond
were in 1428 to ward off the cost of an archiepiscopal visitation
to themselves by offering the archbishop an indemnity for
his pains. The archdeacon at that date well knew how useless it would be for himself to attempt a visitation, and, as a
matter of fact, during the period of rather more than a century
from 1361 to 1477, there is no trace in the records of the
archdeaconry that any visitation of it was held by an archdeacon.[5]

Archidiaconal visitations, indeed, became rare in the course
of the fourteenth century. The formal payment of procurations
absolved the parishes of the archdeaconry from an expensive
and unwelcome burden. Archdeacons with increasing frequency
obtained papal indults authorizing them to visit by deputy and
receive procurations up to a stated daily maximum.[6] There is

[1] See *A.J.* lxxii. 230–1.
[2] For such a complaint on the part of the clergy of Holderness see *R. Wick.*,
pp. 248, 249.
[3] Guido da Baisio, archdeacon of Bologna, ob. post 1300, author of the commentary on the Decretals known as *Rosarium* and of its supplement, a commentary on
*Liber Sextus*.
[4] The complaint is Dante's, *Par.* ix. 136.
[5] See the edition of the archidiaconal registers noted above, p. 4, note 4.
[6] Numerous instances occur in *C.P.L.* An early instance is that of the archdeacon
of Sudbury in 1363, an indult for two years, 'the archdeaconry being of small value,
and having no manse or church annexed to it' (iv. 33). Nothing is said here about
a deputy or procurations. Indults of this kind are constant from the last decade
of the fourteenth century onwards, granted for varying periods of time from two to
seven years. The legal limit of procurations thus received was thirty silver pounds

no trace that such visitations by deputy were ever held in any formal shape, nor have we, so far as I know, any very distinct trace of an archidiaconal court sitting, at any rate before the sixteenth century, for cognizance of the defaults which a visitation might bring to light. The archdeacon had his own official, usually one of his parochial clergy, appointed by himself, a business officer who saw that procurations were collected and sinners, where discoverable, were fined.[1]  No doubt the prevailingly judicial aspect of the episcopal dignity brought many hangers-on to depend upon a small income out of the menial business of the courts of officials-principal; but Chaucer's Sompnour, an undesirable but not exceptional member of this dependent class, was, it will be remembered, attached to the service of an archdeacon. 'Purs is the archedeknes hell, quod he', and visitation by deputy meant in practice the sending round of collectors who exacted fees and inculcated the easy avoidance of ecclesiastical correction by a sufficient money payment. It is not very likely that archdeacons who accepted money payments in lieu of visitation took any warm interest in the church fabrics of whose soundness or need of repair they were expected to take notice; and parochial visitations from various sources reveal a large proportion of churches in which there were broken windows, leaking roofs, and much dilapidation of the buildings and their internal furniture.[2]  Another duty of the archdeacon was to induct incumbents into benefices on receipt of episcopal mandates *ad hoc*. It was possibly the frequent absence of archdeacons, many of whom spent their time industriously in government offices, that made bishops direct mandates for induction, not exclusively to archdeacons, but to their officials as deputies, or sometimes to the local rural dean or other commissaries as they pleased.[3]

Tournois, twelve to the golden florin of the Camera, but the sum occasionally is stated merely as 'moderate procurations'. The value of procurations was fixed in 1336 by the constitution of Benedict XII, *Vas electionis Paulus* (*Extrav. comm.* x, c. un.).

[1]  The archdeacon's official was often, if not habitually, a beneficed incumbent in the archdeaconry. One of these, who acted for more than one archdeacon of Richmond, was master Giles Redman, rector of Bentham, Yorks, W.R.

[2]  See the records from dio. Hereford, *c.* 1397, printed *E.H.R.* xliv. 279, 444; xlv. 92, 444, and from the peculiar of the dean and chapter of York, 1462–1550, ap. *Fabric Rolls of York Minster* (Surtees Soc.), pp. 242–74.

[3]  Any episcopal register will supply examples of variations in the address of such

The part played by archdeacons in diocesan affairs was therefore at this period active enough, so far as raising money for themselves and their assistants was concerned, but from any other point of view was of no great spiritual or other utility. Considering the vast amount of business which came under the cognizance of certain archdeacons in the post-Reformation period—and some of the strangest and least decorous records in existence are to be found among the muniments of archidiaconal courts where they have been well preserved—it is curious that there should be so little evidence of their doings at an earlier date. But the fifteenth-century archdeacon probably regarded his benefice and the cure of souls which it involved[1] without any very lively interest and with very little personal knowledge. If he were a member of the cathedral chapter or a constant resident in the bishop's household, he had interests which took precedence of the affairs of the large group of rural parishes on which he levied tribute; and, if the story told over and over again by Gascoigne of the half-witted archdeacon of good family who lived in Oxford is not exaggerated, there were some archdeacons to whom their offices were no more than comfortable sinecures which provided them with means for doing nothing.[2]

There can be no doubt that the appointment of archpriests or rural deans to the oversight of areas formed by subdivisions of archdeaconries was an established fact in the third quarter of the twelfth century. As the limits of dioceses became clearly defined, the country parishes were grouped together on the

mandates. Generally it runs *archidiacono vel officiali suo*, but bishops appear to have exercised discretion freely in this connexion.

[1] The act of 21 Hen. VIII, c. 13, placed dignities and parsonages in cathedral churches, which included archdeaconries, in the category of sinecures. Up to that time such *dignitates* and *personatus* or *officia* had been regarded as involving cure of souls and, as such, were incompatible with the tenure of another *beneficium curatum*, as may be seen from records of dispensations in *C.P.L. passim*. See Lyndwood, tit. *de praeb.*, cap. *Audistis*, ver. *curam animarum* (p. 135): 'Et sive sit dignitas, vel officium, sive ecclesia, sicut sunt multi archipresbyteri, archidiaconi, et decani, qui nullam habent ecclesiam cui praesint: habent tamen jurisdictionem super multas ecclesias. . . . Dicuntur etiam *beneficia curata* illa, quorum ministris, ratione beneficiorum hujusmodi, competit visitare, inquirere, procuratione exigere, suspendere, excommunicare, a talibus sententiis absolvere de consuetudine, vel de jure, quocunque nomine censeatur.'

[2] See *Loc. L. V.* 166: 'sacerdotem inscium, viciosum et ideotam qui nec scit nec potest nec vult ea facere que necessaria sunt ad curam animarum.'

principle upon which, in cathedral cities and the larger towns in which the process naturally had its origin, parish churches were placed under the supervision of a dean of Christianity, usually one of the local incumbents, as the immediate officer of the spiritual court or court Christian.[1] As the archdeaconry, generally speaking, corresponded in extent to a county or to a substantial division of it marked out by civil boundaries, so the rural deanery corresponded, in a large part of England, though not in the west and south, to the hundred or to a group of hundreds;[2] and the ecclesiastical geography of England, singularly untouched by change, retained many traces until within the last hundred years of civil divisions which have long since disappeared. One interesting example is afforded by the deanery of Bulmer in the archdeaconry of Cleveland and diocese of York, which throughout its history included, in addition to its members in the North Riding, the small East Riding wapentake of Ouse and Derwent. This arrangement lasted until 1896, when the parishes of this wapentake were transferred, as the deanery of Escrick, to the archdeaconry of East Riding. Geographically, this wapentake, in the angle formed by the two converging rivers, belongs more naturally to the North than to the East or West Ridings, from which it is cut off by water. Scarborough and its neighbourhood, again, locally in the North Riding, but lying between the upper course of the Derwent and the sea, had a geographical connexion with the East Riding which was preserved till quite recently for ecclesiastical purposes. Of the five archdeaconries, already referred to, of the diocese of York, two, York and East Riding, covered the West and East Ridings of the county: such exceptions as existed have just been stated. While Cleveland corresponded to the eastern part of what is now the North Riding, the north-western part of the county, known as Richmond-shire, belonged to the archdeaconry of Richmond, which also stretched far beyond the western moors into Lancashire,

---

[1] The title is still used of the deaneries of the cities of Lincoln, Exeter, and Leicester, and was long applied to that of the city of York. It has thus clung to urban deaneries in early centres of Christianity, but there is plenty of evidence for its more general application, for which see the lecture on 'Diocesan Organization' referred to p. 58 above, note 1.

[2] See 'Diocesan Organization', u.s., for the treatment of this subject in detail.

Cumberland, and Westmorland, and took in a few parishes from the West Riding north of the Nidd and near the borders of Lancashire and Westmorland. The fifth archdeaconry corresponded to the county of Nottingham.

Within these areas the rural deaneries corresponded roughly to the civil areas of the wapentakes. In the East Riding and Nottinghamshire this correspondence is almost exact, and in the East Riding the four wapentakes of Buckrose, Dickering, Harthill, and Holderness, gave their names to deaneries. In the large deaneries of the West Riding two or more wapentakes were combined, with here and there a slight overlapping of boundaries. The three deaneries of the archdeaconry of Cleveland were less systematically arranged, but in the archdeaconry of Richmond the deaneries of Richmond and Catterick followed, the first the boundaries of the wapentake of Gilling, the second those of the wapentake of Hang, while including some border parishes in neighbouring wapentakes. The deanery of Boroughbridge lay for the most part in the West Riding, between the Ure and the Nidd. In spite, however, of some irregularity the general identity of rural deaneries and wapentakes or groups of wapentakes is clear.

In the collection of *Early Yorkshire Charters* to which reference has been made already the names of rural deans begin to appear about 1150, at first described by the names of their abodes or benefices, e.g. Walter, 'decanus de Rudestein' (1148–54), Robert, 'decanus de Eclesfeld' (1150–60).[1] This method of description prevails until the decade between 1180 and 1190. But already between 1160 and 1170 there is a reference to the dean and the (ruridecanal) chapter of Whitby,[2] and similarly a charter which may be as early as 1154 and as late as 1180 refers to the chapter of Holderness held by William of Gilling, the vice-archdeacon, in the church of Mappleton.[3] The transition

---

[1] *E.Y.C.* ii. 485; iii, 1.

[2] Ibid. 461. At a later date the churches of the liberty of Whitby Strand were usually counted as part of the rural deanery of Cleveland, though sometimes visited separately. The name of the dean, William of Herleso, probably Harlsey near Northallerton, suggests that in this case Whitby is simply an alternative name for Cleveland.

[3] Ibid. 108. This seems to have been part of an archidiaconal visitation held by a deputy. *Vice-archidiaconus* is a title which appears several times in *E.Y.C.* (e.g. i. 191, 343), and there are other examples of its use in the later part of the twelfth century. See p. 60 above, note 2, and Pet. Bles., epp. lviii, clvii (Migne,

from a merely local description of the dean to the description which was adopted as his official designation may be clearly traced in two instances. At periods between the limiting dates 1170 and 1184 several charters are witnessed by Robert, 'decanus de Helmesle',[1] but in a charter between 1181 and 1189 he becomes Robert of Helmsley, 'decanus de Ridale'.[2] Similarly, Hugh, 'decanus de Silkestun' in earlier and also in later charters,[3] appears between 1191 and 1193 as Hugh of Silkstone, dean of Doncaster.[4]

This same charter mentions two other deans under the title of their deaneries, viz. Roger of Ledsham, dean of Pontefract,[5] and Paulinus, dean of Ainsty, and a third as James, 'decanus de Waldo', a name which seems to imply 'the Wold' and may signify the deanery of Harthill in the East Riding. That the new custom was not generally adopted at once is quite clear: thus Laurence, dean of Cleveland in a charter of 1180-8, witnesses another between 1189 and 1204 as Laurence, 'decanus de Seilton', side by side with Helias, described in the new way as dean of Ryedale.[6] A definite date, 1175, can be given to a mention of Alan, 'decanus de Burhscyr', i.e. the deanery known later as that of Boroughbridge in the archdeaconry of Richmond.[7] Finally, it is not at all improbable that where a witness to a charter is described as 'presbiter', with the name of a place added, the title implies a rural dean. Thus Paulinus, dean of Ainsty in 1191-3,[8] is at an earlier date Paulinus, 'presbiter de Ledes',[9] and we know him to have been parson of Leeds, which was in that deanery.[10]

P.L. ccvii. 73, 450). Another vice-archdeacon of East Riding occurs 1180-90 (E.Y.C. i. 492). The church of Mappleton was a peculiar of the archdeacon.

[1] E.Y.C. i. 483; ii. 100, &c.

[2] Ibid. iii. 492.                              [3] Ibid. 51, 377, 419.

[4] Ibid. ii. 415. Another dean of Doncaster, Thomas de Bosevill, occurs between 1190 and 1200 (ii. 165); but there is later evidence from the archbishops' registers that the large deanery of Doncaster was occasionally divided between two deans.

[5] Jordan of Kellington, probably Roger's predecessor, is called dean of Pontefract in a charter of which the limiting dates are 1177 and 1193 (ibid. i. 298).

[6] Ibid. 444, 452. 'Seilton' is Over Silton, on the western edge of the Cleveland moors.

[7] Ibid. 69.                                    [8] Ibid. ii. 415.

[9] Between 1160 and 1183 (ibid. iii. 366, 367).

[10] Other instances of territorial titles of deans from E.Y.C. are Jordan, clerk of the dean of Craven 1185-1200 (iii. 477), Roger, dean of Catterick 1173-81 (iv. 121, 123), Murdac, dean of Westmorland, dio. Carlisle, 1170-90 (iii. 449), and two deans from dio. Glasgow, viz. of Annandale and Dumfries 1174-91 (ii. 112).

The rural dean, or, as he was often called upon the continent, the archpriest,[1] was the supervising officer of the deanery. In England the title dean was habitually in use from the twelfth century, and that of archpriest was confined to the heads of a few small collegiate establishments in the southern dioceses and of comparatively late foundation.[2] The appointment of the rural dean seems to have been originally in the hands of the archdeacon, but by the thirteenth century at any rate it had fallen in England to the bishop, a change which no doubt was rendered more easy by the frequent non-residence of archdeacons and the view of their office as a means of support for their occupation in external study or business. Rural deans at all events were episcopal officers, acting under commission from the bishop and appointed and removed at his will.[3] In one English diocese, however, that of Norwich, the rural deanery was by old-established custom a freehold benefice with a small annual income, to which the bishop instituted the incumbent by collation.[4]

[1] So, in the constitution *Vas electionis Paulus* (see p. 61 above, note 6), we find: 'decanis ruralibus duntaxat exceptis, qui in aliquibus regionibus archipresbyteri nominantur.' See 'Diocesan Organization' for the use of the title archpriest abroad. In France to-day the terms are interchangeable.

[2] Barton in the Isle of Wight, dio. Winton (1289), Haccombe in Devon (1335), and Ulcombe in Kent (before 1291) are cases in point, quoted with references in 'Diocesan Organization', u.s. In such instances the archpriest corresponded to the dean, in collegiate and cathedral establishments, and his office bore no analogy to that of a rural dean. *Extra* I. xxiv, c. 4, *Ut singulae*, deals with the duties of the *archipresbyter ruralis*. To Lyndwood the title had a merely general meaning; the two constitutions which he includes *sub. tit. De officio archipresbyteri* refer simply to priests in charge of a cure of souls, and he glosses the phrase *quilibet sacerdos plebi praesidens* with the remark *sc. per viam curae* (p. 54).

[3] Lyndwood, tit. *De iudiciis*, c. *in causis*, ver. *decani rurales* (p. 79) quotes *Extra de off. archidiaconi*, c. *ad haec* (I. xxiii. 7), where Innocent III lays down the rule that, as the rural dean exercises an office belonging both to the bishop and to the archdeacon, his election and amotion is their business in common. Lyndwood himself, however, tit. *De constit.*, c. *quia incontinentiae*, ver. *decanos rurales* (p. 14) defines rural deans as 'decani temporales ad aliquid ministerium sub episcopo vel archiepiscopo constituti', and the actual appointment appears to have been made by the bishop. The direct relation between bishop and rural dean is implied by the address of mandates recorded in episcopal registers *suo decano de A.*, &c.

[4] Lyndwood, ibid., stresses the temporary nature of the office, habitually held *ad beneplacitum domini*, citing Innocent IV and other eminent canonists: 'nec habent institutionem canonicam tanquam in beneficio, secundum doctores praedictos.' But the case of Norwich forms an exception: institutions to rural deaneries were recorded in the episcopal registers. Unlike an archdeaconry, such deaneries were sinecures—e.g. the rural deanery of Sparham is described R. Langham,

Thus the dean was not a mere subordinate of the archdeacon. Archdeacons availed themselves of his services, but his authority within his local area could be called into use without reference to them. It amounted, in fact, though technically the rural dean was not reckoned among *ordinarii locorum*,[1] to an ordinary jurisdiction closely parallel to theirs. This point is well illustrated by the circumstance that the obedientiary who exercised spiritual jurisdiction in peculiars subject to monasteries was styled indifferently archdeacon or dean.[2] Further, the deans appointed by the archbishop of Canterbury in his peculiar jurisdictions of Croydon, Shoreham, Bocking, Pagham, South Malling, and Risborough, had a jurisdiction which Lyndwood defines as archidiaconal. Their letters of appointment were couched in terms similar to those addressed to the commissary general, and their title was equivalent to that given to the dean of Arches.[3] The rural dean had his seal of office;[4] unlike the archdeacon, he was always on the spot, for he was usually selected from among the resident clergy of the deanery, and non-beneficed clergy, parochial curates and chantry chaplains, were eligible for the office.[5]

fo. 4*b*, as 'beneficium non curatum nec taxatum sed valoris annui v marc. et non ultra'. See 'Diocesan Organization', u.s., pp. 39–41.

[1] See Lyndwood, pp. 36, 37.

[2] e.g. the archdeacons of Westminster and St. Albans, the dean of the Vale of Evesham. In these cases the offices were exactly similar.

[3] Lyndwood, tit. *De jud.*, c. *quia incontinentiae*, ver. *committatur* (p. 80). He discusses whether these deans have the prescriptive right of jurisdiction in matrimonial cases: 'Videtur quod sic: nam tales in locis suis habent iurisdictionem archidiaconalem, nec alicui subsunt nisi solum archiepiscopo eos deputanti; cum tamen caeteri decani rurales etiam ut communiter subsint archidiaconis.' Lyndwood, however, denies prescription on the ground that they are not perpetual, but *remotivi ad nutum*. 'Et idem . . . etiam dico de decano ecclesiae de Arcubus quoad subditos illius decanatus; sc. quod ex sola consuetudine absque commissione archiepiscopi non potest cognoscere in causis matrimonialibus; cum commissione fateor quod bene potest.' For letters of appointment see Churchill, ii. 19–27.

[4] The seal of the rural dean is mentioned, e.g. in the constitution *Quia ruralium*, where Lyndwood notes, ver. *decani ruralis* (p. 81): 'cuius officium est in causis ecclesiasticis citationes et transmissas exequi . . . et cuius sigillum in talibus est authenticum.' The last clause of the same constitution, requiring rural deans to swear every year in the episcopal synod to observe its provisions, is said by Lyndwood (ibid., p. 85) to have been inserted 'quia per eos potius quam per alios qui habent sigilla authentica multae fiebant fraudes'. See 'Diocesan Organization', u.s., p. 38, note 2.

[5] Examples are given ibid., pp. 41–3. A few early sixteenth-century appointments in dio. Hereford are recorded in *R. C. Bothe*, in each case of a beneficed priest within the area of the deanery.

It would be interesting to know more about the proceedings of rural deans than has been vouchsafed to us. From the constitution *Vas electionis*, which regulated procurations payable to ordinaries, it appears that they had the right of visitation.[1] On the other hand, there seems no existing record of a regular visitation held by a rural dean in England, nor was there any stated time set apart for it; and we may probably confine the performance of this duty to visits, on commission from the bishop or the archdeacon, to inquire into cases of dilapidation or other misconduct on the part of incumbents. With regard to rural deans Lyndwood is judiciously vague. The provincial constitutions included in his work under the title *De officio archipresbyteri* deal, not with rural deans, but with incumbents with cure of souls. He distinguishes indeed between rural deans, as holding a temporary and amovable office, and archpriests, as holding perpetual benefices, like the deans in the diocese of Norwich.[2] He also quotes Pope Innocent III to the effect that their appointment belongs to the bishop and archdeacon in common.[3] He is certain, however, that whatever they do is done, not on their own responsibility, but in the name of their principals. And this is borne out by the evidence of diocesan records, where they occasionally appear as mandataries for the induction of parochial incumbents, and sometimes also for holding inquiries into vacancies of benefices. Such inquiries are recorded with great frequency in episcopal registers of the fifteenth century and are full of interesting detail. In neither case, however, was the commission often directed to the rural dean: it is more often addressed to the archdeacon's official or to one or more special commissaries, who preside for the occasion over the assembly called together for the purpose.[4]

[1] See p. 61 above, note 6.

[2] Tit. *De constit.* c. *Quia incontinentiae*, ad v. *Decanos rurales* (p. 14): 'Et sunt hi decani temporales ad aliquid ministerium sub episcopo vel archiepiscopo exercendum constituti . . . nec habent institutionem canonicam tanquam in beneficio.' Id. tit. *De iudiciis*, c. *Statuimus*, ad v. *Decani rurales* (ibid., p. 79): 'Jo. An. in addi. aliter intelligit, quod decani dicuntur archipresbyteri, tales videlicet qui perpetui sunt, et non amoventur sine causa.'

[3] Ibid. eod. loco: Innocent's statement is to the effect: 'quod sunt personae habentes quaedam officia communiter spectantia ad episcopum et archidiaconum: et ideo communiter eorum receptio et amotio pertinet ad utrumque.' See *Extra de officio archid.*, c. *Sane consuluit*, § 6 (I. xxiii. 7).

[4] A number of commissions of inquiry in *R. Lacy* (Exon.) show that the normal recipients of such mandates were the officials of the local archdeacons, who also

If we come, therefore, to a general conclusion with regard to the organization of English dioceses in the fifteenth century, we find that it has become highly centralized. The power of local ordinaries is somewhat indefinite: the office of archdeacon is exercised largely in the collection of fees through subordinates, while the rural dean is employed as a commissary for whom on occasion, in matters which concern his deanery, other persons may be substituted. The ordinary jurisdiction of the bishop is exercised through the vicar-general and the official. The second of these is a permanent delegate: the first, although his delegacy is in abeyance or merely used on special occasions while the bishop is in the diocese, holds a standing appointment and steps automatically into the shoes of an absent or non-resident diocesan. There is, moreover, a general tendency to combine the two offices into one, and so simplify the complicated relations which might otherwise exist between their holders at a date when the vicar-general is in charge of the diocese for long periods. The appointment of suffragans under commissions renewable at frequent intervals is general. Some bishops, like Alnwick at Lincoln, dispensed with such help, although the same prelate at Norwich continually employed it; but in any case the suffragan is a subordinate at the beck and call of the bishop or the vicar-general, and holds no ordinary jurisdiction, performing only such functions as cannot be delegated to persons not in episcopal orders. We may note that in quasi-episcopal jurisdictions, such as that of the archdeacon of Richmond, these features of diocesan organization are closely followed: mandates go out in the name of a vicar-general, the official holds his court, and commissaries are deputed for special objects. The whole character of the business thus carried on is somewhat formal and mechanical. The language of the episcopal chancery is pious and edifying; the preambles of its common forms are full of unction; but the objects for which the whole organization has been built up are

dealt normally with inductions. In *R. Bek.* the mandates are in most instances addressed to the bishop's commissary-general and another, or to special commissaries. An inquiry into a vacancy of Combe Hay church in the deanery of Frome in 1445 (*R. Bek.* i. 44), is addressed to one of the bishop's usual commissaries, John Sperhauke, who was vicar of South Stoke in the neighbouring deanery of Bath, and the vicar of Wellow, also in the deanery of Frome. The latter may have been rural dean, but no official mention is made of this. Mandates to rural deans for induction come for the most part from the diocese of Lincoln.

legal and judicial. The system was not of course peculiar to the end of the Middle Ages. Its methods may be studied at work at a much earlier date; but it was in the fifteenth century that it assumed that completely stereotyped character which survived the ecclesiastical troubles of the next century, so that the post-Reformation Church continued its administrative course in the well-worn grooves marked out for it on these lines.

# III

## CATHEDRAL AND COLLEGIATE CHURCHES AND CHAPTERS

IT was by the clergy beneficed in cathedral and collegiate chapters that the system of which the principal features have been described was administered: it was naturally from this class that the rulers of the Church were chosen. There was a strongly drawn line of distinction between the higher clergy, the *sublimes* and *litterati*, men of birth and lettered clerks,[1] and the crowd of inferior clergy, vicars, curates, and chantry chaplains, whose education was rudimentary and who lived on small stipends. The prizes of the Church were reserved for a class which may definitely be called professional. We may pass over the younger sons of noble houses, represented by such men as Beaufort and Archbishops Stafford and Bourchier, for whom the way of preferment was made easy and its advantages obtained through gifts of practical shrewdness rather than through any learning.[2] The higher ranks of the clergy were largely filled by men who, of respectable but comparatively humble origin, won their way to administrative posts through a university education and through practice in the ecclesiastical courts or the service of the Crown or of some nobleman or bishop.[3] For

---

[1] This distinction occurs Conc. Lateran. IV (1215), cap. 29 (*Extra.* III. v. 28) *De multa*, where the clause 'ut in eadem ecclesia nullus plures dignitates aut personatus habere praesumat', &c., is followed by a qualification applying to the whole constitution: 'Circa sublimes tamen et literatas personas, quae majoribus sunt beneficiis honorandae, quum ratio postulaverit, per sedem apostolicam poterit dispensari.'

[2] Youth was no bar to such preferment. Beaufort had collation of preb. Thame in Lincoln, 5 Jan. 1389–90, at an early age, and of Sutton-cum-Buckingham, the most wealthy preb. in the church, 16 Feb. following (R. D. & C. Linc. vi, ff. 24*b*, 25, 29*b*). He obtained preb. Riccall in York 22 Aug. 1390 (Le Neve, iii. 209), and the deanery of Wells by royal grant, following a papal provision, 5 Jan. 1396–7 (*C.P.R.* 1396–9, p. 46). In such a case sublimity of rank did not affect the prohibition of the tenure of two benefices in one church *etiamsi curam non habeant animarum*. Beaufort resigned preb. Thame on obtaining preb. Sutton Bucks., in which he was installed personally 6 Sept. 1394 (R. D. & C. Linc. vi, ff. 53, 53*b*).

[3] See e.g. *Linc. Vis.* ii, pp. xiv sqq., for the career of William Alnwick, bishop of Norwich 1426 and of Lincoln 1436–49, a typical example of the kind.

these men the best parochial benefices provided suitable sources of revenue, swelled by canonries and prebends in the greater churches, archdeaconries and deaneries, until for some of them the quest of profitable preferment ended in a bishopric, held with high office in the realm.[1]

Some reference already has been made to the liberties enjoyed by cathedral and collegiate chapters. The chapters of the diocese of York were extreme examples of such enfranchised bodies, the undisputed ordinaries, not only of their churches, but of large and, in the case of York, scattered republics of parishes subject to their jurisdiction.[2] Although the patronage of canonries belonged to the archbishop, his power in the great churches of his see was simply a nominal superiority acknowledged by courtesy; his right of visitation was so carefully fenced about by concessions to the chapters that it became a mere formality.[3] In other dioceses the franchises of chapters were more limited,[4] but, nevertheless, in all cathedral churches of secular canons custom had decreed that attempts on the part of a bishop to assert his authority within the church or its precincts were interferences which provoked justifiable opposition. Even where, as at Salisbury, the bishop retained the prebendal stall

[1] The returns of pluralities in R. Langham, made in 1366 in consequence of the constitution *Dudum* of Urban II (see Wilkins, iii. 62, 63) include many examples, of which the most conspicuous is that of William of Wykeham (fo. 12*b*), with an archdeaconry, a parish church, and sinecure benefices in eleven cathedral and collegiate churches. For the statement made by master Roger Otery, see App. IV.

[2] In addition to a number of parish churches in York, of which 7 remain to-day, the liberty of the dean and chapter or of St. Peter consisted of 20 churches in the West Riding, 32 in the East Riding, 20 in the North Riding, 6 in Nottinghamshire, and the churches of Kirkby Ireleth in North Lancashire and Thockrington in Northumberland. These numbers include dependent chapelries. There were some other parishes in which the dean and chapter possessed temporal but had no spiritual jurisdiction. Most of these churches were appropriated to dignities, offices, and prebends in the church of York, and in all the dean and chapter were ordinaries, instituting to vicarages and exercising the right of visitation. Similar jurisdiction was exercised by the chapter of Beverley in Beverley and some 13 other parishes in the East Riding, and by the chapter of Southwell in 23 Nottinghamshire parishes, the churches of several of which formed prebends in the church of Southwell.

[3] See the composition between Archbishop Melton and the dean and chapter of York in 1328, printed *Surt. Misc.* 280–90. The earlier composition, made with Archbishop Romeyn in 1290, is printed *H.C.Y.* iii. 216–20.

[4] e.g. in dio. Lincoln the bishop instituted to vicarages of prebendal churches. Such churches, however, were not included in his ordinary visitations and were exempt from the authority of the local archdeacons and rural deans.

from which elsewhere he had retired at an earlier date,[1] and consequently had a voice in the chapter, his right to sit there was merely that of any canon in the republic of which the dean was president, and he probably exercised it as seldom as the abbot of Sherborne or the prior of Loders, to whom other prebends were appropriated.[2] Although the principal house of a bishop was in his cathedral city, and although he was often found there on great festivals and at synods and ordinations, the jurisdiction of the chapter within the precincts and city made continuous and prolonged residence there undesirable and even dangerous. In consequence, he preferred the freer atmosphere of his country houses, where he could stir outside his doors without fear of trespassing upon some cherished privilege of a vigilant chapter, and where his yeomen and grooms were free from the temptation of brawling with the servants of the dean and canons.[3] The caution of a bishop in

[1] The bishop's prebend in Salisbury was originally that known as *Maior pars altaris*, consisting of oblations made at the high altar. In 1219 he quitted it for preb. Horton (in Gloucestershire) and this in 1254 for preb. Potterne, still held by his successors (Jones, 393, 399, 409). The history of the bishop's prebend is elsewhere not so clear. At York none was appropriated to the archbishop. At Lincoln the bishop had his part in the division of the psalter among the chapter for daily recitation, but whether he held any fixed prebend at first is uncertain. See Bradshaw and Wordsworth, ii (ii), 796, for some inconclusive remarks on the point. In the division of the psalter at Salisbury the psalms allotted to the bishop's original prebend of *Maior pars altaris* were i to v. At Lincoln psalms i–v appear in an early list (ibid. ii (ii), 789) as divided between the bishop and preb. Aylesbury, a stall held by the dean before the middle of the thirteenth century: it is thus possible that the bishop may in the first place have held preb. Aylesbury undivided.

[2] The Norman abbots of Bec and Saint-Wandrille also had prebends in Salisbury, known as Ogbourne and Upavon respectively. Similarly, the abbots of Lyre and Cormeilles had prebends in Hereford, the abbot of Grestein in the church of Chichester. The abbots of Athelney and Muchelney had stalls in the church of Wells, and the two Augustinian priors of St. Oswald's (Nostell) and Hexham held the prebends of Bramham and Salton in the church of York. The case of the prior of Thurgarton, who had a stall in the choir at Southwell, but no prebend or voice in chapter, is unique.

[3] A very full episcopal itinerary, such as that printed in *R. Green.* v. 299–328, shows how very seldom a bishop was present in his cathedral city. Greenfield, archbishop of York 1306–15, was very diligent in his diocesan duties, and, save for occasional visits to London for parliaments and a year's absence at the Council of Vienne in 1311–12, was constantly resident in the diocese. But, while dates from the manor-houses of Bishopthorpe and Cawood, within easy distance of York, are abundant, dates from York itself are few and far between. The same thing will be noticed as habitual elsewhere: it was convenient for a bishop to be near his see, but unadvisable for him to make a habit of dwelling in his palace.

his dealings with peculiar jurisdictions could not be too great; and one may well contemplate with pity the hard case of the bishop of Chichester, who had no less than three such peculiars at his own door. The city and the close in which his palace stood were the peculiar of the dean and chapter; he had only to cross a street to find himself in a detached fragment of the diocese of Canterbury;[1] while the parishes west of his park were in the jurisdiction of the canons of Bosham, a royal free chapel immediately subject to the bishop of Exeter.[2]

Where the cathedral chapter was monastic, similar difficulties existed, as at Durham. There is very little ground for the often repeated statement that in such churches the bishop was regarded as abbot. The abbot's stall in choir, it is true, was allotted to him;[3] but more than one episode in the history of the church of Durham shows that, if he endeavoured to play the part of an abbot, he was speedily undeceived by the prior and convent, and, where a bishop, who was usually a secular and only now and then a monk, came into conflict with the monastery, he was generally worsted.[4] In fact, the independent position of cathedral chapters was so firmly established in the fifteenth century that bishops adopted towards them a policy of *laissez-faire* undisturbed by mutual quarrels.

It is unnecessary to discuss in detail the constitution of cathedral chapters, but a few leading facts may be recalled. At the head of the chapter was the dean, holding his office by election and episcopal confirmation, its chairman *ex officio*, but only as *primus inter pares*.[5] In theory his seat in chapter depended

[1] The south-east quarter of the city, still known, from the archbishop's palatine jurisdiction as the Pallant (*Palatinum* or *Palentinum*). The church of All Saints formed a member of the exempt deanery of Pagham, consisting of the churches in West Sussex which were *mere de iurisdictione archiepiscopi*. See Churchill, i. 63, 64n; *V.E.* i. 311.

[2] For the claim of the bishops of Exeter to the church of Bosham see *C.P.L.* ii. 149–50, and the series of documents in *R. Stapeldon*, 61–82. Institutions to the prebendal portions in Bosham are regularly recorded in the Exeter episcopal registers.

[3] On the nature of the relation of a bishop to a monastic chapter see introd. to *Dur. Stat.* xxi–xxvi. A brief and excellent summary of the question involved is given by Dom David Knowles, *Rel. Houses*, 25–7.

[4] For the quarrel between Bek and the convent of Durham see *Gesta Dunelmensia a.d. MoCCCo*, ed. Richardson (Camden, 3rd ser. xxxiv. 1–53), and *Scr. Tres* (Surtees Soc.), 82–90.

[5] The position of the dean with regard to the chapter is clearly and forcibly stated in the *Liber Iohannis de Schalby*, the work of a canon of Lincoln who died in

upon his possession of a canonry and prebend, and we often meet with appointments to canonries and prebends obviously intended to anticipate elections to deaneries. Where this had been omitted, or where a prebend was not permanently annexed to his dignity, the question naturally arose whether the normal president of chapter had a right to sit in chapter at all.[1] The three other dignitaries, the precentor, chancellor and treasurer, and the subdean, who held an office or parsonage in the church, were canons with prebends;[2] and their dignities and offices, like that of the dean, were held to involve a cure of souls—it was not until 1529 that such benefices were declared to be sinecures[3] —and to require continual residence. The remaining canons, varying in number in different churches, and holding prebends of varying values, fell into two classes. The majority were non-

1333, with reference to the claim of Roger Martival, dean of Lincoln 1310–15 and afterwards bishop of Salisbury, to a jurisdiction separate from and superior to that of the chapter. The claim rested upon his appointment by the special method of election and episcopal confirmation, and upon the statement 'quod canonici singulariter sibi ut superiori suo obedientiam repromittunt'. The argument of the chapter, in presenting the case for arbitration to Bishop Dalderby, is thus put by Schalby: 'Item de iure cautum non reperitur quid spectat ad officium decani ecclesie cathedralis a capitulo separatim: quia sede vacante decanus subest capitulo de iure et episcopo sede plena de consilio seu assensu capituli iudicandus. Unde nec sede vacante nec sede plena in capitulum imperium ullum habet nec in aliquos de capitulo; quia quilibet subest capitulo sede vacante et episcopo sede plena.' For the purposes of this argument emphasis is laid upon the position of the bishop as the true head of the chapter: 'Item sunt tantum in una ecclesia cathedrali episcopus et capitulum de iure qui faciunt unum corpus cuius corporis episcopus est capud et capitulum membra. Ponere ergo decanum aliud capud est ponere in uno corpore duo capita, quod est monstruosum et episcopo preiudiciale.' (B. & W. ii (i), p. lxxvii.) It is hardly necessary to add that, convenient as it was to recall the original relation of the bishop to his *familia* on occasion, a too liberal interpretation of the theory by the bishop would not have been welcomed by the chapter.

[1] This question arose at St. Paul's in 1365, when John Appleby, appointed dean by papal provision, held no stall in the church. In order to qualify for his place in chapter he exchanged his preb. in Southwell for preb. Chamberlainwood in St. Paul's. Next year he obtained a preb. in Lincoln by exchanging Chamberlainwood for it, but recovered Chamberlainwood a day later by exchange with its new holder of his chapel of St. Mary in the Palace—a good example of the intricacies of exchanges at this period. See Newcourt, i. 42; Hennessy, 20; *R. Sudbury* i. 253.

[2] Prebends were usually annexed to the three dignities, as at Salisbury, where the treasurer held preb. Calne and the chancellor held preb. Bricklesworth from c. 1240 onwards. The treasurer of York held two prebs., Wilton and Newthorpe. Prebs. Laughton and Driffield were not permanently attached to the dignities of chancellor and precentor till 1484, and at Lincoln the annexation of prebs. Sutton in Marisco and Kilsby to similar dignities took place about 1380.

[3] 21 Hen. VIII, c. xiii, § 20 (*S.R.* iii. 295).

resident, whose connexion with the church was their possession of a stall in choir and voice in chapter which they very seldom occupied or exercised, enjoying, nevertheless, their prebendal incomes. A smaller section, after fulfilling the arduous and expensive conditions which were the qualifications for the privilege of residence, lived in their prebendal houses and, in addition to their prebends, shared in the common revenues belonging to the chapter, that daily distribution, as it was in its original form, from the common fund whose advantages made the residentiaries anxious to keep their numbers as low as possible. At Lincoln also the common fund was increased by the 'sevenths' paid from their prebendal incomes by non-residents.

It may be added that the distinction by which residents are called canons, and non-residents prebendaries, is comparatively modern.[1] A prebend, as Lyndwood teaches, is the consequence of a canonry;[2] and although, when provisions to canonries with the expectation of prebends were frequent, men were constantly admitted to simple canonries,[3] it was not until they acquired prebends that they became full members of chapter. The capitular canon was a canon with a prebend, *canonicus preben-darius* or *prebendatus*, canon of the church of A, and prebendary

[1] In cathedral churches of the new foundation the official title of the members of the chapter varies between 'canon' and 'prebendary'. At Durham the lands constituting the *corpus* of each prebend were specified in a chapter of the statutes (*Dur. Stat.* 121): in this chapter, however, the office is called *canonicatus*, and in the following chapter, opening with the words *Decanus et prebendarii, canonicus* is used elsewhere. 'Prebendary' seems to have prevailed in ordinary use, under the abbreviated form 'prebend': hence the Prebends' Bridge over the Wear at Durham. The custom which gave territorial titles to the stalls in churches of the old foundation was not followed in those of the new, which were known simply by their numbers. It was probably a desire on the part of the old foundations to assert the equivalence of their prebends with those of the new that led to the adoption of the title prebendary for general use in most of them, before the distinction between the resident canon and the non-resident prebendary had fully arisen.

[2] Tit. *De concess. praeb.*, cap. *Esurientis*, ver. *praebendas* (p. 144): 'Praebenda differt a canonia. Nam canonia est ius spirituale quod aliquis assequitur in ecclesia per receptionem in fratrem et assignationem stalli in choro et loci in capitulo . . . Praebenda vero est ius spirituale recipiendi certos proventus pro meritis in ecclesia competentes percipienti ex divino officio cui insistit, et nascitur a canonia tanquam filia a matre.'

[3] Such admissions on expectation are recorded in some number in episcopal registers of the early fourteenth century, e.g. in R. Melton, R. Dald., and R. Burg. In some of these cases the subsequent offer of a vacant prebend is noted with its acceptance or refusal. Records of these admissions bear no proportion to the large numbers of expectative grants in *C.P.L.*

of the prebend of B in the same.[1]   And if, under such an
arrangement as has been described, the number of canons in
choir at any time was small, and if the residentiaries appeared
at services in rotation, each canon, resident or non-resident, had
his vicar or deputy with his stall in choir, and the vicars choral,
corresponding in number to the dean and canons, formed a
separate corporation which in process of time acquired an
important and privileged position in the affairs of the church.[2]
In addition to these, a third corporation, of which St. William's
College at York is a good example, was formed by the chantry
priests who served the altars of the church and were bound to
daily attendance in choir.[3]   The attendance of vicars and
chantry chaplains no doubt was subject to a rota, but it is
necessary to remember that such attendance was not confined
to canons, but was incumbent also upon a large body of resident
priests.

The same system was followed in the older collegiate
churches.   The constitutions of collegiate foundations exhibit
considerable varieties of detail, and the foundations themselves
may be classified in various ways.   More important than any of
the others were the three great churches of the diocese of York,
the minsters of Beverley, Ripon, and Southwell, each of which
played the part of a departmental cathedral church for outlying
portions of what in actual area was the largest diocese in
England.[4]   The divergence between their capitular constitu-

---

[1] An early instance of the description of a secular canon as prebendary of a
church *tout court* is the epitaph of William Hogeson, bishop of Dara, in Beverley
Minster. 'Of your charite pray for the soule of William sometyme bysshop of
dariens and prebendary of thys churche.' See *Y.A.J.* xxiv. 232, 253*n*.

[2] The corporate existence of bodies of vicars choral seems to have been recognized at an early date, at Lincoln as early as 1190 (see *B. & W.* i. 59, with its
reference to Maddison, *The Vicars Choral of Lincoln Cathedral*, 1878), at Lichfield
*c.* 1240 (*Mon.* vi. (iii), 1466).   The charter of Ralph of Shrewsbury to the vicars
choral of his church of Wells bears date 7 Apr. 1347 (ibid.).   The regular incorporation by royal letters patent comes later: the college of minor canons, supplementary
to and eventually superseding vicars at St. Paul's, 1 Aug. 1394 (*C.P.R.* 1391–6,
p. 490, and see ibid. 1399–1401, p. 192); the vicars' colleges at Salisbury, 18 Nov.
1409 (ibid. 1408–13, p. 152), York, 26 May 1421 (ibid. 1416–22, p. 360), Lincoln,
9 Nov. 1440 (see *V.C.H. Linc.* ii. 82), Chichester, 30 Dec. 1465 (ibid. 1461–7,
p. 422).                              [3] See *V.C.H. Yorks.* iii. 385.

[4] Beverley for the East Riding, Ripon for the north-western part of the diocese,
Southwell for the archdeaconry of Nottingham.   For the collection of Whitsuntide
oblations from the parishes of Nottinghamshire at Southwell, see the document
from R. Zouche quoted *A.J.* lxxi. 225–6.

tions was very curious: throughout the Middle Ages the chapter of Beverley preserved the clearest traces of its pre-Conquest origin as a college of seven canons, which later additions failed to obscure.[1] Ripon and Southwell had similar origins, but developed on somewhat different lines.[2] In none of the three churches was there a dean, and in all three the dean's stall was reserved for the archbishop. The officer called the provost of Beverley had no status as such in the chapter, and here and at Southwell the normal president of chapter was the senior canon: at Ripon the president was the precentor.[3] None of them, however, possessed the regular quota of cathedral dignities. At Southwell there was a chancellor, who was one of the canons,[4] and, though at Beverley there were a precentor, chancellor, and treasurer, these were merely officers who took rank below the canons and had no voice in chapter.[5]

Other churches in episcopal patronage could claim a pre-Conquest origin. St. John's at Chester, with its dean and seven canons, had a quasi-cathedral status, and gave to the bishop of Coventry and Lichfield the title of bishop of Chester, which survived in popular use as late as the middle of the fifteenth century.[6] The collegiate church of Crediton, with a precentor at its head, recalled the period when Crediton was the see of the bishop of Devon, before Leofric transferred his see to Exeter

[1] See the full discussion of the constitution of Beverley by A. F. Leach (*Bev. Ch. A.* i, introd., pp. xxvii sqq.). The eighth prebend (altar of St. Katherine) was never accepted as possessed of full capitular rights (ibid. i, pp. xlvii–xlix); while the ninth prebend, appropriated to the archbishop, was regarded merely as his portion in the fruits of the church (ibid. i, p. xlvii).

[2] See the introd. to *Mem. Ripon* iii and to *Vis. & Mem. Southwell.*

[3] This arrangement was established in 1230 by Archbishop Gray, who created the preb. of Stanwick and appropriated it to the precentorship (*R. Walt. Gray*, 51–2). To this period probably belongs the undated draft of the collegiate constitution of Ripon entered *R. Cor.* ii. 19: see also *Mem. Ripon*, ii. 25. This marks the conversion of a church of six non-resident portioners into a college of seven canons with a permanently resident head. The responsibility for the cure of souls at Ripon was delegated to six vicars-choral: the precentor had no vicar choral at Ripon, but had his vicar at Stanwick St. John in Richmondshire.

[4] With the preb. of Normanton. See *Vis. & Mem. Southwell*, pp. xli, xlii.

[5] On this peculiar arrangement see *Bev. Ch. A.* i, pp. lv–lix. Although there were no *dignitates* among the canons of Beverley, the title *personatus* seems more appropriate than *dignitas* to these subordinate officers. See Lyndwood, u.s. ver. *Dignitates, Personatus, Officia*, for the somewhat delicate distinction between these terms.

[6] See Ormerod, i. 306 sqq., *Mon.* vi (iii), 1447–8. For the title 'bishop of Chester' see, e.g., Gascoigne's reference to William Bothe, *indignus episcopus Cestrie* (*Loc. L. V.* 40).

in 1050.[1] The church of Westbury-on-Trym, near Bristol, with its dean and five canons, appears to have taken its origin in an early minster of secular clerks; and, at the close of the thirteenth century, Bishop Godfrey Giffard, impatient of the privileges of the monastic chapter at Worcester, made a fruitless attempt to establish an augmented secular chapter at Westbury which might form such a makeweight to Worcester as Wells formed to Bath and Lichfield to Coventry.[2]

A similar impulse to that which moved Giffard in the case of Westbury had moved other bishops at the same period to create secular chapters in which, having no benefices at their disposal in monastic cathedral churches, they might place clerks of their own choosing. Thus Anthony Bek, at war with his cathedral priory, had converted the three churches of the widespreading parishes to the west and north-west of Durham, St. Andrew's Auckland, Lanchester, and Chester-le-Street, into collegiate churches, each with a dean, and with canons deriving their prebends from the tithe of hamlets in the several parishes.[3] To much the same period belonged the collegiate church of St. Mary's-in-the-Fields at Norwich, with a dean and canons.[4] The endowments of all these churches, however, were comparatively small, nor did they ever rise to anything like the importance of Beverley, Ripon, and Southwell. On the other hand, the secular chapter of St. David's, the cathedral of a large and geographically most difficult diocese, was somewhat over-shadowed by the two collegiate churches founded by Thomas Bek, the brother of Anthony, at Llangadock in Carmarthen-shire and Llanddewi-Brefi in the wilds of Cardiganshire. The chapter of Llangadock was transferred at a somewhat later date to Abergwili, the episcopal residence near Carmarthen,

[1] *Mon.* u.s. 1450–1.

[2] Ibid. 1439. For a summary account of Giffard's efforts on behalf of West-bury see *B. & G.A.S.* xxxviii. 109–12. Much information with regard to the history of the college is given, not without many errors in detail, by H. J. Wilkins, *Westbury College from 1194 to 1544,* 1917.

[3] See 'The Collegiate Churches of the Bishoprick of Durham' *D.U.J.* xxxvi. 33–42. Bek's ordinances for Lanchester bear date 25 Mar. 1283; those for Chester-le-Street 9 Nov. 1286; and that for Auckland, 14 Jan. 1292–3 (*Mon.* u.s. 1333–9).

[4] See Blomefield, iv. 169–77, *Mon.* u.s. 1459. The collegiate establishment appears to date from 1280, when John le Brun, who had founded the hospital *c.* 1250, became dean. There were ten prebends, of which five were appropriated to the offices of chancellor, treasurer, precentor, provost, and sacrist.

and was eventually annexed by Henry VIII to his foundation of Christ College at Brecon, in connexion with which it still nominally exists, though its prebends have long been vacant.[1] In a somewhat similar diocese, that of Exeter, including the large counties of Devon and Cornwall, Bishop Bronescombe in the third quarter of the thirteenth century had founded a college of a provost and twelve canons at Glasney near Falmouth;[2] and at the opening of the Hundred Years' War that magnificent prelate, John Grandisson, had bought the dean and chapter of Rouen out of the patronage of the church of Ottery St. Mary and established there a chapter of eight canons.[3]

An important, though somewhat inactive, class of collegiate churches was constituted by those which had their origin as royal free chapels. A certain number of churches in the midlands claimed Edgar the Peaceful as their original founder, and their origin might at any rate be traced to the period of quietude and ecclesiastical reform which followed the Danish wars of the tenth century. Such were St. Mary's at Shrewsbury, and the churches of St. Edith at Tamworth and St. Michael at Penkridge; while the foundation of St. Peter's at Wolverhampton can be dated within 20 years of Edgar's death.[4] In these there were colleges with deans, whose appointment lay with the Crown, and varying numbers of canons, normally appointed by the deans.[5] We may add to these a few other colleges, All Saints'

[1] Bek's ordinance for Llangadock is printed *Mon.* vi (iii), 1332–3. For Abergwili see ibid. 1376, where the ordinance of Bishop Gower, 26 Apr. 1334, is printed. Llanddewi-Brefi is treated ibid. 1475: see also *C.P.R.* 1348–50, p. 27. Gower may be regarded as completing the beginnings of Bek's work in both colleges.

[2] *Mon.* vi. (iii), 1344, and see *R. Brones.* 94–5.

[3] *Mon.* vi. 1347. See *C.P.R.* 1334–8, p. 569; Dalton, *The Collegiate Church of Ottery St. Mary, being the Ordinances and Statutes, 1338–9*, 1917.

[4] The attribution of these colleges to Edgar in the Chantry Certificates of 1548 was purely traditional. Equally traditional was the attribution of St. Mary's at Stafford to the Lady of the Mercians, while the legend of a foundation by Edgar was also applied to St. Michael's at Tettenhall. The Staffordshire Chantry Certificates ascribe the church at Stafford to King John, and that at Tettenhall to Edward III; and the reigns of these kings may mark constitutional stages in the history of both. But for these and for the foundation of Wolverhampton see Mrs. Styles's paper on 'The Early History of the King's Chapels in Staffordshire'. (*Trans. Birm. Archaeol. Soc.* lx. 56–95).

[5] Such appointments are recorded on the patent rolls, those of deans with fair regularity. In view of the attribution of the foundation of the church of Stafford to John, it may be noted that in 1207, when John made a grant of the deanery to the archdeacon of Stafford, a mandate *ad intendendum*, addressed to the canons, shows

at Derby, St. Martin's-le-Grand in London,[1] Wimborne Minster in Dorset,[2] St. Buryan in Cornwall,[3] and St. Mary Magdalene's at Bridgnorth, the last of which, though said to have been founded by the Conqueror, actually came to the Crown in the reign of Henry I by the forfeiture of Robert de Bellême.[4] In these the deaneries and canonries were Crown preferments, exempt from episcopal jurisdiction.[5] Two of them, however, had been permanently given into the charge of ecclesiastics: the deanery of All Saints', Derby, was held by the dean of Lincoln,[6] and that of Penkridge, from the reign of John, by the archbishop

that the collegiate establishment was already in existence (*Rot. Litt. Pat.* 70). The attribution of Tettenhall to Edward III was certainly modest. In 1341, on the attempt of a provisor to intrude himself into preb. Codsall, it was stated that the chapel of Tettenhall was a king's free chapel, exempt from ordinary jurisdiction, and from time immemorial the collation of prebends had belonged only to the dean or in his default to the Crown (*C.P.R.* 1340–3, p. 320). The earliest grant of the deanery of Tettenhall on the patent rolls occurs in 1226 (*C.P.R.* 1225–32, p. 63; see also p. 92). The church of Tamworth, however, was not originally counted among royal free chapels, but was a free chapel in the hands of the lord of the manor and castle, and appointments to the deanery and prebends until the middle of the fourteenth century were made by the Crown only for reasons of escheat and custody of lands, &c., held in chief. See *C.P.R.* 1327–30, pp. 301, 420; 1340–3, p. 515; 1345–8, p. 333; 1358–61, pp. 12, 14, 186, 192. For the patronage in 1348 see ibid. 1348–50, pp. 44, 45. A number of appointments to prebends from 1363 to 1366 were made by the Crown without qualification (*C.P.R.* 1361–4, p. 431; 1364–7, pp. 18, &c., and in 1367, 1372, and at later dates the church is definitely called the king's free chapel (*C.P.R.* 1364–7, p. 418; 1370–4, p. 190; &c.).     [1] *Mon.* u.s. 1323–5; Newcourt, i. 424–8.

[2] *V.C.H. Dorset,* ii. 109. The date of the establishment of a secular college at Wimborne, the seat of a Saxon nunnery, is unknown: the settlement of canons may have been due to Edward the Confessor, but this rests purely on tradition.

[3] *Mon.* u.s. 1448–9.

[4] See *A.J.* lxxxiv. 1–87. The attribution of the foundation to the Conqueror comes from the Chantry Certificates (*Trans. Salop. Arch. Soc.*, 3rd ser. x. 317).

[5] Lyndwood, tit. *De cohabitatione,* c. *Ut clericalis,* ad v. *Beneficiati* (pp. 125–6), has a long discussion of the question whether such deaneries as that of St. Martin's-le-Grand, a royal donative, requiring neither institution by the bishop nor induction by his authority, can be reckoned ecclesiastical benefices.

[6] See *C.P.R.* 1272–81, p. 313, for the statement that All Saints', Derby, was the king's free chapel, exempt from the jurisdiction of the ordinary, and appurtenant to the deanery of Lincoln by grant of the king's predecessors: see also *Reg. Antiq. Linc.* i. 185; iii. 100, 101. The grant of All Saints' and the church of Wirksworth by Henry I as a preb. to the church of Lincoln and its confirmation by Henry II are printed ibid. i. 29, 92–3. All Saints' is not included among the nine royal free chapels enumerated *C.C.R.* 1313–18, p. 596. These are St. Martin's-le-Grand, Wolverhampton, Stafford, Wimborne, Bridgnorth, St. Mary's at Shrewsbury, Tettenhall, Penkridge, and St. Oswald's at Gloucester. For the history of this last and its transformation from a secular establishment to a church of canons regular see *B. & G.A.S.* xliii. 185–280.

of Dublin,[1] both of whom appointed the canons. In the others the deans, appointed by letters patent and installed by lay officers, usually had control of nominations to canonries; but all the benefices in St. Martin's-le-Grand and Bridgnorth were retained at the disposal of the Crown. The result was that the deaneries and canonries in both churches became the perquisites of king's clerks. The late Professor Tout has noticed the close connexion which existed between St. Martin's-le-Grand and the clerks of the Wardrobe,[2] and a very similar union of offices is seen at Bridgnorth, though in neither church the Wardrobe had the entire monopoly of appointments.[3] The chapel in Hastings Castle, with a dean and twelve canons, is a further instance in which the Crown had the patronage of all benefices and filled them with its clerks; but here the bishop of Chichester instituted the royal presentees and retained his ordinary jurisdiction.[4]

There were other collegiate churches of a similar type, St. Mary's at Warwick and St. Mary's in the Castle at Leicester, founded by earls after the Norman Conquest, which remained outside the royal jurisdiction.[5] At Warwick the church came

[1] The grant was made by John to Henry de Loundres, archbishop 1213–28, conveying to him and his successors, not being Irishmen, the deanery and ordinance of the church. See *C.P.R.* 1225–32, p. 97.

[2] Tout, i. 279; ii. 15 *n.*, &c.

[3] See the list of deans and canons, *A.J.* lxxxiv. 50–62. The canonries were filled in much the same way. Appointments are entered with some regularity on the patent rolls; but less regularly towards the close of the fifteenth century, owing to the habit of making grants of the next presentation to lessees.

[4] Lists of the canons of Hastings from the patent rolls are printed in C. Dawson, *Hist. of Hastings Castle*, 1910. The chapel is called the king's free chapel temp. Edw. I: see, e.g., *C.P.R.* 1272–81, p. 9; 1281–92, pp. 362, 505. This, however, is not invariable, and Hastings was not one of the free chapels mentioned in 1318 (see p. 82, note 6 above). Institutions to canonries by the bishop of Chichester are entered in such episcopal registers as remain (see *R. Rede* and *R. Praty*), but the absence of such registers before 1396 makes it impossible to say for how long the bishops had exercised this right. In 1305 the exempt status of the chapel is clearly stated as against the claim of the metropolitan to visit it (*C.P.R.* 1301–7, p. 397); but in 1311 and 1312 grants of canonries and prebends take the form of presentations to the diocesan for institution (ibid. 1307–13, pp. 408, 428, 489). At the same time, mandates for induction were not issued by the bishop of Chichester to the archdeacon of Lewes, but by royal letters patent addressed to the sheriff of Sussex or to some other minister of the Crown.

[5] See *Mon.* u.s. 1325–30 for Warwick, and 1456 for the church at Leicester, inaccurately described as St. Martin's the Less. The founder of the first was Henry Beaumont, earl of Warwick, *c.* 1088–1119, of the second Robert Beaumont, count of Meulan and earl of Leicester (d. 1118).

under the spiritual jurisdiction of the bishops of Worcester;[1] at Leicester the appointment of dean and canons was given by Robert le Bossu to the abbey of St. Mary-in-the-Meadows, which he founded in 1143.[2] This earlier college at Leicester, although it survived into the sixteenth century, was put in the shade by the college which, under the protection of the house of Lancaster, rose in the outer ward of the same castle. In 1330 Henry, earl of Lancaster, founded the hospital of the Annunciation in the Newarke of Leicester: in 1355 his son, the first duke, largely increased the endowments given by his father and attached the hospital to a new college of a dean and twelve canons, whose church was intended to be the memorial and mausoleum of his family.[3] While the abbot of Leicester was ordinary in the older college, the new foundation was subjected to the bishop of Lincoln. There is no doubt that the duke of Lancaster's ambitious and successful project at Leicester was suggested by Edward III's foundation of colleges in connexion with his principal residences, the colleges of St. Stephen at Westminster and St. George at Windsor, each with a dean and twelve canons, whose benefices were royal donatives.[4]

These later colleges were founded upon the old lines after the cathedral pattern, and as late as the last quarter of the fourteenth century the college of St. Peter at Irthlingborough in Northamptonshire, with a dean and five canons, was established in pursuance of the will of a wealthy merchant, John Pyel.[5] The distinctive marks of such colleges were the separate prebend held by its occupant as a freehold benefice, and con-

---

[1] Lists of deans and canons from the Worcester episcopal registers are given in *Antiq. Warw.* i. 433–8.

[2] See *Mon.* vi (i), 1462. No consecutive records of admissions to canonries, known by the letters A to H, exist, though details can here and there be recovered from records of exchanges preserved in various episcopal registers and in *C.P.R.* (see, e.g. *R. Stretton*, 124, 125, 145, 203–4). In these instances the admission of canons by the bishop of Lichfield is in pursuance of commissions from the abbot of Leicester. An admission by the abbot to the deanery and the A prebend in 1382 is recorded *Wyggeston Hosp. Rec.*, p. 320, no. 552.

[3] See Thompson, *Hist. of the Hospital and New College of the Annunciation of St. Mary in the Newarke, Leicester*, 1937.

[4] The letters patent founding both these royal free chapels bear date 6 Aug. 1348 (*C.P.R.* 1348–50, pp. 144–7). These are printed *Mon.* u.s., 1348–9, 1354–5.

[5] See 'The Early History of the College of Irthlingborough' (*A.A.S.R.P.* xxxv (ii), 267–92), which corrects the brief and extremely inaccurate account in *V.C.H. Northants*, and is supplemented by lists of deans and canons.

ditions of residence which, if they were nominally obligatory, did not in practice preclude the tenure of other benefices by canons.[1] But side by side with these we see the development of a new type of collegiate establishment which will be discussed more fully in connexion with chantry foundations. Here it need only be said that the contrast between the old and new types is well illustrated by a comparison of the constitution of the Lancastrian college at Leicester with that founded some sixty years later at Fotheringhay by Edward, duke of York.[2]

Reference has already been made to the origin of certain colleges in those Saxon 'minsters' of which so many traces remain in Domesday Book, and in which bodies of secular clergy resided, each member having a share in the annual revenues of the community.[3] This system was derived from the continental organizations initiated by St. Chrodegang at Metz in the eighth century, and it was developed in England in the tenth and eleventh centuries. At the Norman Conquest it was gradually superseded by the adoption of the system usually considered to have been borrowed directly from the customs of such churches as Rouen and Bayeux.[4] The older minsters gradually disappeared or were transformed. Some, after a lingering and unsatisfactory existence—conspicuous examples are Christchurch in Hampshire and Waltham in Essex—were turned into houses of canons regular:[5] the canons of Stow in Lincolnshire were transferred to the Benedictine abbey of Eynsham,[6] and the canons of Dorchester accepted the rule of St. Augustine.[7]

---

[1] Cf. the above lists for Irthlingborough and the lists of deans and canons of the Newarke college, p. 84, notes 3, 5.

[2] See *A.J.* lxxv. 241–309. The earlier type of foundation is discussed at length ibid. lxxiv, 139–239, 'Notes on Colleges of Secular Canons in England'.

[3] The standard discussion of the subject is by W. Page, 'Some Remarks on the Churches of the Domesday Survey' (*Arch.* lxvi. 61–102).

[4] The view which has long prevailed was that of Henry Bradshaw, enunciated in *B. & W.* i. 35, 36, viz. that the system was derived from Bayeux, of which Thomas, the first Norman archbishop of York, had been treasurer. This view was founded mainly upon the order of the *quatuor personae* or dignities. But this order, though it may have existed at York from the beginning, was not stereotyped until much later. This was shown by the late Dean Savage in his Introd. to the Lichfield *Magnum Reg. Album*, pp. xxvi, xxvii, where he adduces reasons for the influence of Rouen on the early statutes of Lichfield.

[5] The story of the change of constitution at Christchurch is in the *Historia fundationis* (*Mon.* vi (i), 303). For Waltham see ibid. 57; Newcourt, ii. 528.

[6] *Mon.* iii, 1 sqq.

[7] Ibid. vi (i), 323 sqq., where Leland is quoted: 'Alexander bishop of Lincoln

In one cathedral church, that of Exeter, the old system of equal prebends from a common fund survived the introduction of Norman dignitaries and the distinction between residentiaries and non-residents.[1] And there remained a number of churches whose origin is often obscure, with revenues divided between a certain number of portioners, usually four or three. It is difficult to distinguish these, on the one hand, from genuine collegiate institutions such as the two colleges of Shrewsbury, the royal free chapel of St. Mary and the bishop of Lichfield's church of St. Chad, both early minsters which became churches of a dean and canons with equal shares in the revenues.[2] On the other hand, they resembled those rectories divided into moieties, common all over England, which were due to the existence of two patrons or the division of the heritage of a single patron. Often treated as collegiate, they nevertheless had none of the corporate signs of a college, no capitular meetings, no common seal or common fund: each member was a corporation sole. Even at Ripon this state of things was only gradually overcome towards the end of the thirteenth century by the establishment of a resident head of chapter and the transference of the parochial cure of souls from non-resident portioners to resident vicars choral.[3] But a number of these indeterminate establishments survived, for the most part in the west midlands and the south-west. In the diocese of Lichfield, for example, there was the church of Gnosall in Staffordshire with four prebendaries or portioners.[4] In the diocese of Hereford there were

erected there an abbey of blak chanons, yet the chirch berith the name of the prebend chirch.' The traditions of the Saxon 'minster', the see in which was transferred after the Conquest to Lincoln, remained strong. Another case of the foundation of a house of canons regular in a church previously in secular hands is that of the priory of Hexham by Archbishop Thomas II of York in 1113; see Introd. to *The Priory of Hexham* (Surtees Soc.), vol. i, pp. lxi–lxvii.

[1] The plurality returns (1366) in R. Langham show the prebs. at Exeter as taxed equally at 6 marks a year, of which half, by a long-continued grant of the whole chapter, was devoted to the fabric fund of the church (ff. 18*b*, 21, 28*b*, &c.).

[2] Four 'minsters' are noted at Shrewsbury in D.B. i, ff. 252, 253, viz. St. Mary's, St. Chad's, St. Michael's, and St. Alkmund's. In the Chantry Certificates, where, as already noted (p. 81, note 4 above), the foundation of St. Mary's is ascribed to King Edgar, the founder of St. Chad's is said to have been 'Roger, bishop of Chester', i.e. Roger Clinton, bishop of Coventry and Lichfield 1129–48 (*Salop. Arch. Soc.* 3rd ser. x. 305, 306).

[3] See p. 79 above, note 3.

[4] See *V.E.* iii. 99, where Gnosall is treated as a college, with the bishop as merely nominal dean, and the four prebends of Mordhall (Morehall), Suterhall, Beverley-

Bromyard and Ledbury in Herefordshire, Burford, Castle Holdgate, Pontesbury, and Westbury in Shropshire.[1] There are many examples in the diocese of Exeter, the castle chapel at Exeter in the patronage of the earls of Devon, the churches of Tiverton and Chulmleigh, each with four portioners, and in Cornwall the churches of St. Endellion, St. Probus, and St. Teath, each with three.[2] The church of St. Crantock near Newquay, although it acquired a definite collegiate organization, probably had a similar origin;[3] and, although each of the four portioners of Bosham in Sussex, a distant possession of the bishops of Exeter, had his special office in connexion with the church, there was no definite president of chapter.[4] All these and others continued until the close of the Middle Ages and some of them much later; and indeed the three portioners of Pontesbury and Burford may still be found in Crockford's *Clerical Directory*, where St. Endellion also claims the dignity of a college.[5]

hall, and Chyltrenhall. In *Tax. Eccl.* 243b, the church is treated as a single benefice. The prebend referred to *Extra*, tit. *De rescriptis*, c. *Ex parte* (1. iii. 2) as *praebenda de Novalis* was probably one of the portions in Gnosall. Friedberg adds to the list of variants *legendum est Northale*, but this reading would apply to no church of portioners in the diocese of Coventry and Lichfield or to any collegiate church at the date required; but it is possible that 'Northale' might indicate the portion of Morehall, which could probably lay claim to this title.

[1] See *Tax. Eccl.* 160 and b, 165, 166b, 167 and b; *V.E. iii.* 42, 47, 209, 213, 214. Castle Holdgate is treated in *V.E.* as a simple benefice. A document in *R. Gilbert*, pp. 60–1, records the findings of an inquiry in 1384 with regard to the status of the churches of Bromyard and Ledbury, which are declared to be not collegiate, but churches of portioners. In the case of the two portions of Ledbury (Overhall and Netherhall) the necessary qualifications of *sigilla communia, cistae communes, campanae communes, domi communes*, and *domi capitulares* were wanting, and there was no *capud principale*. The three portions of Bromyard were in similar case: 'de anno in annum separatim equaliter currunt, nec habent aliqua jura alia sibi accidencia super.'

[2] See *Tax. Eccl.* 143 and b, 146, 147b, 148b; *V.E. ii.* 317, 330, 350, 397, 401. The portions of St. Probus are not noticed in *V.E.* and in *Tax. Eccl.* Chulmleigh is treated as a simple benefice.

[3] See *Tax. Eccl.* 148b (nine prebs. and a portion, no dean); *V.E. ii.* 399 (dean and nine prebs.). The first mention of a dean of St. Crantock in the Exeter episcopal registers is in 1309 (*R. Stapeldon*, 249); but the benefices in the church were habitually known as prebends at an earlier date. It may be noted that, although St. Probus never acquired collegiate status, a dean of the church appears in 1268–9 (*R. Brones.* 177). [4] See p. 75 above, note 2.

[5] The 'rehabilitation' of St. Endellion as a prebendal church with a rectorial prebend and the prebends of Marny, Bodmin or King's and Trehaverock by the late Bishop Frere, with statutes attached, is printed in a valuable account of *St. Endellion Prebendal Church, its Constitution and History*, ed. T. Taylor, vicar of St. Just-in-Penwith, Truro, 1929.

But such a catalogue, though not exhaustive, may well be wearisome, and we may turn to the internal life of cathedral and collegiate establishments as we see it in the later Middle Ages. In most cathedral churches it was quiet and peaceful. The affairs of the church were administered by the close chapter of residentiaries, which tended gradually to diminish in numbers. At York during the fifteenth century the old causes of strife between the archbishop and his powerful chapter had been adjusted by tacit consent. In the time of Archbishop Bowet, indeed, something like the primitive relation between a bishop and his *familia* seems to have prevailed: the splendid windows of the choir of York Minster, completed during this period, bear witness to the unity of purpose which guided the relations between the archbishop and his canons, with a mutual respect of each other's privileges.[1] The conduct of diocesan affairs was largely entrusted to members of the chapter; and, in the constant absence of later archbishops, such business practically became centralized at York. The residentiary chapter had its own difficulties. The masons of the cathedral church were unruly: when the king lent his master-mason William of Colchester to the chapter, the masons on the spot, jealous of a stranger, conspired against him, wounded him, and killed his apprentice.[2] The records of the dean and chapter contain the usual examples of negligence and irreverence in church, especially on the part of the vicars choral;[3] but possibly cathedral choirs, with all their virtues, have never been nurseries of single-minded piety. The parish churches in the jurisdiction of the dean and chapter showed signs of dilapidation, broken windows, leaking gutters, torn vestments, imperfect books, and non-resident canons doubtless showed as little anxiety as the lay rector of our own day to spend money over the repair of the chancels

[1] Thus three of the windows in the north aisle of the choir, very similar in treatment, were the gifts of one of the archbishop's family, of Robert Wolveden the treasurer, and of Thomas Parker, prebendary of Ampleforth. See Harrison, *The Painted Glass of York*, pp. 89, 90.

[2] *Fabric Rolls of York Minster* (Surtees Soc.), p. 201. The anonymous letter which records this bears no date. We know, however, that William of Colchester was master-mason at York in 1415. His arrival may have been some years earlier: if so, he may have been sent by Henry IV, possibly to make some amends for his treatment of Archbishop Scrope.

[3] For the Minster and the parish churches of the liberty see the extracts from visitation records, ranging from 1362 to 1550, printed ibid., pp. 242–74.

of their prebendal churches; but such defects were not peculiar to this group of churches, as the returns of earlier and later diocesan visitations show abundantly. Moreover, anyone who takes the trouble to compare these sources of information with the architectural evidence of the buildings themselves will have reason to suspect that their conventional phrases often convey an exaggerated impression of damage, and that the stock phrase *cancellus est ruinosus* need not be taken too literally. Of dissensions in the chapter there is no record. There was some variety in the character, so far as we can discern it, of the deans. After Bowet's death, William Felter, a Somerset man who may have come first to York from the diocese of Bath and Wells in the household of Bowet—such instances of importations from other dioceses are frequent—acquired the favour of Archbishop Kempe, became dean in 1436, and was certainly active in the service of his church.[1] The appointment of his successor, Richard Andrew, secretary to King Henry VI, seems to have been due to an arrangement between the Crown and the papacy in the face of an election made by the chapter, and Gascoigne had uncomplimentary remarks to make about it.[2] But on the whole the deans and canons of this period were highly respectable and competent men of business, zealous for the honour and liberties of their church and punctual in the discharge of their duties.[3]

During the first half of the century at Lincoln, however, matters were different. Here there had long been some doubt with regard to the rights of the dean in the church and chapter, and more than one bishop had been called in to arbitrate upon this vexed question.[4] At the opening of the century the dean, John Shepey, claimed the right of holding visitations of the chapter, correcting and punishing their excesses and those of their spiritual subjects, and dealing at his free will with the appointment and removal of the vicars, chantry chaplains, and other ministers of the church. At the end of 1400 Henry IV intervened in the dispute and ordered Bishop Beaufort, his half-brother, to take measures to stop it. Letters apostolic were

[1] See *Surt. Misc.* 294–5.
[2] *Loc. L. V.* 37.
[3] See *Surt. Misc.* 291–302 for biographical notices of canons of York, Beverley, &c., prominent in the records of the pontificates of Bowet and Kempe.
[4] See the section headed 'The Lincoln Awards 1245–1439', *B. & W.* ii (ii), 232–67.

obtained from Boniface IX to the same effect, and in July 1404 Beaufort decided against the dean.[1] When Shepey died in 1412 he was succeeded in the deanery by John Macworth, chancellor of Prince Henry. Macworth, a member of a Derbyshire family, already had a dispensation to hold two cures of souls and was archdeacon of Norfolk and of Dorset. The first of these he resigned, but continued to hold the second, while he also obtained the rectory of Tredington in Worcestershire.[2]

From the beginning of his rule at Lincoln, Macworth was haughty and uncompromising. He neglected his obligation to reside as dean or to protest residence in virtue of his prebend in the church, but insisted upon claiming *ex officio* all the advantages of a residentiary, while refusing to pay the sevenths which each non-resident paid by custom to the common fund. A protest containing thirteen articles of complaint was drawn up by some of the residentiaries somewhere before 1418 to three arbiters, of whom the bishop was one.[3] It was not, however, until May 1421 that an award on a number of disputed points was made by Bishop Flemyng.[4] But, although the dean and one of the canons, William Derby, on behalf of the chapter, bound themselves in £100 to observe this compromise, the quarrel continued. A long list of forty-one *gravamina* against the dean by the residentiaries was presented to Flemyng's successor, William Gray, in 1434.[5] Gray conscientiously made his award, in which the dean was ordered to remedy his defaults. It is perfectly clear that his endeavour to show that a dean was above all rules was in flat contradiction to the customs of the church, and that he took advantage of any ambiguity in their terms to justify an untenable position by obstinacy in which he hoped to break down custom. But the residentiaries, though not wholly of one mind among themselves, were equally obstinate, and their opposition was strengthened by a disgraceful scene that took place in the cathedral a year after Gray's award. On 28 June 1435, the eve of St. Peter's day, while vespers were going on in choir, and the cathedral was full of people and pilgrims, the dean came into church with a band of armed men, who with drawn swords and daggers attacked Peter Partrich the chancellor and dragged him about by his almuce, maltreating

[1] *B. & W.* ii (ii), 249–56.    [2] For Macworth's career see *Linc. Vis.* i. 69, 174.
[3] *B. & W.* ii (ii), 257–8.    [4] Ibid. 182–6, 258–9.    [5] Ibid. 259–66.

him and threatening him.[1] Bishop Gray held an inquiry into the matter, but he died shortly afterwards, and the disputes which his award had failed to settle came before his successor William Alnwick.

The documents relating to the visitation of the cathedral church which, begun by Alnwick on 1 October 1437, lasted for a week, have been printed at length in Bradshaw and Words-worth's *Lincoln Cathedral Statutes*.[2] The dean and canons were examined separately by the bishop himself, but the examination of the vicars, chantry chaplains, and inferior ministers of the church, ninety-four persons in all, was committed to the bishop's official, Robert Thornton. The dean, orally and in writing, brought a number of charges against the residentiaries, including a charge of organized conspiracy against six of the residentiaries, the chancellor Partrich, the treasurer John Haget, John Southam, archdeacon of Oxford, William Derby, archdeacon of Bedford, Thomas Warde, and Richard Ingoldsby. His other complaints concerned various sins of omission on the part of the chapter, neglect of the fabric of the church, the habit followed by the canons of taking persons from the choir to assist them at the altar instead of supplying proper clerks and servers, and the tendency of the canons chosen as provosts to conduct the financial business of the chapter on their own account. He asked for a clear and definitive ruling upon the terms of residence of the dean and canons; and, anticipating the charge of non-residence against himself, stated that William Derby had been allowed all the privileges of a residentiary during an absence of two years in London, when he was an officer of the Exchequer, and that during that time the chapter had provided him with money for their legal business which ought to have been paid to the ministers of the church. All this had been done without a word to bishop or dean.

To the argument that, as the governing body of the church was the dean and chapter, the chapter could not act independently of the dean, there was no reasonable answer.[3] But the

---

[1] Ibid. 380–1.

[2] Ibid. 364 sqq. Of a paper read by the Rev. A. R. Maddison, said to have been read before the Archaeol. Institute 30 July 1889 and printed in their transactions for 1891, there is no trace in the records of the Institute contained in *A.J.*

[3] The corporate unity of dean and chapter is manifest in the fact that letters

point of view of Peter Partrich and the other confederates was
that a dean who did not keep residence lost the rights which
residence conferred on him. Moreover, the dean's behaviour
to the canons went beyond all that a dean could claim. He
treated his office as a separate jurisdiction which could be
exercised without reference to the chapter.[1] He had entirely
disregarded his undertaking to observe Bishop Gray's award,
even after he had entered into a concord with the residentiaries
by indentures signed in April 1436 before the treasurer of
England. Even during the present visitation he was issuing
orders to the canons and their officers, in spite of the fact that
the jurisdiction of dean and chapter was at such a time superseded by that of the bishop. Although not resident, he demanded
the so-called quotidians, his dividend from the commons of the
church, reckoned according to days of residence. More than
this, he had attempted to withold from William Derby the rent
from the chapter's estate at Little Bytham, which had been
assigned to Derby on the death of the last residentiary who had
received it. If he kept no residence, he was often enough in
Lincoln to make his presence felt, worrying the canons by
summoning chapter meetings at all hours of the day, hindering
the provost of the chapter and the clerk of the common in their
administration of the common fund, keeping a body of hired
partisans in his house, and neglecting the discharge of the special
duties incumbent upon a dean. His behaviour in processions
was open to criticism: he walked where and how he liked, often
hurrying along by the officiant and talking to him.[2] On great
festivals, when processions went outside the precincts, his cope
was held up by a train-bearer. He kept, contrary to the customs
of the church, one of the keys of the common seal; he appropriated the book of customs, the famous Black Book; he privately
opened letters addressed to the dean and chapter in common;
he had broken down part of the close wall to build himself a

addressed to the chapter without the dean are habitually qualified *capitulo decano
absente* or *decanatu vacante*.

[1] See especially the three schedules of *detecta* submitted by William Derby in
1438, all *gravamina contra decanum, B. & W.* u.s., 379–86.

[2] See the evidence of Peter Partrich, ibid. 374: 'Item quod decanus con-
fabulatur cum canonico coexecutore officii in processionibus, dominicis diebus,
incedendo, vel iuxta, vel post eum, contra solitum morem et consuetudinem lauda-
bilem ecclesie cum secundum huiusmodi consuetudinem pergeret linealiter in
ordine post ultimum canonicum ex parte sua.'

stable.[1] Altogether, a study of the depositions and scheduled complaints of the canons confirms the impression that Gascoigne's description of Macworth as *decanus superbus* was not misapplied.[2]

With regard to the dean's complaint of the preferential treatment shown to William Derby, the residentiaries showed that it had been the act of the subdean and chapter in the absence of the dean, and therefore that there was no irregularity about it. As a matter of fact, it was generally recognized in all chapters that a residentiary, if absent anywhere on the business of his church, should be treated in all respects as though he were actually in residence.[3] The residentiaries, however, showed no disposition to extend this rule too far, and when the precentor, Robert Burton, accepted the office of a proctor of the clergy of the province of Canterbury at the Council of Basel and remained there for four years, his brethren endeavoured to extract from him a promise that he would abandon his resident privileges for the time being. He did not consent, and he had in his favour decrees passed at Constance and Basel to cover such cases as his; but the chapter kept his profits and would not restore them. Consequently Burton, though not in love with the dean, had his own quarrel with the confederate canons.

A full examination of all the points raised at this visitation would provide a fairly complete picture of the life of the church of Lincoln and its ministers; but we must confine ourselves to the main dispute. At the close of the visitation the long series of *detecta* and *comperta* was duly published, and the dean and canons for the time being were left to their own devices. In the following January, however, Alnwick resumed his visitation, saying pointedly 'who is in fault God knows, but you are not ignorant'.[4] The result of the second visitation was that, after some persuasion, the dean consented to submit to the bishop's arbitration. In June 1438, in pursuance of instructions communicated to them, the ten residentiaries, including in addition

---

[1] Ibid.: 'Item dicit quod decanus, inconsulto capitulo, edificavit stabulum suum infra mansum suum decanalem super murum claustri borialem, per cuius stillicidia dampnificatur tectum claustri, et eciam plures lapides politos de ipso muro ad hoc opus et pro illo tempore prostrauit per quod timetur de maiori dampnacione in futurum quam modo suspicatur.'

[2] *Loc. L. V.* 153.

[3] So in the Hereford statutes (*B. & W.* ii (i), 48): 'Dicuntur autem vere residentes ... qui de licencia capituli sunt absentes pro expediendis ecclesie negociis.'

[4] 'Quis est in culpa, nouit Deus, non ignoratis' (ibid. ii (ii), 364).

to the six confederates the precentor, the subdean, William Lassels, archdeacon of Huntingdon, and John Marchall, presented forty-one articles against the dean, while he, then residing at his prebendal manor of Nassington in Northamptonshire, presented fourteen articles, among which there appears no definite charge of conspiracy, but merely the statement that certain canons had usurped the rights of the dean as officials of the church of Lincoln during the vacancy of the see, i.e. after the death of Bishop Gray in 1436, and had claimed to exercise jurisdiction over the dean himself. It was not until a year later that Alnwick issued his award or *Laudum*, a document which had the merit of establishing a clear definition of the constitutional relations between the dean and canons, resting upon the distinction between the position of the dean as dean and his position as a canon and prebendary, in which he could lay no claim to exceptional privileges by virtue of his dignity.[1] In this award Alnwick was aided by the advice of the clerical lawyers of his household, among them his chancellor John Depyng, who had been one of the papal commissaries in the famous award known as the Barnwell Process which established the right of the chancellor and university of Cambridge to independent ecclesiastical and spiritual jurisdiction.[2] Alnwick's decision, thus arrived at, made no further resort to an award necessary, and, although its details on certain points, such as the duty of dean and canons to provide sufficient stipends for the minor officers of the church, were more honoured in the breach than in the observance, it was henceforth regarded as authoritative.[3]

Before the award was formally issued the bishop held a visitation on 8 June 1439, at which he urged its acceptance upon the dean and chapter and begged them to turn their attention to the pressing needs of the fabric of the church.[4] He also raised a point which, without design on his part, was more efficacious than any award in promoting a temporary agreement between the dean and his opponents. At the visitation of 1437 it had become quite clear that the statutes of the church were in in-

---

[1] The *Laudum* is printed *B. & W.* ii (ii), 187–228.

[2] See *C.P.L.* viii. 484–5 (confirmation by Eugenius IV, 18 Sept. 1433).

[3] On the *Laudum* see *B. & W.* ii (i), pp. clxxi–clxxxii. Its authority is still maintained in the latest series of Lincoln Statutes, and dean and canons are sworn to obey it.

[4] Ibid. ii (ii), 427–38. The bishop's speech is given in *oratio recta*, pp. 431–3.

extricable confusion, amounting to a mass of customs, in many respects ambiguous and mutually contradictory, contained in repertories whose comparative weight of authority was doubtful. The Book of Customs could be pleaded against the Black Book and vice versa, and the precentor had brought up a case in point, when he refused to accept the authority of the first of these for the duty of entertaining the choir incumbent on residentiaries. Alnwick proposed to bring harmony into this discord by producing a new and authoritative volume which should supersede the existing sources of reference.[1] The canons present at the visitation agreed to this offer; but the dean and the archdeacon of Huntingdon stipulated that the Black Book and Bishop Flemyng's award should not be touched. More than a year went by before the bishop with great pains got his work into shape. When he next visited the chapter on 3 October 1440, four-fifths of the new book were completed, and a committee of canons was invited to inspect it and make suggestions.[2] By this time, however, he must have seen that, if the chapter had been willing to accept his award, any further work of reform would meet with opposition. His intention of visiting the prebends of the church was opposed by the dean, who protested that they were exempt, like the prebends of Salisbury, from episcopal jurisdiction. Alnwick was content to point out that the relation of the bishop of Lincoln to prebends in his church was quite different from that of the bishop of Salisbury; for he could institute vicars to prebendal churches, whereas such institutions at Salisbury belonged to the dean and chapter.[3]

[1] Ibid. 432. The bishop summed up the matter thus: 'Nam, dum tot sint libri, registra, siue lauda, et occurrerit aliquis casus, propter quem ad huiusmodi libros, registra, siue lauda oporteret haberi recursus, propter eorundem librorum, registrorum, siue laudorum diuersitatem, siue contrarietatem, cicius forte resultaret ambiguum vel controuersia, quam decisio.'

[2] See ibid. 443–9 (3–8 Oct. 1440).

[3] The bishop's words were: 'prebende Linc' et prebende Sarum non sunt eiusdem nature, cum episcopus Linc' habeat institucionem et destitucionem vicariorum huiusmodi prebendarum et ecclesiarum, ipsique vicarii recipiant curam animarum ab episcopo, et [eidem] iurent obedienciam, et e contra episcopus Sarum nullam habet in prebendis sue ecclesie iurisdiccionem, nisi solum collacionem ipsarum prebendarum, sed capitulum' (ibid. 444). This, however, did not affect prebendal churches of Salisbury in other dioceses, to which the local ordinaries instituted prebendaries and vicars, e.g. the bishop of Lincoln in the cases of prebs. Brixworth, Shipton, and the two prebs. of Grantham, the bishop of Bath and Wells in those of prebs. Bedminster and Writhlington, and the bishop of Worcester in those of prebs. Bitton and Horton.

This matter seems to have been dropped a few days later when Alnwick disclaimed any wish to exact fees for the proposed visitation. There were other points at issue. The precentor complained that the dean had nominated a thurifer without asking his permission. The dean refused to accept an arrangement by which his stable was to be allowed to stand, provided that he made an annual contribution to the repair of the adjacent wall of the close. The burning question of the new statute-book was adjourned for consideration to the following April.

When that time came, dean and canons were united in their unreadiness to admit the book. The dean denied that he had consented to the making of such a book and took his stand upon the existing muniments and awards. The precentor objected to certain points in it, notably its provisions for disposing of the fruits of vacant prebends, and Partrich and the rest were unanimous in the decision to hold it over for examination and revision.[1] A year later, in April 1442, in the presence of a commissary appointed by the bishop,[2] the dean called the attention of his brethren to the existence of a papal privilege confirming the statutes and customs of the church, and protested against any further proceeding which might prejudice them or this. The precentor followed: 'I profess myself an obedient son of the Roman church: I protest therefore that I will not go back upon such its graces.'[3] Under these protests, however, they joined with the other canons in agreeing to an adjournment of the meeting. On 29 May, before the bishop in person, Macworth flatly refused to have anything to do with the new ordinances, asserting that they were prejudicial to his dignity.[4] This led to proceedings against him by the bishop. He was summoned before a commissary in the Lent of 1443, but sent a messenger, without any formal proxy, to say that he had gone to his parish church at Tredington, where he went every year in Lent to hear the confessions of his parishoners, and that the case was too

---

[1] *B. & W.* ii (ii), 450–3: 24 Apr. 1441.

[2] Thomas Ryngsted: 9 Apr. 1442 (ibid. 453–6).

[3] Ibid. 454: 'Profiteor me filium obedientem ecclesie Romane. Protestor igitur me nolle recedere a talibus eius gratiis.'

[4] Ibid. 457–8: 'dixit . . . quod nunquam preberet consensum eidem, nec ipsis nouis ordinacionibus quouis modo consentiret, ymo pocius reclamaret, et ibidem pro tunc contra predicta penitus reclamaret, cum talia ordinaciones et statuta, vt asseruit, in graue preiudicium dignitatis sue per consensum ipsius redundarent.'

important to go on without his personal presence.[1] Thus, with further delays, and with an appeal by the dean to the court of Canterbury, the case dragged on to no settled end. Alnwick indeed in May 1443 obtained the consent of the chapter *nem. con.*, for the dean kept silence, to a statute which prescribed the method of censing the choir, with regard to which there had been hot disputes between the dean and canons;[2] but this did not prevent the precentor, at vespers on the feast of the Circumcision 1445, from attacking, in a fit of bad temper, the acolyte who was censing him, striking the censer from his hand and hitting him on his cheek.[3] The dean continued to disregard details of the award: at Alnwick's death in 1449 bickerings were still in progress; and active strife ended only at Macworth's death in 1451.

Although at a later date Alnwick's *Novum Registrum* was regarded as a valuable source of reference upon disputed points, it was never accepted as a code of statutes abrogating all that had gone before; and the long story illustrates the extraordinary complications which might arise in the interpretation of cathedral statutes and customs.[4] The bishop's well-meant and, from a literary point of view, highly skilful effort to reform the statutes imperilled for the time being the permanence of his award.[5] Fortunately, the next dean, Robert Flemyng, was a man of peace whose humanistic tastes led him to obtain a dispensation from residence and retire to the more congenial climate of Tivoli, where he dedicated his *Lucubrationes Tiburtinae* to Pope Sixtus IV.[6] If Macworth found his Lenten visits to Tredington, where he lies buried, a convenient excuse for contumacy, we may at any rate sympathize with Peter Partrich, who at an early period of the quarrel was granted a papal dispensation from residence at Lincoln, enabling him to seek his

---

[1] Ibid. 458–60: 22 Mar. 1442–3. The dean's proctor argued: 'est causa grauis et ardua tangens sedem episcopalem et consequenter ipsum episcopum.'

[2] Ibid. 463–4.

[3] Ibid. 466, 519.

[4] Ibid. ii (i), pp. clxxxii, clxxxiii, is shown the relation between the *Novum Registrum* and the Lincoln Black Book, with its close relation to the statutes of St. Paul's Cathedral, compiled a century and a half earlier, of which it is an adaptation. See Simpson, W. Sparrow, *Registrum statutorum et consuetudinum ecclesiae cathedralis S. Pauli*, 1873.

[5] The text of the *Novum Registrum* is printed *B. & W.* ii (ii), 268–363.

[6] See *D.N.B.*, s.v. 'Flemming'.

country parsonage at Biddenden in Kent and recreate his parishioners with preachings.[1]

For the most part, however, as an examination of the chapter acts of Wells, for example, will show, life in cathedral and collegiate churches was peaceful.[2] The question of the declaration of doubtful statutes arose from time to time. From Bishop Alnwick's visitation of the New College at Leicester in 1440, it is quite clear that considerable reformation was necessary; and some fifty years later the statutes were entirely revised by Bishop Russell.[3] Revision, however, did not prevent the outbreak of a bitter quarrel in 1516 between an overbearing dean with powerful family connexions, Lord George Grey, and a party among the canons. This, however, was due to the presence of the dowager Lady Hungerford and her husband, Sir Francis Sacheverell, as boarders in the college: their enmity to Grey led to constant brawling between their servants, and on one great festival, when the church was full, the dean showed such an active objection to the presence of one of their serving-men who stood near his stall that one of the canons, Thomas Wigston, a brother of the celebrated Leicester merchant, was heard to say in exasperation: 'Jesus! that a man may not say his prayers but if he must be thus spoken unto!'[4] We may of course be thankful that private animosities such as modern writers of fiction discover in cathedral chapters are to-day concealed in church beneath a superficial decorum of demeanour. But it would be a mistake to suppose that in the Middle Ages behaviour in church was strictly guided by a code of good manners and a sense of reverence which are comparatively modern.

The idea which to-day converts such churches into active centres of diocesan life is certainly quite modern. Mother churches they were, to which at stated times of the year, as at mid-Lent and Whitsuntide, representatives of the diocese repaired with their offerings; to whose fabric also testators, as in duty bound, from the whole diocese left bequests of money. The possession of shrines and relics, the grant of indulgences for rebuilding and enlargement, made them constant resorts of pilgrims. But primarily they were founded for corporations of

---

[1] *C.P.L.* vii. 497.    [2] *D. & C. Wells.*
[3] In 1490–1. See Thompson, *Hist. Newarke Coll.* 120–35.
[4] Ibid. 153.

clergy, whose sole duty, whether in person or by deputy, was to maintain a continual succession of services, in choir and at their altars, for the good estate of founders and benefactors while living and for their souls after death. The special functions ascribed to resident dignitaries and officers were all closely connected with this object. Even though in all such foundations there grew up large bodies of non-resident canons, their places were supplied by permanent deputies. Outside church the interests of a corporation whose members by their training were for the most part better lawyers than theologians were occupied largely by matters of financial and legal business: the care of the fabric, building projects which required the constant retention of a staff of masons, the management of large estates and endowments, the maintenance of discipline in a staff of vicars-choral and chantry priests, jealous of their own corporate privileges, choristers, lay officers and servants, the defence of the rights of the church against importunate litigants, the exercise of jurisdiction over tenants and spiritual subjects—all these things, emerging from and dependent upon the main object for which the church was founded, implied a preoccupation with interests which, highly local and circumscribed, often developed strong differences of opinion and were mainly secular. In such an atmosphere those conflicts of rival jurisdictions, of which medieval Church history furnishes so many examples, became of absorbing interest and were waged with remarkable obstinacy. The attitude of the Crown and other patrons to prebends as convenient sources of income for statesmen and government offices overstocked certain churches with canons whose interests lay elsewhere, and thus some of the collegiate churches which already mentioned had a corporate life which was little more than nominal and suffered greatly from neglect and structural decay.[1] In the foundations of later colleges the provisions for

---

[1] See, e.g. the dilapidations of which Columb Dunbar, the Scottish dean of Bridgnorth, had been guilty, as specified in the letters patent, 19 Oct. 1412, revoking the grant of the deanery to him (*C.P.R.* 1408–13, p. 435). Commissions for the visitation of chapels royal entered on the dorse of patent rolls reveal great negligence. See, e.g., such documents relating to the chapel in Hastings castle, 28 Sept. 1334, 20 Nov. 1336 (*C.P.R.* 1334–8, pp. 66, 374), 16 Nov. 1341 (1340–3, pp. 362–3), 6 Apr. 1343 and 10 Mar. 1344–5 (1343–5, pp. 79, 501), 8 May 1361 (1358–61, p. 586, and 1361–4, pp. 68–9), 5 June 1403 (1401–5, p. 274), 8 Mar. 1407–8 (1405–8, pp. 473–4). Such disorders were enhanced by lawless interference from outside (see, e.g., ibid. 1343–5, p. 79, and 1364–7, p. 369), but the root of the

residence and for adequate maintenance of divine service were carefully drawn up in compact bodies of statutes. As already said, a new type of collegiate establishment, the college composed of resident chantry priests, began to supersede the older cathedral model during the fourteenth century. Such colleges as Ottery St. Mary mark the transition to this type: if its canonries and prebends were individual freehold benefices, the majority of their holders were intended to be resident. And we may note a certain attention to their duty, in a collegiate church which was also parochial, in the petition of the warden, canons, and ministers of Ottery St. Mary to the pope in 1423 for an indult by which they were allowed to transfer the hour for matins from midnight to 4 a.m., as a more convenient time for the attendance of parishoners.[1]

evil lay in the constant neglect of a body of clergy who regarded their prebends mainly as a source of revenue.

[1] *C.P.L.* vii. 277.

# IV

## PARSONS, VICARS, AND CURATES

THERE is a general impression that Chaucer's famous portrait of the Parson represents an entirely exceptional type
of medieval clergyman; and it is true that in describing him
Chaucer contrasted him with other types, with the incumbent
who made the most of spiritual menaces to exact his tithes, and
with him who deserted his parish to seek a lucrative chantry
in London. But, if we accept the Monk and the Prioress, two
very respectable people, or the less reputable Friar as types of
their several vocations, it would be unfair to assume that the
Parson is presented to us as a rare example of a saint in a world
whose priesthood was generally irreligious and corrupt. The
idea, without any substantial ground, that Chaucer was drawing a portrait of Wycliffe, whose antecedents and circumstances were totally different,[1] has coloured our conception of
the character and read into the Parson's simple orthodoxy the
reforming zeal of the innovator. Further, looking back upon
that age from the standpoint of our own, in which so high a
value is set upon the correspondence of conduct with religious
profession, we are not unnaturally prone to lend a ready ear to
anti-clerical satire and the invective of the medieval Puritan,
well-versed in the prophetical language of Scripture, and to
derive from these diatribes a prejudiced view of the ecclesiastical
system in which the Parson played a humble part. It is not
improbable that our habitual equation in this context of the
divine discontent of Langland, the seer, with the impartial
irony of Chaucer, the tolerant man of the world, is a hindrance

---

[1] To describe Wycliffe as the 'poure persoun of a toun' would be far from the
truth, as Wycliffe's cures of souls were all substantial benefices; and, even if
Chaucer transferred qualities of Wycliffe to another type of parson, it was not until
the last years of his life that Wycliffe showed any sign of activity in parochial duties.
Of his three successive livings Fillingham was assessed (*Tax. Eccl.* 75) at £20;
Ludgershall (ibid. 41) at £6. 13s. 4d., and Lutterworth (ibid. 63) at £20. If the
exchange from Fillingham to Ludgershall meant a considerable drop in income, it
might at any rate be pleaded that the church was within easier reach of Oxford
and that such travelling expenses as the rector chose to incur were light. See
p. 103 below, note 1.

rather than a help to a true estimate of that system as the average man of the period regarded it.

At the same time it cannot be denied that, unless Chaucer used the term Parson in the loose and general sense of the word familiar to modern ears, he was drawing a somewhat exceptional picture of a beneficed clergyman. For to medieval ears, and indeed until a much later period, the parson, the *persona*, was a rector, the incumbent of the great tithe of the parish, and the title belonged not only to individual incumbents but to corporate bodies with regard to the churches which they held in appropriation.[1] At a visitation or an inquiry into the vacancy of a benefice the question might be aked, Who is the parson of this church? And the answer might be either some individual name, or the name of some abbot or abbess and convent, or some dean and chapter. In the first case of course the parson usually had the cure of souls; in the second the cure was usually deputed to a vicar by the corporate parson. Chaucer's parson, we may assume, was a rector with cure of souls; and, although rectories of parish churches varied greatly in value, and there were some with revenues so small that there may have been difficulties in the way of inducing priests to accept them, yet as a rule it may be said that the normal rectory was like a prebend in a cathedral church, which often consisted of the fruits of a parish church, a benefice sought after by members of the higher clergy as a source of income.[2] The residence of rectors was intermittent:

[1] The earliest example in *O.E.D.* of the popular use of 'parson' as a synonym for a clergyman or minister of any denominations is from *Love's Labour's Lost*, where Shakespeare can hardly have used it with any thought of its strict sense. 'The appellation of parson', says Blackstone, as quoted in *O.E.D.* '(however it may be depreciated by familiar, clownish, and indiscriminate use) is the most legal, most beneficial, and most honourable title that a parish priest can enjoy.' For the special sense of 'parish priest', however, see below, p. 122. The medieval parish priest was not a parson.

[2] See p. 13 above, note 2, for the rectory of Bishop Wearmouth, taxed at £52. 13s. 4d. and held by the former archbishop of Canterbury, Cardinal Langham. Other valuable rectories in the bishoprick of Durham were Haughton-le-Skerne (£54. 1s. 8d.), Easington (£53), Sedgefield (£51), and Houghton-le-Spring (£50), usually reserved by bishops for clerks assisting in the work of the diocese. Each of these was above the average value of a prebend in York (£48), or in Lincoln (£40), though individual prebends in each church were considerably in excess of the average sum. In the archdeaconry of Northumberland several rectories were of even larger annual value, rivalling the best prebends in cathedral churches: one of them, Ovingham, taxed at £96. 4s. 10¼d., when appropriated to Hexham Priory in 1378, afforded maintenance for four canons of the monastery, one as vicar and

we have already seen how the dean of Lincoln evaded an episcopal summons by retiring to hear the Lenten confessions of his
flock at Tredington, and how the chancellor sought to soothe
his ruffled feelings by preaching to the country folk of Biddenden.
If Chaucer's parson had anything in common with Wycliffe,
it was that Wycliffe was also a rector. But in the twenty-three
years during which Wycliffe held three parish churches in succession, from 1361 to 1384,[1] his habitual residence was at
Oxford, and it was not until 1382, when he was obliged to retire
from Oxford, that, for the last two and a half years of his life, he
took up his residence at Lutterworth. Episcopal registers contain an immense number of memoranda of dispensations
granted to rectors for non-residence. There was the rector who
was constantly engaged in the royal service, the rector who was
a member of the household of some nobleman, the rector who,
under the papal constitution *Quum ex eo*, sought, like Wycliffe,
to reside in a university, and might stay there for seven
years without proceeding to holy orders higher than the
subdiaconate,[2] or the rector who, like Partrich, armed with a

the others as chantry priests (R. Hat., ff. 148b–149b). The church of Simonburn,
taxed at £136. 14s. 2d., and probably the richest parochial benefice in England,
was at one time estimated at fabulous figures, 700 marks (*Chr. Lan.* 158) and 500
marks (*R. Rom.* i. 397).

[1] Workman, i. 151, assumes that Wycliffe resided at Fillingham in Lincolnshire
between his institution in 1361, and his first recorded licence for non-residence in
1363. Id. i. 195 suggests that his exchange of Fillingham for the poorer living of
Ludgershall in 1368 was prompted, as noted p. 101 above, note 1, by the neighbourhood of Ludgershall to Oxford. Both these hypotheses are possible in default of
positive evidence to the contrary, but they can hardly be taken as facts. His
prebend of Aust in Westbury-on-Trym was a manorial prebend which required no
residence on the spot, and Wycliffe's shortcomings, as set forth by Wilkins, *Was
John Wycliffe a Negligent Pluralist?* 1915, concerned his periods of residence in the
church of Westbury, not in that of Aust, which was, and is still, a chapel dependent
upon the church of Henbury.

[2] Examples of persons engaged in the royal service are numerous among the
returns of pluralists in R. Langham (see below). From the long series of licences
in R. Melton may be selected the following cases of rectors in noblemen's households: William Wirkesworth, rector of Slaidburn, at the petition of Thomas, earl
of Lancaster, and Sir Robert Holand, 30 July 1320 (fo. 138b); Roger Pokelington,
rector of Wath, at that of John, bishop of Winchester, 28 May 1319 (fo. 134b);
Roger de la More, rector of a moiety of Kettlewell, at that of Sir Henry le Scrop,
knt., king's justice, 1 Mar. 1319–20 (fo. 137); William de Cusaunce, rector of
Wakefield, at that of John Warenne, earl of Surrey, 1 Oct. 1327 (fo. 171), and of
John the son of Edward II (John of Eltham), earl of Cornwall, 3 Feb. 1331–2
(fo. 184). Licences for study 'in loco congruo et honesto ubi generale studium
litterarum dinoscitur vigere' are very numerous under such forms as 'Attendentes

dispensation for plurality, might prefer to reside in another benefice. Such dispensations, granted for periods of one, two, or three years, were periodically renewed, with extensions to periods of seven years or without a specified limit.[1]

An immense number of presentations to rectories by the Crown are recorded on the patent rolls. These for the most part were benefices in the patronage of tenants-in-chief which escheated to the Crown during the minority of an heir or the vacancy of a religious house, or in consequence of a forfeiture of estates. Such presentations did not always take effect: they were frequently made upon false information, and instances of two or more concurrent presentations to the same benefice through mere inadvertency are not uncommon.[2] But they gave the Crown a good opportunity of providing for its clerks. It was thus that Wycliffe in 1374 obtained a Crown presentation to the church of Lutterworth.[3] The returns of pluralists made in 1366, in pursuance of Urban V's constitution *Dudum*,[4] show how many of the best livings in England, in addition to dignities and pre-

tue indolis habilitatem tuumque propositum laudabile insistendi scolasticis disciplinis ut fructum in ecclesia dei processu temporis afferre valeas oportunum tecum . . . dispensamus'.

[1] The case of Alan Conyngesburgh, rector, first of Thrybergh and then of Hickleton, may be taken from the same register: unspecified period from the date of his institution to Thrybergh, 11 May 1318 (fo. 126b); as rector of Hickleton, 1 Feb. 1319–20, till Michaelmas (fo. 137); 8 Aug. 1320, for two years from Michaelmas (fo. 140); 30 Apr. 1323, for a year (fo. 157b). These licences were for study in accordance with *Quum ex eo* (*Sext* I. vi. 34): between the second and third, Conyngesburgh had proceeded from the order of subdeacon to that of deacon. Of licences for seven years that of Adam Ayreminne, rector of Gargrave, is an example, 11 Jan. 1317–18 (fo. 133).

[2] See, e.g., *C.P.R.* 1391–6, p. 130: revocation, 1 Aug. 1392, of the grant of the archdeaconry of Leicester to Richard Holand by letters patent, 'issued by inadvertence and inforgetfulness of others' of a previous grant made to John Elvet. For revocations of the same period, issued on grounds of false suggestion by the presentee or errors in assuming vacancies or overriding rights of patrons, see ibid., pp. 22, 50, 100, &c.

[3] The letters of presentation are dated 7 Apr. 1374 (*C.P.R.* 1370–4, p. 424). The cause, not stated in the letters as calendared, was the minority of the patron, Henry de Ferrers of Groby (Workman, i. 209). There is no record of institution in R. Buck.

[4] For the text of the constitution see Wilkins, iii. 62–3. The returns for the province of Canterbury are entered in R. Langham, ff. 3 sqq. There are also lists for separate dioceses in some contemporary registers, e.g. Lincoln. Reg. xii, ff. 43–7 and *R. Stretton*, ii. 216–23. For pluralists beneficed in dio. Lincoln at this date, see the present writer's 'Pluralism in the Medieval Church' (*A.A.S. R. P.* as p. 12 above, note 1).

bends in cathedral and collegiate churches, were occupied by king's clerks; and, in the golden days before pluralism had been regulated by the constitutions *De multa*[1] and *Execrabilis*,[2] the opportunities for servants and favourites of the Crown in this direction were unlimited.

It is also worth noting that the patronage of religious houses was constantly used for the promotion of clerks whose services could be used to advantage by the patrons. Although the gifts of churches—that is to say, of the advowsons of churches—to monasteries and collegiate churches before the statute of Mortmain were frequently followed as a matter of course by the appropriation of their rectories, nevertheless most monasteries kept some of their benefices unappropriated, and presented to them a succession of clerks whose influence at court or experience in the practice of ecclesiastical tribunals made them useful assistants in legal business as attorneys or counsel in the litigation to which monasteries were constantly exposed, or as agents in *ardua negotia* involving conveyances or leases of property. The numerous churches in the gift of the abbot and convent of Peterborough are cases in point. Among others, the church of Cottingham in Northamptonshire, eventually transferred to Brasenose College, the church of the adjoining parish of Bringhurst in Leicestershire, and the church of Oundle were constantly given to clerks of high repute:[3] and it was not until the last quarter of the fifteenth century that, under the pressure of growing poverty Bringhurst and Oundle were appropriated to the abbot and convent.[4]

A word, too, may be said of those parish churches which were appropriated to prebendal stalls in cathedral and collegiate foundations. In these the prebendary was rector, but without

---

[1] *Const. Lat.* 4, c. 29 (*Extra* III. v. 29).

[2] *Extrav. Joan.* XXII. iii. c. un.; *Extrav. comm.* III. iv. 4.

[3] Thus William of Edington, afterwards bishop of Winchester, was rector of Cottingham (Bridges, ii. 299). John Thoresby, afterwards archbishop of York, was rector of Oundle at the time of his promotion to the see of St. David's in 1347, and similarly John Delaber, bishop of St. David's, a clerk closely associated with Peterborough, was rector in 1443 (ibid. i. 408). Among the rectors of both Oundle and Bringhurst (Nichols, ii. 514) occur names of several well-known clerks in the service of the Crown or of prelates.

[4] Licences for Oundle 29 May 1477 (*C.P.R.* 1476–85, p. 41); for Bringhurst 25 Feb. 1485–6 (ibid. 1485–94, p. 81). The series of documents relating to the appropriation of Bringhurst is in R. Assh., ff. 126b–134.

cure of souls, for his duty to the greater church in which as a canon he held his prebend absolved him from any duty to his parishioners; and the cure of souls was delegated to a vicar. At York the institution of prebendal vicars lay with the dean and chapter as ordinaries within their peculiar jurisdiction. But custom varied in this respect, and in the diocese of Lincoln, although the prebendal churches were omitted from episcopal visitations, the bishop kept institutions to their vicarages in his own hand.[1] It should be noted that such churches occasionally lay in other dioceses. In spite of the sinecurist position of the prebendary, he was still the rector of his church, and while, by the act of collation, the bishop put him in possession of his pre-bend, yet, if the church which formed its *corpus* lay outside the diocese and in the ordinary jurisdiction of its local bishop, it was necessary for him to obtain institution from that ordinary. Thus in the diocese of Lincoln the churches of Brixworth, Grantham, and Shipton-under-Wychwood were prebends in the cathedral church of Salisbury: Brixworth was appropriated to the chancellor of the church, and Grantham was divided into two prebends. In each case the prebendaries were insti-tuted by the bishop of Lincoln, who also instituted to their vicarages. Similarly the prebendaries of Clifton, Farndon, South Scarle, and Stoke, all Nottinghamshire churches, in the church of Lincoln, sought institution from the archbishop of York and presented their vicars to him.[2] In speaking, however, of prebendal churches, it should be remembered that not all prebends by any means consisted of churches. In all cathedral churches there were some formed out of the landed estates of the

[1] See p. 95 above, note 3, for the similar distinction between the prebendal vicarages of Lincoln and those of Salisbury.

[2] The notification, 12 Aug. 1268, of a collation of preb. South Scarle by the bishop of Lincoln, was made to the archbishop of York by the dean and chapter. His answer, to the effect that he was delaying institution until certain inquiries had been made, contains the sentence: 'Scituri quod in prebendis Wellensis ecclesie, dum ei prefuerimus, modum ipsum quo ad prebendas extra diocesim constitutas servavimus, et venerabilis frater, dominus Sarisberiensis, quo ad prebendam (? prebendas) Sarisberiensem (?-es) in Wellensi diocesi idem fecit' (*R. W. Giff.* 89). Institutions by the bishop of Lincoln to the prebendal churches of Brixworth and Shipton in Salisbury were made in 1224 according to an ordinance made by the bishops of Bath and Lincoln with consent of the bishop of Salisbury (*Rot. Hug. Welles*, ii. 116–17) and are subsequently recorded, as are those of the two Grantham prebends, in the Lincoln registers. The extra-diocesan prebends of Wells included the distant church of Shalford in Essex: see Newcourt, ii. 518.

dean and chapter, like the prebends in St. Paul's; and, where a parish church went together with a manor, the manor occasionally formed one prebend and the church another. At Great Milton and Langford in Oxfordshire, for example, church and manor formed separate prebends in the church of Lincoln, while the prebends of Hova Villa and Hova Ecclesia in Chichester mark a similar distinction with regard to Hove in Sussex.

In the course of the fourteenth century the custom of exchanging ecclesiastical benefices had reached serious proportions. The methods and consequences of this custom need a much more detailed examination than can be given here; but by the end of that century it had developed into an abuse. The existence of brokers who arranged exchanges led to the issue of Archbishop Courtenay's strongly worded mandate against 'chop-churches' in 1392.[1] Among the articles set forth in the schedule of *reformanda* produced in the Convocation of 1399 is one relating to fraudulent and fictitious exchanges, requiring the parties in such transactions to exhibit their letters of institution to the benefices which they desire to exchange.[2] The two great volumes of institutions which form part of the register of Bishop Buckingham of Lincoln (1363–98) are full of records of exchanges, entered with great particularity. More often than not these are exchanges to churches in another diocese. One of the ordinaries concerned issues a commission to the other to carry out the business and institute to both churches: this done, the ordinary who has expedited the exchange sends his certificate to the other, to whom the new rector of the church in his diocese resorts in person or sends his proxy to do obedience. There is no lack of exchanges which may be taken as genuine. But there are also many instances in which a man exchanges one church for another, and then, a day or two later or even on the same day, exchanges this for a third.[3] The obvious

---

[1] R. Court. (Cant.), fo. 225*b*, 5 Mar. 1391–2: see Wilkins, iii. 215–17. The mandate is entered at length in the contemporary R. Wake., ff. 37–8.

[2] R. Arundel i, fo. 51*b*: 'Item, quod propter fictiones et fraudes varias in permutationibus beneficiorum exercitas, *persone ignote* nullatenus expediantur, nisi institutiones duorum beneficiorum permutandorum realiter tunc exhibeant. Et si partes permutare volentes hinc inde sub pena pecuniaria vel iuramento, ea occasione, *se* obligaverint, nullo modo expediantur.' The text in Wilkins, iii. 240, omits some necessary words, here italicized.

[3] A good example of a quick series of exchanges is provided by the deanery of Chester-le-Street in 1408, after the death of Thomas Hexham. John Thoralby

explanation is that the first of these exchanges is a transaction with a middle-man who negotiates the second; and we must conclude that the bishops who, by going through the form of institution in such cases, gave their sanction to the proceedings, were not ignorant of what was passing under their eyes and connived at the dealings of these 'accursed consorts in guilt of Gehazi and Simon Magus'.[1] Further, in spite of the number of these records and the care with which they are entered again and again with repetitions of identical common forms, there is no doubt that many institutions which ought to have taken place are not recorded at all. Everyone who has attempted to compile lists of incumbents of parish churches from episcopal registers knows how frequent the gaps in institutions become, even where the registers are quite complete, in the last quarter of the fourteenth century. It is difficult for example to explain the absence of any record of Wycliffe's institution to Lutter-worth, and, though it would be wrong to suggest that his pre-sentation to the church in 1374 was the result of a simoniacal transaction, yet such omissions, taken into account with the evidence for the actual prevalence of the abuse of exchanges, show that there were many people who stepped into benefices through the backdoor of the chop-church's London office. This, too, is borne out by the insinuation in the article of 1399 that, when the would-be parties to an exchange put forward their request, letters of their previous institutions were not forthcoming.[2] Exchanges continued to be frequent in the fifteenth century, but institutions were recorded with much

had collation on 6 Apr., but on 12 Apr. exchanged for the rectory of Lockington, Yorks E.R., with John Dalton, who was Bishop Langley's official. On 15 Apr. Dalton resigned, having accepted the vacant deanery of Lanchester, and was succeeded at Chester-le-Street next day by Walter Bosum. But a fortnight later, on 1 May, Bosum exchanged the deanery for the vicarage of St. Oswald's, Durham, with Robert Assheburn (R. Langley, ff. 14, 14b, 15), who held it till his death in 1412–13 (ibid., fo. 65b). A preb. in the same church was resigned by Thomas del Hay in 1411 and collated to Robert del Hay on 27 Dec. On 22 Jan. 1411–12 Robert exchanged this preb. with Thomas for a preb. in Howden, but Thomas again resigned it on 13 Mar., and next day Robert again had collation (ibid., ff. 51, 51b, 52b, 53b).

[1] Courtenay's phrase, f. 226, Wilkins, iii. 216: 'predictos iniquitatis alumpnos, clerum et ecclesiam blasphemantes maledictos Giezei et Simonis consortes in crimine Choppechurches vulgariter appellatos, in civitate vestra Londoniensi pro maiori parte degentes, ut dicitur.'

[2] See p. 104 above, note 3.

greater regularity, and, if Courtenay's mandate did not stop the abuse, at any rate it seems to have warned the traffickers in benefices to proceed with more caution. But it is possible to trace the existence of rings of persons who, by obtaining advowsons by purchase or lease, kept up a brisk trade in benefices. In particular, three canons of Lincoln, John Baysham, Thomas Baldyng, and Nicholas Wymbysh, are found in close association during the first half of the fifteenth century;[1] and numerous bodies of feoffees throughout most of the century were busy in securing long leases of the advowsons of churches in the gift of religious houses or grants of the next presentation with a regularity which indicates that these were not wholly unprofitable.[2]

The statutes of Mortmain in 1279 and 1391 are often referred to as if they put an end to the alienation of real property to religious corporations. Actually, their effect was to put alienations under control and subject them to licences from the Crown and other parties concerned for which, although they increased the expense, constant applications were made. Appropriations of churches to monasteries went on, though they were often delayed by the procedure necessary for their fulfilment. The endowment of the New College at Leicester, founded in 1355, consisted largely of the revenues of appropriated churches— Irchester, Higham Ferrers, and Raunds in Northamptonshire, Hannington and Inglesham in Wiltshire, Llandyfaelog, Llanelly, and Pembrey in Carmarthenshire, all churches previously in the patronage of the house of Lancaster. To these Simon Symeon, a devoted servant of Henry of Lancaster and his son-in-law John of Gaunt, added in 1381 the church of Cransley in Northamptonshire, and in 1406 and 1416, after some delay, the college entered into the rectories of Preston in Lancashire

[1] For their careers see *Linc. Vis.* i. 81, 192, 200, 201. See also a copy of Baysham's will, somewhat different from that in Lincoln R. Gray. in *R. Chich.* (C. & Y. Soc.), ii. 303–5: Wymbysh was one of his executors and had the bequest of a little silver-gilt goblet with a similar cover. Baysham died in 1434, surviving Baldyng by a year: Wymbysh lived until 1460–1.

[2] Examples of grants of next presentation are common in R. Assh. Thus 14 Feb. 1439–40 Richard Reynhill and William Hathvile, both clerks in holy orders, obtained the next presentation to North Collingham, Notts., while 1 Apr. 1440 two other clergymen, William Garnet and Roger Gury, obtained that to Barnack, Northants, contingent upon the life of Richard Reynhill (ff. 7, 7b). Reynhill died rector of Castor in 1449 (fo. 33b). On 7 Nov. 1445 the next presentation to Oundle was granted to Thomas Catworth, alderman of London, John Everdon and John Parke, clerks of the green cloth of the king's hostel (fo. 18).

and Bradford in Yorkshire, given to them by the Crown in virtue of its duchy of Lancaster.[1] To this striking example of appropriation upon a large scale may be added those frequent appropriations of benefices already in the gift of religious houses for reasons stated at length and with considerable variety in their petitions. The stock explanation, amounting to common form, was the growing poverty of the monastery: it is heavily burdened by debt, its revenues are impaired by the recurrence of pestilence, murrain, and flood; it stands close to the king's highway and is constantly beset by a crowd of visitors of all conditions to whom it is bound to give hospitality. What with all these expenses, with the obligation of repair of buildings and upkeep of property and with the continual wastage caused by taxation, it is very likely that the convent will be compelled to abstain from works of piety and be dispersed, unless an opportune remedy and succour be found for its needs.[2] But sometimes the reasons are more precise and have a specific local bearing. The abbot and convent of Cockersand, on the bare

---

[1] See Thompson, *Hist. New Coll. Leic.*, chs. ii, iv. The deeds of appropriations and ordinations of vicarages in the churches in dio. Lincoln are there summarized. The ordination of the vicarage of Bradford is in R. Bowet, i, ff. 118–19. The licence for the appropriation of the church of Preston was issued in 1354–5, but nothing further was done for nearly fifty years until, on 8 Feb. 1400–1, Boniface IX issued letters for its appropriation in consequence of a fresh grant by Henry IV (*C.P.L.* v. 411). The execution of these was delayed until after the death of Boniface IX, and fresh letters were issued to the same effect by Gregory XII, 19 Dec. 1406, addressed to Thomas Langley, bishop of Durham, one of the executors of John of Gaunt (ibid. vi. 110). These documents are rehearsed in the deed of appropriation and ordination of the vicarage in R. Langley, ff. 7–9. The register of the archdeacons of Richmond, where one would expect to find such entries, is wanting for this period.

[2] So, in the deed appropriating the church of Geddington, Northants, to the abbot and convent of Pipewell, 30 Jan. 1357–8: 'Sane dilectorum filiorum [etc.] nobis exhibita peticio continebat quod dictum monasterium in quo pulcher et amplus numerus monachorum et conversorum virtutum domino die nocteque iugiter famulatur propter sterilitatem terrarum et carenciam famulorum ac cessacionem reddituum per obitum tenencium suorum et consumpciones bladorum et fenorum suorum per feras bestias forestarum domini regis iuxta quas et viam regiam est idem monasterium situatum ad quod pro hospitalitate habenda cotidie hominum confluit multitudo necnon ex incendio maneriorum suorum et irrupacione [*sic*] subitanea stagnorum aquaticorum piscabilium eorundem ad tantam inopiam est redactum ac ab ere alieno vehementer oppressum per alia infortunia insperata adeo quod facultates ipsius ad sustentacionem dictorum monachorum et conversorum hospitalitatemque tenendam erisque alieni solucionem et alia onera ordinaria et extraordinaria in dies gravius solito ingruencia non sufficiunt supportanda nisi eis de alicuius subvencionis remedio, etc.' (R. Gyne., fo. 171*b*.)

and wind-swept flats by the shore of Morecambe Bay, ask leave to appropriate the church of Mitton, at the confluence of the Ribble and the Hodder, because, among other disadvantages,

'the walls of their monastery, which is notoriously situate between the western sea and the marshlands, are so beaten and shaken twice in the day and night by the waves and heady tides of the said sea, lashed by the storm-wind, that, inasmuch as its own resources, which are very slight and slender, are insufficient to meet the defence and repair of the same walls, the monastery will shortly be brought without fail to pitiable ruin, unless succour come to it from some other source.'[1]

In 1347 the church of Manfield was appropriated to Easby, and in 1348 that of Great Ouseburn to Eggleston Abbey, because the English army in the campaign of Neville's Cross had been billeted in these houses and had so consumed their resources that they were left nearly destitute.[2] The presence of their defenders was as disastrous as the invasions of the Scots who in 1320 had wrecked the possessions of Bolton Priory and compelled the canons to seek shelter in other monasteries;[3] and the proverb was justified which says: 'Whether you throw a stone at an owl or an owl at a stone, the bird will always have the worst of it.'[4]

These are examples from the fourteenth century, but the work of appropriation continued in the fifteenth, during the course of which old appropriations and the taxations of vicarages which followed them were frequently revised. Out of numerous instances in the York registers may be selected the appropriation of the church of Hutton Bushell, near Scarborough, to Whitby Abbey in 1453, on the ground that the

[1] R. Melton, fo. 218. 'Sane vestra nuper nobis exhibita peticio continebat quod muri monasterii vestri inter mare occidentale et loca palustria notorie situati bis in die et nocte adeo undis et impetuosis fluctibus dicti maris venti turbine agitatis concuciuntur et quassantur quod propriis facultatibus que valde tenues et exiles existunt ad ipsorum murorum defensionem et reparacionem non suppetentibus monasterium ipsum in breui nisi aliunde succurratur ad miserabilem ruinam ineuitabiliter deducetur.'
[2] R. Zouche, ff. 70b, 71b. The documents, in which the same common form is employed with variations, are collated in the text printed ap. *Hist. Essays in Hon. of James Tait*, 336–9.
[3] See Thompson, *Hist. of Bolton Priory* (Thoresby Soc.), p. 91.
[4] See Wals. *H.A.* i. 375, commenting on the ill-fortune of English arms in 1378:
Si bubo lapidi iactetur, vel lapis illi,
Ictus damna gravis semper habebit avis.

monastery, from its exposed position by the sea, was continually
threatened by hostile attacks, and, in addition to the expense
and labour of transport caused by its difficulty of access by land,
was heavily burdened by the cost of a thorough restoration of
the nave of the abbey church.[1]  In 1455 the reduction of much
of their arable land to pasture and the general deterioration of
their rents led the prior and convent of Bolton to apply for new
ordinations of the vicarages of Kildwick and Preston-in-Craven.[2]
In the same year we have a rare example of a disappropriation:
owing to the depopulation of the village of Thorpe-by-Newark,
the vicarage of the church, which had long been appropriated
to the prior and convent of Haverholme, was suppressed and
the rectorial tithes restored to the vicar, on condition of an
annual pension from the church to the priory.[3]  But this is a

[1] R. W. Bothe, fo. 224.  The petition of the abbot and convent contained that
'dictum suum monasterium in littore maris situm crebris inimicorum insultibus
vndique expositum necnon propter longa et periculosa viarum discrimina et
hominibus et iumentis per terram de difficili accessione illos insuper sumptus
pregrandes et continuos quos hactenus circa reparacionem navis ecclesie dicti
monasterii impenderunt in presenti impendunt et in futurum impendere habent
vera manifesta et notoria existere et idcirco pium et meritorium esse eorum necessi-
tati et indigencie modis congruis rationabilibus et honestis subveniri facere et
subvenire'.

[2] Ibid., fo. 226.  The appropriation of Kildwick Church had been decreed in
the thirteenth century by Archbishop Gray and reinterpreted in the fourteenth by
Melton, who is said to have decreed the appropriation of Long Preston (see,
however, *Hist. Bolton Priory*, u.s., pp. 80–3, 85–6, for the original appropriation by
Archbishop Corbridge and its supplement by his successor Greenfield).  The preambles of the *novae dotationes* are identical: 'ipsi prior et conventus per concursum
et adventum hospitum ad eorum dictum monasterium sive prioratum plus solito
indies confluencium quibus in esculentis et poculentis oportet necessario provideri
sunt multipliciter onerati ac pretextu appropriacionis ecclesie predicte variis et
magnis oneribus supportandis astringuntur de fructibus et proventibus eiusdem
ecclesie persolvendis qui tamen citra tempus dicte appropriacionis pro eo et ex eo
quod terre ibidem quondam arabiles modo steriles sunt et ad pasturam redacte
adeo sunt diminuti quod ad onera dictis priori et conventui ratione appropriacionis
ipsius ecclesie imposita vix sufficiunt hiis diebus quodque preterea reliqui redditus
et proventus dicti prioratus qui in loco silvestri terraque sterili et inculta situatur
ab eorum solito valore valde sunt collapsi diminuti ac deteriorati et iidem prior et
conventus in onus non exiguum eris alieni quo variis eorum creditoribus tenentur
et obligantur ex causa illa sunt delapsi et astricti ita quod nec se et onera eis
incumbencia ex tunc sustinere nec predicto ere alieno se exuere poterant nisi provisione et auxiliis nostris presertim vt asserunt in moderacione porcionis vicarie
predicte [que] multipliciter crevit in augmentum et satis habundat hiis diebus eis
vberius succurratur.'

[3] Ibid., ff. 229–30.  The petition runs: 'quod propter raritatem paucitatem et
paupertatem incolarum et inhabitancium villam de Thorp predicta terre ibidem
quondam fertiles et arabiles modo steriles sunt et exiles ac ad pasturam redacte

very exceptional instance. An interesting reason is given for the appropriation of the churches of Heversham and Burton-in-Kendal to St. Mary's Abbey at York in 1459. The abbot and convent owed an annual rent of 200 marks to the duchy of Lancaster for the manor of Whitgift, in the marshland at the head of the Humber. But the manor and its members were

'so close to the water of Ouse, which so ebbs and flows, both salt and fresh, that, by reason of the flooding of the said water in and upon the aforesaid manor and its members with their appurtenances, because of the flow and reflux, so premised, of the stream, which rise to a great height and swell in these days more than ever, the same manor, etc., cannot be kept safe or defended without heavy costs and almost daily toil and expense in the making, repair and maintenance of divers walls, catchwaters, sewers, sluices, dykes, banks, causeways and drains, adjoining and appertaining thereto, the making of and the outlay on which falls upon the said abbot and convent and their successors, to the very serious damage and no small grievance of them and their monastery.'[1]

In 1461 the church of Barnbrough, a portion from which had been applied in the thirteenth century to the maintenance

fructus redditus et proventus dicte ecclesie de Thorp ab eorum solito valore valde sunt collapsi diminuti et deteriorati ita quod congrua porcio de fructibus et redditibus dicte ecclesie de Thorp pro sustentacione vicarii et oneribus eidem incumbentibus deducta vt necesse fit et fieri debet modica et exilis pars sive porcio fructuum tum propter exilitatem eorundem fructuum vt supra dicitur multum diminutorum et deterioratorum tum propter distanciam inter monasterium sive prioratum prefatum et ecclesiam de Thorp predicta ad vtilitatem et sustentacionem predictorum canonicorum et monialium remanet.'

[1] The royal licence to appropriate was granted 16 Nov. 1448 (*C.P.R.* 1446–52, p. 207), but the decrees of appropriation were not issued until 19 Oct. 1459 (R. W. Bothe, ff. 238–41). Both have the same preamble, rehearsing the petition of the abbot and convent. The passage quoted above runs thus: 'Predictum tamen manerium ipsiusque membra cum suis pertinenciis predictis ita adiacent aque de Usa que tam salse quam dulce fluit et refluit quod ex superinundacione aque predicte de et super dicto manerio ac membris cum suis pertinenciis predictis causa fluxus et refluxus dicte aque de Usa ut premittitur se in altum elevancium et plus solito hiis diebus ingruencium ipsa manerium ac membra cum pertinenciis salvari nequeunt nec muniri absque sumptibus gravibus et quasi cotidianis laboribus et expensis circa facturam reparacionem et sustentacionem diversarum wallearum gurgitum sewerarum clusarum fossatarum et riparum [*the letters patent add* calcetorum gutterarum] eidem manerio cum membris et pertinenciis suis contiguorum et pertinencium ac per vos abbatem et conventum predictos et successores vestros fiendis et exponendis in vestrum ac monasterii vestri predicti onus gravissimum dampnum non modicum et gravamen in tantum quod ex fructibus reddiditbus et exitibus dicti manerii membrorum et pertinenciorum [*sic*] suorum pensionem huiusmodi dicti domino regi et heredibus suis racione ducatus predicti debitam nisi vobis aliunde uberius succurratur solvere non poteritis.'

of the clergy who served an altar in Southwell Minster, was appropriated to the chapter of Southwell because the rectors of the church, 'sometimes being of no good conversation or honest life, but living voluptuously', had become very irregular in their payments.[1] Scottish raids were responsible for the petition of the abbot and convent of Alnwick to appropriate the church of Leconfield in the East Riding: the letters patent authorizing this were issued in 1459,[2] but, doubtless owing to the disturbed state of the north in the Wars of the Roses, the appropriation remained unexecuted for thirty years.[3] A final example is the appropriation in 1499 of the church of North Collingham, near Newark, to the abbot and convent of Peterborough, for the special support of a service founded by the famous Sir Reynold Braye at the rood-altar in the abbey church. Here the chief reason is as follows:

'Because the rivers, streams and other watery places, and especially the great water of Nene, that lie near to and round about the said monastery, and wherein from of old time for years together fish were wont to teem and be bred in great multitude, to the very

[1] Ibid., fo. 255. The petition runs: 'quod rectores dicte ecclesie de Barnbrugh pro tempore existentes quandoque non bone conversacionis et vite honeste ymmo voluptuose viventes huiusmodi porcionis annue dictis ministris ut prefertur debite obliviosi; et in solucione eiusdem porcionis iuxta ordinacionem inde factam valde negligentes adiu extiterunt ex quorum culpa et negligencia propter non debitam solucionem prefate annue porcionis iidem ministri aliunde non habentes sufficienter unde se sustentare poterunt penuriam paciuntur cultusque divinus propter hoc in dicta ecclesia nostra collegiata Suthwell' minuitur ac in eadem devocio subtrahitur et inde scandalum non modicum generatur.'
[2] 4 May 1459, in pursuance of previous letters of 3 Mar. 1456–7 (C.P.R. 1452–61, pp. 483, 350).
[3] 31 Mar. 1489 (R. Roth. i., ff. 280b–282). Petition as follows: 'quod dictum monasterium in marchia versus Scociam ad quam adversarii Scoti notorii inimici domini nostri regis et regni Anglie in brevi possunt accedere sicco pede notorie situatum existit possessionesque dicti monasterii ac redditus et proventus eiusdem per invasionem et frequentem insultum Scotorum et guerrarum discrimina in illis partibus ingruencia annis retroactis et hiis diebus plus solito fuerunt et sunt nimium diminuti et attenuati ac quasi inutiles iam effecti ac edificia domus et tenementa eorundem religiosorum in dictis partibus existencia per immanitatem et crudelitatem Scotorum sepius combusta et devastata sunt quod ad onera eisdem religiosis et eorum monasterio incumbencia supportanda domorumque edificiorum et tenementorum suorum consumptorum et devastatorum reedificacionem et refeccionem ac hospitalitatem debite observandam non suppetunt dicti monasterii possessiones redditus et proventus nisi eis de alicuius subvencionis remedio succurratur oportuno presertim cum dictum monasterium prope et inter vias publicas sit notorie constitutum et ex recepcione hospitum ad dictum monasterium indies confluencium multipliciter oneratur.'

great profit and nourishment of the said lords abbot and convent,
who are notoriously bound by the appointment of law as well as by
the rule of St Benet to a fish-diet in many of their repasts, on account
of the exceeding and unusual dryness of the weather which has
befallen of recent years, are become almost dry and waterless, or at
any rate empty of fishes and unproductive, to the grievous damage
of the said lords abbot and convent. Wherefore, for the purchase
and buying of the fish, which they were in time past accustomed, to
their abundant profit, to have and get in the aforesaid waters and
waterish places at light expense to themselves and almost ready to
hand, they are now compelled to send, to their very heavy expense
and intolerable burthen, to other parts and other places and markets
far removed and distant from them and their said monastery.'[1]

This is one of the latest appropriations recorded in the episcopal registers at York, and this series contains only three further
examples before the end of the reign of Henry VIII.[2] The
actual number of benefices in any given diocese is always a
difficult matter to determine, as the actual status of some
parochial benefices is somewhat uncertain, and probably no
two calculators will exactly agree in their results. Taking the
county of York alone, an approximate reckoning shows that at
the period of the Reformation it contained 622 parish churches,
of which no less than 392 were appropriated, i.e. 63 per cent.
In the county of Lincoln the percentage of appropriations was
smaller, 311 to a total of 628, i.e. just under 50 per cent. The
large number of appropriations in Yorkshire was considerably
above the ordinary average, and the county was in more than
one respect exceptional. The parishes varied in extent from the
vast parishes of the western moors to the comparatively small
parishes of the vale of York and its neighbourhood, a dis-
crepancy which did not occur in the much smaller county of
Lincoln. The existence of those peculiar jurisdictions to which

---

[1] The royal licence for appropriation bears date 20 Apr. 1499 (*C.P.R.* 1494–1509,
p. 175). The decree of the archbishop's commissaries followed on 4 June and was
confirmed by the archbishop on 1 Aug. 1499 (R. Roth. i., ff. 284*b*–289). The essential statement of the petition is printed *A.A.S.R.P.* xxxiv. 273*n*.

[2] Licence for appropriation of Arksey church to Lenton Priory 8 May 1504.
This licence applied also to the church of Middlewich in Cheshire (*C.P.R.* 1494–
1509, p. 367). See Ormerod, iii. 180 for Middlewich. The church of Brompton
in Pickering Lythe was appropriated to Malton Priory and a vicarage ordained
1 Mar. 1518–19 (R. Wolsey, fo. 119*b*). Later still is the appropriation of the church
of Lythe to the archbishop of York in 1544, in which a vicarage was ordained
20 Sept. 1546 (R. Hol., fo. 21*b*).

reference has been made swelled the number of churches appropriated to collegiate foundations; but in addition to these there
were large groups of churches appropriated to houses of canons
regular, especially to the priories of St. Oswald at Nostell,
Guisbrough, Bridlington, and Bolton, the first three of which
were among the most important houses of Austin canons in
England. A somewhat similar group was gathered round the
Benedictine abbey of Whitby, and St. Mary's at York held a
considerable number of churches, especially in the north-
western part of the county. Such groups were much fewer in
Lincolnshire, in spite of its large number of religious houses;
and in Lincolnshire there were no secondary collegiate churches
of the importance of Beverley and Ripon.

In most of these churches vicarages were ordained; but
Yorkshire again provides an exception to the general rule in
this respect, as more than a hundred churches in the county
thus appropriated were served simply by curates put in and
removed at the will of the rectors. Of some seventeen churches
appropriated to Guisbrough at least ten or eleven were without
vicars.[1] We may, of course, find parallel instances in other parts
of England, as in the group of churches which formed the peculiar jurisdiction of the abbot and convent of Dorchester;[2] but
the Yorkshire examples are unusually numerous. From these
calculations have been omitted the parochial cures inherent in
the collegiate churches of Beverley, Ripon, and Howden, in
the first two of which the parish was divided between the
vicars-choral, while in the third it appears to have been delegated by the canon who held the parochial prebend to a chaplain. It is also perhaps worth remarking that the appropriations
held by those Cistercian abbeys, whose remains in Yorkshire
are so valuable to students of monastic architecture, were few.
Kirkstall alone possessed any appreciable number, and most of

---

[1] Danby-in-Cleveland, East Harlsey, Guisbrough, Kirklevington, Seamer,
Skelton with the chapel of Brotton, Upleatham, Wilton, and Yarm. Ingleby
Arncliffe, afterwards transferred to the prior and convent of Mount Grace, is
reckoned with these in a list of 1308–9, from which Seamer and Wilton are omitted, while Yarm is counted as a chapel of Kirklevington (*R. Green.* v. 238). The
chapel of Nether Silton in Allertonshire and the church of Leake are said by Lawton
(p. 492) to have been appropriated to Guisbrough.

[2] There were nine of these churches: Dorchester, Benson, Chislehampton,
Clifton Hampden, Drayton St. Leonard, Nettlebed, Pishill, Stadhampton, and
Warborough.

those belonging to Kirkstall came to it at a late period, when it was put in possession of the churches in the East Riding which had belonged to the alien abbey of Aumale.[1]

In times past the usual method of ordaining vicarages had been to assign the small tithes of the parish, together with the oblations or altarage and the casual offerings accruing from various sources to the vicar. A more satisfactory alternative was the allocation of a fixed yearly stipend out of the net profits of the church, which was adopted in certain cases, though, where this stipend was more liberal than usual, it was sometimes charged with a pension to the proprietors. The burdens which fell upon the church, the payment of visitation fees, synodals and subsidies, the provision of lights and service-books, were customarily divided between proprietors and vicars. Repair and rebuilding of the chancel was the business of the rectors; but in certain parts of England it was usual from an early date to lay a third of this charge upon the vicar.[2] But early statements of the endowments and duties of a vicar were usually brief: frequently they were nothing more than summary rehearsals in which a bishop confirmed and gave official sanction to existing arrangements of a somewhat vague and general character.[3] Vicars were under the canonical obligation of residence, and early provisions for the supply and upkeep of a vicarage

[1] Aldbrough, Kilnsea, Owthorne, Paull, Skeckling and Withernsea (Hollym), all in Holderness. Licence was granted, 7 Aug. 1394, for the abbot and convent of Aumale to grant to the abbot and convent of Kirkstall their manor or priory of Burstall with the advowsons of the church of Burstall (in the parish of Skeckling) with those mentioned above (*C.P.R.* 1391–6, p. 585).

[2] The general rule is laid down in the constitutions for the diocese of Exeter (1287): 'Onus huiusmodi constructionis et reparationis cancelli matricis ecclesiae ad ipsius ecclesiae rectorem; navis vero ecclesiae ad parochianos . . . verum onus capellae, quae distinctam habet parochiam, ad ipsos capellae parochianos totaliter pertinebit' (Wilkins, ii. 138). In this diocese the repair of the chancel at Fowey in 1314, with windows, books, and ornaments, was divided between the proprietors and the vicar in proportions of two-thirds to one-third (*R. Stapeldon*, 160). An ordinary method was to charge the proprietors with the entire repair of the chancel for one time after appropriation and leave subsequent repairs of windows to the vicar, as at Barnstaple and Walkhampton (ibid. 41, 399). At Brixham all repairs were left to the vicar after the proprietors had done their duty *hac vice prima* (p. 87); at St. Budock and St. Gluvias he was charged with roofs and windows (p. 327); but at Burlescombe the whole upkeep of the chancel was charged as an extraordinary burden upon the rectors, the abbess and convent of Canonsleigh (p. 91).

[3] See, e.g., the ordinations of vicarages recorded in *Rot. Hug. Welles* and *Liber Antiquus* and very briefly in *R. Brones*.

house were rare and insufficient. Ambiguities in such ordinations, coupled with the extremely uncertain nature of endowments derived from the various sources specified, led constantly
in the fourteenth and fifteenth centuries to re-endowments, in
which the fixed stipend often took the place of an earlier arrangement,[1] and the proprietors were ordered to provide a dwelling
for the vicar, usually by the partition of their rectory house and
its outbuildings, which must often have been in the occupation
of their farmer.[2] For any further repair, after they had set all in
order, the vicar became responsible. These are the characteristic features of the ordination of vicarages in such churches as
have been mentioned, and occasionally the clauses relating to the
vicarage house are so detailed that they enable us to obtain a
satisfactory plan of the building and its surroundings.[3] Sometimes a small stipend was augmented by the addition of certain
of the more productive small tithes, as at North Collingham, where the tithe of ducks and porkers supplemented a
stipend of £8.[4] Arrangements with regard to the chancel
varied. Generally its repairs were charged to the proprietors.
In the re-endowment, however, of the vicarage of Preston-in-
Craven, which included somewhat elaborate redivisions of the
great and small tithe, without the provision of fixed stipends,
a third of the repair fell upon the vicar.[5] But the ordinations of
the vicarages of Heversham and Burton-in-Kendal, churches

---

[1] Thus in 1438, at the petition of the prior and convent of Haltemprice, the
vicarage of Kirk Ella was reordained, with an annual stipend of 20 marks to the
vicar, who was to contribute to all burdens, ordinary and extraordinary, *pro rata*
(R. Kempe, ff. 178b–179b). An ordination of the vicarage of Leeds at an early
date (1241) is worth notice, where, in consequence of disputes between the vicar
and proprietors, the vicar was to receive the whole altarage and tithe of mills, out
of which he was to pay the proprietors £10 a year (*R. Walt. Gray*, 89).

[2] For the frequency of rectories farmed out to laymen in the later Middle Ages
see *Linc. Dioc. Vis.*, i, ii.

[3] Thus in the ordination of the vicarage of Brantingham, Yorks. E. R., 1 June
1458 (R. W. Bothe, ff. 236b–238) the vicar was to have the west part of the existing
rectory-house, viz. the hall, parlour, and upper chamber at the east end of the
hall and the tower on the north side of the hall, the lower and upper chambers at
its west end with the kitchen. These divisions seem to be the result of the partition
of the rectory-house into two dwellings, while the east part of the house was
probably partitioned in a similar way.

[4] R. Roth. i, fo. 288b.

[5] R. W. Bothe, ff. 227, 228. In the simultaneously issued ordination of the
vicarage of Kildwick, the prior and convent of Bolton, the rectors, were charged
with the entire repair of the chancel (ibid., ff. 226, 226b).

of large parishes, laid the entire responsibility for the chancel upon the vicars. Here, however, their endowments were larger than ordinary. They were charged upon certain specified portions of the fruits of the churches, farm of certain lands, small tithes, and various obventions and oblations, estimated in the case of Heversham at £28. 17s., and in that of Burton at £24 yearly. Out of these the vicar of Heversham was charged with a pension of £5. 16s. 8d., and the vicar of Burton with one of £5. 3s. 4d. to the proprietors; and with the upkeep of the chancel in both cases went all responsibility for the furniture and services and the fees payable to ordinaries. With such deductions from the gross amount of endowment the yearly stipend at Heversham was reckoned at £20 and that at Burton at 20 marks; and, in vacancies of the vicarages, the taxation of Heversham was reduced to 10, and that of Burton to 6 marks.[1]

Such documents, though in the second half of the fifteenth century they run to tedious length, show extreme care and full knowledge of local circumstances. Vicars, as already said, were required to be resident, and vicarages were often so small in value that it was no doubt difficult to find suitable incumbents. It is certain that, although in the thirteenth century bishops had endeavoured to compel religious houses to present secular chaplains to vicarages of their patronage,[2] this rule had never

---

[1] For the deeds of appropriation of these churches see p. 113 above, note 1. The ordination of vicarages followed some months later, 6 June 1460 (R. W. Bothe, ff. 250b–252b).

[2] This is implied by Langton's constitution at the Council of Oxford in 1227: 'statuimus igitur ut nullus episcoporum ad vicariam quemquam admittat, nisi velit in ecclesia, in qua ei vicaria conceditur, personaliter residere' (Wilkins, i. 587). Cf. const. x of Otho: 'iuret [vicarius] residenciam ibi facere, ac eam faciat continue corporalem' (ibid. i. 651). A constitution of St. Richard of Chichester (ibid. i. 693), containing a direction for the appointment of vicars in appropriated churches 'qui velint et valeant saluti intendere animarum', does not forbid religious to reside in churches, but requires that at least two shall reside together. This rule of residence was enforced by Ottobon: 'quod si forte pauperes habeant ecclesias, quae duobus non sufficiant exhibendis, faciant illis per seculares clericos deserviri, ut sic nec debitis ecclesiae fraudentur obsequiis, nec regularis frangatur integritas disciplinae' (ibid. ii. 16). In the Lincoln institution rolls of the thirteenth century such institutions as those of canons of Dunstable to the vicarage of Flitwick (Rot. Gravesend, 191, 193, 195) are rare. In the later Middle Ages the most conspicuous examples of the admission of monks to cures of souls are occasional institutions of abbots with dispensations to augment their incomes. Thus in 1498 John Langton, the Cistercian abbot of St. Mary Graces in London, was instituted to the church of Stoke Albany (Bridges, ii. 340). The institution of another

been uniformly enforced. Where monks were concerned, it hardly came into question: parochial cures were entirely alien from any strict conception of the religious life, and although monks in the later Middle Ages frequently obtained dispensations to hold parochial benefices, yet advantage of such grants was certainly not always taken. On the other hand, there is sufficient evidence for the conclusion that one of the reasons for which houses of canons were founded was the establishment of centres from which ministrations could be furnished to neighbouring parish churches. It is true, as bishops clearly saw, that the employment of canons as parochial incumbents interfered with their monastic duties, and, where vicarages were ordained, bishops were generally unwilling to institute canons. But Premonstratensian canons seem to have been always privileged to hold cures of souls. One of the earliest ordinations of a vicarage which survive is that of Kirkby Malham Church in Craven, followed by the institution of a canon of the appropriating house, the abbey of West Dereham in Norfolk; and this meant that he had to take with him a fellow-canon, as he was not permitted to leave his monastery without a companion.[1] It would be difficult to find, then or later, the institution of an Austin canon to a vicarage at so inconvenient a distance from his house. But there were certain houses whose prescriptive right of presenting canons to appropriated churches in their neighbourhood seems, at any rate after a certain date, to have been recognized and, as time went on, the prejudices of bishops were gradually relaxed. From the middle of the fourteenth century the vicarages in the gift of Bolton Priory were habitually given to canons.[2] In 1349, during the Black Death, the prior and convent of St. Oswald's presented one of their canons to the vicarage of Tickhill, which hitherto had been held by a secular: the

Cistercian abbot, John Brompton of Jervaulx, in 1458, to the free chapel of West Witton (*Y.A.J.* xxx. 122–3), was indeed to a sinecure, but was unusual. An early instance of the admission of a monk to a living is the collation in Sept. 1380 of the vicarage of Stoke Gifford, near Bristol, to a monk of the priory of Little Malvern, which held the church in appropriation (R. Wake., fo. 14*b*).

[1] *R. W. Giff.* 255–6.

[2] See lists of incumbents of Skipton, &c., in Whitaker's *Craven*. From 1307 to the dissolution of monasteries all the recorded vicars of Sheffield, with one exception in 1458, were canons of Worksop (*Fasti Paroch.* ii. 54–5). The church of Harewood in the deanery of Ainsty, dio. York, was served by canons from the time of its appropriation in 1353: see Thompson, *Bolton Priory*, p. 100.

archbishop of York instituted him as a special favour, and the privilege seems not to have been converted into a precedent.[1] It was, in fact, during this period, owing to the scarcity of clergy, that licences of this kind began to be freely conceded. The Trinitarians of Knaresborough, often reckoned as friars, but in reality canons, were allowed, for instance, to present their brethren to appropriated churches.[2] In later days it became usual, when a church was appropriated to a house of canons, to mention that it might be served by a canon as an alternative to a secular vicar.[3]

Whether such canons, however, permanently resided on their vicarages is a question which is not easily determined. A canon of Newburgh who was vicar of Kirkby Hill, near Boroughbridge, suffered so severely from the visits of highwaymen that he sought a papal dispensation from residence in 1411.[4] The canon of Dorchester who served the cure of Stadhampton in 1445 received such treatment at the hands of his parishioners and subsequently of his abbot that he begged Bishop Alnwick with solemn asseverations to send him anywhere else.[5] It is certain too that, in spite of the canonical obligation to reside, seculars who obtained vicarages of more than the average value did not trouble to do so. Such vicarages were not common; but here

---

[1] R. Zouche, fo. 36b: 'ad vicariam . . . vacantem *que per capellanum secularem solita est gubernari pro raritate* personarum secularium per plagam mortalitatis iminentem de medio sublatarum ista dumtaxat vice suplenda admittimus'. Italicized words interlined.

[2] Ibid., fo. 24b. On 5 Nov. 1348 John Broun, brother of the house of St. Robert, Knaresborough, was instituted to the newly ordained vicarage of Pannal, at the presentation of the minister and brethren of St. Robert's.

[3] This alternative was a condition in the indenture for the foundation of the chantry of six priests at Harewood, which included the appropriation of the church, and appointment of a vicar (Thompson, u.s., p. 101). In 1398–9, when the church of Healaugh was appropriated to Healaugh Park Priory, the vicar to be appointed was definitely to be a canon regular (R. Scrope, ff. 21b–22b). The abbot and convent of Newbo in Lincolnshire were Premonstratensians, so that it is perhaps natural that the ordination of the vicarage of Acaster Malbis, appropriated to them in 1358–9, should decree that the vicar should be a canon regular in priest's orders (R. Thores., fo. 99b); but, in spite of the considerable freedom allowed in this respect to Premonstratensians, it was necessary for the abbot and convent of Coverham in 1336 to apply for and receive a licence to serve their church of Sedbergh by a regular vicar (R. Melton, fo. 467). For the service of churches appropriated to the Augustinian priory of Canons Ashby *c.* 1400 'per canonicos seu alios capellanos seculares ad nutum prioris pro tempore existentis ponendos amotiuos canonicos vero ad claustrum reuocandos' see *Linc. Vis.* i. 32–3.

[4] *C.P.L.* vi. 322.          [5] *Linc. Vis.* ii. 81–3.

and there the profits of a vicarage rose in value, especially in populous centres of trade and industry, until they became desirable objects for the ambition of pluralists. Dr. William Felle, vicar of Newcastle-upon-Tyne in 1499, followed the example of many rectors by going to study in one of the universities;[1] and in the days of Henry VIII, a singularly successful pluralist, Thomas Magnus, archdeacon of the East Riding, added the vicarage of Kendal, one of the wealthiest benefices in England, to his exorbitant list of parish churches and prebends.[2]

In rectories and vicarages alike the parochial incumbent, whether resident or absent, was assisted or his place was supplied by an unbeneficed priest known as the parish chaplain, curate, or priest, hired for a small annual salary. The term parish priest was used exclusively of this type of chaplain. He was the parish priest whose name so often occurs among the witnesses to last wills and testaments: his distinction from the clerical freeholder is marked in the Canons of 1604 by the mention of 'parsons, vicars and curates'. The beneficed clergyman who bequeaths a legacy to his priest refers to the parish priest whom he has hired.[3] All clergy with a cure of souls were, of course,

[1] *Eccl. Proc. Barnes*, app., p. xxiii.

[2] In 1535 Magnus's preferments, with their yearly value, scattered over *V.E.* were as follows: archdeaconry of East Riding, £62. 14s. 7d.; sacristy of St. Sepulchre's chapel, York, £6. 13s. 4d.; mastership of St. Leonard's Hospital, York, £367. 17s. 9½d. net; canonry in St. George's Chapel, Windsor (value not stated); rectory of Kirkby-in-Cleveland, £20; rectory of Sessay, £17. 0s. 2d. net; rectory of Bedale, £89. 4s. 8d.; vicarage of Kendal, £92. 5s. 0d.; wardenship of Sibthorpe, Notts., £25. 18s. 8d.; rectory of free chapel of Whipstrode, Hants, £3. 6s. 8d.; deanery of St. Mary Magdalene, Bridgnorth, and rectory of Claverley, Salop, £40; prebend of Corringham in Lincoln, £38. 16s. 6d.; prebend of Llanbadarn Odwyn in Llanddewi-Brefi, dio. St. David's, £6. Total: £769. 17s. 6½d. and more.

[3] So Thomas Whitby, vicar of Marske in Cleveland, refers in his will, 22 Jan. 1516–17, to 'Sir Richard Grymesby my prest', and William Appilton, vicar of Huntington near York, to 'Sir John Dalle my parish preste', 17 Dec. 1517 (R. Wolsey, ff. 143, 145b). 'Maister Robert Nevill, parson of the church of Grove and Sir Thomas Elton his parishe prest' were witnesses to the will of Humphrey Hercy of Grove, Notts., 11 June 1517 (*Test. Ebor.* v. 25); and Laurence Wright, rector of Crathorne, and William Pacok, parish priest (either of Crathorne or Rudby), to that of Cuthbert Conyers, archdeacon of Carlisle and rector of Rudby in Cleveland, 29 March 1517 (R. Wolsey, fo. 144). Much earlier, in 1405, William Noion, canon of York and rector of Haddenham, Cambs., made bequests *capellano parochiali de Hadenham*, and in 1416, Richard Rede, 'capellanus de Ryngwod', was executor of John Prophet, dean of York and rector of Ringwood, Hants (*Test. Ebor.* iii. 29, 55). In 1526–7 occurs the will of Robert Wildon, parish priest of Kirkby Moorside and rural dean of Buckrose (ibid. v. 218–19), interesting as

*curati*, curates; but in England the word became specially applied to the *capellanus curatus*, the hired assistant who looks after the cure of souls.[1] He belonged to the class of priest from which chantry chaplains were chosen, and of which more will be said in the next chapter; but he was definitely attached to the service of the rector or vicar, and his duties lay at the high altar where, in the absence of his principal, he celebrated the parish mass, and to him also frequently fell the responsibility of hearing the confessions of parishioners and administering the last sacraments to them. But it should also be remembered that in many appropriated churches, in which no vicarage was ordained, the entire cure of souls was committed to him by the proprietors.[2]

Parochial chaplains, however, were by no means confined to parish churches. In large parishes there were scattered hamlets from which access to the mother church was difficult, especially in winter: the roads were bad, and, where a parish was divided by watercourses, the difficulty of access was increased. The provision of local chapels for such outlying areas no doubt began at an early day. In Leicestershire, for example, early in the thirteenth century, there were in a little over two hundred parishes more than a hundred dependent chapels.[3] Their

showing an unbeneficed priest as a rural dean, not of the deanery in which Kirkby Moorside was situated, but of one adjoining it and in another archdeaconry.

[1] An interesting document in R. Thores., fo. 204*b*, is a letter from the archbishop to the rural dean of Harthill at the instance of the rector of Hotham, a small country parish in the East Riding, during the pestilence of 1361–2. 'Nobis est grauiter conquerendo monstratum quod licet pestilencia in dicta parochia sua in tanto viguerit et vigeat in presenti quod omnes capellanos quasi in dicta parochia celebrantes subtraxit ut dicitur ab hac luce et eo pretextu requisierit quemdam dominum Adam de Brantyngham capellanum anniversarium in dicta parochia celebrantem quod prefate ecclesie parochiali de Hothom loco capellani parochialis pro salario competenti iuxta ordinacionem inmediati predecessoris nostri inde factam debite deseruiret: idem tamen dominus Adam ordinacioni prefate . . . parere non curans dicte ecclesie loco capellani parochialis deseruire penitus recusauit in ipsius rectoris dampnum ac animarum parochianorum dicte ecclesie periculum manifeste.' The dean is to warn Adam to comply with the rector's wish. The letter shows that in ordinary circumstances there was no difficulty in finding a parish chaplain.

[2] Hence the term 'perpetual curacy', long applied to cures of souls in which no vicarage had been ordained.

[3] See *Rot. Hug. Welles*, i. 238–72. The *Matriculus* for the archdeaconry of Leicester there printed was previously printed by Nichols as one of the preliminary documents to his *History of Leicestershire*, i, pp. lv–lxii.

geographical distribution is often of great interest as illustra-
ting what may be called the manorial origin of the parish. Thus,
in the great Templars' manor of Rothley, its detached members
studded over the county were ecclesiastically all chapelries
subject to the church of Rothley.[1] In the small village of Blaston,
near Market Harborough, there were and still are two chapels,
one, in the abbot of Peterborough's manor, dependent upon
the church of Hallaton, the other, in the king's manor, nominally dependent upon the church of Medbourne, but claiming
the status of a free chapel with a rector of its own, but without
full parochial rights.[2] A similar case to the relation between
Blaston and Medbourne is that which existed, in a very large
parish, between the chapels of Windermere and Grasmere and
the mother church of Kendal. These were manorial chapels,
founded at a time whereof the memory of man runneth not,
the patronage of which, like that of the church of Kendal, had
come to the abbot and convent of St. Mary's, York. They had
their own rectors, but in order to bury their dead they had to go
to Kendal, miles away. The inconvenience of this necessity
must have been obvious at all times of the year, and there were
periods of frost and flood in which, as they represented to the
archbishop of York, they were compelled to dispose of dead
bodies without Christian burial in the lakes and woods. In the
course of 1348 Archbishop Zouche issued licences for the consecration of graveyards in both places.[3]

There are several other instances, such as the chapels of the
large Shropshire parish of Wenlock, of chapels governed by
their own rectors which were yet dependent upon a mother
church,[4] whether by the payment of a yearly pension or by the
subjection which obliged the inhabitants to resort to the mother

[1] Rothley itself was in the deanery of Akeley. Its subordinate chapels of Gad-
desby, Keyham, Grimston, Chadwell, and Wartnaby were scattered over the
deanery of Goscote. See *Rot. Hug. Welles*, i. 259.

[2] Both are mentioned ibid. i. 261. There is an interesting record of an inquiry,
early in the fourteenth century, into the status of the chapel of St. Giles, Blaston, as
a free chapel in R. Dald. i, ff. 219–221*b*.

[3] R. Zouche, ff. 71, 78*b*, 79. See *Hist. Essays in Hon. of James Tait*, pp. 332–3,
339–42, where the Grasmere ordination of burial is printed with the preamble of
the commission for Windermere.

[4] Broseley with Linley, Willey, Barrow (at any rate for a time) and Hughley,
reckoned as free chapels, had their own rectors. See Eyton, ii. 39, 42, 59; iii. 280–1;
vi. 307–8.

church for burials and for the sacrament of marriage. Such chapels in the beginning were manorial free chapels. It is interesting to notice how, in the western midlands, especially in Shropshire and Staffordshire, some churches, even after they had acquired full parochial status, were still from time to time styled free chapels.[1] The fact seems to be that, while some of these gradually achieved independence of their mother churches, others continued for long to be bound by the old tie. Such chapel rectories were regarded as sinecures, the cure of souls belonging to the incumbents of their parish churches. Early in the fourteenth century Roger Martival, bishop of Salisbury, founded a chapel in his manor of Noseley in Leicestershire and procured its exemption from the parish church. In this free chapel he established a small college, consisting of a warden and two priests. But, as the population of Noseley, such as it was, lived for the most part near the manor-house and chapel, the parish church was eventually abandoned and the cure of souls vested in the warden of the chapel.[2]

The ordinary parochial chapel, however, was treated merely as an offshoot of the parish church, served by a curate who was appointed by the incumbent to say mass daily at its altar. In this dependence it remained, for nothing was more alien to the mind of the medieval rector and vicar than the formation of a new parish with the damage that it inevitably would cause to his income. As late as 1634 the consecration of St. John's at Leeds was delayed because the vicar of Leeds feared that his oblations and fees might be diverted to a chapel in a new and growing quarter.[3] So it was that through a great part of their history two of the most noble churches in England, St. Mary Redcliffe at Bristol and Holy Trinity at Hull, were chapels, one attached to the prebendal church of Bedminster, the other to

[1] Frodesley, Salop, is a case in point. Although it appears as a parish church in *Tax. Eccl.* 244*b*, it is called a free chapel in *R. Stretton*, ii. 11, 206, 208, and a chapel ibid. 193. Eyton, vi. 295, thought that it might originally have been a chapel of Condover. If this was so, its freedom may have been an acquired independence of its mother church, but it may also have been from the beginning a free manorial chapel within the limits of the parish. The advowson was appendant to the manor.
[2] See *Trans. Leices. Arch. Soc.* xii. 214–71; xiii. 73–9.
[3] *V.C.H. Yorks.* iii. 58. Objections were raised by the archbishop to the grant of the patronage to the corporation and the vicar of Leeds; he insisted that the vicar should have a veto on appointments. In view of Puritan tendencies there was a danger of 'rival pulpits'.

the parish church of Hessle. At Newcastle-upon-Tyne, a town broken up by streams, now built over, which found their way down lateral valleys to the main river, the churches of St. Andrew, All Saints, and St. John were all chapels of the parish church of St. Nicholas, built within the town walls. Decrees which united parishes were not uncommon in the later Middle Ages,[1] but it would be difficult to point with any certainty to a decree which created a new parish.[2] Occasionally the question arose whether a church was a parish church or a chapel. In 1454 the chancel of the church of Ollerton in Nottinghamshire fell into disrepair, and the question arose, who was responsible for repairs. The rectors of the church were said to be the dean and chapter of Lincoln, who had apparently appropriated it on the death of the last rector two centuries before. No vicarage had been ordained, but for years past the church had fallen into dependence upon the neighbouring church of Edwinstowe, also appropriated to the dean and chapter; and the vicars of Edwinstowe had undertaken the repairs of the chancel, the expense of which the proprietors wished them to meet out of their own

[1] See, e.g., the decree in R. W. Bothe, fo. 236, uniting the church of Broxtow in Nottinghamshire to that of Bilbrough, 26 Apr. 1458, on the petition of Robert Strelley, esq., 'quod integri fructus redditus et proventus annui prefate ecclesie de Brokesstawe alias Brocholwestouwa in eam iam diu devenerunt et deducti sunt tenuitatem et notoriam exilitatem per destruccionem domorum mortem et recessum inhabitancium sterilitatemque agrorum quod nullatinus sufficiunt aut sufficere poterunt ad sustentacionem congruam vnius capellani ad celebrandum in eadem ecclesia divina officia et ministrandum sacramenta et sacramentalia parochianis eiusdem ecclesie: quamobrem cum iam a nonnullis retro effluxis annorum curruculis nullus potuisset reperiri capellanus qui onus cure eidem ecclesie incumbentis admittere vellet vel curam suscipere eiusdem ullo modo eadem ecclesia remansit inofficiata taliter quod parochiani eiusdem ecclesie quamuis pauci sunt [sic] ea de causa compulsi sunt necessitate quadam alias ecclesias adire vicinas pro audiendis inibi diuinis ac sacramentis et sacramentalibus ibidem recipiendis.'

[2] An interesting example comes from Scotland in the St. Andrews Formulare 1514–46 (Stair Soc.), ii. 291–4, unfortunately without definite names of places. Cardinal Betoun was moved to make this decree by the complaint that the river called E. ran swiftly between the vills. of N. and N. and their mother church of A. Those who attempted to come to church by boat were sometimes drowned, with the corpses which they were carrying for burial; often parishioners died without the sacraments; 'mulieres partui appropinquantes timore partus aborsum fecerunt et quandocunque submerse sunt', and children died without baptism. At Christmas, when the river and the flooded fields froze and wind and storm swept the country, the mother church was sometimes inaccessible. The inhabitants of N. and N. had built themselves a chapel, but the vicar of A. refused to let another priest serve it. Fortunately the sinecure rector of A. was otherwise well endowed and had no objection to the formation of a new parish of which he presumably remained rector.

pockets. Here there was no doubt about the original parochial status of the church, and the vicar of Edwinstowe maintained that, if he made himself liable for repairs, the dean and chapter ought to pay for them.[1]

If the dependence of parochial chapels was strongly emphasized, and their independence carefully guarded against, their necessity was nevertheless quite obvious. In the widespreading parishes of West Yorkshire there were many parochial chapels of whose origin nothing is known. In the course of the fifteenth century the population of the hamlets in the great parish of Halifax appears to have been rapidly growing. In 1466 licence was given to the inhabitants of certain townships south of the Calder to have mass celebrated in a chapel at Ripponden;[2] and again a similar licence was granted in 1496 to the inhabitants of Midgley, Sowerby, and Warley for a chapel which they had recently built at their own expense at Luddenden.[3] It is noteworthy that in the first instance not only the rights of the mother church of Halifax were safeguarded, but also those of the chapel of Elland, an old dependency of Halifax which had acquired a quasi-parochial claim over the district on that side of the river.[4] In the document which relates to Luddenden the chaplain was allowed in cases of necessity to administer the last sacraments to the dying; but it is expressly stated that no tithes, mortuaries, or oblations were to be withheld from the mother

[1] R. W. Bothe, fo. 169.

[2] R. G. Nev. i, fo. 51b. The inhabitants of Soyland, Rishworth, Bothomley, and Barkisland had licence 8 Jan. 1465–6 'ut in capella situata in Riburneden de parochia de Halifax predicta missas et alia divina officia voce submissa per quoscunque capellanos idoneos in vestra aut alicuius vestrum et aliorum quorumcunque ibidem adueniencium presencia licite valeatis facere celebrari dumtamen locus ad hoc decens sit et honestus ac ecclesie parochiali de Halifax predicta et capella de Elande eiusdem parochie in decimis oblacionibus et aliis obuencionibus et emolumentis debitis et consuetis preiudicium nullum inde generetur'.

[3] R. Roth. i, fo. 93 (29 June 1496). The petition of the inhabitants stated 'quod dicta ecclesia sua parochialis de Halifax per non modicum spacium a locis siue hamelectis predictis ita quod incole et inhabitantes huiusmodi senio confracti ac variis langoribus detenti necnon mulieres pregnantes ac alii plerique occasione longe distancie in dominicis et aliis festiuitatibus missarum celebracioni et horis canonicis in dicta sua ecclesia parochiali de Halifax minime interesse queant ut eciam frequenter cum ad eandem suam ecclesiam parochialem diebus festiualibus ex causa predicta aduenerint infra eandem ecclesiam suam parochialem quamuis tempus fuerit pluuiosum vel aliis procellarum turbinibus intemperatum pre multitudine populi et parochianorum hiis diebus augmentata intrare vix valeant'.

[4] Lawton, p. 129.

church, nor any contributions to its fabric or repair or to the upkeep of its churchyard enclosure. The inhabitants of the chapelry, moreover, were bound to visit the church of Halifax on all the great feasts of the year, including that of its dedication and the patronal festival of All Saints.[1] Such directions are typical of the obligations which lay upon such chapels, which were intended for the convenience of districts isolated and self-contained, which were kept up by the offerings of those whom they were intended to benefit, and the chaplains of which were probably chosen by them subject to the approval of the parochial incumbent.

In conclusion, something should be said about the fabric of the parish church, to which occasional allusions already have been made. There is no period at which money was lavished so freely on English parish churches as in the fifteenth century, and there is a curious contrast between the complaints of dilapidation and decay so common in the reports of visitations and the building activity which was prevailing all over the country. In church after church in Norfolk and Suffolk, Somerset and Devon, in the churches of the great cities, London, Bristol, York, and Norwich, the stone-mason provided the framework for the exhibition of the full powers of artists and craftsmen in wood-carving and stained glass, in painting and in tomb-making. No part of England is without splendid examples of their art, and few churches are without some trace of the handiwork of the period. The complaints to which reference had been made are usually concerned with the state of the chancel, and, where decay was due to the negligence of proprietors, it can hardly be wondered at. A monastery with heavy expenses to meet at home naturally looked upon an appropriated church, not as an artistic treasure whose needs were a first charge upon its means, but as a source of income which enabled it to meet its liabilities; and this is clearly indicated by the terms of appropriation deeds which have been already quoted. The parish church was a remedy by which the poverty of a monastery might find succour, not an additional burden upon the funds of a community which was already faced with drains upon its resources. Those splendid chancels which occur so frequently in Lincolnshire, Nottinghamshire,

[1] R. Roth. i, u.s.

and Derbyshire in the earlier part of the fourteenth century were, almost without exception, provided at the cost of individual rectors, men of means who were well able to hire first-rate masons.[1] It is rare to find a chancel, either then or in the fifteenth century, which was entirely rebuilt by proprietors; and it is much to the credit of the warden and fellows of New College that, early in the fifteenth century, they reconstructed the fine chancel at Adderbury.[2] Such instances are rare: far more often the chancel of an appropriated church was patched and cobbled as occasion arose, and frequently there is a strong contrast between its insignificance and the splendour of a nave rebuilt at the expense of parishioners.[3] Nor would the farmer to whom the rectory of an appropriated church was usually let show much enthusiasm in repairing a part of the fabric which lay outside the province of the ordinary fabric fund. His aim and that of the proprietors would be to find any excuse by which a portion of their duties could be shifted to the shoulders of others. At intervals for some two centuries the prior and convent of Pontefract disputed with the parishioners of Silkstone, the mother church of Barnsley, the responsibility for the repair of the west part of the ritual choir beneath a central tower, which had formed part of the original chancel, subsequently prolonged eastwards, of the church of Silkstone. The matter was settled in 1496, when the central tower was taken

[1] The most famous of these, the chancel at Heckington, near Sleaford, has frequently been quoted as owing its origin to the connexion of the church with Bardney Abbey. The abbot and convent held the advowson and presented the rector, Richard Pottesgrave, a clerk in the service of the Crown, whose effigy occupies the recess for the founder's tomb and indicates his responsibility for the fabric. Such responsibility would not have fallen upon the abbot and convent until the middle of the century, when the church was appropriated and a vicarage was ordained (see *Mon.* i. 636–7).

[2] See the accounts in *Adderbury Rectoria*, ed. Hobson (Oxfordshire Record Soc.).

[3] Yatton, Somerset, is a striking example. The result of the rebuilding of the nave in the fifteenth century, on a very handsome scale (see *Somerset Church-Wardens' Accounts* [Som. Rec. Soc.], pp. 78 sqq.) contrasts strongly with the fabric of the chancel, which received no alteration at the date. The rector was the prebendary of Yatton in Wells Cathedral, who happened during part of this period to be John Macworth, the dean of Lincoln whose doings with his chapter have already been discussed. On the other hand, when, towards the middle of the fifteenth century, the parishioners of Thirsk in Yorkshire rebuilt their nave, the rectors, the prior and convent of Newburgh, seem to have done their duty by the chancel and apparently employed the same master-mason, whose design, though more modest, was thoroughly harmonious with that of the nave (See *Y.A.J.* xxii. 205–10).

down and the parishioners constructed a new tower at the west end of the church; the liabilities were then divided in proportional parts between the parishioners and the prior and convent.[1]

With regard to the conduct of the fabric fund, the 'fabric' or 'works' from which building expenses were met, the arrangement in parish churches was to all intents and purposes the same as that which prevailed in the greater ecclesiastical foundations. Just as in a monastery the sacrist or the master of the works, just as in a cathedral church a canon or vicar-choral, the clerk or warden of the works, kept the gifts and contributions arising from various sources, with an associate as comptroller to share or check his accounts, so in a parish church two wardens of the fabric received, paid out, and accounted for the money which accrued to the fund in the form of special oblations, bequests by will, or the gifts in certain cases of pilgrims. The variety of material in those interesting documents known as churchwardens' accounts is due to the fact that the fabric fund, raised in the first instance for purposes of building and repair, became in process of time a fund for general purposes. Years often passed by during which expenses on the building were slight, but during which contributions to the fund were made at the usual rate; or, when any special piece of building was urgent, a new fund was started concurrently with the other for a limited period. For the surplus of the regular fund there were many uses of a general parochial character. The payment of subsidies, the supply of the local quota of men for the king's service, the repair of roads, causeways, dikes, and bridges, the provision of dowries for needy spinsters, a host of matters in which the interest of the community of professing Christians was concerned, came under the eye of the churchwardens and were met, when occasion offered, by a grant from the works chest, whose three keys of divers forms were in the custody of the wardens and the incumbent; and it was thus that churchwardens obtained so prominent a place in the village life of the post-Reformation era and until a period at which the close connexion between every department of such life and the parish life was remembered only in the practical politics of the vestry meeting. Not that the modern vestry meeting differs greatly from such a gathering in the fifteenth century, when local

[1] See discussion of the relevant documents, *Y.A.J.* xxviii. 342–4.

objectors and obstructionists probably made their views known with equal and even greater vigour, and much language flew about. It is rather that the post-medieval growth of a sharp contrast between the sacred and profane in ordinary matters of life has emphasized the secular character of the business discussed by vestrymen. It would be interesting if we had, for example, the minutes of the meetings at which the parishioners of Wyberton, near Boston, discussed the conduct of the mason whom the wardens had engaged to remodel the nave and the steeple of the church in 1419, and who exceeded the sum named in his contract. The record of his suit in Chancery with the wardens incidentally serves to explain certain unusual architectural features of the building, a virtue rare in such documents, which sometimes leave matters darker than we found them.[1] Building contracts unfortunately are rare; but in those which have survived, such as the nearly contemporary contracts for the building of the south aisle at Hornby Church in Richmondshire and the rebuilding of the neighbouring church of Catterick,[2] we have types which show us the usual procedure in such matters; and we can still go to the magnificent nave at Fotheringhay, and with a copy in our hand of the contract made in 1434 between Richard duke of York and the local mason William Horwode— for most of our church-builders were local masons trained in the handling of local material—study the execution of the proposed design and note the variations that arose in the course of work.[3]

[1] See the paper by Sir W. H. St. John Hope, 'The New Building of Wyberton Church, Lincs.' (*Lincs. Notes & Queries*, xiv. 225–34).

[2] Both are printed by McCall, *Richmondshire Churches*, pp. 37–40, 62. His version of the Catterick contract of 18 Apr. 1412 was taken from the original document at Brough Hall in the parish of Catterick and collated with the version by James Raine, sen., published in 1834. The Hornby contract of 28 Jan. 1409–10 was among the muniments formerly preserved at Hornby Castle, N. Yorks. It is more than possible that Richard of Cracall, the mason at Catterick, was identical with Richard of Newton in the parish of Patrick Brompton, employed at Hornby.

[3] Printed in *Mon.* vi (iii), 1414–15, with some hiatuses and doubtful readings. The original, formerly in the possession of Lord Manvers, has disappeared, being no longer among the muniments at Thoresby.

# V

# CHANTRIES AND COLLEGES OF CHANTRY-PRIESTS

A<small>T</small> the basis of all medieval pious foundations there lies the idea of continual intercession for the living and the departed. That remarkable memorial, the *Liber Vitae* of the church of Durham,[1] begun in the early days of the congregation of St. Cuthbert at Lindisfarne, preserved throughout the migrations which brought the successors of that community more than two centuries later to Durham, crowded thickly with names of twelfth- and thirteenth-century monks, noblemen, and miscellaneous lay-folk, and continued fitfully at intervals until the very eve of the Reformation, is a long record of the names of friends and benefactors from far and near who desired to be remembered at the altar on which the book was laid. With this intention masses, accompanied by the prayers of the faithful, were offered daily at altars throughout the church. The landowner who founded a parish church or endowed a monastery with lands and churches did so not merely with the idea that such acts were for the good of his soul in a general sense, but with the express purpose that he and his should be remembered daily at the altar, and that the salvation of their souls and their deliverance from the cleansing fires of purgatory should be constant topics of prayer with the priests and ministers of their foundations. Grants of property in frankalmoin were made upon the understanding that the service done for them should be a service of prayer. Religious houses furnished benefactors with letters of confraternity, admitting them to share vicariously in the works of piety and the suffrages of the community.[2] Chaucer's Clerk of Oxenford, maintained by patrons at the university, 'bisily gan for the soules preye of hem that yaf hym wher-with to scoleye'.[3] Every form of pious benefaction, in fact,

---

[1] Ed. J. Stevenson (Surtees Soc. vol. xiii), 1841. In 1923 the Surtees Society published a collotype facsimile of the original MS. as vol. cxxxvi of its publications, to which a new text, rectifying the many errors in Stevenson's text and supplemented by a biographical index of names, is promised as a sequel.

[2] See the papers by W. G. Clark-Maxwell (*Arch.* lxxv. 19–61; lxxix. 179–216).

[3] *Cant. Tales* A, 301–2.

carried with it the obligation of intercession upon the bene-
ficiary; and from this point of view every church, from the
cathedral or abbey to the humble chapel of a remote hamlet,
was a chantry foundation.

Needless to say, however, the chantry, properly so called, was
a service founded and endowed by one or more benefactors at
an altar in a church or chapel for the special objects already
mentioned. The foundation of chantries was, of course, an
ancient custom, although the habitual use of *cantaria* to signify
a special mass did not begin until the thirteenth century.[1] Thus
the deed by which Archbishop Gray founded his chantry at the
altar of St. Michael in the south transept of York Minster contains no mention of the word chantry: the service is simply a
celebration of mass.[2] But, for the most characteristic foundation
of the later Middle Ages, at a time when the foundation of
monasteries had almost ceased, the term came into regular use;
and throughout the fourteenth and fifteenth centuries chantries
came into being in very large numbers. The greater churches
of the country were full of them, and no parish church was
without them, although in the ordinary parish church they
generally assumed a merely temporary form.

In classifying these foundations, which played so large a part
in the life of the later medieval church and bring us so close to
the popular religion of the day, we may begin with those whose
permanence was guaranteed by the founders. From the end of
the reign of Edward I onwards the patent rolls record licences for
the alienation in mortmain of lands and tenements to chaplains
who are to celebrate divine service daily in specified churches
for objects stated by the founders. The chaplain who celebrates
at a given altar in a given church is placed in possession of

---

[1] An early example of its use in this sense is the foundation of a *cantaria* by
Robert of Akeld in the chapel of Akeld, parish of Kirknewton, Northumberland
(Kirkham Cartulary, fo. 84, quoted in *Hist. Northumb.* xi. 238). This in all prob-
ability marks the foundation of the chapel itself, the service in which would be
regarded as a *cantaria*. The date seems to be early in the thirteenth century.

[2] *R. Walt. Gray*, 190–1 (among supplementary documents): 'Noveritis nos de
consensu capituli nostri Ebor. ordinasse quod unus sacerdos ab eodem capitulo
constituendus apud Ebor. sub se duos alios habeat sacerdotes et clericum idoneos,
quos sibi duxerit eligendos, et quod omnes iidem sacerdotes in ecclesia B. Petri
Ebor. ad altare S. Michaelis quotidie pro animis praedecessorum, nostra, successorum nostrorum et canonicorum Ebor. ac omnium fidelium defunctorum divina
officia cum plenis exequiis mortuorum imperpetuum celebrent.' The date is
22 Mar. 1241–2.

certain property to be continued to his successors for ever. He enters into a freehold like that of a rector or vicar: he is presented by the founder and instituted and inducted in the usual way. He is thus quite independent of the parochial incumbent: his tenure of the chantry ceases with his death, resignation, or deprivation. In the church of Newark-on-Trent there were by the end of the Middle Ages no less than fifteen of these perpetual chantries, each of them being a presentative benefice. For the general ordering of the services of the church the vicar of course was responsible, and the presentation to several of the chantries at Newark was made by him, acting with bodies of local trustees or with parishioners whom he associated with himself.[1] The chantry-chaplains also were bound to take part in the services of choir and to pay due respect to the vicar; but their own altars were part of their freehold, and they were wardens of their chantries and had control over the sums bequeathed to their embellishment and upkeep.

These chaplains are often distinguished as chantrists, *cantaristae*. The chantrist, that is to say, is properly speaking the

---

[1] For the Newark chantries see *Thor. Soc.* xvii. 68–88; xviii. 138–49. See also Cornelius Brown, *Hist. Newark*, 1904, i. 208–38. To one, the earliest of these, no institutions remain. The vicar, with four or six *fidedigniores*, presented to six, the rectors (the prior and convent of St. Katherine, Lincoln), and *fidedigniores*, to one. Six more were in the gift of the alderman and members of the guild of the Holy Trinity, and two in that of the alderman and members of the guild of the Blessed Virgin. The alderman of the Holy Trinity guild was constantly among the *fidedigniores* summoned by the vicar to present with him, and now and then the aldermen of the guilds of the Virgin and Corpus Christi appear in a like capacity. The chantry of St. Nicholas, probably founded in the thirteenth century, from at any rate 1332 onwards was in the gift of the commonalty of the town of Newark (R. Melton, fo. 376*b*), and at the head of those presenting is regularly named from 1412 the alderman of the Trinity guild (R. Bowet, i, fo. 222*b*, &c.), with one apparent exception in 1438, when the presentation seems to have lapsed to the vicar and four *fidedigniores* (R. Kempe, fo. 394*b*). In the last recorded presentation, in 1533, a list of 34 names 'and many others' is headed by the name of the well-known native of Newark, Thomas Magnus (see p. 122 above, note 2), followed by that of the alderman of the guild (R. Lee, fo. 48*b*). Once the alderman of the guild is called 'alderman of Newark' (R. Sav., fo. 76*b*), and it seems probable that when the town received its charter of incorporation from Edward VI, this guild formed the basis of its governing body. The probable origin of the corporation in the earlier guilds is suggested by Dickinson, *Hist. Newark*, 1816, pp. 27, 28, followed by Brown, op. cit. i. 253–4. Anthony Forster, the first alderman of Newark, who was certainly the last warden of the Trinity guild, was one of those who presented to Alan Flemyng's chantry of Corpus Christi, 20 Oct. 1535, and the occurrence of his name after that of the vicar makes it probable that he was alderman of the Trinity guild in that year (R. Lee, fo. 56*b*).

incumbent of a permanently endowed benefice, the revenues of which have been made over in perpetuity to him and his successors. This is the normal state of things where the patronage remains in private hands. But a great impulse to the foundation of chantries was given by the action of confraternities and guilds, who, from the middle of the fourteenth century, showed great activity in buying up property under licences in mortmain for the endowment of chantries. The Newark chantries, for example, were largely founded by prominent members of the guilds of Holy Trinity, St. Mary, and Corpus Christi.[1] The guild of Corpus Christi at Leicester had its chantry of three chaplains in St. Martin's, while another guild had its chantry of two chaplains in the suburban parish church of St. Margaret.[2] It was these religious guilds or confraternities which supplied the chief impetus, apart from private founders, to the movement.[3] Wealthy associations, many of which, it may be conjectured with some reason, were survivals of the decline of guilds merchant before the growing importance of craft guilds, existed mainly for religious and charitable purposes, including persons of both sexes, and sometimes enrolling among their members personages of distinction, like the guilds of St. Mary and Corpus Christi at Cambridge, which, under the presidency of the first duke of Lancaster, founded Corpus Christi College in 1353. Outside the towns they abounded in prosperous agricultural and industrial districts. In the southeastern district of Lincolnshire, the parts of Holland, they sprang up in great numbers during the fourteenth century, when the prosperity of the great mart of Boston and its port reflected itself upon the whole neighbourhood. There is some indication that the chantries which came into being under these auspices

[1] See previous note.

[2] *A.A.S.R.P.* xxx. 511–13, 507–8.

[3] The importance of a great local guild in connexion with chantry foundations has been illustrated in the case of the Trinity guild at Newark (p. 143 above, note 1). Instances in which the presentation to chantries lay with bodies of parishioners or members of a municipal corporation are the chantry of Our Lady at Gateshead, to which twelve parishioners presented in the name of the rest (R. Langley, ff. 167 bis *b*–168) and that of the Annunciation at Hartlepool, where the presentation was made by the mayor and *duodecim sibi consultos* (ibid. ff. 221, 303*b*). On chantries in general see the valuable essay by K. L. Wood-Legh, *Studies in Church Life in England under Edward III*, 1934. A more extended work on the point is promised by the same author.

were founded in more than one instance without the necessary licences. The inquisition which followed the parliament of Cambridge in 1388, promoted in the first instance as a precaution against political associations masquerading under the name of guilds, revealed the number of these foundations; and it is significant that in 1391 the statute of mortmain extended the provisions of the old statute *De religiosis* to corporations in general.[1] The patent rolls for the years immediately following the statute are full of licences in mortmain, including several granted to the Lincolnshire village guilds, which indicate that guilds were hastening to make up for lost time and regularize their position.[2]

Property thus amortized was usually held by the guilds for the use of their chantries, and their chaplains received annual stipends out of its profits. This distinguishes the stipendiary chaplain from the chantrist proper. There were chantrists, it is true, regularly instituted to their benefices, who were actually stipendiaries, inasmuch as their yearly income consisted in a salary paid by trustees. But the stipendiary is obviously a hired priest, *capellanus conductitius* or *conductivus*, a conduct, *amovibilis* or *amotivus*, removable at the pleasure of his employers. The great array of choir-stalls in St. Botolph's at Boston and St. Lawrence's at Ludlow remind us of the multitude of chantry priests maintained in each church; but nearly all of these were stipendiaries, like the seven priests kept by the guild of Palmers at Ludlow.[3] The stipend, moreover, which proceeded from landed property,

---

[1] *S. R.* ii. 80. For the writs issued by authority of the parliament of Cambridge to which returns were made in 1389 see *C.C.R.* 1385–9, p. 624. Translations are printed in Toulmin Smith, *English Gilds* (E.E.T.S. Orig. Ser. xl, 1870), pp. 127–31. Summaries of the returns form a valuable appendix to H. F. Westlake, *The Parish Gilds of Mediaeval England*, 1919.

[2] Thus six licences for chantries in churches of Holland were granted within the space of a few days in 1394 as follows: 27 June, Swineshead (*C.P.R.* 1391–6, p. 101); 1 July, Algarkirk, Cowbit and Kirton (ibid., pp. 105, 107, 120); 2 July, Donington (ibid., p. 101); 3 July, Wigtoft (ibid., p. 109). A licence for a second chantry at the same altar in Kirton was granted 2 Sept. (ibid., p. 143).

[3] See the certificate returned in 1547, printed *Salop Arch. Soc.* 3rd ser. x. 327–8. The certificate among the guild returns of 1388–9 is printed in full, with royal letters patent of 4 July 1392, ibid. 4th ser. i. 150–63. On the guilds of Boston see Pishey Thompson, *Hist. Boston*, pp. 113–57, and documents printed in 'Lincoln & Lincolnshire Chantry Certif.' *A.A.S.R.P.* xxxvii. 255–72). Here, on the establishment of the borough in 1545, the property of the guilds of St. Mary, the Trinity, Corpus Christi, St. Peter and St. George was made over to the mayor and corporation.

did not represent its average annual income: it was merely a first charge upon its revenues. We may compare the Works chantry in Lincoln Minster, whose priests, two to four in number, were paid yearly salaries as a charge upon the fabric fund of the church.[1] The surplus arising from the lands of stipendiary services was open to employment in other directions, like the surplus of the fabric fund of a parish church. Occasionally, where there was urgent need, the chantry was dropped, and the income devoted entirely to other purposes. At Henbury in Gloucestershire, a parish embracing a large trace of the Severn marsh and often for that reason called Henbury Salt-marsh, there was a stipendiary service in the hands of a body of trustees, who reported to the Chantry Commissioners of Henry VIII and Edward VI that rents and profits of the chantry had been at recent and earlier intervals appropriated to the maintenance and repair of sea-walls ruined some sixty years before by one of the disastrous inundations caused by the high tides of the Bristol Channel.[2]

Such churches as St. Michael's and Holy Trinity at Coventry, whose fabrics were enlarged in the later Middle Ages by the addition of chantry chapels, bore witness to the activity of craft guilds, as well as confraternities, in founding stipendiary chantries. Here the stipends were usually paid out of the profits of land or stock procured by the subscriptions and fines of members, and administered by the officers of the body.[3] There is one important point which remains to be noticed in this context. Where chantry lands were put into trusteeship, they

[1] See *B. & W.* ii (ii), 899. So (ibid. 443) in July 1440 'Item debentur eisdem ministrantibus et cantantibus in dicta missa de fabrica ecclesie. ixs.' The object, of course, was prayer for contributors to the fabric fund; ibid. 168: 'custos autem fabrice tres capellanos celebraturos pro subuenientibus fabrice capitulo nominabit.' The number, thus stated in 1330, appears to have grown to four by 1432 (ibid. 472: cf. 383); but Alnwick's *Novum Registrum* after some hesitation reduced it to three (ibid. 358), and ultimately only two are mentioned, at any rate by name (*A.A.S.R.P.* u.s, 293).

[2] Certificate of 1547, printed *B. & G.A.S.* viii. 252–3. The incumbent of the chantry, whose yearly salary was £5. 6s. 8d. assisted the parochial curate 'for that the parishe stretchethe farre & is of a greate compasse & many people inhabitinge within the same'. 'The same parishe is verie greate & poore nott able to defend the grete ragez of the water beatynge agaynst the towne.'

[3] See, e.g., the large number of stipendiary services and endowments for lights and lamps recorded in 'Shropshire Chantry Certif.' (*Salop Arch. Soc.* 3rd ser. x. 372–83). At Clun a stock of money, producing £19. 6s. 8d. yearly, maintained a stipendiary priest in addition to contributing to repair of the fabric (ibid. 382).

were sometimes committed to the care of a monastery. This was the case as regards most of the Newark chantries. As previously stated, these owed their foundation largely to guilds. But they were not all guild chantries in the ordinary sense, but chantries in the patronage of committees of townfolk, nominated by the vicar and composed of members not necessarily representative of a single guild. Further, their founders, like Alan Fleming, whose magnificent brass remains in the south transept of the church, were individual guildsmen acting privately for the benefit of their guilds, keeping the patronage in their own hands during their lifetime, and sometimes giving a preference to their kindred in the choice of future members of the patronage board.[1] Consequently the chantry property was handed over neither to any guild nor to the townsmen at large, but to various convents in the neighbourhood, the abbots and convents of Newbo,[2] Rufford,[3] and Wellow,[4] the priors and convents of St. Katharine's at Lincoln (the proprietors of the church),[5] Shelford,[6] and Thurgarton,[7] each of whom paid salaries of £5 or £6 a year apiece to various priests. Similarly, the abbot and convent of Vaudey were trustees of the three chantries founded at Grantham in 1349, one of which, it may be noted, was the chantry in the parish church at the rood-altar, where, at the ringing of the day-bell, the morrow mass was sung for the benefit of travellers who were about their day's work betimes.[8] The *missa pro itinerantibus* was general in English towns; but nowhere are records of it so numerous as in the towns busily frequented by wool-traders on their way to Boston from the

---

[1] Thus, in the case of Sausemer's chantry at Newark, the foundress remained patron for her lifetime. After her death the vicar presented the chaplain with the aid of six trustworthy parishioners in the choice of whom *sufficientes de parentela* of William and Maud Sausemer were to be taken into account (R. Melton, fo. 373*b*).

[2] Robert Caldewell's Trinity chantry (*Thoroton Soc.* xvii. 81).

[3] Robert Caldewell's chantry of Corpus Christi, ibid. 78.

[4] Chantry of St. Lawrence (Maud Sausemer's) and Morrow-mass chantry (William Sausemer's) at the same altar, ibid. 71, 73.

[5] Chantry of St. James, ibid. 70.

[6] Alan Flemyng's chantry of Corpus Christi (mostly), ibid. 75.

[7] Chantry of St. Katharine, ibid. 74 (partly); Alan Flemyng's chantry of Corpus Christi, ibid. 75; and Isabel Caldewell's chantry of Corpus Christi, ibid. 77.

[8] Inspeximus and confirmation, 16 Oct. 1349, of letters of the abbot and convent of Vaudey, the trustees of the chantries, dated 14 Aug. previously (*C.P.R.* 1348–50, pp. 414, 415).

sheep-farms of Yorkshire and Lincolnshire[1]—those wool-traders, who have left substantial memories of their thriving in the upland villages of the parts of Kesteven, and to one of whom, Anthony Ellys, we owe the beautiful tower of Great Ponton Church in the meadows by the springs of the Witham, carved with his woolpacks, his merchant's mark, the arms of the Staple of Calais, and his motto 'Thynke and thanke God of al'.

In this connexion it is perhaps unnecessary to emphasize what has already been sufficiently implied, the close relation between the growth of the chantry system and the growth of the middle class. We all remember that group of tradesmen in the Prologue to the *Canterbury Tales*, the Haberdasher and his companions, clothed all in the livery of one 'solempne and great fraternity', all worthy to sit in a guildhall upon a dais, each with a wife who liked to be called Madame 'and goon to vigilies al before' or, like the Wife of Bath, go up first to give her offering at the altar of her parish church.[2] This was the type of man like Alan Fleming or John Flore of Oakham, like the civic knights William Walworth and John Philipot, who came forward with substantial aid in the financial stress of the early years of Richard II, like William Canynge of Bristol in the reign of Edward IV, and, later, like John Tame of Fairford or like John Greneway, whose chantry chapel on the south side of Tiverton Church, with its elaborate sculptures of merchant vessels, cogs, balingers, and barges,[3] recalls at once that Merchant of more than a century earlier, who 'wold the sea were kept for anything bitwixe Middelburgh and Orewelle'. That unscrupulous sea-dog, the Shipman—'for ought I woot, he was of Dertemouthe'—at once recalls John Hawley, the indefatigable

[1] At Wakefield the morrow mass was said at 5 a.m. 'for all servaundes and laborers in the said paroche' (*Yorks. Chantry Surveys* (Surtees Soc.) ii. 311). In the large parish of Doncaster, where seven other priests were resident, mass was said every hour from 5 to 10 a.m., 'as well for th'inhabitauntes of the sayd towne as other strangers passing through the same' (ibid. i. 175). The morrow mass at Newark was said at 4 a.m. (*Thoro. Soc.* xvii. 72). The morrow mass chantry at the altar of St. John Baptist in Southwell Minster was founded by the celebrated Thomas Haxey, canon of Southwell and treasurer of York (ibid. xv. 120). For a curious survival of the *missa pro itinerantibus* in the form of morning prayer at 6 a.m. in St. Alkmund's at Shrewsbury for the brethren of the Drapers' guild before starting for Oswestry market see *Salop Arch. Soc.* 1st ser. vi. 184.

[2] *Cant. Tales* A, 376-7, 449-50.

[3] See E. F. Prideaux, 'Late Medieval Sculpture from the Church of St. Peter, Tiverton' (*A.J.* lxxv. 209-40).

scourge of the galleys of France and Castile, and the benefactor of the parochial chapel of St. Saviour at Dartmouth,
where his initials may be seen in juxtaposition with the leopards
of England in the ironwork of the south door.  If we can connect
the Wife of Bath with no specific chantry in the churches of
Somerset or Wiltshire, we know at any rate that, apart from her
own good estate, there were at least five good reasons which
might have prompted her to found one; and nowhere in the
competitive energy of traders, not only in founding chantries,
but in building chantry chapels, more conspicuous than in the
district between the Cotswolds and Salisbury Plain.  One has
to remember only such churches as Burford, Cirencester, and
Northleach, the chantry chapels in the churches of Lacock and
Bromham near Devizes, and the handsome village church of
Steeple Ashton, to realize the extent of the contribution of the
successful merchant to the amenities at once of divine worship
and of art.

Hitherto reference has been made only to those permanent
chantries, founded by individuals or by guilds, of which records
are abundant.  There were others, of course, founded with less
chance of perpetuity by small groups of humble villagers, who
contributed according to their means to common stocks of
money, cattle, or sheep.  Such stocks—the interesting church-
wardens' accounts of Croscombe in Somerset furnish good
examples[1]—were insufficient for the regular support of a priest,
and some of them served merely to keep a light burning before
an altar or image.[2]  The fund, however, was capable of maintaining a yearly anniversary or obit, such as formed part of every
chantry foundation.  All classes of the community, in fact,
furthered the growth of chantries or kindred institutions.  From
King Henry V founding his tomb-chapel at the east end of
St. Edward's chapel at Westminster, from the great series of
episcopal chapels beneath the arches of Winchester Cathedral,
it is a long way to the yearly obits and feasts kept by the village
people of Croscombe, or to the service of Our Lady at Ellesmere,
maintained by annual subscriptions of fourpence from each
married man and twopence from every servant taking five
shillings wages or above; but the idea which lay beneath both

[1] See *Church-Wardens' Accounts* (Somerset Record Soc.), pp. 1–48.
[2] Cf. the list of endowments mentioned p. 137 above, note 3.

these extremes was the same.[1]  To quote from the pious preambles of deeds by which chantries were ordained:

'It is befitting to encourage with affectionate sympathy the sincere devotion of those who desire to give of their worldly goods to the increase of divine worship, the multiplication of the number of them that minister in God's Holy Church, and the establishment of celebrations of masses which are the more profitable to Christ's faithful people unto salvation, inasmuch as in the same the King of Heaven is placated by mystic gifts, and remedies for sins are more easily obtained by asking.'[2]

And again:

'The Spirit of counsel from on high breathes into the devout hearts of God's worshippers the delights of good intent, out of whose abundance there follow healthful works of piety.  For what is so sweet in the memory, what more soothing in a clean heart, what sound more loud in God's ear, what more perfect thing dwells in the soul than the sacrifice to the glory of His name and in the spirit of purity, of the body of Christ, the Son of God, which was stretched forth for sinners upon the altar of the Cross?  Surely nought can be pondered in the breast that in this life can surpass a work so august and so holy.'[3]

Formal language, no doubt, turned neatly by clerks who prided themselves upon adding to their treasury of common forms new variations upon an old accustomed air.  But that air embodied a deep and widespread conviction: 'the spinners and the knitters

---

[1] *Salop Arch. Soc.* 3rd ser. x. 349.

[2] R. Zouche, fo. 75*b*. Ordination of the chantry of William Nesfeld in the chapel of Scotton near Knaresborough. 'Illius devocionem sinceram convenit pia mentis intencione fovere qui ad divini cultus augmentum multiplicandum numerum ministrancium in ecclesia sancta dei ac instituendum missarum celebraciones que eo christi fidelibus magis proficiunt ad salutem quo in ipsis rege celorum per mistica munera complacato peccatorum remedia facilius impetrantur sufficientem perpetuam porcionem de possescionibus [*sic*] et facultatibus suis, libertate cupit grativa (*rectius* gratuita, fo. 83) elargiri.'

[3] R. Melton, fo. 182, 182*b*. Ordination of a chantry at the altar of St. Mary in Rothwell Church, Yorks. 'Inspirat divinitus consilii spiritus in pia corda cultorum dei bone intencionis oblectamina ex quorum affluencia salubria insequuntur opera pietatis. Quid enim tam dulce in memoria quid suavius in mente pura aut quid sonorius in aure divina seu perfeccius in anima quam corpus christi dei in ara crucis pro peccatoribus extensum ad nominis sui gloriam in spiritu mundicie patri suo diebus singulis inmolare?  Profecto nichil in corde revolvi poterit quod tam celebre tamque sanctum opus excelleret in hac vita.' The same preamble occurs fo. 221*b*, for the chantry of St. John Baptist at Bailey in the parish of Mitton in Craven.

in the sun did use to chant it', and to the Shropshire labourer the light to which his penny went was his part in the general harmony which applauded the supreme act of Christian worship.[1]

In addition, however, to these more or less perpetual masses, there were the vast number of chantry masses depending upon bequests in wills and extending over periods of varying length from several years to a few days, trentals, month's minds, and anniversaries. With regard to these the most important point is the number of chaplains who were available for such duties. The study of wills reveals surprisingly large legacies for this purpose. There is probably none more imposing than that of Nicholas Hugate, provost of Beverley, who in 1338 left £200 for distribution for a year among sixty chaplains, to celebrate daily for his soul.[2] Large as this seems, it came to only 5 marks a year for each priest, and it is at least conceivable that the chaplains may have taken advantage of other bequests to combine more names with his in their masses. The higher clergy in their last wills spread their bequests lavishly over churches and monasteries.[3] It is certain that for these objects there was no

---

[1] The preamble of the charter by which in 1334 Adam Oxenhoppe founded a chantry in the Lady Chapel of Batley church is worth quoting (R. Melton, fo. 201): 'Omnibus christi fidelibus, etc., salutem in eo qui est salus omnium et in se sperancium refugium singulare. Mundi fallax et vana gloria de quo Ecclesiastes vanitas vanitatum et omnia vanitas oblectamentis huius caducis et vanis transactis temporibus ultra quam oporteret meum ut fateor animum occupavit dum terrena felicitate excecatus in agibilibus mundi frivolis et fugitivis delectatus sum secundum quod etas iuvenilis assolet et utitur diversimode in subiectis. Quamobrem ad instar apostoli dicentis cum essem parvulus sapiebam ut parvulus cum autem factus sum vir evacuavi ea que erant parvuli puerilia que exercui opitulante domino iam vir factus evacuare disposui ac talia imminencia precavenda pericula aliquod hoc sementis tempore proficui seminare quod veniens cum exultacione metere valeam in futurum.'

[2] Bev. Ch. A. ii. 122–5.

[3] Thus John Chitterne, canon of Salisbury and other churches, in 1419, left bequests for distribution among the poor of the parishes of Newchurch, I.W.; Steventon, Romsey, Timsbury, and Lackford, Hants; Ditchling and Hove, Sussex; Olveston, Glouc.; Chute, Fittleton, Horningsham, Tytherton, South Newton, Winterbourne Dauntsey, Swallowcliffe, Heytesbury, Imber, Figheldean, Newton Toney, Collingbourne Abbas (Kingston), Berwick St. John, and Minety, Wilts.; Winterborne Steepleton, Dorset; Compton Beauchamp, Berks.; and St. Nicholas, Guildford. Some of these churches formed the *corpus* of prebends held by the testator. Bequests to monasteries for obits were left to the cathedral priories of Canterbury and Bath, the abbots and convents of Hyde, Malmesbury, and Stanley, the abbesses and convents of Lacock, Romsey, Shaftesbury, Tarrant, and St. Mary, Winchester, the priors and convents of Bradenstoke, Breamore, Christ-

difficulty in securing unattached priests who made their living by such temporary duty. Ordination lists show what a number of clergy, promoted quickly from one order to another, were ordained in the course of a year; at Advent, the two Lenten ordinations, Trinity, and in September. Much surprise has often been expressed at the apparent insufficiency of their titles. How was it possible, for example, for poor nunneries to make themselves responsible for the maintenance of chaplains from whom there is no indication that service in the conventual church was required?[1] There is one simple answer. Religious houses always had at their disposal trust-money for chantries committed to them by testators. We have seen how the payment of the Newark chantry priests was entrusted to monasteries, and each of the houses so concerned would undoubtedly have money or securities in its keeping which would have enabled and required it to grant titles to applicants for orders. The wealth or poverty of such houses does not come into question, and we need not suspect that titles were given by a series of illicit pacts, though it is, of course, possible that a prudent convent might manage its business in this respect on the practical lines of a modern scholastic agency.

The unbeneficed chaplain, at any rate, ready to take payment for casual duty, was a familiar figure in medieval society. Reference has been made already to the unbeneficed parish priest or parochial curate, and we have seen how, in one small rural parish in the East Riding, when the post of parish priest was vacant, the offer of it was made by the rector to one after another of the chaplains who lived in the parish. It is obvious that in normal times there could have been little difficulty in finding such a priest. At this time, however, the 'second pestilence' was afflicting the district, and the rector was at last obliged, with the aid of the archbishop, to exercise compulsion upon a priest to undertake work which might well at such a

church, Easton [sic], Maiden Bradley and Marlborough, the prioress and convent of Kington St. Michael, and the rector and convent of Edington. The chapters of St. Paul's and Salisbury also had bequests, and provision was made for a chantry mass for ten years in Westminster Abbey in St. Edmund's chapel, where Sir Bernard Brocas, of whom Chitterne had been an executor, is buried (P.C.C. 44 Marche).

[1] Such a register as that of Bishop Sudbury of London (Cant. & York Soc.) supplies, in the ordination lists printed in vol. ii, numerous instances of titles granted by insignificant priories in Essex and farther afield.

time be dreary and unprofitable.[1] No doubt during the prevalence of plague the local chaplains found it possible to make a fair income out of the work that fell their way. For, while we fully recognize the ideal which guided this perpetual work of intercession at the altar, we must not forget that in the nature of human things it was pursued in an eminently business-like spirit. The whole round earth was every way bound by gold chains about the feet of God, but the gold was not a little tarnished. The life of the ordinary chantry chaplain in a parish church was not very busy. He had no cure of souls. Apart from his daily mass, the recitation at such a time as suited him of the office of the dead, *Dirige*, *Placebo* and the commendation of souls—that 'torrent of prayer'[2] which is the most noble and inspiring of all liturgical forms—he was under a general obligation to take part in the daily choir offices. He might be chosen to teach the elementary sciences, grammar, writing, and song, with some rudimentary arithmetic by means of the abacus, to the village children; and to some chantries this office was specifically attached, while in most churches it was probably executed with some degree of diligence.[3] It was not until long after the Reformation and the suppression of chantries that the 'pedagogue who teaches school in the church'[4] left his old quarters, and the grammar school above the south aisle of the collegiate church of Howden was still in use in recent years; while the grammar schools at Ewelme and Higham Ferrers still bear witness to the connexion between elementary education and the parish church. At Easter the duties of the chantry priest were augmented by the help which he was expected to afford in hearing the confessions of parishioners before their yearly communion.[5] But, when all is taken into account, he

---

[1] See p. 123 above, note 1.

[2] This phrase is applied by Charles Reade, *The Cloister and the Hearth*, ch. xciv, to the Lenten antiphon included in the Burial Service of the Book of Common Prayer. Noble as those solemn words are, the phrase is even more true of the farewell to the departing soul *Proficiscere anima Christiana* in the *Ordo Commendationis animae*.

[3] See A. F. Leach, *English Schools at the Reformation*, 1896, in which are printed the certificates (1546-8) of chantries with details of schools included, and his later work, *The Schools of Medieval England*, 1915.

[4] Shakespeare, *Twelfth Night*, III. ii. 83-4. At Dennington in Suffolk the chantry chapel at the east end of the south aisle was long used as a school, and the abacus used to teach arithmetic, and the wooden tray for sand in which the letters of the alphabet were formed are still preserved there.

[5] So at Doncaster (*Yorks. Chantry Surveys*, i. 175) 'The same chauntery [of St.

had plenty of time on his hands and not much with which to occupy it. Chantry-priests had to be reminded of the maxim *dum colitur Martha expellitur Maria*, 'while Martha is cherished, Mary is banished': so, among others, said Sir Robert Umfraville who in 1429 founded a chantry of two chaplains in his manorial chapel of Farnacres near Gateshead.[1] Visiting in the parish was discouraged as leading to loitering and gossip; country walks had more temptations than were afforded by the beauties of inanimate nature. These were precisely the dangers which Archbishop Thoresby feared when in 1363 he ordered the rural dean of Nottingham to inquire into the behaviour of the chantry-chaplains of St. Mary's Church. Public rumour and clamorous insinuation had brought to his ears the news that they said their masses as early in the morning as they could, without attention to their customary duty of beginning them after the offertory at the parish mass. Such premature haste beguiled worshippers from the parish mass and diverted to the chantry-priests' offerings that were the vicar's due. When their masses were over, it was uncertain how they spent their time: it was to be feared that they went paying calls and strolling about where they pleased, and, while they asserted that they said their daily office, it was not in church, and there was strong suspicion that its recitation was mutilated and syncopated.[2]

The conduct of the Nottingham chantry-priests might have been less open to criticism had some provision been made for their association as a body of priests connected by some

Nicholas] is within the sayd church. The necessitie is that there are mm howslyng people and above within the sayd paryshe, wherof the sayd incumbent and other vij prystes, now resiaunt in the sayd churche, can skant here the confessions of the sayd parochians from the begynnyng of Lente unto Palme Sunday; and then ministre the blessed sacrement all the sayd weke, with other requisite besines to be doon in the sayd churche.'

[1] *Inspeximus* and confirmation 7 May 1437 of the founder's ordinance dated 26 Aug. 1429 (*C.P.R.* 1436–42, p. 53). See a licence granted 27 June 1428 (ibid. 1422–9, p. 454), previous to the licence granted by the bishop of Durham, 20 Mar. 1428–9.

[2] R. Thores., fo. 254*b*. It was complained that the chantry-priests 'seorsum in cameris campis et locis aliis minus congruis evagantur et inibi matutinas et alias horas canonicas absque devocione debita dicunt quinimmo cincopant et transcurrunt et ut verisimiliter credi potest cum sufficienti testimonio careant in hac parte quidam eorum horas prorsus transiliunt et omittunt', &c. The dean was enjoined to warn them to be present daily at matins and the canonical hours, especially on Sundays and feasts of nine lessons, and not to begin their daily masses 'nisi prius ad prefacionem misse parochialis in dicta ecclesia sit processum'.

corporate bond. At Newark, early in the fourteenth century, some of the chantry-priests were lodged in a common dwelling-house given by a lay benefactor,[1] and, although there was no further attempt at incorporation, Archbishop Thoresby gave directions for their attendance in choir on feasts of nine lessons in a common habit like the choral habit worn by the vicars of Southwell.[2] It is rather surprising that nothing further was done in a church where there were so many chaplains; but, where each chaplain was supported by a separate endowment, it is obvious that there were difficulties in the task of bringing them all together under a system which involved a common life in one establishment, with shares in a common fund and under the presidency of one of their number. On the other hand, the process of founding collegiate bodies of chantry-priests in parish churches on this system became a marked feature of the church life of the fourteenth and fifteenth centuries. Some attempt has already been made to describe how the communities of secular clergy which existed in many churches at the time of the Norman Conquest developed in two separate directions. Some acquired constitutions which approximated closely to those of the secular cathedral churches: others were transformed into houses of canons regular, in obedience to the strong movement which imposed a monastic complexion upon the canonical life. Thus, during the reign of Stephen the canons of the free chapel of St. Oswald at Gloucester, a possession of the see of York, took advantage of the disturbed condition of their neighbourhood to abandon their church and live upon the estates which formed their several prebends. Arch-

[1] The house is described in the covenant made 15 May 1326 between the prior and convent of St. Katherine, Lincoln, and William Duraunt and Isabel his wife, for the foundation and maintenance of a chantry at the altar of St. James in Newark Church (R. Melton, ff. 366b, 367: see also *Thor. Soc.* xvii. 70).

[2] R. Thores., fo. 247. 'Cum igitur in ecclesia parochiali de Newerk nostre dioceseos sint capellani perpetui per nos et predecessores nostros in cantariis suis quibus intitulati existunt canonice instituti [eleven names follow, serving eleven chantries at six altars] continue celebrantes nos archiepiscopus predictus cultum divinum in ecclesiis nobis subditis augere sinceris affectibus cupientes recensita humili postulacione parochianorum dicte ecclesie de Newerk predictis capellanis ac eorum successoribus qui pro tempore fuerint in cantariis predictis et aliis in eadem ecclesia imperpetuum creandis canonice instituendis ut decetero in omnibus festis novem leccionum nigris amiciis cum superpelliciis mundis more vicariorum in ecclesia nostra collegiata Suthwell. libere vti valeant auctoritate nostra pontificali specialem concedimus facultatem.'

bishop Murdac, however, a rigorous Cistercian, recalled them from dispersion and converted St. Oswald's into a priory of Austin canons.[1] At the same time, there are instances of efforts to found secular minsters during the twelfth and thirteenth centuries in which the old principle of the common life and the common fund play some part. A genuine example is the college of four priests established by Henry of Blois, the famous bishop of Winchester, at his manor of Marwell.[2] During the thirteenth century, among new colleges which cannot be placed with colleges of chantry-chaplains, there are nevertheless colleges of a transitional type, such as Wingham in Kent and Glasney in Cornwall.[3] In these, as was also the case with Marwell, the canonries and prebends were distinct benefices, but the head of the chapter received the title of provost, a title which definitely connotes financial management, and which in the greater churches was applied to the officer elected from among the residentiary canons every year to administer the common property.[4] When, at the beginning of the fourteenth century, John of Pontoise, bishop of Winchester, founded his chapel of St. Elizabeth of Hungary at the gate of Wolvesey Castle, it was for a provost and six chaplains; and, although each of the chaplaincies was a benefice in the bishop's collation, yet the college was definitely a chantry foundation for residents.[5]

The early colleges of Oxford and Cambridge, although primarily places of study, nevertheless cannot be dissociated from chantry foundations and are among the earliest examples of fully developed organizations of residential colleges in which a body of priest-fellows were placed under the rule of an officer

---

[1] See *B. & G.A.S.* xliii. 98, 99.          [2] See *Mon.* vi (iii), 1343–4.

[3] For the ordination of the college of Wingham, 18 Feb. 1286–7, with relevant documents, see *R. Pecham*, 55–67. The ordination is also printed in *Mon.* vi (iii), 1341–3. The ordination of Glasney is in *R. Brones.*, pp. 94–5: see also the charter of Bishop Quivil (18 Dec. 1288) for the appropriation of the church of St. Allen by the college, from an *inspeximus* (*C.P.R.* 1313–17, p. 280).

[4] At Lincoln in 1437 one of the chaplains of the works chantry complained of the confusion caused by the union of the separate offices of provost of the common fund and provost of the works, which defrauded the chantry-priests of their salaries (*B. & W.* ii (ii), 406). For the provost of Newarke College, Leicester, see Thompson, op. cit. The 'provost of Wells' was actually provost of the fifteenfold prebend of Combe, an office similar to that of the four provosts in the church of Chartres, each of whom administered the revenues of a divided prebend.

[5] The ordination is in *R. Pont.*, 128–33. The copy in *Mon.* vi. (iii), 1339–41, is from an *inspeximus* in the patent rolls.

elected from their number, admitted by the ordinary who is
the visitor, and entitled provost, master, warden, rector, president, or principal. Indeed, as time went on, the chantry
element was strongly emphasized in these colleges. Not only
the name of All Souls, but the sculpture of the souls in purgatory above the gateway, recall the pious object of the founder.
When Bishop Alcock founded Jesus College at Cambridge in
the buildings of the suppressed nunnery of St. Radegund, the
licence which he obtained is indistinguishable from a licence
for a chantry college with a school attached.[1] Further, in the
early part of the fourteenth century, owners of castles and
manor-houses began with some frequency to endow chantries
of several priests in their chapels. There was, for example,
Roger Martival's chapel at Noseley in Leicestershire, with its
warden and two priests.[2] Guy Beauchamp, earl of Warwick,
endowed a chantry of eight chaplains at Elmley Castle;[3] John
Beauchamp endowed one of five at Stoke-under-Hamdon in
Somerset;[4] Sir John Lercedekne founded a college of an archpriest and five chaplains in his manor of Haccombe in Devon;[5]
and Roger Beler, the judge who was murdered by a body of
lawless neighbours on the highroad, founded a manorial chapel
of a warden and twelve chaplains at Kirkby-on-Wreak near
Melton Mowbray.[6]

In the last instance the several chaplaincies were founded as

---

[1] *C.P.R.* 1494–1509, p. 72. The foundation was for a master, six fellows, and a
certain number of scholars to be instructed in grammar, to pray and celebrate
divine service daily for the king and queen, the king's mother and children, the
bishop of Ely, and the soul of the king's father. The grammar-school, with its
hired master, formed no part of the immediate duty of master and fellows. A.
Gray, *Hist. Jesus Coll.*, p. 48, calls the governing body of Alcock's foundation 'a
claustral community of student priests, not concerned with education', and so it
remained under the body of statutes granted by Bishop Stanley in 1514.

[2] See p. 125 above.

[3] Licence for endowment 11 Aug. 1308 (*C.P.R.* 1307–13, 136). See Nash, i. 383.

[4] Licence 17 Oct. 1303 (*C.P.R.* 1301–7, p. 161). The ordination of the chantry,
4 Oct. 1304 (*R. Drok.*, p. 292), is printed in full by Collinson, *Hist. Somerset*, iii.
316–18.

[5] Licences 8 and 18 Nov. 1335 (*C.P.R.* 1334–8, pp. 183, 197). For the *ordinatio
archipresbiteratus* 8 Dec. 1337, see *R. Grand.* ii. 852–5.

[6] *Inspeximus* and confirmation 15 Oct. 1319 of the founder's deed of endowment and ordinances (*C.P.R.* 1317–21, pp. 392, 393). Translations of these with
other documents from the Lincoln episcopal registers are given in *Leices. Arch.
Soc.* xvi. 129–212. See also *Mon.* vi (i), 511–14, where the founder's ordinance is
printed from an *inspeximus* by Richard II.

freehold benefices, and the statutes contained careful directions with regard to their patronage. But the obvious difficulty of combining a number of presentative benefices with freehold tenure into a single organism of the type desired was proved by practice; and after forty years of trial and failure the chapel in 1359 was turned into a priory of Austin canons. Meanwhile, in more than one instance, parish churches had been converted into collegiate churches of chantry-chaplains, a work in which the foremost place was taken by distinguished and wealthy clerks. The colleges of a rector and six chaplains at Lowthorpe in the East Riding founded by John of Heslerton in 1333,[1] of a provost and twelve chaplains at Cotterstock in Northamptonshire, founded by John Giffard in 1337,[2] and of a master and six chaplain-fellows at Sibthorpe in Nottinghamshire, founded by Thomas Sibthorpe, which, after a gradual process of endowment, reached its final form in 1342,[3] were all established on similar lines. The cure of souls of the parish was vested in the head of the college; the church was appropriated to the college. The one freehold benefice was the headship, under its various names, of the foundation: the chaplain-fellows were admitted by the head after consultation with the remaining chaplains, and held their offices without any security but their good behaviour. It is true that here and there founders still provided for presentative fellowships in collegiate parish churches. When the last Lord Thweng of Kilton, just before the Black Death, obtained the conversion of the church of Kirkleatham in Cleveland, of which he was rector, into a college, all the twelve chaplains were duly presented and instituted.[4] But this college was stillborn and nothing more was done; and later the only conspicuous example of this practice was John Pyel's college of St. Peter at Irthlingborough, where it continued until the suppression of colleges and

---

[1] Licence 25 Jan. 1332-3 (*C.P.R.* 1331-4, p. 413). Ordinances dated 26 Mar. 1333 were confirmed by letters patent 3 May following (ibid. 426-8).

[2] Licence 2 Sept. 1337 (*C.P.R.* 1334-8, p. 515). See further licences 9 May 1338, &c. (ibid. 1338-40, pp. 61-2, &c.). See also App. V.

[3] See App. V.

[4] See R. Zouche, ff. 161*b*-163*b*. Ten chaplains were instituted 19 June 1348: the remaining two 9 Mar. 1348-9. The first chaplain died in 1348-9 and the fifth died later in the year; their places were filled 12 Feb. and 31 July respectively; but no further institutions occur. There is no licence for the foundation upon the patent rolls.

chantries.[1]    At Irthlingborough, however, the somewhat ambitious design of the founder gave the clergy the title of dean and canons.

The erection of parochial into collegiate churches was the most general method employed by founders of such colleges; and, while Bishop Grandisson gave the outward semblance of a small cathedral establishment to the college which he established at Ottery St. Mary,[2] there is really little but outward forms to differentiate it from the college which Sir Guy Brien founded at Slapton in the same diocese in 1369.[3]  In both instances a parish church was appropriated to the services of a college in which the parochial cure was vested.  But we must also take into account the extra-parochial colleges founded in chapels built for the purpose in connexion with the cathedral and the older collegiate establishments, St. George's at Windsor, St. Stephen's at Westminster, and the New College at Leicester, all of which were founded upon the older model.  On the other hand, the college of nine chaplains founded by Thomas, duke of Gloucester, in his castle at Pleshy, though doubtless suggested by the example of his father and his cousin of Lancaster in thus augmenting the dignity of their residences, was definitely a college of resident chantry-priests.[4]  And although Fotheringhay, of which more later, was eventually associated with a parish church, the original idea, as contemplated by another son of Edward III, Edmund of Langley, was that of a college in a castle chapel.[5]

[1] See 'The Early History of the College of Irthlingborough', *A.A.S.R.P.* xxxv. 267–92: also *Mon.* vi (iii), 1384–5.

[2] Licence 15 Dec. 1337 (*C.P.R.* 1334–8, p. 569), printed with other documents in *Mon.* vi (iii), 1346–8. See the *Ordinacio primaria* of the college, 22 Jan. 1337–8, with ratification by Clement VI, 27 June 1342, printed in *R. Grand.* i. 121–30. The statutes, issued at length 29 Sept. 1339, are printed in Oliver, pp. 268–75, and with elaborate comment by Dalton, *The Collegiate Church of Ottery St. Mary*, pp. 133–259, who also printed the *Ordinacio primaria* and other relevant documents.

[3] Licences 26 July and 29 Aug. 1369 (*C.P.R.* 1367–70, pp. 299, 322). See *Mon.* vi (iii), 1351–2. There is no ordinance in the Exeter registers and the first institution to the *ministeriatus* of the parish as a separate benefice occurs in 1382 (*R. Brant.* i. 76), but a document relating to endowments treats the college as an existing foundation in 1374, with William Batokeweye as its head (ibid. i. 145); but the first institution to the rectory of the chantry is in 1375 (ibid. i. 41).

[4] Licence 25 Jan. 1393–4 (*C.P.R.* 1391–6, p. 363), printed, with another of 3 Feb. in *Mon.* vi (iii), 1393–4. The foundation was in the parish church: there was a free chapel in the castle. See Newcourt, ii. 469–72.

[5] *Mon.* vi (iii), 1411–15, where the letters patent for foundation and endowment,

We must distinguish again, between the collegiate church, whether parochial or extra-parochial, and colleges which were merely founded in a church. The most obvious examples of these are found in cathedral churches, where the colleges of vicars-choral and chantry-priests, like the Mountrey College at Wells and St. William's College at York, were bodies with their own endowments and buildings. In churches where there were many chantry-priests we sometimes find them incorporated as a college, usually towards the close of the Middle Ages. This happened, for example, at All Saints', Northampton, in 1460,[1] and the church has therefore been reckoned sometimes as collegiate. But the government of the church, which was appropriated to St. Andrew's Priory and had its own vicar, was not changed, and the college was merely an organization attached to it, in fact, a fulfilment of the idea which, as has been said earlier, seems to have been entertained at Newark in the fourteenth century. Or, again, a collegiate chantry of several chaplains might be founded in a parish church without any attempt to appropriate the church to it, as at Wappenham in Northamptonshire, where Gilbert Middleton, archdeacon of Northampton, founded such a chantry in 1323.[2] Such chantries of more than one priest are common, but the smaller chantries very seldom assumed the title of college, though technically they had a right to it. At Towcester, however, in 1448, the executors of William Sponne, archdeacon of Norfolk, who had been rector of the church, founded a chantry of two chaplains which by his wish was known as the college of Towcester. Here one of the objects was educational and the secondary chaplain was charged with the duty of keeping a free school.[3]

The three main types of chantry college are well illustrated

18 Dec. 1412, and a second licence of 5 Aug. 1415 (*C.P.R.* 1413–16, pp. 349–50) are given. See also 'The Statutes of the Collegiate Church of St. Mary and All Saints, Fotheringhay' (*A.J.* lxxv. 241–309).

[1] Licence 13 Mar. 1459–60 (*C.P.R.* 1452–61, p. 601). The college included the vicar and an unspecified number of stipendiary priests, occasionally amounting to sixteen. See Serjeantson, *Hist. of the Church of All Saints, Northampton*, 1901, pp. 67–72.

[2] Licence 5 Apr. 1323, in an indefinite form and including licence of appropriation to a body unspecified (*C.P.R.* 1321–4, p. 272). The founder subsequently issued a charter and ordinances for six chaplains 9 Apr. 1327, confirmed by letters patent 24 Apr. following (ibid. 1327–30, pp. 107, 108; *R. Burg.* i, ff. 198–201).

[3] Licence 17 Nov. 1448 (*C.P.R.* 1446–52, p. 204).

by three foundations in that part of Shropshire which was in the diocese of Lichfield, all belonging to the first half of the fifteenth century. The collegiate chapel of Battlefield was founded and built in 1406 by a clerk named Roger Ive at Adbrighton Hussey, north of Shrewsbury, on the site of the battle fought there between Henry IV and the Percies in 1403.[1] In 1410 the parish church of St. Bartholomew at Tong, near Shifnal, was converted by the patron, Dame Isabel Pembridge, into a collegiate church of a warden and four other priests.[2] Thirdly, in 1442 Thomas Draper, an inhabitant of the small town of Newport, founded a college of a warden and four other priests to serve a guild chantry attached to the parish church.[3] The constitution of these colleges was similar, with a warden or master as the head of each; but the first was founded to serve an extra-parochial chapel, the second absorbed the government of the parish church in which it was founded, and the third was attached to a parish church without affecting the position of its incumbent.

Again, in the valley of the Nene in Northamptonshire there were three parish churches, already mentioned, which became collegiate. These were Cotterstock, a comparatively early foundation, St. Peter's at Irthlingborough, completed early in the fifteenth century, and Fotheringhay, which received its final form in 1410. Of these, as we have seen, Irthlingborough has a constitution allied to that of the older type of college. In 1425 Archbishop Chichele founded a fourth college in the same district at Higham Ferrers, a parish adjoining Irthlingborough on the opposite side of the river. This consisted of a warden or dean and seven fellows. Although the foundation deed was delivered in the parish church, and although the parish church

---

[1] See *Salop Arch. Soc.* 3rd ser. iii. 171–284. Licence for the alienation of the site by Richard Huse to Roger Ive and another chaplain was granted 28 Oct. 1406 (*C.P.R.* 1405–8, p. 263). The college of a master and seven other chaplains was founded under licence of 17 Mar. 1408–9 (ibid. 1408–13, p. 59). See also ibid. 173–4, where the foundation is specified as for a warden and six other chaplains. It was finally fixed at a master or warden and five other chaplains: see royal charter of 27 May 1410, printed in *Mon.* vi (iii), 1426–7, from *inspeximus* of 17 Nov. 1425 (*C.P.R.* 1422–9, p. 321).

[2] Licence 25 Nov. 1410 (*C.P.R.* 1408–13, p. 280), printed in *Mon.* vi (iii), 1401–3.

[3] Licence 29 Mar. 1442 (*C.P.R.* 1441–5, pp. 64, 112). The second form is printed in *Mon. u.s.* 1438.

came under the control of the college, yet the arrangements were quite exceptional. The church had been appropriated in 1355 to the New College at Leicester, whose rights, including the presentation of the vicar, were maintained in it. Chichele's foundation included a bedehouse and a grammar school, which remain in the churchyard and afford a close parallel to the similar arrangement of bedehouse and school in connexion with the church of Ewelme. The collegiate buildings, however, were at some distance from the church, built round a quadrangle with their own chapel. Chichele reserved the appointment of the master to himself and his successors in the see of Canterbury, but secured for the college a status in the parish church by arranging that the master should be nominated to the dean and canons of the New College for presentation to the vicarage and for institution by the bishop of Lincoln.[1] To this arrangement there is no exact parallel: the nearest instance, perhaps, is that of the older collegiate church at Leicester, the deans and canons of which were instituted by the abbot of Leicester; while the abbot, as proprietor of the church, presented the parochial vicar, who stood outside the collegiate body, for institution.

These details illustrate the variety of the constitutions of chantry colleges. Among collegiate churches may be mentioned the group of small foundations in Norfolk, of which the most noteworthy was Edmund Gonville's college of Rushworth (now Rushford),[2] the foundation of four priests at St. Michael Penkivel on the Fal, near Truro,[3] and the college of seven chaplains at Bunbury in Cheshire, founded by the famous

[1] Licence of foundation granted 2 May 1422 (*C.P.R.* 1416–22, p. 441; printed in *Mon.* u.s. 1425–6). See *inspeximus* of this and other documents relating to the foundation and endowment, 7 Nov. 1427 (*C.P.R.* 1422–9, pp. 472–4), from which it appears that the actual foundation of the college took place 28 Aug. 1425.

[2] See Blomefield, i. 287–90. The foundation was for a chantry of two priests, by licence 15 May 1341 (*C.P.R.* 1340–3, p. 188). The master and chaplains appear in the licence for the alienation of the advowson of the church and its appropriation to them, 28 Jan. 1347–8 (ibid. 1348–50, p. 19). Two further licences of 13 Rich. II are printed in *Mon.* u.s. 1386, only one of which (25 Jan. 1389–90) is in *C.P.R.* (1388–92, p. 176). The ordinances for the master and four chaplains, issued by Bishop Percy of Norwich 14 July 1360, are printed in *Mon.* u.s. 1386–7.

[3] Founded by Sir John Trejago, lord of the manor of Fentongollan. The head of the chantry was called archpriest. See the *Ordinacio archipresbiteratus*, 7 Feb. 1319–20, in *R. Stap.*, pp. 339–41, and *inspeximus* and confirmation of the same, 4 June 1320 (*C.P.R.* 1317–21, pp. 454–5).

captain Sir Hugh Calveley, whose tomb remains, surrounded by its iron hearse, in the middle of the chancel.[1] Although it is not usually reckoned among colleges, the chapel of Chaddesden, near Derby, is an excellent example of a small church rebuilt in the fourteenth century in consequence of the foundation of a chantry of three chaplains.[2] But the total number of such churches is considerable, and, from Lingfield in Surrey,[3] Shottesbrook in Berkshire,[4] Archbishop Kempe's college of St. Gregory and St. Martin at Wye in Kent,[5] and the college in St. Lawrence Poultney in London,[6] to the two collegiate churches of Cumberland, Greystoke,[7] and the latest of all such churches to be turned to this use, Kirkoswald on the Eden,[8] few English counties were without some foundation of the kind. The oddest, perhaps, was at Kirkby Overblow in Yorkshire, on the north bank of the Wharfe. Here in 1362 executors appointed by Henry Percy obtained the appropriation of the church to a body of priests known as the college of Kirkby Overblow, of whom one only, the rector, was resident in the church. Of the other four, one served an altar in York Minster, while three resided as chantry-priests in the chapel of Alnwick Castle.[9]

In the two famous colleges of St. Mary at Winchester and Eton the colleges of warden and provost and fellows became

[1] Licence for foundation 12 Mar. 1386–7 (*C.P.R.* 1385–9, p. 310). See also ibid., p. 444, 8 May 1388. See Ormerod, ii. 256–8.

[2] Licences for endowment granted 15 and 20 July 1355 (*C.P.R.* 1354–8, pp. 268–9, 272).

[3] Licence for foundation 16 Mar. 1430–1, for a master, five chaplains, four clerks, and thirteen poor (*C.P.R.* 1429–36, pp. 146, 147).

[4] See letters patent 8 Apr. 1337 (*C.P.R.* 1334–8, p. 424). For a master and five chaplains.

[5] Licence for foundation 27 Feb. 1431–2 (*C.P.R.* 1429–36, pp. 189–90, 218), printed in *Mon.* vi (iii), 1430–1. For a provost and an unspecified number of chaplains.

[6] The foundation of a chantry of seven priests in honour of Corpus Christi and St. John Baptist was about 1333: see papal letters of 24 Aug. in that year (*C.P.L.* ii. 383). See also letters patent 16 Jan. 1334–5 (*C.P.R.* 1334–8, p. 60). The number of chaplains had been increased to thirteen by 1 July 1345 (ibid. 1343–5, p. 489).

[7] Licence for foundation 30 Apr. 1358 (*C.P.R.* 1358–61, p. 46). It did not take effect and was renewed to Ralph, Lord Greystoke, the son of the founder, 8 Nov. 1374 (ibid. 1374–7, p. 27).

[8] Founded before 5 Dec. 1523 for a warden and five chaplains: see *L. & P. H. VIII*, iii (ii), 1499 (no. 3606).

[9] Licence for foundation 1 Feb. 1362–3 (*C.P.R.* 1361–4, p. 301). The chantry-priests at Alnwick, holding their endowments as members of this college, were admitted by the archbishop of York.

somewhat overshadowed by the fame of the schools attached to them; and here we come again to the colleges in which definite provisions were made for education.[1]  When Ralph, Lord Cromwell, Henry VI's treasurer, founded the college of Tattershall in 1440, he transformed the parish church, just outside the precincts of the castle which he so imposingly remodelled, into a collegiate church, with special provisions for almshouses and teaching;[2] and it is not at all improbable that the project of a school in close connexion with the college was suggested by the contemporary action of Henry VI at Eton.  The associates whose names are united with Cromwell's in the foundation were persons of high importance, and, when he made his last will at Collyweston in 1451, he appointed as his chief executor Bishop Waynflete, whose part in the early history of Eton and King's College is well known, and to whom the completion of Cromwell's design at Tattershall is probably due.  In view of the multitude of chantry masses said for a single person, it is worth remarking that Cromwell left money for three thousand masses to be said for his soul, a thousand of the Holy Trinity, under whose invocation Tattershall Church was dedicated, a thousand of Our Lady, and a thousand of Requiem.[3]  How the school at Tattershall prospered we do not know; but the need of an Eton or Winchester for that corner of England was felt in the following century, when Henry VIII established a college and school in the dissolved monastery of Thornton. Neither this nor the similar foundation which took the place of the abbey of Burton-on-Trent had much more than a nominal and temporary existence; but the history of Christ College in the Black Friars at Brecon was more fortunate.[4]

---

[1] Licence for foundation of Winchester College 6 Oct. 1382 (*C.P.R.* 1381–5, p. 186). The foundation of Eton is dated 11 Oct. 1440; the charter of endowment followed 25 Mar. 1441 (*Mon.* vi (iii), 1434–7: cf. *C.P.R.* 1436–41, p. 556).

[2] Licence for foundation 14 July 1439, for a master, six chaplains, six clerks, and poor (*C.P.R.* 1436–41, p. 292), printed in *Mon.* vi (iii) 1432–3.  See also papal confirmation 16 Oct. 1441 (*C.P.L.* ix, 159–65).

[3] Cromwell's will (R. Ched., fo. 36) is briefly summarized by Nicolas, i. 276, and with some more detail, by Gibbons, *Early Lincoln Wills*, p. 182.

[4] The abbey of Burton-on-Trent was reconstituted as a college with a dean and four prebendaries, 14 Aug. 1541 (*L. & P. H. VIII*, xvi. 536 [g. 1135/9]).  A similar reconstitution of Thornton Abbey took place 12 Jan. 1541–2 (ibid. xvii. 28 [g. 71/8].  The college at Brecon, founded by letters patent 19 Jan. 1540–1 (ibid. xvi. 241–2 [g. 503/30]), was formed by the translation of the college of Abergwili, near Carmarthen, to the Dominican friary of Brecon.  The college of Thornton

One of the most interesting of late chantry establishments, in which the educational idea was very prominent, was Jesus College at Rotherham, founded in 1480 by Thomas Rotherham, archbishop of York.[1] The chantry-priests of the parish church up to that time lived in whatever lodgings they could get, with obvious risk to their conduct and reputation; and Rotherham thought it well that they should lodge together in a single house. Their accommodation, however, was a secondary matter to the primary object of the college, which was the provision of a school for a rough and uncultivated neighbourhood; and the establishment, presided over by a provost, included three masters, one of grammar, one of writing, and a third of music. The college owed its dedication to the popularity of the devotion to the name of Jesus, and there is reason for thinking that, when John Alcock, Rotherham's friend and successor in the see of Rochester, founded Jesus College at Cambridge, it was partly under the influence of Rotherham's example.[2] With such foundations in view, the contribution of the chantry system to later medieval learning cannot be overlooked; for at the root of that type of college which has so impressed itself upon our minds that to most people the word college is synonymous with an educational institution there lay the conviction of the duty of offering up masses and suffrages for the souls of benefactors as an essential factor in the collegiate life. No more striking illustration of this principle exists than the famous pictures of the *alumni* of the two colleges of St. Mary of Winton, John Chaundler, Thomas Bekynton, Andrew Holes, and the rest of that illustrious group, united in the commemoration of the founder who had given them 'wher-with to scoleye'.[3]

survived until the dissolution of colleges and chantries: see the certificate printed *A.A.S.R.P.* xxxvii. 251–3.
    [1] Licence for foundation 28 July 1480 (*C.P.R.* 1476–85, p. 209), printed in *Mon.* vi (iii), 1440, 1441.          [2] See Gray, *Hist. Jesus Coll.*, pp. 29 sqq.
    [3] See *Arch.* liii. 229–32 (T. F. Kirby, 'On Some Fifteenth-century Drawings of Winchester; New College, Oxford', &c.). One of these drawings represents Wykeham seated, holding his colleges in his hands. On either side of him is an archbishop, Chichele of Canterbury and Thomas Cranley of Dublin, next each of whom is a bishop, Bekynton of Bath and Wells, and Waynflete of Winchester. The lower part of the drawing is occupied by seven figures, each marked with his Christian name and cathedral preferment, viz. Thomas [Chaundeler], chancellor of Wells; Andreas [Holes], archdeacon of Wells; Johannes [Norton], archdeacon of Berks.; Hugo [Sugar], treasurer of Wells; Johannes [Selot], archdeacon of Cornwall; Ricardus [Andrew], dean of York; and Willelmus [Say], dean of St. Paul's.

Statutes of chantry colleges exist in some quantity, many of which are still unprinted. They have a strong family likeness, as is natural; for the life in one college differed in no important respect from life in another. The ritual and liturgical directions which they embody are often elaborate. The Sibthorpe statutes, for example, were drawn up with great care and with the special object of incorporating the chantries already founded by Thomas Sibthorpe in the church which he began by enlarging and ended by rebuilding. In these, with those which he added later, we have the most detailed provision for the varying number of tapers to be burned according to the season at the high altar, at the altars in the aisles of the nave, and before the rood, fully rivalling on the great feasts the expenditure of light which is condemned by modern purists as incorrect and appropriate only to churches that put out their fullest strength for harvest festivals. Equally minute are the ordinances for the collects to be said at special services and seasons, for the votive masses on weekdays, and for the performance of obits with their accompanying distributions to members of colleges and to the poor. Choir services were to be recited daily as part of the duty of the college, and the intention of the founders was that they should be said as regularly as in a monastery. The custom, however, prevailed of saying the lesser choir offices by accumulation without strict regard to the hour: terce, sext, and nones were recited together at the end of the morning, and, after the meal which followed, the afternoon was free for recreation until it was time for vespers and supper. In such rural places as Sibthorpe, still an extremely remote spot in a network of by-roads, or Fotheringhay, there can have been little to do after the services of the morning were over, and during the afternoon hours there was plenty of opportunity for considering the rival claims of Martha and Mary. There was no provision for contemplation or manual work, and such daily educational tasks as were incumbent upon the chaplains of a normal chantry college were slight. One of the objects of such colleges was to give a definite organization to the life of the chantry-priests and to provide against the negligent and slipshod way of living into which they might easily fall. The system was to some extent a revival of the old canonical life followed by priests grouped together in minsters, and there was a strong superficial likeness between a chantry college and a house of Austin canons, a likeness all the more noticeable at a time when canons regular had grown lax in monastic observances. At the same time, chantry colleges observed no rule but their statutes, and it was impossible to force a monastic life upon secular clergy. They had their common hall, they lived upon their statutory allowances from the common fund; but they had no common dormitory, no chapter-house, no claustral observances. Their residence within college, however, was strictly enforced, and at supper-time the gate of the quad-rangle was closed. Perhaps their most distinctive custom, in which all members joined together, was their nightly meeting after compline, when, gathered beneath the tower while the great bell swung overhead, warning the country-side that the college was at its prayers, they sang *Salve Regina* and uttered their last suffrages for the souls of the faithful before dispersing for the night.[1]

Here and there, as in the range of buildings occupied by Archbishop Courtenay's chantry-priests at Maidstone or in Chetham's hospital at Manchester, the habitation of the chaplains who served, under their warden, the collegiate church founded by Thomas Lord La Warre, rector and lord of the manor of Manchester, we can picture to ourselves the life for which such places were intended.[2] It must be owned, however, that priests bound down to very limited duties, with-out parochial work or cure of souls, save in so far as the cure might be deputed by the warden to one or other of the chaplains, engaged in the sole business of saying masses, attending the choir services, and putting in an appearance at obits, found their spare time hang heavy on their hands. Visitation reports show that their leisure was not infrequently spent in bickering. At Fotheringhay the college was divided into parties by the misdeeds of an overbearing and pilfering steward, who supplied his wife, family, and friends with victuals for which he sent his maidservant.[3] At Irthlingborough one of the fellows attacked

---

[1] See App. V.

[2] Licence for foundation 22 May 1421 (*C.P.R.* 1415–22, p. 366), printed in *Mon.* vi (iii), 1424. See Raines, *The Rectors of Manchester and the Wardens of the Collegiate Church of that Town*, 2 vols. (Chatham Soc., N.S., v and vi), 1885.

[3] *Linc. Vis.* ii. 92–107. This was in 1438. Although in 1442 this source of trouble had gone, the two parties in the college were still active (ibid. 108–12).

another on the steps of the college hall, haling him about by the hairs of his head.[1] If there were unsatisfactory monasteries at this period, secular communities got out of hand even more easily, and the prolonged discord which prevailed in the cathedral church of Lincoln cannot have failed to make its baneful influence felt in smaller secular foundations. In these matters, however, we may distinguish more severely than the normal man of the fifteenth century between profession and conduct; and though no doubt unpunctuality, talking in church, and strolling about the nave of the church during divine service were not uncommon faults of those engaged in the high and holy task of perpetual intercession, yet the main object which was in the founders' minds was accomplished. The tasks which they had enjoined were performed, and, compared with that, the negligence and *incuria* of celebrants and officiants were of purely secondary importance.

In conclusion, we should not forget that the foundation of a chantry college was a long and expensive process, not lightly to be undertaken. The procedure through the ordinary diocesan channels was long and intricate; the appropriation of a parish church to a college meant a readjustment of existing arrangements by which a bishop might lose, especially in the matter of sequestrations, for which the bishop would require substantial indemnities. Certain founders, anticipating difficulties with the diocesan, went directly to a higher source and obtained a bull from the pope entrusting the fulfilment of their purpose to executors. This, however, was not always successful. The story of the foundation of the college of Irthlingborough is a curious instance of the employment of papal protection against the unreadiness of a diocesan to act.[2] The whole tale is too complicated to tell here; but from the first bull which John Pyel obtained in 1375 nearly eighteen years passed before the college actually came into being, and by that time the hindrances which the bishop of Lincoln seems to have put in the way had led to the removal of his control from the proceedings, and the existence of the college was actually decreed and its statutes promulgated by a papal executor from another diocese. Even so, so much expense had been incurred that it

[1] Ibid. ii. 162.
[2] See p. 150 above, note 1.

was not until 1415 that it was possible to get the college into full working order.

On the other hand, whatever may have been the drawbacks of the chantry college, it was an organization which fulfilled its ends better than the old colleges of the cathedral type, whose original purpose was obscured by the non-residence of canons and the tendency to treat its benefices as perquisites of government clerks. The transformation which in 1455 Bishop Carpenter effected in the old and moribund college of Westbury-upon-Trym, establishing a body of dean, subdean, and priest-fellows instead of the previously existing dean and five canons, and erecting the residence of which the gateway and part of the quadrangle still remain, shows that in the opinion of a prudent and active bishop the chantry college had its practical uses.[1] And, in the reign of Henry VIII, the cathedral bodies established under the new foundation were modelled on the lines, not of the old secular cathedral churches, but on those of the later type of college in which the authority of a single head was supreme, and the number of members was limited according to the resources of the common fund. In practice the cathedrals of the new foundation departed considerably from the ideals of the chantry college; but a comparison of their statutes with those of any college of the type will clearly indicate the source from which the first were derived.[2]

---

[1] See ordinances, dated 13 June 1455, and papal confirmation, 25 Sept. following (*C.P.L.* xi. 229–32).

[2] See introd. to *Durham Stat.*

# VI

## THE MONASTERIES

IN the course of these lectures there have been from time to time allusions to the relation of the religious orders to the ecclesiastical institutions amid which they attained their maturity. In particular, their relation to parish churches as patrons and as proprietors has been treated in some detail. We have seen something of the light which deeds of appropriation throw upon their financial condition in the fourteenth and fifteenth centuries, and, though the language of such documents is often very similar, and the needs which produced petitions for appropriation were much the same, the information thus obtained is sometimes of a special nature and of considerable use. In this concluding lecture some general remarks will be made upon the state of monasteries at the close of the Middle Ages. Nothing in the world is easier than to pick holes in religious institutions. It is one inevitable result of human imperfection that, the higher the ideal aimed at by any endeavour, the more likely it is that practice will constantly fall short of profession, and the more watchful will critics be to mark what is done amiss and put the worst construction upon it. No candid student of documents can fail to admit that, throughout the Middle Ages, even in those early days when the monastic movement was at its height, the internal condition of religious houses often called for correction and reform. It is one of the most remarkable features of that treasury of states-manlike wisdom, with its biblical pregnancy of phrase, the Rule of St. Benedict, that the patriarch of western monachism fore-saw so clearly the risks that attended the cenobitic life and endeavoured to guard against them without undue optimism.[1] The history of the system which he founded is in no small degree a history of alternating decline and revival. The reforms of St. Benedict of Aniane were followed too closely by the political strife which dismembered the Carolingian empire to have a fair chance of succeeding. Cluny, after its exceptionally long

---

[1] See the text of the Rule with Abbot Delatte's commentary, trans. Dom Justin McCann, 1921.

and brilliant career of reform and missionary effort, lasting for nearly a century and a half, turned its attention to internal affairs and, though its support strengthened the papacy in its conflict with the secular power, there were periods at which that support was somewhat inactive.[1] The puritan austerity of Cîteaux and the spread of the Cistercian Order are among the most striking phenomena in the history of medieval Christendom. But the movement lost its first vigour after the death of St. Bernard in 1153, and, although the prudential measure of the General Chapter a year earlier, which attempted to check the foundation of new houses, was a dead letter after the end of the twelfth century, such ardour as remained visibly slackened.[2] Finally, if the friars in their first generation of activity outshone the older religious orders, the temptations which beset their manner of life soon overcame their early zeal.

By the end of the thirteenth century the foundation of monasteries had practically ceased, and those founded in the fourteenth century are few and far between. New houses of Austin canons are occasionally found, as at Haltemprice (Haute Emprise) near Hull, founded in 1325–6 by Lord Wake of Liddell;[3] and the interesting fact of the conversion of the chantry college at Kirkby Bellars into a priory has already been noted.[4] The object of this move was to secure a resident body of priests to perform the objects contemplated by the founder; for the method of patronage which he had arranged was extremely cumbrous, and some of the chaplaincies had practically lapsed. There was certainly no other advantage to be gained, for between a house of Austin canons and a college of

---

[1] Miss L. M. Smith in her paper 'The Evidence for the Connexion of the Cluniacs with the Reform of Gregory VII' (*E.H.R.* xxvi. 20–33) and her work on *The Early History of the Monastery of Cluny*, 1920, clearly showed that what evidence there was for the old theory of the relations of Gregory VII with Cluny in the work of ecclesiastical reform was untenable. His attitude to Abbot Hugh was indeed one of impatience at Hugh's cautious unreadiness to support his efforts. See *R. Greg. VII*, i, ep. lxii: 'Grata nobis et dulcia sunt verba vestra, sed multo uberiori delectatione nos caperent si vestra charitas ardentius erga Romanam ferveret ecclesiam', &c. (*M.P.L.* cxlviii. 338).

[2] See the statute of the general chapter in 1152 'ne ulterius alicubi construatur nova abbatia nostri ordinis' (Guignard, *Monuments primitifs de la règle cistercienne*, 1878, p. 273; *Nom. Cist.*, p. 231) and the statute of 1256 'ne ulterius alicubi construatur nova abbatia nostri ordinis', *Y.A.J.* ix. 338: see also *Nom. Cist.*, p. 288. For the chronological foundation of houses see Janauschek.

[3] *Mon.* vi (i), 519–22; *V.C.H. Yorks.* iii. 213–16.     [4] See p. 149 above.

chantry-priests there was no great difference. In 1359 the
canons appear to have taken over the buildings of the college
as they stood, without attempting to institute a regular claustral
life, though the total disappearance of the buildings makes this
uncertain.[1] Some eighty years later the state of things was so
far satisfactory that the house contained its requisite comple-
ment of thirteen canons; but their behaviour was more that of
seculars than regulars, and they cultivated an unbecoming
dressiness, wearing clasps to their boots, while the young canons
carried at their belts silken purses with bands of gold thread
hanging to their knees.[2]

The abbey of St. Mary Graces, founded near the Tower of
London by Edward III in 1353, is the only instance of an
English Cistercian monastery founded after the end of the
thirteenth century.[3] Its situation, on the outskirts of a great
and populous city, was a most unusual site for a Cistercian
house.[4] By this date, however, there was probably not much
to choose between the Cistercian and other orders. The isola-
tion which the Cistercians had cultivated in their earlier days
was much less practicable in the fourteenth century. It had
been made possible in the first instance by the self-contained
nature of Cistercian communities. The lay brothers who,
though not peculiar to this order, were admitted to it in large
numbers and supplied most of the manual labour which the
monks needed, had diminished and seem, after the period of
the Black Death, to have abandoned the houses generally.[5]
The monks had to employ lay servants in their place, and the

[1] See 'The Chapel of St. Peter at Kirkby-upon-Wreak. Documents from the
Lincoln Episcopal Registers' (*Leices. Arch. Soc.* xvi. 129–212).

[2] *Linc. Vis.* ii. 166.

[3] *Mon.* v. 717–20.

[4] See the early statute in *Consuetudines*, sect. II, i: 'In civitatibus castellis et villis
nulla nostra construenda sunt coenobia sed in locis a conversatione hominum
semotis.' Renewed in 1240 and 1256 (*Nom. Cist.*, pp. 212, 287) in identical terms.

[5] This was the view taken by Sir William Hope: see, e.g., his 'Fountains Abbey'
(*Y.A.J.* xv, p. 105). The clearest architectural evidence for the change is at Hayles
Abbey, where the *domus conversorum* west of the cloister was made into the abbot's
lodging in the fourteenth century and a new doorway into the church was made
from the west walk of the cloister. Definite historical evidence comes from Meaux
in the East Riding. Here long before, in the thirteenth century, the *importunitas*
and *protervia* of *conversi* employed on the manor of Waghen had so disturbed the
peace of a local landowner that he made an exchange of property with William des
Fors, earl of Albemarle. During the rule of Abbot William Scardburghe (1372–96)
'conversi omnes de monasterio defecerunt; pro quorum numero monachos

conjecture may be hazarded that this reason had something to do with Edward III's choice of a site for his abbey. It must also be remembered that by this time the constitution of the order was being modified in other respects. Benedict XII, himself a Cistercian, had given it a new code of statutory observances,[1] as he gave also to the Benedictines and the Austin canons; but throughout the subsequent period the tendency of the order was towards a relaxation of custom and a liberal interpretation of the Rule of St. Benedict on whose literal observances the early Cistercians had laid such stress. Had those monks who in 1132 left the flesh-pots of St. Mary's, York, for the wilderness in which the abbey of Fountains was to rise, been able to revisit their home in later days, they might have wondered whether that exodus, with all its spiritual and physical inconveniences, had been worth the trouble. They would certainly have been surprised to find their successors rejecting their simple vegetarian ideals and demanding flesh-meat three days a week.[2] This demand was responsible for one of the most interesting features of the remains of Cistercian abbeys. Custom strictly forbade meat to be cooked in the monastic kitchen or eaten in the refectory. In some abbeys, therefore, the infirmary kitchen, in which the preparation of 'more subtle and delicate meats' for the aged, and sick, and the convalescent, had always been allowed, was used for the new form of indulgence, and the existing misericord, a dining-room in close connexion with the infirmary, became the refectory on flesh-days.[3] In certain houses a new meat-kitchen and a

supplevit, et annuum pensum pro victu conventus augmentavit. Infirmitorium conversorum et secularium ab incolis et invalidis destituit. Coquinam infirmitorii conversorum diruit', &c. (*Chronicon de Melsa* [Rolls Ser.], ii. 4; iii. 229). The latter passage is quoted by Hope, u.s.

[1] The constitution *Fulgens sicut stella*, dated at Sorgues (Vaucluse), 12 July 1335, is printed *Nom. Cist.*, pp. 473-95.

[2] Strict regulations for the use of flesh-meat were laid down in the constitution of Benedict XII, u.s., pp. 484-6, restricting it to the refectory of the infirmary and its cooking to the infirmary kitchen, and revoking licences produced by certain abbeys. In spite, however, of emphasis laid from time to time on this rule, the articles of reform drawn up at Paris 15 Feb. 1492-3 show that the use of flesh-meat on Sundays, Tuesdays, and Thursdays had become general (ibid., pp. 552-3).

[3] The flesh-meat refectory or 'misericord' at Fountains, on a site between the great hall of the infirmary and the abbot's lodging, is described by Hope, op. cit., pp. 62-3. The building seems to have been adapted to this purpose in the time of Marmaduke Huby, abbot 1494-1526.

special refectory were built, or, as an alternative, the old refectory was divided into two stories, the lower one of which was used for the new purpose.[1] Again, the departure of the lay brothers led to indifference to a feature of the Cistercian plan which had been originally introduced for the sake of this portion of the community towards the close of the twelfth century. In order to bring the kitchen into direct communication, through turntables in the wall, with the monks' refectory on one side and the refectory of the lay brothers on the other, the monks' refectory had been set at right angles to the adjoining cloister walk instead of parallel to it, as in the houses of other orders, thus leaving room for the insertion of the kitchen between it and the western range of cloister buildings.[2] The coming of ordinary lay servants put an end to this custom; and so when, in the fifteenth century, a new refectory was built at Cleeve Abbey in Somerset, the builders reverted to the normal monastic arrangement, with the main axis from east to west.

Further, as years had passed, there are signs that the old relations between the abbeys of the order prescribed by the Carta Caritatis in 1119 had become radically altered. It was no longer practicable for the abbot of such a monastery as Clairvaux to visit all the houses, many of them in distant lands, which were directly bound to it by affiliation. How, again, could the abbot of Fountains, one of the most prolific daughters of Clairvaux, be expected to brave the dangerous passage of the North Sea at intervals to visit his Norwegian offspring at

[1] Hope, ibid., p. 63, notes this division at Kirkstall, Jervaulx, and Ford, with the building of special kitchens for flesh-meat at Kirkstall and Jervaulx. See Hope, *Kirkstall Abbey*, pp. 46–9. At Jervaulx, however, there was no division of floors, but the misericord was a room built in the fifteenth century at right angles to the south-east end of the refectory. The new kitchen at Kirkstall adjoined the refectory at its south-east corner, but the great new kitchen at Jervaulx lies farther east. For Jervaulx see Hope and Brakspear, 'Jervaulx Abbey' (*Y.A.J.* xxi. 334–8). For the possible arrangement at Furness, where the fifteenth-century refectory may have been divided into two floors, see Hope, *Furness Abbey*, pp. 51–3. The evidence for such divisions from written documents comes from two Cistercian nunneries in Lincolnshire, both in 1440: see *Linc. Vis.* iii. 249 (Nuncoton): 'unum refectorium superius in quo vescuntur piscibus et lacticiniis, et aliud in quo ex gracia vescuntur carnibus'; 357 (Stixwould): 'in superiori refectorio vescuntur piscibus et lacticiniis, et in inferiori carnibus.'

[2] Before the close of the twelfth century Cistercian refectories in England seem to have been built on the ordinary Benedictine east to west axis. There are clear traces of this at Fountains, Kirkstall, and Rievaulx, and this arrangement continued without change at Merevale in Warwickshire and Sibton in Suffolk.

Lyse, near Bergen, or the abbot of Kirkstead, a child of Fountains, to pay a similar call upon the abbot and convent of Hovedø, on an island in the fjord of Oslo?[1] The abbeys of Ireland, over whose life tribal factions and animosity to the English of the Pale had an undue but unavoidable influence, were divided from one another and from their natural parents. Thus it was that the old system of affiliation, by which every Cistercian house traced its ultimate origin to Cîteaux, the mother of the order, left its regular course, and constant revisions took place by which, temporarily or permanently, monasteries were removed from the care of their natural parents and placed under more convenient supervision which, it may be suspected, was often little more than nominal.[2] The desire to assign a definite use to each room in the ruins of Cistercian monasteries has produced a rule by which makers of monastic plans, when in doubt with regard to the purpose of some apartment or building, label it, Visiting Abbot's Lodging; but one may doubt whether such an ascription has any definite justification behind it.[3] In any case, the practice of regular visitation, though an excellent ideal, must always have been difficult.

The Hundred Years War with France, however, combined with the constant hostility of Scotland, had the effect of isolating English monasteries from the brotherhoods to which they belonged. In one sense this was fortunate, for they escaped that disaster and ruin into which so many foreign houses fell during that period. On the other hand, while surviving in comparative prosperity, they none the less would have profited by that zeal for reform which, amid the general decay of the religious life abroad, produced new congregations of monks and canons within the older orders. In England we can point to no movements such as those which, in the era of the councils, gave

---

[1] Plans of Lyse and Hovedø are given by Gerhard Fischer, *Cistercienserne og Hovedøya (Foreningen til Norske Fortidsminnesmerkers bevaring*, 1935. See also Sigurd Curman, *Cisterciensersordens Byggnadskonst*, Stockholm, 1912, i. 185–9.

[2] Numerous examples can be gathered from *Statuta Capitulorum Generalium Ordinis Cisterciensis*, ed. Canivez, vols. i–vi, Louvain, 1933–8.

[3] Thus the substantial thirteenth-century house on the east part of the site at Netley has been called the Visiting Abbot's lodging. But the visiting abbot of Netley was the abbot of Beaulieu, on the other side of an arm of Southampton Water, who would hardly have needed such a lodging; and there is no reason to suppose that its ordinary tenant was not the abbot of Netley himself.

birth to the Benedictine congregation of Santa Giustina at Padua and to the Augustinian congregation of Windeshem, the agent of a widespread revival of religion in the Netherlands and North Germany.[1] Amid great activity in the multiplication of chantries and chantry colleges the religious orders remained stationary. The great exempt Benedictine abbeys, subject immediately to the pope, steadily maintained their independence against the encroachments of bishops. The abbey of St. Edmunds, which in the middle of the fourteenth century withstood with success the attack of Bishop Bateman of Norwich upon its privileges, fell upon evil days in the reign of Richard II. The attempt of Edmund Bromfield, a turbulent and ambitious monk, to intrude himself into the abbacy by virtue of a papal provision obtained surreptitiously, ousted for the time being the abbot elected by the convent and approved by the Crown, and filled the monastery with brawling, while Bromfield kept himself in possession with the aid of partisans from the neighbourhood. Before these troubles had entirely subsided, the revolt of the lesser commons and villeins in 1381 broke out: the abbey was invaded by the mob, and the prior and some of the monks were murdered.[2] In spite of these catastrophes, half a century later Abbot Curteys was able to employ all the vigour of his predecessors in opposing Bishop Alnwick and his archdeacon. The house of St. Edmund, founded upon a rock, was proof by God's grace against the blasts of the north wind: even as Berith and Ashtaroth fled before the face of blessed Bartholomew the Apostle, so did the bishop and the archdeacon turn their backs and in the pit which they had made for other privily was their foot taken.[3]

Strength and solidarity, no doubt, had been given to the Benedictine houses and to houses of Austin canons by the institution of general chapters of the orders which met triennially and received their final form under the constitutions of

[1] See Heimbucher, i. 217–18 (S. Giustina), 424–8 (Windeshem). For the latter see especially Johann Busch., *Chron. Windeshemense* and *Liber de reformatione monasteriorum*, ed. Grube, 1897.

[2] Wals. i. 414–18, 423–30; ii. 2–4, &c.

[3] *Mon.* iii. 136: 'Sed S. Edmundi monasterium super firmam fundatum petram ut mons stetit immobilis faciesque ipsorum confusio [*sic*] cooperuit. Et quemadmodum Berith et Asteroth a facie fugierunt [*sic*] beati Bartholomei Apostoli sic isti fugierunt [*sic*] impii nemine persequente. Deo tunc volente postea capti fuerunt et in foveam quam fecerant merito inciderunt.'

Benedict XII.[1] These provided for some degree of mutual supervision between monasteries, each of which led a virtually independent existence, an order, as Benedictine writers are fond of pointing out, in itself,[2] allied to its neighbours merely by pious treaties of fraternity and mutual support.[3] The Benedictine ideal of the abbot as the father of his monks, to be implicitly obeyed, gave the head of the house supreme authority. In his hands lay the appointment of the officers, the obedientiaries of the monastery. In the greater houses he kept up an establishment for the support of which a large proportion of the convent revenues were set aside and to the service of which special obedientiaries were told off.[4] The abbot had his own chamberlain, his own cellarer, his own almoner and chaplain. He kept his household of esquires, yeomen, and grooms, the well-known three estates of a medieval nobleman's household. The entertainment of royal and distinguished guests was the share of the convent's duty of hospitality which he fulfilled. The expense of his position was greatly increased when he was one of those abbots who were regularly summoned to parliament; and an abbot who obtained exemption from that duty deserved the gratitude of his convent.

There is no better description of an ideal abbot, as the ordinary man of the Middle Ages saw him, than Knighton's account of the Augustinian William of Clown, abbot of St. Mary's in the Meadows at Leicester, who died in 1378, after ruling the monastery for thirty-three years.

'Of his great piety and patience, of all his discreetness and moderation to them that were set under him and stood in need of his help and advice, or sought his aid in any justifiable cause, the tongue fails to tell, the mind waxes dull in thinking, the hand in writing slackens, the will that would trust to memory is but lukewarm. I am indeed afraid to think that in the ears of my hearers I may possibly seem to have covered the truth of my story with a veil of flattery. He was a lover of peace and quiet in his own neighbour-

---

[1] The Benedictine Constitutions for Benedictine houses are printed by Wilkins, ii. 585–613; for Augustinian houses, ibid. ii. 629–51 and a corrected text by Salter, *Chapters of Aug. Canons*, pp. 214–67.

[2] See Butler, *Benedictine Monachism*, pp. 28–9, 258–9.

[3] Such as that between the abbeys of Peterborough and Ramsey, printed *Mon.* i. 395; ii. 586.

[4] For the double arrangement of abbot's and convent's obedientiaries at Peterborough see *Linc. Vis.* iii. 273.

hood; everywhere he was a reformer of quarrels and wrongs, which, wheresoever in his days they happened, he never omitted to endeavour, so far as he could, to set right and put at rest with all his strength, labouring zealously and ever abhorring and dreading bloodshed. He was an untiring follower of good works, kind and obliging to his underlings and persons of the lower orders, unspeakably amiable to great men and the magnates of the realm; how earnestly craved his countenance and presence were by all, both rich and poor, is past telling. This most pious abbot of devout memory, in token and sign that he was wholly a servant of God and a lover of peace and quiet, at the season of peace and the hour of rest, to wit at midnight on a Sunday, supported by the arms and hands of his brethren who bewailed his decease and commended his soul to God, he passed from this world to the Lord who, as seems very probable, loved him in all his works. What more shall I say? Out of that laudable community, which followed in the footsteps of so respectable a shepherd, two members in his days were preferred to be abbots, to wit of the abbeys of Missenden and Wellow by Grimsby, and two to be priors, to wit at Tortington and Mottisfont. Two sought the life of anchorets at Chester and St. Michael's at Leicester, and two migrated to ecclesiastical benefices with cure of souls. In his days two churches were appropriated . . . two manors were acquired . . . likewise also rents and possessions (in various places). He also obtained a charter from the king for himself and his successors, excusing them from attending parliament. He likewise acquired the right of the voidance of the abbey after the death of every abbot, so that, if an abbot chance to leave this world, the king's escheator shall merely enter the abbey and there take simple seisin in the king's name for all its possessions; and so shall he stay there a day and a night only, not annoying anyone or intermeddling with any thing within or without, and then shall he depart. And if he be unwilling, they shall have the right to expel him thence in his own despite by the charter of King Edward III, which was ratified by his successor King Richard, so that no king's escheator shall intermeddle with any manor or place of the said abbey, save with the abbey only. To this kindly abbot William, God gave so great grace in the eyes of all men, lords and others, that there was scarce a man who could deny him what he asked. On such good terms was he with the lord King that he asked the King in jest to grant him a fair for buying and selling harriers and hounds of all sorts. The King actually thought that he meant it seriously and granted him the fair; but he would not insist on the matter. In hunting of the hare he was reckoned the most notable and renowned among all the lords of the realm, so that the King himself and his son Prince

Edward and divers lords of the realm had an annual engagement to hunt at his entertainment. Nevertheless he would often say in private that the only reason why he took delight in such paltry sports was to show politeness to the lords of the realm, to get on easy terms with them and win their good will in matters of business.'[1]

'A manly man, to ben an abbot able.' Those qualities of character which Chaucer discovered in his Monk were conspicuously manifested in the life and conversation of William of Clown, and for these the chronicler has nothing but praise. The alliance of the monastery with the world under so politic a ruler was all to its advantage. The character of a monastery depended largely upon the personality of the abbot; and of Leicester Abbey in these days, even though one or two of its younger canons, notably Philip Repyngdon, were becoming notorious for heterodox opinions, it might well be said that its respectable pastor led his flock along the road where 'abundant is the thriving, if the flock strays not.'[2] Very different was the state of things rather less than sixty years later, when Abbot William Sadyngton, bent only upon expensive building schemes, neglected the services of the church, kept the offices of treasurer and cellarer in his own hands, rendering no accounts for them or for receipts from the stewards of the manors, employed a large and useless body of lay servants, and missed no opportunity of making money, to the extent of maintaining a resident alchemist. His treatment of his brethren was a great contrast to the paternal assiduity of Abbot Clown: when according to custom they took their meals in his hall during their 'seynies', the period of convalescence after the customary blood-lettings with which a medieval religious purged the humours engendered by a sedentary life, he looked on them very despitefully and with a sour visage and would not talk to them, confining his conversation to his secular servants. In particular, he detested one of the canons called Thomas Asty, and, missing some money— it may be the lost piece of silver for which his serving-man went

[1] See App. VI.
[2] Dante, *Par.* x. 94-6:

> Io fui degli agni de la santa greggia
> che Domenico mena per cammino
> u' ben s'impingua se non si vaneggia

William of Clown's methods, however, were of a different type from those of St. Dominic, holding as they did 'after the newe world the pace'.

to consult a wise woman at Market Harborough—he took a youth, one Maurice, who possessed clairvoyant powers, to Ingarsby, one of the manors acquired by William Clown, and there in a house which is still standing he smeared the adept's thumb-nail with some magic ink and, reading from a book of incantations, bade him tell him what he saw in the fluid. Maurice, probably knowing what he was expected to see, gave an answer which emboldened the abbot to return in wrath to his brethren in the chapter and charge Asty with the theft. We can hardly wonder that the number of canons had decreased, or that the boys brought up in the almonry were much fewer than the number which the house ought to have supported, and, being without an instructor, spent their time in running errands for the canons.[1] The multitude of hounds which was kept in the house may not have been any larger than in Abbot Clown's day; for, although the harrier no longer occupies the place of honour among the dogs of the county, Leicestershire, lay and clerical, has never been backward in its appreciation of the hound.

The Lincoln visitation records, in which the story of Sadyngton's misdoings survives, contain more than one striking example of the decline of a religious house under the rule of a weak or headstrong abbot. Bardney is a case in point, where the abbot was old and either lazy or incapable, and the house was managed by the sub-cellarer and a few accomplices who helped themselves to the common seal and sealed blank charters with it, sending them to be engrossed to order by a scrivener at Lincoln.[2] At Peterborough the abbot in 1438 was also old and was obliged to resign; and here the management of property had fallen into the hands of his brother and other laymen.[3] The abbot of Ramsey at this date was either incredibly lax or utterly incompetent: this was a house which certainly was in need of reform from every point of view, and the cellarer's grange at Bury, conveniently situated on the road to the cell of St. Ives, was the scandal of the neighbourhood.[4] Of the lesser monasteries it is less easy to judge: many were small and poor, and visitation returns display a general state of financial weakness. Although cases of serious moral lapses are certainly

[1] *Linc. Vis.* ii. 206–18 (A.D. 1440).
[2] Ibid. ii. 29–31 (A.D. 1440).
[3] Ibid. iii. 269–82 (A.D. 1437).
[4] Ibid. iii. 303, 304, &c. (A.D. 1439).

not uncommon, the general moral decline which is conspicuous
at Ramsey was rare. The only case which approaches it is that
of Dorchester.[1] It must be owned, however, that the suspension
and relegation to a cell of so important a person as an abbot of
Peterborough for immoral conduct is a somewhat startling
fact.[2] Nunneries were ill protected and exposed to violence and
licence; and it is impossible to forget Walsingham's detailed
story of the outrages committed by Sir John Arundel and his
troops in an unnamed nunnery on the south coast.[3] The nuns
of Rothwell, a small Northamptonshire nunnery, were mal-
treated by marauders who attempted to abduct one of those
lady boarders who were often a serious problem to their hostesses,
like the dowager lady Audley at Langley Priory in Leicestershire, who came to church with a dozen pet dogs, all vocal, so
that the nuns in choir were sadly put out.[4] Oxford scholars
would wander out to Godstow;[5] when the prioress of Ankerwyke,
a lady very like Chaucer's prioress, was blamed for blocking
off the end of the dormitory to make a private room for herself,
her excuse was that the nuns would talk out of the window to
loiterers beside the Thames.[6] The prioress of Catesby, a woman
of ungovernable temper, much under the thumb of her mother,
whom she maintained in the monastery, fell into rages with her
spiritual sisters, dragged them about by the hair, and called
them names which ladies never use. Her nuns certainly did not
improve the reputation of the house, for two of them, on an
errand to Northampton, spent the evening in dancing and play-
ing the lute with friars.[7] St. Michael's outside Stamford, close
to the main road from south to north, was an ill-governed
house, and one of the nuns was beguiled into apostasy by a
wandering harper from Newcastle-upon-Tyne.[8] At Gracedieu
in Leicestershire, a house popular with the daughters of the
well-to-do local middle class, a lively and self-willed sub-prioress,
who went haymaking with the chaplain, *sola cum solo*, set all the
nuns by the ears.[9] More than one writer has ingenuously used
the contents of a Gracedieu account-book of much the same

---

[1] *Linc. Vis.* ii. 68–83 (A.D. 1443, 1445). 'Abbas immundissimus est' (p. 70).
[2] Ibid. iii. 300, 301.
[3] *H.A.* i. 419–23; *Chr. Ang.* 247–53.
[4] *Linc. Vis.* i. 107–9; ii. 175.                  [5] Ibid. i. 67; ii. 114.
[6] Ibid. ii. 3.                                                  [7] Ibid. ii. 47–50.
[8] Ibid. iii. 348, 350.                                    [9] Ibid. ii. 120, 123.

period to illustrate the beauty and simplicity of nunnery life;[1] but hard facts prove more than sentiment, and bishops' threats than tradesmens' bills.

Still, allowing for all this—and monks and nuns, after all, were only human, and their vocation for the monastic life was seldom, if ever, properly tested[2]—the fundamental weakness of the system lay in the difficulty of making two ends meet. Appropriation deeds, as we have seen, constantly allude to the decrease of revenues through bad seasons, murrain, pestilence, famine, and other casual disasters. The appropriation of the church of Geddington to Pipewell Abbey in 1358 was due in part to the devastations of the beasts of game from the king's forest of Rockingham:[3] the fenland abbeys were menaced by wet and dry seasons alike. Above all, there was the constant drain of hospitality, the continual complaint of the necessity of receiving and entertaining the multitude of travellers who turned aside to monasteries from the high roads. No doubt pious kings like Richard II, busily engaged in touring from monastery to monastery while the bishop of Norwich's Flemish crusade was coming to its inglorious end,[4] left handsome gifts at the shrines which they visited; but we may ask how far their generosity went to cover the cost of their entertainment. A monastery like

[1] See Gasquet, *English Monastic Life*, pp. 158–76. Of the internal discipline of Gracedieu in the years covered by the account-book (1414–18) we know nothing; but in 1440–1, when the convent was disturbed by bickerings and the sub-prioress reported that *sub ista priorissa tota religio perit*, five out of the fourteen nuns recorded at the earlier date were still in the priory. The prioress in 1440–1 was one of these, but was said to be old and incapable, though still evidently able to correct wrong-doers; and the fact that two of the older nuns adhered to her may show some loyalty to a past and better order of things. But the results were certainly unpromising, and the cellaress into whose hands much of the business of the monastery had been allowed to slide was unsuitable and unpopular. See *Linc. Vis.* ii. 119–27.

[2] This is, at any rate, the general impression which visitation documents convey. It is strengthened by the prevalence of the habit, especially in nunneries, of admitting members for a consideration, a frequent cause of warnings. Alnwick, e.g., forbade the prioress and convent of Harrold to exact any 'earthly good' for the receiving of any nun 'otherwise than that they or their friends of their charity without any paction or covenant or promise made before will give you' (ibid. ii. 252).

[3] See p. 110 above, note 2.

[4] Wals. *H.A.* ii. 96: 'Dum haec aguntur in Flandria rex Angliae et regina cum suis Boemiis abbathias regni circueunt visitando quibus tanto tristior fuit eorum adventus quanto gravior quia et accesserunt in excessivo numero et non "offerre" sed "auferre" venerunt.' For Richard's sudden departure from Daventry Priory on learning of the imminence of the surrender of Gravelines, see ibid., p. 103.

Bardney, with only a moderately good income, must have found itself worse off after a visit from Henry IV, with a band of attendant courtiers and his noble Scottish prisoners.[1] Money flowed like water; and, although in certain houses there was a tradition of regular account-keeping, it was over and over again reported to visitors that accounts were never or seldom rendered, and then imperfectly with summary totals in place of details. In many places convents could give only rough and approximate statements of their incomes and outgoings: the head of a house would say that the revenues or the debts of the house at his entry upon office amounted to about so much, and that now they were about so much more or less.[2] The credit balance of the state of the house was at best small, and usually the balance was on the debit side. Houses were burthened with yearly pensions and annuities; there was the weight of taxation to meet; and all this at a time when the benefactions which earlier had been devoted to monasteries were diverted elsewhere. Appropriations of churches brought solid advantages which served for a time to stem the tide of debt; but the number of churches that could be appropriated were few, and appropriation itself was an expensive proceeding. Monasteries great and small found it easy, however, to get ready money by gambling in life insurance—for that is the simplest description of the corrody system. The present writer once heard a distinguished archivist say in all good faith that a corrody was so called because it corroded or gnawed upon monastic finances. That certainly was a result of the custom; but a corrody means nothing more than an allowance consisting of a share in a common fund.[3] Men secured annuities for themselves and their wives by buying from a monastery a daily supply of victuals and drink, often

[1] Leland, *Collectanea*, vi. 300; *Mon.* i. 625.

[2] See, e.g., *Linc. Vis.* ii. 240: the prior of the small house of Newstead by Stamford said that his monastery had a credit balance of 40 marks as against 20 marks debit (£26. 13s. 4d. to £13. 6s. 8d.). The debit side, however, had grown from £5 at the time of his installation, and the house had been *pene destructa* by the alienations made by the last prior. At Ulverscroft in Leicestershire the credit amounted to 80 marks and the prior thought that £5 would cover all debts: he had presented no account for three years, but proposed to have one ready for the Michaelmas audit (ibid. iii. 386). In spite of the unsatisfactory state of things at Gracedieu, the prioress claimed to have reduced by £10 a debt of £48 which existed when she took office (ibid. ii. 119).

[3] See *O.E.D.* s.v. 'Conrey', 'Corrody': also 'A corrody from Leicester Abbey A.D. 1393-4' (*Leices. Arch. Soc.* xiv. 113-34).

combined with a lodging within the precincts, for a lump sum calculated over a certain number of years, to last for the purchaser's life, not infrequently, though not always, with remainder to his widow for her lifetime.[1] How easily a corrody could become a pension without return in process of time is quite obvious. The system in itself was vicious, and bishops attempted to check it by ordering that corrodies and those pensions and annuities which convents granted freely should be subject to episcopal licence. But the practice went on, and little could be said against it when kings and other patrons were in the habit of nominating protégés to corrodies in monasteries already overburthened with such charges. Religious houses thus involved in debt, continually endeavouring to lessen the load by such makeshift expedients, could hardly keep their pristine fervour. Their more capable members, faced with these administrative problems, were forced, willing or unwilling, to leave the word of God and serve tables. This indeed was the habitual lot of such officers as the cellarer and chamberlain, the caterers for the provisions and stores of the monastery; and the life of a monk with business abilities, like Chaucer's monk or Abbot Islip of Westminster, might be conducted with decorum, but was not conducive to holiness.[2] Monasteries whose incomes were still above the average became worldly; attendance in choir was relaxed or regulated by a rota; as at Durham in its later days, the refectory was left, except on feast-days, and the monks dined together in a more comfortable parlour;[3] occasionally the inmates took to dining in separate messes in various parts of the monastery; the desire for privacy, as may be seen in several

---

[1] Thus, in an early fifteenth-century Peterborough register (B.M. Add. 25288), fo. 60 b, a corrody granted to one Robert Bulwer, 5 May 1414, includes a suit of livery of the abbot's yeomen without fur for himself, and for his wife Agnes a cloth dress of the colour of the said livery yearly. After Robert's death Agnes, if she remains continent, is to have half the corrody for her lifetime. A similar grant of half a corrody to a widow in survivorship, with details specified, occurs in the grant to Henry Hopkyn of Peterborough, 28 July 1447, in R. Assh., fo. 21 b.

[2] See H. F. Westlake, *Westminster Abbey, the last days of the monastery, as shown by the life and times of Abbot John Islip, 1464–1532*, 1921.

[3] For the regular use of the loft at the west end of the 'frater-house' at Durham, see *Rites of Durham* (Surtees Soc.), ed. Fowler, pp. 82, 86, 87. The refectory was used when 'the Prior and the whole Covent of the Monkes held their great feast of St. Cuthberts day in Lent' (20 Mar.). During all the rest of the year 'a fair table with a decent skrene of wainscott over it' at the east end of the building was kept 'for the novices and their master' (pp. 82, 83).

Cistercian abbeys, led to the partitioning of some of the larger chambers of the monastery and the infirmary hall into separate rooms.[1] In fact, the whole tendency was to abandon the common life essential to the monastic system, and live like members of a club. In the smaller monasteries whose financial depression was permanently acute, need produced a general carelessness of living; the sin of *accidia*, spiritual torpor, and discontent, always the greatest temptation of the monk and provocative to other sins, led to mutual dislike and bickering; and apostasy to a secular life became a common danger.

In such matters it is dangerous to generalize and very easy to be censorious, and there is nothing more misleading than to apply the moral standards of a later age to the shortcomings of medieval religion. Moreover, we must remember that the *comperta* of visitation records deal with offences that had long been familiar to visitors: the material for episcopal injunctions usually is found to cover much the same field as the injunctions of Innocent III to the abbot and convent of Subiaco, contained in what Rabelais called the 'terrific chapter' *Quum ad monasterium.*[2] We need not put too much faith in the denunciations of unofficial Jeremiahs; for prophets are prone to rhetorical variations on common forms. Nor must we assume that, because we hear nothing positive about them, there were not individuals who in cloisters 'kept their feet firm and their hearts sound'.[3] Visitors framed their questions upon breaches of rule and custom, not upon points in which they were observed.[4] It does not follow that a canon of Ulverscroft who had the amiable weakness of going out bird's-nesting by night in the groves of Charnwood Forest,[5] or monks who liked gardening and spent too much time in tending flower-beds in the cloister garth,[6] led lives of impiety

---

[1] This is conspicuously illustrated by the subdivision of the dormitory sub-vault at Jervaulx (*Y.A.J.* xxi. 322 and plan).

[2] *Extra*, iii. xxxv. 6: see Rabelais, *Pantagruel*, iv. 53, for this and other 'terrificques chapitres'.

[3] Dante, *Par.* xxii. 50, 51:

Qui son li frati miei che dentro ai chiostri
Fermâr li piedi e tennero il cor saldo.

[4] See App. VII.

[5] *Linc. Vis.* iii. 386: 'Item dicit [prior] quod Robertus Rodyngtone discurrit in silvis et nemoribus absque licencia, querendo nidos avium silvestrium et capiendo alias bestias silvestres.'

[6] The sacrist of Bardney in 1440 (ibid. ii. 33) prayed *quod gardinus quem colit non*

and iniquity. And if the canons of Dorchester and Nutley were found to dishonour their profession, we have no right to assume that because, apart from a few individual complainants on trivial matters, Abbot Hooknorton of Oseney and his canons in 1445 answered that all was well,[1] they were linked in conspiracy to hoodwink their bishop. It is impossible, however, to escape the conclusion that English monasteries in the fifteenth century needed spiritual quickening to justify their existence as a whole. The monastic ideal was forgotten; religion, as Bishop Alnwick often had to remark, was perishing.[2] Learning was at a standstill; there was a very general lack of teachers to train novices in the rudiments of knowledge. Abbot Wheathampstead of St. Albans liked to engage his leisure in elegiac verse, solemnly lampooning the derogators of the privileges of his house, but the quality of his verse was poor, and its quantities, to say nothing of its concords, were infamous.[3] Exhibitions for student monks at Oxford and Cambridge were withheld; a monk of Spalding, who afterwards became abbot of Bardney, was obliged to pawn the books which he borrowed from the monastic library to meet his expenses.[4] These are facts which cannot be overlooked, and the state of things which Cardinal Morton, at the end of the century, found at the illustrious monastery of St. Albans is a sign of the stagnation which had beset that portion of the church most entirely set apart for God's service.[5]

In view of the abundant evidence which comes to us from records of episcopal visitations, we naturally ask ourselves how far such visitations were capable of effecting reform. Some bishops may have been careless: after collecting what evidence

*auferatur.* His petition was allowed: another monk complained that he had been rebuked *pro factura gardini claustri.* At Thornholm in the same year (ibid. iii. 365) the canons were refused licence by the prior 'ad faciendum gardina ad eorum recreaciones et decorem monasterii.'

[1] Ibid. iii. 263–4.

[2] Thus at Daventry (ibid. ii. 65): *tota religio inter vos periit*; at Elsham (ibid. ii. 88): [*religio*]*que inibi quasi perit.* Cf. Nutley (ibid. iii. 259): 'comperimus nonnulla puritati religionis contraria et inimica indies ibi committi', and Ramsey (ibid. iii. 311). See also the stern preamble of Alnwick's injunctions to Markby Priory (ibid. iii. 225–6).

[3] See Amundesham, *Annales* (Rolls Ser.), i. 364–7, for the hexameters written against Bishop Alnwick and the treasurer Cromwell and in congratulation of the judge, John Juyn.

[4] *Linc. Vis.* iii. 334.

[5] Wilkins, iii. 632–4. See also *Linc. Vis.* ii, introd., pp. lxii–ix.

exists for Archbishop Kempe's arrangements for the visitation
of his diocese during twenty-seven years, one is bound to conclude that a partial primary visitation begun some three years
after his enthronement, deferred for twelve years and completed,
as the programmes show, by commissaries, does not imply
exemplary vigilance.[1] While a bishop in person, even if he
came as a judge, was also by his vocation a shepherd of souls,
whose duty was to treat the lost sheep with discriminating kind-
ness and mingle the sharp wine of correction with the oil of
charity, a commissary, with no personal responsibility, treated
matters in a more summary way. But the fifteenth-century
bishops of Lincoln, at any rate, were diligent in visitation.
Richard Flemyng and William Gray, between 1421 and 1436,
have both left records of their zeal for the maintenance of monastic life at a reasonably high level.[2] Of Alnwick's visitations a
rich collection of documents remains, and although for the rest
of the century there is not much to show, the visitation books of
William Atwater and John Longland, covering the period from
1518 to 1530, are of very great value for the period immediately
preceding the suppression of the monasteries.[3] Even though
much of Atwater and Longland's work was done through commissaries, chiefly through John Rayne, who was murdered at
Horncastle by the Lincolnshire rebels, and the reports of their
visitations are often of the brief kind of which the contemporary
Norwich reports also furnish examples,[4] it would be ridiculous
to argue that such visitations were wholly formal. The bishop
came to the monastery and was solemnly received at the church
door and led to the altar. He sat judicially as a tribunal in the
chapter-house, and, after the sermon had been preached, he
proceeded to examine the members of the convent severally
and privately. Their *detecta*, that is, their disclosures made by
deposition, were taken down by the bishop's notaries, and were
read out publicly at the end of the visitation, together with the
*comperta*, that is, the discoveries obtained from them after their
review by the bishop and his assessors. Verbal injunctions were
frequently delivered by the bishop before leaving, and written

---

[1] *Surtees Misc.* 201–80, 145–51.
[2] See *Linc. Vis.*, vol. i.
[3] Ibid. ii, iii; *Linc. Dioc. Vis.* ii, iii.
[4] *Visitations in the Diocese of Norwich, A.D. 1492–1532*, ed. Jessopp (Camden Soc.), 1888.

injunctions with statutory force were dispatched later, composed as a rule by the registrar, but corrected by the bishop or his chancellor.[1] The language of these, of course, was modelled upon common forms, and we cannot always estimate the seriousness of the evidence upon which they were founded; but we may at any rate remark the habitual skill of clerks in moulding their style to suit the special nature of the *comperta*, and sometimes the *comperta* themselves are included in the preambles to the several injunctions which concern them.[2] The bishop usually dealt with individual offenders before he left the monastery, although occasionally a detailed examination of serious charges was deferred until a later period. There were certain exemplary penalties which lay in his power. He could compel the head of a house to resign, at any rate if a clear majority of the convent urged this course;[3] he could command a troublesome monk to be transferred temporarily to another house of the order where he might acquire profit for his soul's health[4]— though whether this arrangement was of advantage to the other monastery is a point on which we may feel some doubt; he could degrade a monk for a fixed period to the lowest place in church and chapter, prescribing a meagre diet and humiliating observances,[5] he could suspend a monk who had incurred irregularity from priestly functions.[6] But he was dealing after all with the domestic affairs of a corporation sheltered within its precincts,

[1] For descriptions of the conduct of visitations see Gray's visitation of his cathedral church (*Linc. Vis.* i. 128) and Alnwick's visitations of Bardney and Peterborough in 1437 (ibid. ii. 9–14; iii. 269–74).

[2] See the *ad interim* injunctions issued by Alnwick to Ramsey followed by the elaborate series of written injunctions embodying the *comperta* (ibid. iii. 306–19).

[3] Thus in 1437 at Peterborough Abbot Depyng's surrender of administration was made 'de consensu fratrum suorum' (ibid. iii. 271).

[4] See, e.g., the case of John Medemenham of Nutley, sent to do penance at Oseney (ibid. iii. 261–2).

[5] This penalty was by no means so common, however, in the fifteenth century as at an earlier date, and in *Linc. Vis.* there is nothing so severe as the penance enjoined by Archbishop Greenfield on a canon of Bolton Priory in 1312–13 (R. Green., ii. 140–1). Additional penalties were enjoined later in 1313, when Appelton had been guilty of violence to a secular clerk: these included the order 'quod omni die ejusdem anni hora capituli convocati dictus frater Willelmus ad terram sedeat in capitulo aliis sedentibus super scanna.' At the end of 1313 he was sent for a time to Thurgarton Priory in Nottinghamshire in exchange for an unsatisfactory canon of Thurgarton who took his place at Bolton (ibid. ii. 153, 169–70).

[6] See the case of William Bryan, canon of Breedon in Leicestershire (*Linc. Vis.* ii. 41).

and tact counselled leniency, so that penalties were often surprisingly light. It was no doubt tedious for a monk convicted
of some serious breach of rule to recite the psalter from beginning
to end a certain number of times within a month, and nothing
less likely to endear the psalter to him can be imagined;[1] but
this mechanical performance had no more permanent effect
upon the soul than an imposition of five hundred lines has upon
the soul of a schoolboy. The penalty was strictly *ad hoc*, without
any wider consideration. Offenders, it may be remarked, had
to bring compurgators to prove their innocence of charges laid
to them. The system has often been blamed as allowing room
for collusion. The facts show, however, that the definitely
guilty persons did not find it easy to make up the number of
compurgators required;[2] and we must allow, on the one hand,
that, unless a convent was bound to a conspiracy of silence, the
notoriety of the transgression would hinder compurgators from
coming forward, and, on the other, that the visitor and his clerks
had sufficient experience of men to know a liar when they saw
him. It is difficult to agree with the point of view that sees infinite duplicity on the part of monks, and infinite credulity on
the part of visitors; still less with the cynicism that views a
visitation as a solemn farce, played upon an understanding of
mutual accommodation by means of fees. But, the bishop once
gone, the convent was left to itself again, and there was little
chance of his return for some years to come. In the meantime,
the convent had to be trusted to keep the injunctions which he
delivered. There was nothing to prevent an angry abbot or
prior from taking vengeance upon some deponent who had
traduced him to the bishop: the *detecta* were not published with
the names of their authors, but in a limited society where each
man knew all about his neighbour, they could easily be traced
to their sources without difficulty, and more than one abbot
was known to warn his brethren with threats to be silent before
the visitor, and to say that he would undo all that the visitor
commanded after his departure.[3] So, while we may admire

---

[1] Thus Thomas Dryby, canon of Markby, was ordered 'quod citra proximum
festum Michaelis dicat in claustro ad duodecim vices sex psalteria Davitica
equaliter' (ibid. iii. 224).

[2] The prior of Daventry, e.g., in 1442 failed to find compurgators in answering
a charge of incontinence and threw himself upon the bishop's mercy (ibid. ii. 64).

[3] At Leicester in 1440 William Coventre said that 'audivit abbatem dicere quod

the methodical conduct of a visitation and the combined zeal
and tact of the visitor, we must admit that their immediate
results were less salutary to the convent than their ultimate
consequences are instructive to the historian.

We must remark, however, that while the monasteries
generally were declining from sheer inanition, without that
spur to encouragement which the sympathetic interest of the
outside public supplies to homes of good works, and while the
friars, active as regards theological and controversial learning,
skilful as confessors, and promoted in large numbers to the less
profitable bishoprics and to bishoprics *in partibus* which enabled
them to work as assistants in dioceses, were nevertheless, upon
the mendicant side of their calling, very far from the ideals of
their founders, one religious order achieved a certain popularity
in the later Middle Ages, and that the most severe and exacting
in its customs. Before 1343 only two Carthusian houses had
been founded in England, and both in Somerset, that house of
Witham from which St. Hugh rose to be bishop of Lincoln,
and Hinton Charterhouse near Bath, whose beautiful and
tranquil site, and the austere dignity of its buildings, still speak
to us of that lonely blessedness and blessed loneliness which
were the Carthusian ideal.[1] In 1343 Sir Nicholas Cantilupe
founded a Charterhouse at Beauvale in Nottinghamshire, and
this was followed during the next half-century or so by five
more, the famous London Charterhouse of the Salutation of
St. Mary, and the Charterhouses of Hull, St. Anne at Coventry,
Epworth in Axholme, and, in 1398, Mount Grace upon its plat-
form beneath the steep escarpment of the hills of Cleveland. It
is remarkable that the last four were founded by four of the chief
actors in the tragic drama of the reign of Richard II. The Hull
Charterhouse was actually begun in the previous reign by
William de la Pole, whose first intention of erecting a hospital
was changed to a project for a monastery of Franciscan nuns:
eventually his son Michael, the earl of Suffolk and chancellor,

visitacio ordinaria non esset nisi trufa quia quod in ea ordinatum est in crastino
vellet subvertere' (ibid. ii. 210). Of a similar temper was the prior of Ulverscroft,
who, blamed for the ruinous condition of the buildings, said 'Vellem quod omnia pro-
strata forent ad terram: satis est michi quod durent tempore meo' (ibid. iii. 387).
    [1] For Witham and Hinton see *Mon.* vi. (i), 1–6, followed by London, Beauvale,
Coventry, Hull, Mount Grace, Axholme, and Shene (pp. 6–34). See also E. M.
Thompson, *The Carthusian Order in England*, 1930, pp. 133–246.

who was the scapegoat of the parliament of 1386 and fled from
the condemnation of the Merciless parliament two years later,
founded it for Carthusians.[1] The Coventry Charterhouse was
founded by Richard II and his queen, the name of whose patron
saint it bore; the Epworth Charterhouse by Thomas Mowbray,
earl of Nottingham, lord of the Isle of Axholme, and duke of
Norfolk, who died at Venice after his banishment in 1398; and
Mount Grace by the King's half-nephew Thomas Holand, earl
of Kent and duke of Surrey, who, in the abortive rebellion of
Christmas 1399, with the object of restoring Richard to the
throne, fell a victim to the townsfolk of Cirencester. Last of all,
in 1414, the greatest and most richly endowed of the English
Charterhouses, the house of Jesus of Bethlehem at Shene, was
founded by Henry V almost contemporaneously with the
Bridgetine abbey of St. Saviour at Syon.[2]

If, in the last days of the monasteries, there were any who
'kept their feet firm and their hearts sound' in cloister, it was
the Carthusians, and the story of their end may awake some
pity even among the least sympathetic students of monastic
history. That silent and solitary life of contemplation in
separate cells, with its consolations of mystical vision which
can be realized so well among the ruins of Mount Grace—of all
English monasteries the one in which the permanent attraction
of the religious life to the pious soul can be best understood—
was proof against the temptations which too often overcame
the fortitude of less secluded orders. But, for our present
purpose, the interest of the Carthusians lies in their endowments. These were in large part derived from those so-called
alien priories which belonged to monasteries in France, chiefly
in Normandy. The Hundred Years War brought about the
confiscation of alien property; and earlier the Statute of Carlisle
in 1307 had legislated against the diversion of English money
to enemy uses caused by the yearly payment of farms by the
guardians of alien priories to the mother houses abroad.[3] There
were two types of alien priory, conventual and manorial. In
the first, typical examples of which are Blyth in Nottingham-

---

[1] In addition to the material printed in *Mon.*, R. A. Nev. at York contains a
document which throws light upon the early vicissitudes of this foundation.

[2] The date of foundation of Shene was 1 Apr. 1414, of Syon 3 Mar. 1414–15.

[3] *S.R.* i. 150–2.

shire, a cell of La Trinité at Rouen, and St. Neots in Huntingdonshire, a cell of Bec, there were full complements of monks leading a claustral life under priors. These also included the Cluniac
priories, whose complete subordination to the abbot of Cluny
and his vicegerents earned them a penalty which the Cistercians,
with their more elastic organization in abbeys under the
presidency of the abbot of Cîteaux, escaped. But much the
larger number of alien priories were of the second class, manors
usually with the advowsons of parish churches, which were by
no means always appropriated,[1] attached to them, where two
or three monks, sent from time to time by the mother houses,
resided, leading no regular conventual life, but acting as land-
agents for the collection of revenues, which they transported
abroad.[2] After the outbreak of war these were allowed to
continue under royal protection, rendering their farms through
royal collectors to the Exchequer; but, throughout the period,
the foreign houses constantly showed their willingness to part
with unproductive property for a compensation, and thus,
before the final act of resumption in 1411, many of the alien
priories were entirely at the disposal of the Crown. Out of these
came endowments for new foundations, and the Carthusian
houses were some of the earliest to profit by them. The whole
story of this transference of property is extremely complicated,
and grants so made were not always permanent: thus alien
priories made over to the Coventry Charterhouse in 1399
appear at a later date among the endowments of Mount Grace.[3]
The acquisition of the alien priory or manor of Monk's Kirby in

[1] Cases in point where the churches were in the patronage of the foreign
monastery but remained unappropriated were Everdon in Northamptonshire, a
priory or manor of the abbey of Bernay, and Ipplepen in Devon, dependent upon
the priory of Fougères in Brittany. Everdon eventually was among the numerous
alien possessions granted to Eton College, while Ipplepen, which in its precarious
existence during the Hundred Years War had from 1351 onwards been contemplated as a grant to the college of Ottery St. Mary, did not pass into the hands
of the warden and canons till 1437. For Everdon see Bridges, i. 58–60, and for
Ipplepen see Dalton, *The Coll. Church of Ottery St. Mary*, pp. 279–91.

[2] Much with regard to the relation of alien priories to their parent houses during
the undisturbed period before the outbreak of war between England and France
can be gathered from the *Registrum* of Eudes Rigaud 1248–75, ed. Bonnin, 1851.

[3] Field Dalling in Norfolk and Long Bennington and Hough in Lincolnshire. See
*C.P.R.* 1396–9, p. 579; 1416–22, p. 395 (8 June 1421). Or, again, the alien priory
of Bonby in Lincolnshire, a 'cell' of the abbey of Saint-Fromond, which its foreign
patrons granted without royal licence to the London Charterhouse in 1389–90,
was granted by the Crown to Beauvale, 4 April 1403 (*C.P.R.* 1401–5, p. 217).

Warwickshire, a cell of Saint-Fromond, by Thomas Mowbray, led to the foundation of the Epworth Charterhouse:[1] Richard II gave to the Coventry Charterhouse the alien priory of Ecclesfield, near Sheffield, which had belonged to the abbey of Saint-Wandrille near Caudebec.[2] The foundation of Shene, which profited greatly by gifts of alien priories, was subsequent to the act of resumption.[3] Throughout the fifteenth century alien priories formed a standing treasury on which the Crown drew for gifts to chantry colleges,[4] the colleges of Oxford,[5] Cambridge,[6] Eton,[7] and Winchester,[8] and sometimes to older religious houses, as when, in 1405, the alien priory of Scarborough, consisting of the revenues of the church, which had been given by Richard I to Cîteaux for the support of the general chapter, was appropriated to Bridlington Priory.[9]

The enrichment of colleges at the universities by this means was accompanied also now and then by the suppression of small religious houses which had fallen into decay. The best example is the nunnery of St. Radegund at Cambridge, which in 1491

[1] C.P.R. 1396–9, p. 77.

[2] See Fast. Paroch. i. 95–106.

[3] The English priories mentioned in the foundation charter of Shene are Ware (cell of Saint-Evroult), Lewisham and Greenwich (of Saint-Pierre at Ghent), Mayling (of Jumièges), and Carisbrooke and Hinckley (of Lyre). See Mon. vi. (i), 31.

[4] Fotheringhay in 1412 obtained the priories of Newent in Gloucestershire (cell of Cormeilles) and Avebury in Wiltshire (of Saint-Georges-de-Boscherville); Higham Ferrers in 1425, that of Mersea in Essex (of Saint-Ouen, Rouen).

[5] As, for instance, Alberbury in Shropshire (a cell of Grandmont), to All Souls, 11 May 1441 (C.P.R. 1436–41, p. 563).

[6] e.g., Allerton Mauleverer in Yorkshire (cell of Marmoûtier), Ruislip in Middlesex (of Bec), Stower Provost in Dorset (of Préaulx), and Winghall in Lincolnshire (of Séez) to King's. See C.P.R. 1441–5, pp. 84, 160.

[7] See the long list of grants to Eton in the foundation charter, Mon. vi (iii), 1434–7.

[8] The priories of Andwell and Hamble, Hants, and St. Cross in the Isle of Wight, cells of the abbey of Thiron, dio. Chartres, were bought by William of Wykeham in 1391 and given by him to Winchester College (R. Wyke. ii. 14, 63). Andover, a cell of Saint-Florent at Saumur, came to the college at the dissolution of alien priories in 1413 (ibid. i. 221). The priory of Harmondsworth in Middlesex, a cell of La Trinité on the Mont-Sainte-Cathérine at Rouen, was granted to Winchester College 10 Mar. 1390–1, and its possessions outside Middlesex to New College; while on the same day New College had a grant of Takeley in Essex, a priory of Saint-Valéry-sur-Somme, whose possessions in other counties went to Winchester (C.P.R. 1388–92, pp. 417, 418).

[9] C.P.R. 1405–8, p. 52; see also C.P.R. 1399–1401, p. 356, and Hist. Scarborough, ed. Rowntree, pp. 75–6.

was converted into Jesus College,[1] and founders of colleges at the beginning of the next century were not slow to follow this precedent. St. John's College at Cambridge entered into the revenues of two derelict nunneries,[2] and everyone knows the advantage to which Wolsey put the bull of Clement VII by which Christ Church, enriched by the possessions of a number of small houses suppressed for the purpose, eventually took the place of the priory of St. Frideswide.[3] The process by which these changes took place was not very different from that by which the priory of Hornchurch had passed to New College,[4] and other alien priories had been applied by Chichele to All Souls and Higham Ferrers, by Henry VI to Eton and King's, and by Waynflete to Magdalen.[5] And this free treatment of monastic property showed the way on a small scale to the wholesale measures of suppression with which the story of the medieval Church closed.

In concluding these lectures, I feel how small a part of a large area they have covered; and, in dealing with the government of the Church and its institutions, there are large and important topics which have been left untouched. But it was impossible to leave the subject without some reference to the religious life of the age, and, if, in so doing, I have treated a

---

[1] *C.P.R.* 1494–1509, p. 72. On the date of the letters patent, in the patent roll 12 July 1497, see Gray, *The Nunnery of St. Radegund*, pp. 44–5.

[2] Bromhall in Berkshire and Lillechurch or Higham in Kent. The bull bears date 28 Sept. 1524: see *Mon.* iv. 383; *L. & P. H. VIII*, iv (i), 305 (no. 686).

[3] The bull for the suppression of St. Frideswide's Priory, &c., is 1 Sept. 1524, is printed by Rymer, xiv. 23–5, with the royal assent, 7 Jan. 1524–5, ibid. 32. See *L. & P. H. VIII*, iv (i), 435–6 (no. 1001). The list is given ibid. 285 (no. 650): the houses, in addition to St. Frideswide's, were the Premonstratensian abbey of Bayham in Sussex, the Augustinian abbey of Lesnes in Kent, the Benedictine priories of Wallingford, Berks., Bradwell and Tickford, Bucks., Little Horkesley (formerly Cluniac) and Stanesgate, Essex, Daventry (formerly Cluniac), Northants, Canwell and Sandwell, Staffs., Snape, Suffolk, and Causey or Pinham, Sussex, the Augustinian priories of Poughley, Berks., Ravenstone, Bucks., Blackmore, Thoby and Tiptree, Essex, Tonbridge, Kent, and Dodnash, Suffolk, and the Benedictine nunneries of Littlemore, Oxon., and Wix, Essex.

[4] See the licence of 18 Dec. 1389, vacated by that of 14 Feb. 1390–1 (*C.P.R.* 1388–92, pp. 262, 417) and H. F. Westlake, *Hornchurch Priory*, 1923. The priory or hospital of Hornchurch in Havering, Essex, was an offshoot of the hospital of St. Nicholas and St. Bernard at Montjoux, dio. Sion.

[5] The priory of Sele in Sussex, a cell of Saint-Florent at Saumur, which Waynflete wished to annex to Magdalen as early as 1459, came into the possession of the college in 1480. See L. F. Salzman, *The Chartulary of Sele Priory*, 1923, introd., pp. xvi, xvii.

rather well-worn theme, yet I may, from independent and not unsympathetic observation, have put some of its aspects in a somewhat different light from that in which they are usually represented. The evidence of facts cannot be overlooked, but to moralize on that evidence is out of place, and the lover of truth will never hesitate, when the interpretation of facts is doubtful, to regard them in the most charitable light.

# APPENDIX I

## VICARS-GENERAL AND OFFICIALS PRINCIPAL

EXAMPLES of forms of appointment of these and other diocesan and provincial officers are given in Churchill, vol. ii and several occur in printed editions of episcopal registers, in which, however, they were not entered with strict regularity.

The ordinary duties of the vicar-general have already been summarized in the text. Attention, however, may be called to specific acts of appointment in which such duties are detailed. On 5 April 1408 Bishop Bubwith, then in London, appointed Richard Bruton, chancellor of Wells, vicar-general in the diocese of Bath and Wells during his absence. The points mentioned in the commission are: (a) the receipt of resignations of benefices and the institution of presentees, including the receipt of their oaths of canonical obedience; (b) the grant of letters dimissory to clerks, natives of or beneficed in the diocese; (c) grants of dispensations *cum ex eo*, limited to one year, to incumbents of benefices; (d) absolution and reconciliation of persons excommunicated, suspended, or under interdict; (e) licences to bishops to hold ordinations in the absence of the diocesan; (f) execution and return of royal writs directed to the bishop; (g) the appointment of a commissary-general in the diocese.

On the same day Richard Bruton was also created official principal of the consistory of Wells, with full power of cognizance and procedure in all causes coming before the consistory court, to hear, discuss, and terminate them, to deal with the admission or rejection of witnesses, to examine their evidence or commit its examination to suitable persons, and to give sentence. The commission also gave him authority to deal fully with appeals and complaints submitted to the bishop's audience. Power of correction and reform, with the imposition of canonical penalties upon offenders, was committed, however, on the same day to a commissary-general, Thomas Barton, in whose hands also was placed the entire business connected with probate of wills, the measures necessary to compel incumbents to reside in their benefices and meet their responsibilities of repair and renewal of buildings and goods, and the recall of sentences pronounced by him, with the absolution of offenders implicated in them.[1]

Later appointments of officials by Bubwith appear to follow the form above described. Under his successors, Stafford and Bekynton,

---

[1] *R. Bub.*, pp. 23–7. The texts are given in full.

probate business continues to be the work of the commissary-general who is also the bishop's official receiver and has jurisdiction within his peculiar, while Stafford commits to him grants of dispensation for non-residence and the appointment of penitentiaries in the diocese.

At Hereford, where the names of officials and commissaries-general have already been noted, corrections and probate of wills were the special province of the commissary, but, in the appointment of a commissary by Bishop Stanbury in 1453, he is granted the cognizance of causes, even matrimonial, which was proper to the official principal, with a special clause prohibiting him from appointing deputies in matrimonial causes. At the same time the title commissary-general has by no means an invariable connotation. While in the diocese, as distinct from the province, of Canterbury, his powers were those of an official principal, we have seen that at Wells his office was sometimes extended to include special duties of a miscellaneous kind, and that in at least one instance at Hereford it was indistinguishable from that of the official. Further, during Edmund Lacy's tenure of the see of Exeter, his commissary-general at various times between 1422 and 1430 instituted to benefices and issued licences which were acts of grace within the special competence of the vicar-general.

The following examples of commissions may be cited from the archiepiscopal registers at York.

1. *Appointment of an Official by Archbishop Alexander Neville, 1374*

Dated at Clavering, Essex, 19 July. To Master Walter de Skirlawe, archdeacon of East Riding, doctor of decrees.

Ad corrigendum et puniendum crimina et excessus subditorum nostrorum tam clericorum quam laicorum et ad cognoscendum et procedendum in omnibus causis et negotiis in curia nostra Eboracensi introductis et introducendis sive ex officio mero vel ad partium instantias procedendum fuerit in eisdem ipsaque causas et negotia fine canonico terminandum ceteraque omnia et singula faciendum que ad generalis officium pertinent
Vobis de cuius fidelitate et industria fiduciam gerimus specialem committimus vices nostras cum cuiuslibet cohercionis canonice potestate vosque officialem curie nostre ibidem auctoritate nostra pontificali tenore presentium facimus, constituimus ac etiam ordinamus.[1]

In this document, expressed in very general terms, the word omitted before *generalis* should probably be *commissarii*, which is appropriate to the powers of correction given to the official. There is no act of appointment of a vicar-general, but this office was

[1] R. A. Nev. i. fo. 14.

exercised by Adam Thorp, *domino in remotis agente*. The probate of wills, however, was granted in London on 11 June to master Thomas Gothmundham, *juris peritus*, on his appointment as the archbishop's receiver at York, as follows:

Ad insinuandum et approbandum testamenta et ultimas voluntates defunctorum in nostris civitate et diocesi administrationemque bonorum huiusmodi defunctorum executoribus eorundem et aliorum ab intestato decidentium [*sic*] in nostra iurisdictione existentium committendum illis quibus de iure fuerit vel consuetudine committendum eosdem executores calcula et ratiocinia reddere et exhibere compellendum ac compotos huiusmodi audiendum acquietantiasque finales eisdem executoribus et bonorum administratoribus concedendum et faciendum ac sequestrum in bonis quorumcumque subditorum nostrorum in casibus a iure permissis interponendum fructus etiam et proventus ac ecclesiastica bona subditorum nostrorum quorumcumque in forma iuris sequestrandum colligendum et recipiendum ac sequestrum huiusmodi cum videbitur expedire relaxandi [*sic*] necnon bona quecumque omnium et singulorum beneficiorum vacantium vel vacaturorum que ad nos spectant seu spectare poterunt infuturum ac etiam quascumque pecuniarum summas et singulos denarios ad nostrum scaccarium Eboracense provenientes percipiendum colligendum exigendum et levandum et de receptis huiusmodi acquietantias faciendum.[1]

## 2. *Appointment of a Vicar-General by Archbishop Bowet, 1408*

The commission, dated at Isleworth, Middlesex, 4 April 1408, is directed to master Richard Pittes, canon of Salisbury and Wells. The division of the clauses into numbered paragraphs has been adopted here for the sake of convenience.

Henricus permissione divina Eboracensis archiepiscopus Anglie primas et apostolice sedis legatus dilecto nobis in Christo circumspecto viro magistro Ricardo Pittes Sarisbiriensis et Wellensis ecclesiarum canonico salutem gratiam et benedictionem.

Quia nos variis et arduis prepediti negotiis ad nostram diocesim adhuc personaliter accedere non valemus vos de cuius fidelitate circumspectionis industria et conscientie puritate plenam in Domino fiduciam reputamus [*sic*] tenore presentium facimus constituimus creamus et solemniter ordinamus nostrum in spiritualibus vicarium generalem

(1) Ad recipiendum videlicet et recipi faciendum de omnibus et singulis personis ecclesiasticis nostrarum civitatis et dioceseos beneficiatis que nobis obedientiam iurare et promittere tenentur de consuetudine vel de iure obedientie debite iuramentum

(2) Et cum iisdem personis ecclesiasticis infra nostras civitatem et diocesim beneficiatis de absentando de beneficiis suis iuxta formam constitutionis *Cum ex eo* vel alia causa rationabili et legitima dispensandum et dispensationis gratiam faciendum

(3) Litteras dimissorias pro ordinibus a quibuscumque episcopis catholicis

[1] Ibid.

infra Angliam intitulatis tam regularibus quam secularibus clericis nostrarum civitatis et dioceseos concedendum

(4) Crimina quoque defectus et excessus quorumcumque subditorum nostrorum canonice corrigendum puniendum et debite reformandum

(5) Testamenta et ultimas voluntates omnium et singulorum subditorum nostrorum defunctorum probandum inventaria bonorum suorum petendum exigendum et fieri faciendum administrationesque bonorum eorundem executoribus propterea deputatis nominatis et constitutis comittendum calculum compotum et ratiocinium ab eisdem inde exigendum petendum et audiendum acquietantiasque et finales liberationes sibi concedendum superinde dandas et faciendas et expletis per eosdem in ea parte requisitis ipsos ab ulteriori impetitione officii nostri absolvendum et pro perpetuo dimittendum

(6) Administrationem bonorum omnium et singulorum subditorum nostrorum ab intestato decedentium suscipiendum et etiam si oporteat personis ydoneis committendum

(7) Sinodos infra nostram diocesim et convocationem cleri eiusdem celebrari consuetas locis et temporibus ad hoc idoneis vel consuetis celebrari mandandum et faciendum

(8) Denarios beati Petri sinodaliaque et pensiones et alia nostra denaria nobis ratione ecclesie nostre Eboracensis de spiritualibus provenientia et debita levandum colligendum et recipiendum levari colligi et recipi faciendum et de receptis acquietantias et finales liberationes faciendum

(9) Suspensionis excommunicationis et interdicti sententiis involutos in omnibus casibus quibus absolvendi facultas nobis competit absolvendum et reconsiliandum

(10) Electionum negotia et decreta super eisdem nobis de quibuscumque personis ydoneis presentandum recipiendum examinandum et discutiendum et fine debito terminandum eademque inventa rite facta et canonice celebrata iuris ordine observato approbandum et auctorizandum et electam personam vel electas personas canonice confirmandum et installandum seu installari demandandum necnon electiones exadverso minus canonice factas reprobandum cassandum et annullandum

(11) Fructus omnium beneficiorum ecclesiasticorum nostre provincie quocumque nomine censeantur qualitercumque vacantium qui nobis tempore vacationis eorundem debeantur colligi levari et recipi faciendum vel committendum

(12) Ordines generales infra nostram diocesim per episcopos catholicos sedis apostolice gratiam et sui executionem officii obtinentes qui clericos nostre dioceseos tam regulares quam seculares et ceteros clericos quoscumque per litteras dimissorias diocesanorum suorum sufficienter dimissos qui ad suscipiendos ordines tam minores quam sacros reperiantur idonei canonice ordinent celebrari faciendum

(13) Negotia quoque presentationum et donationum de quibuscumque beneficiis ecclesiasticis nostre dioceseos examinandum discutiendum et in eisdem legitime procedendum ipsaque fine debito terminandum presentatas ad huiusmodi beneficia personas idoneas et ceteras personas idoneas quibus donari contigerit beneficia ecclesiastica nostre dioceseos admittendum

instituendum et prout moris est in corporalem possessionem iurium et pertinentium eorundem induci canonice faciendum et recipiendum canoni-cam obedientiam ab eisdem

(14) Quoscumque subditos nostros ex causa rationabili et legitima desti-tuendos seu beneficia ecclesiastica in nostra diocesi illicite occupantes vel minus iuste aliqualiter detinentes destituendum et eosdem servato iuris processu legitimo realiter ammovendum

(15) Clericorum incarceratorum purgationem et compurgatores idoneos admittendum et eos prout iustum fuerit de nostro carcere liberandum

(16) Brevia regia nobis directa debite exequendum et sicut convenit retornandum

Omniaque alia et singula que premissa contingunt seu dependere ab eisdem vel emergere poterunt et generaliter omnia alia et singula exercendum expediendum et exequendum que per vicarium episcopi generalem fieri exerceri et exequi poterunt de consuetudine vel de iure etiam si talia sint expressata maiora de quibus mentionem hic oporteret facere specialem

Collationes vero et presentationes omnium beneficiorum ecclesiasticorum que ad nos ratione ecclesie nostre Eboracensis mere pertineant vel iure devoluto seu alia quacumque de causa infra nostram provinciam quovismodo poterunt pertinere et ecclesie nostre Eboracensis atque cleri nostrarum civitatis et provincie visitationem nobis specialiter reservantes

Vobis committimus vices nostras et plenam tenore presentium cum cuiuslibet cohercionis canonice potestate donamus et concedimus potestatem quousque illam revocari duxerimus duraturam

In cuius rei testimonium sigillum nostrum quod ad manus habemus una cum impressione signeti nostri in maiorem roboris firmitatem presentibus est appensum.

Data in manerio nostro de Ystilworth quarto die mensis Aprilis Anno Domini millesimo quadringentesimo octavo et nostre translationis anno primo.[1]

It will be noticed that this commission includes the powers of correc-tion and of probate which are attributed frequently to the com-missary-general in other dioceses, but the office of vicar-general was not combined with that of official. Bowet's official was master Richard Conyngeston, LL.D., whose terms of appointment are left unrecorded in the register.

### 3. *Later Appointments from the York Registers*

The register of Archbishop William Booth (1452–64) contains distinct forms of appointment for vicars-general and officials. On 16 September 1452, at Hackney in Middlesex, of which he had at one time been rector, Booth committed the office of vicar-general *conjunctim et divisim* to four persons, masters John Barningham, treasurer of York, Richard Tone or Toone, archdeacon of the East

[1] R. Bowet, i, fo. 2.

Riding, Stephen Wilton and John Marshall, U.I.B., canons residentiary of York. The form used is closely allied to that of Alexander
Neville's commission to his official, but the opening clause is common
also to Bowet's commission to the vicar-general, of which it expands
the fourth special clause. Its conclusion states the reservations
given in Bowet's mandate.

(1) Ad corrigendum puniendum et debite reformandum crimina et delicta
quecumque ac excessus et defectus quorumcumque subditorum nostrorum
et pro premissis penas et penitentias canonicas infligendum et iniungendum

(2) Ac in omnibus causis et negotiis ex officio mero mixto seu promoto vel
ad alicuiuscumque partis instantiam in quibus de iure et consuetudine
iurisdictio ecclesiastica ad nos dinoscitur pertinere qualitercumque mouen-
dum cognoscendum et procedendum ac eas et ea cum omnibus et singulis
incidentibus emergentibus dependentibus et connexis fine debito terminandum et finiendum

Ceteraque omnia et singula in premissis seu circa ea necessaria vel
quomodolibet oportuna exercendum et expediendum ac si mandatum
magis exigant speciale

Vobis coniunctim et diuisim de quorum circumspectionibus et industriis
fiduciam habemus specialem committimus vices nostras et plenam in
Domino potestatem cum cuiuslibet cohercionis canonice exequendi que
decreueritis in hac parte potestate

Vosque coniunctim et diuisim nostros in spiritualibus vicarios generales
nobis in remotis agentibus ordinamus deputamus et facimus per presentes
ad nostrum beneplacitum duraturas

Collationibus vero dignitatum et prebendarum hospitalium et liberarum
capellarum et aliorum beneficiorum ecclesiasticorum quorumcumque
nostrorum collationis et patronatus tam infra nostram diocesim sive
provinciam Eboracensem quam extra necnon beneficiorum ecclesiasticorum et pensionum ad nos tam infra diocesim sive provinciam nostram
Eboracensem quam extra ut premittitur spectantium dumtaxat exceptis et
nobis in hac parte specialiter reservatis prout eadem sic reservamus per
presentes.[1]

Two days later, on 18 September, the duties of official were committed to Richard Tone, one of the four vicars-general above named,
in the following terms:

(1) Ad cognoscendum in omnibus causis et negotiis etiam tuitoriis in
curia consistoriali ecclesie nostre Eboracensis tam ad partis instantiam quam
ex officio mero seu promoto intentatis motis seu movendis necnon in omnibus causis et negotiis ad eandem curiam nostram per viam appellationis vel
querele aut alias qualitercumque devolvendis ipsaque causas et negotia
cum omnibus suis emergentibus incidentibus dependentibus et connexis
decidendum et fine debito terminandum

(2) Crimina (&c. as Bowet, VG, cl. 4) nostrorum corrigendum et
puniendum et super eisdem inquirendum

[1] R. W. Bothe, fo. 147.

(3) Testamenta quoque et ultimas (&c., as ibid. cl. 5) probandum approbandum et insinuandum inventaria . . . administrationes quoque bonorum . . . ab eisdem exigendum . . . acquietantias et finales liberationes in ea parte concedendum et faciendum . . . dimittendum

(4) De bonis insuper ab intestato decedentium disponendum et administrationes eorum suscipiendum et personis idoneis si oporteat committendum (cf. ibid. cl. 6)

(5) Sententiasque interlocutorias et diffinitivas juris ordine observato ferendum et promulgandum

Ceteraque omnia et singula in premissis et ea contingentibus necessaria seu quomodolibet oportuna faciendum exercendum et expediendum que per officialem curie consistorii nostre supradicte fieri exerceri et exequi poterunt de consuetudine vel de jure

Vobis (&c., as ibid.) potestatem

Vosque officialem curie nostre antedicte cum omnibus et singulis que ad illud officium pertinent constituimus et preficimus per presentes ad beneplacitum nostrum duraturas.[1]

The appointment of the four vicars-general was renewed on 5 November 1453.[2] It is of course obvious that, while Tone's commission as official referred to the consistory court in which he was the archbishop's standing delegate, the judicial powers of the vicars were exercised in cases which normally would have come before the archbishop in person, and such powers ceased when he was present in the diocese. On 14 May 1455 Booth appointed Tone his sole vicar-general.[3] Tone retired from the officiality in 1458 and was succeeded on 24 August by master Adam Copendale;[4] and at the next appointment of vicars on 7 June 1461 Copendale was associated with master John Sendale.[5] The principle is thus established that, while the official can act by himself as vicar-general, he is as a matter of course one of the partners when the latter office is entrusted to more than one person.

This is further illustrated by the appointments made by Archbishop Rotherham on his translation from Lincoln to York in 1480. On 18 September in that year there occur two commissions, one of the officiality, in the form used by William Booth, to master William Poteman, archdeacon of Cleveland,[6] the other, of the vicariate, to master Robert Booth, dean of York, with Poteman as his associate.[7] The second repeats the form employed in Bowet's register, with a little change in the order of clauses. Clause 12 becomes clause 3, clauses 3 to 8 become 4 to 9, clause 11 becomes 10, and clause 9 becomes 11, the rest following as before. Verbal changes are insignificant, but in clause 2 the words *et non beneficiatis*, probably

---

[1] Ibid., fo. 2b.    [2] Ibid., fo. 157.    [3] Ibid., fo. 174.
[4] Ibid., ff. 203b, 204.    [5] Ibid., fo. 211b.
[6] R. Roth. i, fo. 199.    [7] Ibid., fo. 1.

omitted by error in Bowet's form, are added to *beneficiatis*, and in clause 13 the words *ad hujusmodi beneficia citra vel ad summam xxli. per annum taxata dumtaxat* are inserted between *dioceseos* and *admittendum.*

In August 1483 master William Sheffeld, doctor of decrees, was associated as vicar-general with Booth and Poteman in a brief and general form:

> Super omnibus excessibus ac delictis quorumcumque subditorum nostrorum inquirendum eaque et eos canonice corrigendum multandum condempnandum et puniendum ac omnia alia et singula que ad officium vicarii in spiritualibus generalis de jure et consuetudine incumbere et pertinere dinoscuntur.[1]

Poteman, who became archdeacon of the East Riding in 1484, died in 1493 and was succeeded in the officiality by Sheffeld, who had a sole appointment as vicar-general in the same form on 25 January 1493–4.[2]

The successor of Rotherham, Thomas Savage, was translated from London to York in 1501. On 12 April in that year he appointed an official in the person of master Martin Colyns, doctor of decrees, treasurer of York.[3] The text of this, with merely slight verbal variations, is that of the first clause of the form in William Booth's register, followed by the final clause 'Ceteraque omnia et singula', &c. Side by side with this, however, was issued a letter appointing Colyns and master John Perott, bachelor in canon law and archdeacon of Colchester in the church of London, commissaries-general of the archbishop and receivers-general of the exchequer of York. This is as follows:

> (1) Ad cognoscendum procedendum et inquirendum tam ex officio mero mixto seu promoto de et super quibuscumque criminibus delictis et excessibus quorum correctio punitio et reformatio ad forum ecclesiasticum pertinere dinoscuntur contra quoscumque subditos nostros de et super huiusmodi criminibus [delictis] seu et [*sic*] excessibus qualitercumque notatos diffamatos sive reos ipsa quoque crimina et excessus qualitercumque claruerint canonice corrigendum puniendum et reformandum
>
> (2) Necnon testamenta et ultimas voluntates (&c., as W. Booth, Off. and Savage, Off. cl. 3) . . . ab omni ulteriori compoto et officii . . . dimittendum (see Bowet, VG, cl. 6: the variations are insignificant).
>
> (3) Bona insuper quorumcumque ab intestato decedentium auctoritate nostra sequestrandum et huiusmodi sequestri custodiam personis ad hoc idoneis quotiens et quando videbitur expediens committendum ac sub arto et tuto sequestro custodiri faciendum et de bonis huiusmodi decedentium disponendum administrationemque eorundem bonorum suscipiendum et personis idoneis si oporteat committendum
>
> (4) Necnon prelatos et clerum ad sinodos in ecclesia nostra metropolitica

---

[1] R. Roth. i, fo. 224.      [2] Ibid., fo. 250b.      [3] R. Sav., fo. 2.

Eboracensi ac aliis locis ad hoc idoneis et consuetis ut moris est celebrandas convocandum huiusmodique sinodis quotiens et quando opus fuerit vice et auctoritate nostris interessendum easque celebrandum et non comparentes in eisdem contumaces pronunciandum ipsosque in penam contumaciarum suarum huiusmodi prout de jure et consuetudine fuerit faciendum puniendum et multandum

(5) Hujusmodique multas necnon procurationes denarios beati Petri pensiones portiones et donaria sinodalia ac omnia alia et singula pecuniarum summas proventus jura et emolumenta nobis qualitercumque debita seu debenda ac ad scaccarium nostrum solvi consueta nomine nostro et pro nobis petendum exigendum colligendum levandum et recipiendum ac de levatis et receptis acquietantias et exonerationes finales faciendum sigillandum et hujusmodi solventes finaliter liberandum et acquietandum

Ceteraque omnia et singula faciendum exercendum et expediendum que in premissis et circa ea necessaria fuerint seu quomodolibet oportuna

Vobis conjunctim et divisim sub infrascripta tamen limitatione committimus vices nostras et plenam in Domino tenore presentium potestatem

Vosque commissarios nostros ad supradicta et receptores in scaccario nostro generales ordinamus preficimus et deputamus per presentes

Proviso tamen omnino quod vos dilecte fili Martine sine consensu assensu et voluntate expressis antedicti magistri Johannis Perott nichil penitus exequamini vel recipietis [sic] in hac parte.[1]

On 15 April Savage issued a commission appointing four vicars-general, two of whom were Colyns and Perott. The others were John Carver, doctor of decrees, and Hugh Trotter, S.T.P., treasurer of York.

Quia ex diversis et rationabilibus causis et negotiis nos ecclesiam nostram ac statum honorem et utilitatem ejusdem concernentibus extra nostras civitatem et diocesim aliquotiens nos abesse necessarium est et oportunum

Cupientes igitur animarum subditorum nostrorum curam et jurisdictionem nostram dum sic absentes fuerimus ad omnipotentis Dei laudem et subditorum nostrorum commodum et quietem provide gubernari

Vos de quorum fidelitatibus et circumspectionum industriis plene confidimus quotiens et quando nos abesse contigerit nostros in spiritualibus vicarios generales conjunctim et quemlibet vestrum per se divisim sub infrascriptis cum provisione et limitatione ordinamus facimus et constituimus per presentes

Et super omnibus excessibus et delictis quorumcumque subditorum nostrorum inquirendi eaque et eos canonice corrigendi multandi et condempnandi et puniendi

Ac omnia alia et singula que ad vicarii in spiritualibus generalis officium de jure seu consuetudine pertinere dignoscuntur faciendi excercendi exequendi et expediendi

Vobis conjunctim ut prefertur et divisim vices nostras committimus et plenam in Domino potestatem

[1] Ibid., fo. 2*b*.

Proviso tamen omnino quod vos dilecti filii Martine Colyns Hugo Trotter et Johannes Perott absque expresso consensu assensu et voluntate prefati magistri Johannis Carver dum presens fuerit nichil prorsus exequamini aut aliquis vestrum exequatur.[1]

Archbishop Bainbridge, translated from Durham to York in 1514, made appointments similar to those of his predecessor, distinguishing the offices of vicar-general, official, and commissary-general. But, while Savage's official had been associated in the other functions, his action as vicar-general and commissary was limited by the consent of a colleague to whom the power of initiative was reserved. Bainbridge, while reappointing Colyns to the officiality, gave him no share in the two other offices. Carver was reappointed vicar-general and master John Withers, *canonicus prebendatus* of St. Paul's and Salisbury, was made commissary and receiver-general.[2]

Carver's form of appointment as vicar-general differs somewhat in wording from the form which he and his colleagues had received from Archbishop Savage, but in no essential feature of its contents:

Quia non nullis arduis causis et negotiis nos et ecclesiam nostram metropoliticam Eboracensem ac statum honorem et utilitatem ejusdem tangentibus et concernentibus extra nostras civitatem diocesim et provinciam Eboracenses ad tempus agere nos oportet

Cupientes animarum subditorum nostrorum saluti prospicere curamque et jurisdictionem nostram dum sic abfuerimus ad omnipotentis Dei laudem et subditorum nostrorum commodum et quietem provide gubernari

Te de cujus fidelitatis industria scientia et conscientie puritate in et circa justitie administrationem plenam in Domino fiduciam obtinemus nostrum in spiritualibus vicarium generalem pro tempore absentie nostre hujusmodi creamus facimus ordinamus et constituimus per presentes et super omnibus (&c., as in the previous form) omniaque alia et singula (&c., as in the previous form) tibi committimus vices nostras et plenam in Domino tenore presentium committimus [*sic*] potestatem.[3]

The commission to the official bears the same date, 3 December 1508, and, save for a few slight verbal variations, is identical with that previously received by Colyns. There is a similar identity between the form of appointment of the commissary, issued on 21 December, and the form seven and a half years earlier, the final clause reading:

Vobis committimus vices nostras et plenam in Domino tenore presentium potestatem

Vosque commissarium nostrum ad omnia et singula suprascripta et receptorem in scaccario nostro generalem preficimus ordinamus et deputamus per presentes.[4]

[1] R. Sav., fo. 2.     [2] R. Bain., ff. 1*b*, 2.
[3] Ibid., fo. 1*b*.     [4] Ibid.

This series of documents may conclude with those issued by Wolsey on 13 November 1514. There is no appointment of a commissary-general, and the vicariate and officiality were both committed to the same man, master Brian Higdon, canon of Lincoln and shortly afterwards dean of York. His commission as official is in the form used in Savage's and Bainbridge's registers.[1] But the commission of the vicariate is a long and elaborate document containing a lengthy catalogue of duties rendered necessary by the fact that Wolsey's absence from his diocese was indefinite and its administration by a vicar-general was in consequence a more or less permanent arrangement. Large portions of it are derived from earlier forms, but there is none in which so many duties are combined.

Thomas permissione divina Eboracensis archiepiscopus Anglie primas et apostolice sedis legatus dilecto nobis in Christo magistro Briano Higdon legum doctori canonico ecclesie cathedralis Lincolniensis prebendato salutem gratiam et benedictionem.

Quia nos variis et arduis domini nostri regis et regni prepediti negotiis ad nostram civitatem diocesim et provinciam Eboracenses adhuc personaliter accedere commode non valemus

Cupientes igitur totis viribus animarum (&c., as Savage, VG) . . . gubernari

Te de cujus fidelitate et discretionis industria ac conscientie puritate necnon administratione justitie fiduciam constantem in Domino obtinemus tenore presentium facimus constituimus et ordinamus nostrum vicarium in spiritualibus generalem

(1) Ad recipiendum (&c. as Bowet, VG 1) . . . juramentum

(2) Capitulis collegiis et conventibus ipsarum nostrarum civitatis diocesis et provincie Eboracensium pastoribus destitutis licentiam eligendi dandum et concedendum electiones sive postulationes ipsarum canonice factas et celebratas quarum ad nos de jure seu consuetudine confirmatio vel infirmatio spectare et pertinere dinoscuntur examinandum discutiendum et fine canonico terminandum ac ipsas et personas electas canonice confirmandum vel suis exigentibus vitiis et defectibus infirmandum cassandum et annullandum

(3) Ecclesias personas et loca ecclesiastica nobis subjecta visitandum inquirendum corrigendum puniendum et reformandum visitationis officium in eisdem vice et auctoritate nostris exercendum procurationem sive procurationes ea de causa nobis debitas exigendum et recipiendum

(4) Ac prelatos et clerum (&c. as Savage, Comm. Gen. 4) . . . multandum huiusmodique multas exigendum levandum et recipiendum

(5) Necnon ecclesias cimiteria monasteria et alia loca ecclesiastica cum pollute sive polluta fuerint auctoritate nostra reconsiliari

(6) Abbatesque et viduas benedici et velari ac perpetue castitatis votum ab eisdem recipi faciendum

(7) Causas querelas et lites omnium et singulorum subditorum nostrorum

[1] R. Wolsey, fo. 3.

etiam causas appellationum ad nos interpositas et interponendas vel per queremonias aut alias qualitercumque devolvendas seu iam devolutas etiam si tendant ad depositionem suspensionem ab officio seu privationem audiendum et audiri committendum examinandum decidendum et terminandum

(8) Iurisdictionem nostram ordinariam ecclesiasticam et metropoliticam in dictis nostris civitate diocesi et provincia Eboracensibus regendum et exercendum ac regi et exerceri faciendum

(9) Sententias proferendum carceris penas et alias quas sacri canones volunt seu permittunt infligendum multandum et mitigandum emendas quoque debitas taxandum et moderandum

(10) Quoscumque subditos delinquentes criminosos et excedentes ac de crimine heresis suspectos sive diffamatos necnon divinatores sortilegos aut in fide nostra male sapientes et devios sive errantes incarcerandum et detinendum ipsosque super excessibus suis criminibus et delictis puniendum corrigendum et eis penas indicendum ac eas relaxandum modificandum et diminuendum juxta et secundum eorum qualitatem et quantitatem ac exigentiam delictorum et propter sua crimina aut suam malam administrationem beneficiis et eorum administrationibus privandum ammovendum et deponendum ipsosque ad penam perpetuam vel ad tempus in carceribus nostris peragendam condempnandum

(11) Sententias interdicti suspensionis sive excommunicationis standum promulgandum et pronuntiandum beneficia absolutionis impendendum et decreta quecumque interponendum

(12) Quascumque presentationes ad quecumque beneficia ecclesiastica cum cura vel sine cura in nostris civitate diocesi et provincia Eboracensibus existentia per mortem resignationem privationem sive dimissionem ex causa permutationis aut pure et simpliciter factam aut quovismodo alias vacantia aut imposterum vacatura per quoscumque patronos ecclesiasticos vel seculares factas vel faciendas dummodo debite fiant admittendum et recipiendum

(13) Inquisitiones super iurispatronatus ipsorum beneficiorum ac informationes personarum presentatarum faciendum et fieri mandandum ac inquisitiones et informationes sic factas recipiendum et aperiendum partibusque copiam tradendum et tradi faciendum decernendum et demandandum

(14) Ipsasque personas sic presentatas habiles et idoneas ad huiusmodi beneficia admittendum et instituendum in eisdem et prout moris est in realem corporalem et actualem possessionem eorundem ponendum et inducendum seu poni et induci mandandum

(15) Litteras institutionum et alias necessarias et oportunas desuper faciendum expediendum et expediri faciendum et mandandum

(16) Renuntiationes sive resignationes quorumcumque beneficiorum simpliciter vel ex causa permutationis recipiendum et admittendum aut etiam si opus fuerit refutandum juramentaque a talibus permutantibus sive resignantibus ac aliis beneficiatis quibuscumque requisita ac fieri et prestari solita recipiendum ipsisque personis beneficia sua huiusmodi sic resignantibus congruam portionem sive pensionem annuam ad terminum vite sue sive ad tempus de fructibus redditibus et proventibus dictorum beneficiorum suorum et quorumcumque aliorum dignitatum canonicatuum et pre-

bendarum ad collationem nostram aut aliorum quorumcumque sive presentationem spectantium sive pertinentium assignandum limitandum et moderandum ac terminis et locis quibuscumque fideliter persolvendum sub quibuscumque sententiis censuris et penis decernendum statuendum ordinandum et vallandum ac decreta in hac parte interponendum

(17) Necnon abbatibus et prelatis suis monasteriis sive prioratibus renuntiare volentibus renuntiandi licentiam dandum et concedendum

(18) In quibuscumque votis et in aliis casibus a iure nobis permissis et concessis cum subditis nostris dispensandum

(19) Atque religiosos nostrarum civitatis et diocesis Eboracensium de uno monasterio ad alium se transferendi licentiam concedendum

(20) Confessiones omnium et singulorum subditorum nostrorum audiendum et absolvendum eosdem etiam de criminibus et censuris ac penis ecclesiasticis a iure vel ab homine latis et inferendis ac in casibus a iure nobis permissis reservatis aut alias nobis commissis penitentias salutares pro modo culparum suarum iniungendo

(21) Confessores et penitentiarios in nostris civitate diocesi et provincia Eboracensibus eligendum deputandum constituendum et ordinandum qui parem aut limitatam in premissis habeant potestatem et eos quotiens opus fuerit revocandum

(22) Atque super bannis una duabus vel tribus vicibus si opus fuerit minime faciendis aut edendis cum subditis nostris matrimonium contrahere aut nuptialem benedictionem matrimonio adhibere volentibus et loco originis partium dispensandum

(23) Necnon licentiam et gratiam celebrandi et desponsandi in oratorio concedendum eisdem

(24) Atque cum rectoribus sive curatis ecclesiarum quarumcumque nostrarum civitatis et dioceseos Eboracensium super residentia sua personali dum tamen ecclesie ipse propter hoc non defraudentur suis obsequiis in eisque cura animarum minime necligatur dispensandum

(25) Ordines insuper tam minores quam sacros necnon sanctum crisma et oleum aquam gregorianam altaria cimiteria et ecclesias per quemcumque episcopum catholicum rite et canonice promotum gratiam et communionem sancte sedis apostolice habentem et obtinentem celebrari confici benedici consecrari reconsiliari seu dedicari faciendum et ad hos eidem episcopo licentiam dandum et concedendum

(26) Necnon subditis nostris promoveri cupientibus litteras dimissorias tradendum et concedendum ac cum subditis nostris de se non promovendo ad ordines dum tamen in studio generali resideant et permaneant dispensandum

(27) Clericosque convictos quoscumque per quoscumque iudices seculares petendum et recipiendum ac peti et recipi faciendum ipsosque carceribus nostris salvo ibidem custodiendos mancipandum ac ipsos ab huiusmodi criminibus pro quibus ut prefertur convicti fuerint legitime purgatos de carceribus nostris deliberandum ipsosque clericos ad purgationes suas sic faciendas admittendum et recipiendum ac admitti et recipi faciendum

(28) Testamenta omnium et singulorum subditorum nostrorum beneficiatorum et ultimas voluntates eorundem defunctorum probandum

approbandum et insinuandum inventarium (&c. as Bowet, VG, cl. 5) . . . dimittendum

(29) Administrationemque bonorum eorundem ab intestato (&c., as Bowet, VG, cl. 6) . . . committendum

(30) Necnon fructus omnium beneficiorum nostrarum civitatis diocesis et provincie Eboracensium quocumque (&c., as Bowet, VG, cl. 11) . . . committendum

Et generaliter omnia alia et singula que ad officium vicarii in spiritualibus generalis de iure vél consuetudine pertinere dignoscuntur faciendum exercendum expediendum et exequendum

Tibi committimus vices nostras et plenam in Domino potestatem cum cuiuslibet cohercionis canonice potestate

In cuius rei testimonium sigillum nostrum presentibus est appensum

Dat. in hospitio nostro prope Westmonasterium tertio decimo die mensis Novembris anno Domini millesimo quingentesimo quartodecimo et nostre translationis anno primo.[1]


# APPENDIX II

# APPOINTMENT OF SUFFRAGAN BISHOPS

A GOOD example of a commission given to a suffragan is the letter addressed in December 1408 by Henry Bowet, archbishop of York, to William of Northburgh, 'episcopus Pharensis', in which his duties are detailed. It is accompanied by a letter of credence addressed to the clergy of the diocese in general and notifying the appointment.

Henricus, etc., venerabili fratri nostro domino Willelmo eadem permissione Pharensi episcopo salutem et fraternam in Domino caritatem.

(1) Ad celebrandum et conferendum ordines minores quibuscumque subditis nostris ad hoc idoneis et aliis a suis diocesanis sufficienter dimissis

(2) Ecclesias cimiteria et altaria quecumque nostre dioceseos non consecrata aut sanguinis vel seminis effusione polluta suspendendum et de eisdem in forma iuris inquirendum nosque superinde rite et congrue certificandum

(3) Sacramentum confirmationis quibuscumque subditis nostris ministrandum

(4) Altaria portatilia que superaltaria nuncupantur calicesque patenas et vestimenta sacerdotalia benedicendum et consecrandum

(5) Abbates moniales et virgines viduasque nostra premunitione canonica previa benedicendum consecrandum et velandum

(6) Confessiones quorumcumque subditorum nostrorum tam virorum quam mulierum vobis confiteri volentium audiendum iniunctaque eis pro commissis penitentia utinam salutari eos ab eorum excessibus in omnibus casibus a iure permissis absolvendum nostreque penitentiarie officium gerendum et exercendum

[1] R. Wolsey, ff. 3, 4.

Dispensationibus nobis seu nostro vicario generali a sede apostolica commissis et demandatis apostolicis necnon parcorum nostrorum fractionibus libertatum nostrarum et ecclesie nostre violationibus necnon iniuriis offensis et violentiis nobis et ecclesie nostre illatis seu inferendis incestibus periuriisque in assisis ubi sequitur exheredatio seu gravis depauperatio alicuius dumtaxat exceptis

Ceteraque omnia et singula in premissis seu circa ea vel eorum aliquod necessaria vel quomodolibet oportuna faciendum gerendum exercendum expediendum et debite exequendum

Paternitati vestre reverende de cuius conscientie puritate et circumspectionis industria plene confidimus vices nostras committimus et potestatem quamdiu nobis placuerit duraturas

Ratificantes insuper quantum in nobis est omnes et singulas indulgentias a vobis hactenus in quibuscumque missis solennibus rite concessas et imposterum concedendas

In cuius rei testimonium sigillum nostrum presentibus est appensum

Dat. in castro nostro de Cawode antepenultimo die mensis Decembris anno Domini millesimo quadringentesimo octavo et nostre translationis secundo.

The letter of credence follows:

Henricus, &c., dilectis filiis universis archidiaconis et eorum officialibus abbatibus prioribus decanis rectoribus vicariis et capellanis quibuscumque curatis et non curatis totique populo per nostram diocesim constitutis salutem gratiam et benedictionem.

Cum venerabilis frater noster dominus Willelmus de Northburgh promerens ex dono scientie decore virtutum et gratia meritorum quibus pollebat in oculis sanctissimi in Christo patris et domini nostri domini Urbani divina providentia pape sexti specialem gratiam invenire per eundem dominum nostrum papam in ecclesie Pharensis episcopum canonice sit prefectus legitimeque creatus et ipsius sanctissimi patris auctoritate rite juxta iuris exigentiam consecratus prout per litteras apostolicas et alia plurima documenta super huiusmodi creatione prefectione et consecratione confectis et coram consilio nostro preostensas liquere poterit manifeste

Nos ipsius conversationem placidam et honestam ac utilis sue devotionis obsequia nobis cleroque et populo nobis lege diocesana subiectis multipliciter profutura de qua consideratione pensantes ipsum in nostrum assumpsimus suffraganeum arbitrantes quod in ipso ecclesie nostre honoris suscipient incrementa unde nostre mentis affectum vobis plenius ostendentes rogamus vos in Domino exhortantes quatinus sic eum in officio per nos sibi tradito unanimiter benevole et gratiose prosequi cum ad vos declinaverit benignius et admittere studeatis quod fervere devotionem vestram per evidentiam operis erga nostra complacita cognoscamus et ad ea que processu temporis grata vobis extiterint debeamus ob id specialiter promptiores effici et magis favorabiles inveniri Valete

Dat. (&c. as before).[1]

[1] R. Bowet, i, fo. 284.

The terms of the first of these letters may be compared with those of the briefer commission addressed by Archbishop Bainbridge to John Hatton, bishop of Negropont, in December 1508, nearly a hundred years later:

Cristoforus (&c.) venerabili confratri nostro Johanni Hatton Dei gratia Nigropontensi episcopo suffraganeo nostro salutem et fraternam in Domino caritatem.

(1) Ad consecrandum per sacrarum manuum vestrarum impositionem quoscumque subditos nostros utriusque sexus sacri baptismatis unda renatos

(2) Ac altaria in quibuscumque ecclesiis capellis sive oratoriis per nostras civitatem diocesim et provinciam Eboracenses ubilibet constitutis existentia quotiens opus fuerit dedicandum

(3) Necnon viatica seu portatilia que superaltaria vulgariter nuncupamus etiam et vestimenta ac alia ornamenta ecclesiastica quecumque in debita forma benedicendum

(4) Temporibus quoque a iure statutis clericis beneficiatis et aliis quibus-cumque nostrarum civitatis et dioceseos Eboracensium predictarum alienis-que per suos ordinarios sufficienter dimissis titulos sufficientes habentibus tam minores quam sacros ordines in locis per nos aut nostrum vicarium in spiritualibus generalem limitandis conferendum

(5) Oleumque et crisma congruis loco et tempore cum solempnitate qua decet consecrandum

Ceteraque omnia et singula que ad officium pastorale in premissis seu eorum aliquo pertinent seu pertinere debeant faciendum exercendum expediendum et exequendum

Fraternitati vestre tenore presentium committimus potestatem

In cuius rei testimonium sigillum nostrum presentibus apponi fecimus

Dat. in hospitio nostro prope Westmonasterium quarto die mensis Decembris anno Domini quingentesimo octavo et nostre translationis anno primo.[1]

On 13 November 1514 Wolsey issued a commission to the same bishop in precisely the same terms, the word *consecrandum* in clause 1 being now rightly given as *confirmandum*.[2] The offices deputed to the suffragan are described in Bainbridge's and Wolsey's letters in some-what different terms from those in Bowet's commission: no clause covers the power of consecrating, blessing, and veiling abbots and nuns, and there is no penitentiary clause. With questions of penance the special diocesan penitencers could deal, while with regard to the work of the suffragan in connexion with religious houses, each benediction of an abbot and each of the other functions mentioned required a special commission which made their insertion in a general commission unnecessary.

In addition to examples noted in the text, the ordinations which took place during the long pontificate of John Kempe and those of

[1] R. Bain., fo. 2.
[2] R. Wolsey, fo. 4.

some of his successors at York, may receive attention. Between May 1426 and September 1452 we have details of 154 ordinations, only 23 of which were celebrated by the archbishop's authority, the rest in his constant absence from the diocese being by the authority of the vicar-general. The archbishop employed two suffragans in succession, one, Nicholas, bishop of Dromore, up to the middle of 1445, and after that time John, bishop of Philopolis.[1] In all only eight ordinations were held by Kempe in person. These were the September ordinations of 1428 and 1440, and the Easter ordinations of 1432, 1438 and 1440, held in York Minster, the September ordination of 1441, in the chapel at Bishopthorpe, and two special ordinations in September and December 1444 at Scrooby in Nottinghamshire. Of the rest, 103 were held by the bishop of Dromore, of which 5 were in the Minster, presumably at the high altar, 11 also in the Minster at the Lady altar, 1 in St. Mary's Abbey, 6 in Holy Trinity Priory, 18 at the Greyfriars, 16 at the Blackfriars, 17 at the Whitefriars, 18 at the Austin Friars, 4 in St. Mary's Castlegate, 3 in St. Michael-le-Belfrey, and 4 in St. Leonard's hospital. Of the 43 held by the bishop of Philopolis, 7 were at the Lady altar in the Minster, 3 at Holy Trinity, 6 at the Greyfriars, 5 at the Blackfriars, 7 at the Whitefriars, 8 at the Austin Friars, and 7 at St. Leonard's Hospital.

Kempe's successor, William Booth, appointed four suffragans, of whom the bishop of Philopolis was again one (23 Mar. 1452–3).[2] He held twenty-one ordinations, being all except one of those recorded between December 1454 and Easter Even 1458. The one exception was that in September 1457, held by John 'Insulensis', presumably John, bishop of the Isles (i.e. Sodor and Man) at this period. He had been appointed 21 October 1452,[3] and the nine ordinations from December in that year to September 1454 are in his name. He acted throughout Booth's primacy, his appointment overlapping that of the other suffragans, and, in addition to the 10 ordinations already noted, held 17 more, 8 of which, from 1459 to 1462, viz., 4 at Southwell, 3 at Scrooby, and 1 at Lenton Priory, indicate that his duties lay in the archdeaconry of Nottingham. Meanwhile Richard Misson, bishop of Dromore, appointed 1 December 1475,[4] was ordaining in the Lady Chapel of the Minster and in the friary churches at York, completing his twenty-fifth ordination in June 1462. He appears to have died about this date and the nine ordinations between September 1462 and the Lent of 1463–4 were held at York by the bishop of the Isles. Misson's

---

[1] Always called Philopolis in the York registers. But probably the right form, as in Eubel, is Philippopolis.

[2] R. W. Bothe, fo. 367b.

[3] Ibid., fo. 367.        [4] Ibid., fo. 638b.

successor in the see of Dromore, William Egremont, was appointed suffragan 25 January 1463–4.[1] In the course of 1464 the last three ordinations of Booth's primacy are in his name, and until his death in 1501 he remained the principal suffragan in the diocese. His successor, John Hatton, bishop of Negropont, has been noted in the text as holding the archdeaconry of Nottingham and as receiving, after his appointment by Savage, reappointment by Bainbridge and Wolsey. He died in 1516 and was succeeded as bishop of Negropont and suffragan of York by Richard Wilson, who became bishop of Meath in 1523. After his time Wolsey's latest suffragan was the ill-fated Premonstratensian Matthew Makarell, abbot of Barlings and bishop of Chalcedon.[2] Of William Hogeson, bishop of Dara, the last, under Archbishop Lee, of the papally licensed suffragans, something has already been said.

William Booth, although he had affection for his diocese and is remembered with his brother Lawrence, who also became arch-bishop, at Southwell, seems to have spared himself the privilege of ordaining its clergy, and, by this time, save on rare occasions, ordi-nations had become the regular feature of the suffragan's duties. This, however, was not always the case. The printed registers of the bishops of Bath and Wells from 1407 yield the following results:

(a) Bishop Bubwith (1406–24) out of 37 recorded ordinations, celebrated 13, 4 in Wells cathedral, the rest in his manorial chapels at Banwell and Wookey. Of the 24 held by three suffragans, John 'Soltoniensis', John, bishop of Ross, and Richard, bishop of Innis-cattery, 9 took place in the elder Lady chapel at Wells, 12 in St. Cuthbert's, Wells, and 3 others at Taunton, Yeovil, and Bruton Priory church respectively.

(b) In the register of Bishop Stafford (1425–43) 67 ordinations are recorded, 18 of which were held by the bishop himself, 4 in his cathedral church at Bath, 3 at Wookey, and the rest at Dogmersfield in Hampshire. The bishop of Inniscattery held 27 at a variety of places, viz. 1 at Bath, 5 at Yeovil, 4 at the Blackfriars, Ilchester, 3 in St. Cuthbert's at Wells, 2 at Bruton Priory and in each of the parish churches of Bridgwater, Crewkerne, Montacute, and Taunton, and 1 in each of those of Axbridge, Bruton, and Ilminster and in St. Mary Redcliffe at Bristol. Of the remaining 22, held by John 'Olenensis', whose titular see appears to have been in Iceland, 1 was at Bath, 11 in St. Cuthbert's, Wells, 4 in the elder Lady chapel, 1 at Bruton Priory and in each of the churches of Axbridge, Crewkerne, Taunton, Yeovil, and the Temple or Holy Cross at Bristol.

[1] R. W. Bothe, fo. 371.

[2] Wilson received his commission before 28 Nov. 1516 (R. Wolsey, fo. 20) and Makarell before 19 Mar. 1424/5 (ibid., fo. 79b).

(c) The episcopate of Bekynton (1443–65) marks a surprising exception to what was elsewhere becoming the rule, for the bishop celebrated no less than 92 out of 138 recorded ordinations in person, 7 in Wells Cathedral, the rest in his palace chapel and oratory and, with three exceptions at Taunton, at his manors of Banwell, Dogmers-field, and Wookey and his inn in London. Of 46 held by the two suffragans, James, bishop of Achonry (subsequently of Bangor) and John, bishop of Tenos, 20 were in the elder Lady chapel by the cloister, 8 in the later Lady chapel at the east end of the cathedral church, 2 in other chapels of the church, 13 in St. Cuthbert's, and 1 in St. John's Hospital at Wells, 1 at Taunton and 1 at Wookey, while the bishop of Achonry held one ordination at Bath.

(d) If Bekynton had been industrious in the work of ordination, his successor Robert Stillington (1466–91) left it entirely to his four suffragans who served in succession. The last of these was the secular Thomas Cornish, who succeeded the Augustinian canon John Valens as bishop of Tenos and, from 1486 to his death in 1513, acted on behalf of bishops Stillington, Fox, King, and Hadrian di Castello. In none of these cases did the bishops celebrate Orders in person, but, like the later archbishops of York, acted by deputy. Later suffragans, after the death of Cornish, were Thomas Wulff, bishop of Lacedaemon, in 1513, and Thomas Chard, either the Cluniac prior of Montacute, or the Cistercian abbot who has left his mark upon his abbey of Ford in the shape of the splendid abbot's lodging.[1]

It is worth noting that no suffragan in this diocese, while both the Lady chapels at Wells were at his disposal as well as the parish church of St. Cuthbert and St. John's Hospital, celebrated at the high altar of the cathedral church. While the high altar at Bath, which Stafford seems to have preferred to Wells, was apparently the scene of more than one ordination held by a suffragan, the list of monastic and parish churches is varied. Under Stillington, ordina-tions at St. John's Hospital reached the remarkable figure of 76 out of 122. Suffragan bishops were very often friars, more often in fact than not; but, even though this is true of some of the suffragans of Bath and Wells, the use of friary churches for ordinations was as rare as it was general at York, and the only friary church used for this purpose seems for a short period to have been one at Ilchester. For the reservation of the high altar to the diocesan bishop we may compare the list of Alnwick's ordinations as bishop of Norwich (1426–36). Out of the 29 ordinations which he held, 18 were in the

---

[1] Both were bishops, one apparently of Selymbria and the other of Solubria, but the similarity in the names of their titular sees makes distinction more difficult.

cathedral church, while none of the 28 held by his suffragan, Robert 'Gradensis', was celebrated there. And at Durham,[1] though a suffragan occasionally seems to have used the high altar, the normal place for his activities was the Galilee chapel.

## APPENDIX III

## BISHOP ALNWICK'S COURT-BOOK (*see p.* 55)

THE substantial fragment of a Court or Correction Book referred to in the text was discovered by the late Canon Foster among a miscellaneous collection of documents in the Bishop's Registry at Lincoln. It consists of 56 paper leaves, of which 23 relate to the archdeaconry of Lincoln, 20 to the archdeaconry of Huntingdon, and 12 to the archdeaconry of Buckingham. They bear no marks of binding, but are in each case the remains of larger gatherings. Of the Lincoln gathering there were originally at least 52 leaves, numbered in Roman figures, of which ff. xi, xvi-xviii, xxii, xxiv, xxv, xxvi, and xlv-lii remain, with seven more from which the numerals have disappeared. The Huntingdon gathering, though not complete, is in somewhat better condition; but the Buckingham portion is fragmentary and in a bad state of decay. The entire fragment has been transcribed by the present writer, and a selection from its contents, with the passages alluded to in the text, is given below.

The contents are records of the hearing of cases reserved to the bishop before him or his commissaries. These follow no regular chronological order, but belong to the three last years of Alnwick's episcopate (1446–9) and extend into that of his successor Marmaduke Lumley (1450–2). While the earlier entries, however, record the procedure followed with scrupulous care, those of Lumley's time, written in an ink which has become faint with years, are merely brief memoranda without detail. The number of cases recorded is: Lincoln, 178; Huntingdon, 131; Buckingham, 43.

A complete edition of the fragment would involve a large amount of tedious repetition and much unimportant matter. The specimens selected here are worthy of preservation as dealing in detail with especially interesting, but not necessarily exceptional cases. We may begin with cases of violence *in casu a jure non permisso.*

1. (fo. 2*b*; Huntingdon, no. 13.) In decanatu de Leghtonstone. Hamerton. Willelmus Hogeson, Willelmus Burgeys, Johannes Graunger, Johannes Tracy, Willelmus Judde et Johannes James, familiares servientes Johannis Knyvet de Hamerton armigeri, de mandato et ratihibicione eiusdem

[1] *Linc. Vis.* iii. 405, 409–13.

Johannis Knyvet 22 die Marcii, a.d. 1445(/6) infra mansum rectorie ecclesie
de Hamerton predicta et 24 die eiusdem mensis in campis de Woldeweston¹
manus violentas in dominum Johannem Marchall, rectorem ecclesie de
Hamerton predicta,² usque magnam sanguinis effusionem de capite et facie
eiusdem in casu a iure non permisso temere iniecerunt, insultum eidem
rectori infra rectoriam predictam more guerrino publice faciendo et eum
ab eorum manibus pro salute sua fugientem usque in campos de Woldeweston
prefata insequendo, sicque eum grauiter vulneraverunt et fustigarunt, sen-
tentiam maioris excommunicacionis contra tales a canone generaliter latam
incurrendo.³

12 die April. a.d. 1446 in ecclesia de Lincolnia coram Derby comparuerunt
Tracy, Judde, Burgeys et Graunger, qui omnes quatuor de veritate dicenda
in forma iuris iurati et singillatim interrogati fatentur se manus violentas in
dictum rectorem iniecisse, &c. ut supra. Unde iurati de stando mandatis
ecclesie et peragendo penitenciam occasione premissa habent diem Mercurii
prox. post festum sancti Marci evangeliste extunc prox. ad recipiendum
beneficium absolucionis in ecclesia Lincoln., in casu quo huiusmodi absolucio
pertineat ad reverendum patrem, vocando ad hoc dicto rectore pro suo
interesse, et habent quemlibet diem citra, dummodo dictus rector intersit.
Et eodem die 12 April. dicti Tracy, Judde, Burgeys constituerunt et eorum
quilibet constituit apud acta Robertum Ufford et Johannem Graunger
predictum suos procuratores licet absentes tanquam presentes coniunctim
et divisim ad petendum et obtinendum beneficium absolucionis &c. et ad
recipiendum et subeundum penitenciam in hac parte et ad cetera facienda
et recipienda que iuris sunt.

15 die April. in domo registri de Nettelham coram Derby comparuit
Graunger tam suo quam nomine procuratorio dictorum Tracy, Jud et
Burgeys, et peciit se et dominos suos huiusmodi a sentencia excommunicacionis huiusmodi absolvi; ad cuius peticionem et de consensu dicti rectoris
eosdem, prestito primitus per eundem procuratorem tam suo quam suorum

¹ Old Weston, the parish adjoining Hamerton on the south-west.
² No institution of Marshall to this church is recorded. On 4 Nov. 1446 he
appeared in Buckden Church before the commissary Leek to answer a charge of
absenteeism *a longo tempore* without cause. He pleaded guilty, but alleged fear as
his reason, which, considering his experiences at the hands of master Knyvet's
servants, was not an unreasonable excuse. He failed, however, to prove his case,
and next day was admonished to reside on his living and minister in person
(Huntingdon, no. 24). About the same time Knyvet himself was charged with
adultery with a serving-woman Joan Brown, who had had a child by him. He
received correction from the commissary, but details are not given (ibid., no. 25).
Marshall resigned in 1454 (Noble, ap. *Trans. Camb. & Hunt. Archaeol. Soc.* iii. 117).
He had already in Oct. 1444 been summoned to appear before the bishop's
chancellor Depyng on the charge of having obtained his presentation to the church
of Hamerton by simony. On this occasion the rural dean had sent word that he
was in hiding, and the sequel is not recorded (Hunt. no. 126). Later in 1449 he
was suspended for failure to answer a summons to a synod, and further contumacy
produced a renewal of the sentence (ibid., no. 108).
³ A marginal note runs: 'Directum mandatum citacionis magistro Johanni
Leek, rectoribus de Buckeworth et Mullesworth, et Johanni Elveden.'

dominorum nomine de peragendo penitenciam iuramento &c., idem Derby dictum Graunger primo, Tracy secundo, Jud tercio et Burgeys quarto, in personam dicti procuratoris, et ipsum procuratorem in personam dominorum suorum absolvit; et quilibet eorum habet quatuor fustigaciones circa ecclesiam suam parochialem, offerendo ultimo die dominico ceram unius denarii, et quatuor fustigaciones circa forum Huntingdonie in forma penitencie, offerendo ad sumpnum altare ecclesie sancte Marie Huntingdonie unum denarium post peractam penitenciam.

2. (Huntingdon, no. 3, fo. 3.) (Hichyn.)  Pirington[1]
    Adam Tydy (non citatus)
    Willelmus Raven alias Taylour de Perington, taylour
    Ricardus Burgeys (peregit penitenciam)
    Thomas Dekes (excommunicatus)
    Johannes Cattesson (ad purgandum)
    Thomas Yvery (purg.)
    Henricus Dawngerys (peregit penitenciam)
    Johannes Dawngerys (excommunicatus)
    Willelmus Dixe (purg.)
    Johannes Samme, sen. (ad purgandum)
    Ricardus Tydy (ad purgandum)
    Thomas Sam' (vocetur)    (Omnes de eadem)

Omnes isti simul combinati notantur super eo quod ipsi, scientes Thomam . . . lond de Polites[2] fore apparitorem generalem reverendi in Christo patris et domini domini Willelmi, Dei gratia Lincolniensis episcopi, in decanatu de Hichyn et pro tali tentum, habitum et reputatum, ac nuncium in hac parte specialem ad citandum Johannem Samme predictum seniorem, Johannem Tydy et Thomam Flynt de Pirington predicta super certis meram animarum suarum salutem concernentibus, eis et eorum cuilibet prout eos coniunctim et divisim concernunt ex officio mero dicti reverendi patris ad meram animarum suarum correccionem dumtaxat obiciendis, eiusdem reverendi patris certi tenoris litteras et mandatum habentem et circa huiusmodi litterarum et mandati execucionem suum officium exercentem ac exercere proponentem, in predictum reverendi patris nuncium memoratum tanquam ecclesiastice libertatis transgressores hostiliter et inhumaniter irruerunt ac manus violentas in casu a iure non permisso iniecerunt eundemque male tractarunt et violenter verberarunt; et hiis malis non contenti, sed mala malis accumulantes, eundem nuncium litteras memoratas in ecclesiastice libertatis vilipendium comedere, necnon magistrum Johannem Elvedon clericum, notarium publicum, pro similibus litteris per eum exequendis contra prefatum Willelmum Raven per comminaciones et timorem mortis subterfugere coegerunt, coartarunt et fecerunt, sentenciam excommunicacionis maioris a constitucione que sic incipit *Accidit novitate perversa* &c. ac aliis constitucionibus in hac parte editis latam dampnabiliter incurrendo.[3]

---

[1] Pirton in the deanery of Hitchin.
[2] Ippollitts, Herts., in the same deanery.
[3] See tit. *De immunitate ecclesiarum* ap. Lyndwood, ed. 1679, pp. 255 sqq. *Accidit novitate*, a constitution of Abp. Stratford, is printed on pp. 260–4.

Secundo die Maii, a.d. 1446, in ecclesia cathedrali Lincoln. decanus decanatus de Hichyn certificavit per suas litteras retroscriptas magistrum Johannem Derby, legum doctorem, dicti reverendi patris commissarium sufficienter constitutum, tunc ibidem iudicialiter sedentem, quod ipse decanus litteras et mandatum dicti reverendi patris ad citandum prefatos septem viros simul combinatos super premissis responsuros, ipsos tamen citare personaliter ausus non fuit propter metum mortis et alium metum qui in ' constantem virum cadere potuit, ipso decano ut asseruit perniciosum exemplum occasione premissorum attendente. Quibus [quidem] certificatoriis receptis et perlectis, dictus magister Johannes Derby commissarius eosdem Willelmum Raven, Ricardum, Thomam, Johannem, Thomam, Henricum &c. personaliter si valeant apprehendi et tutus ad eos pateat accessus, alioquin publice citacionis edicto ac aliis viis et modis de iure in hac parte requisitis super premissis responsuros premissorum occasione . . . citandos fore decrevit; super quo quidem decreto eodem secundo die Maii emanavit decretum, presentibus in premissis magistro Johanne Tylney Johanne Smeton et Bugg.

Primo die Junii, a.d. 1446, in ecclesia de Lidyngton decanus decanatus de Hichyn per suas litteras certificatorias retroscriptas prefatum reverendum patrem tunc ibidem iudicialiter sedentem certificavit; quas quidem litteras certificatorias idem reverendus pater per magistrum Thomam Colston[1] perlegi fecit. Quibus perlectis idem reverendus pater prefatos Willelmum Raven, *Ricardum Burgeys*, Thomas Dekes, *Johannem Catesson, Thomam Every,* *H. Daungerys*, Johannem Dawngerys, *Willelmum Dixy, Johannem Samme et Ricardum Tydy*[2] ad ipsos diem et locum litteris citatoriis preconizari fecit. Et, ipsis sic preconizatis, comparuit prefatus Willelmus Raven, qui iuratus de veritate dicenda obiectum sibi articulum fatetur, et se una cum aliis complicibus suis dictum nuncium suum mandatum lacerare, mastigare [*sic*] et comedere fecisse et cogisse [*sic*]. Quam quidem confessionem idem reverendus pater ut asseruit sequens, dictum Willelmum Raven nichil proponentem ad sui excusacionem, sed se gracie domini submittentem, in sentenciam excommunicacionis maioris in constitucione provinciali que sic incipit *Novitate perversa* [*sic*] [latam] incidisse declaravit, et extunc idem reverendus pater eundem Willelmum se ab huiusmodi sentencia excommunicacionis absolvi humiliter petentem, prestitito [*sic*] primitus per eum iuramento de stando mandatis ecclesie et parendo iuri, perficiendo penitenciam sibi occasione premissorum iniungendam, et quod similia imposterum non perpetrabit, a sentencia excommunicacionis maioris huiusmodi absolvit et iniunxit sibi pro modo culpe penitenciam, videlicet quod ipse per sex dies dominicos seu festivos circa ecclesiam parochialem de Pyrington coram processione nudus caput et pedes, braccis et camisia suis tantum retentis, cum cereo ponderis libre cere in manu sua, et per alios sex dies circa mercatum de Hychyn cum alio cereo ponderis libre cere in manu sua in simili forma penitencie peragat, huiusmodi cereos, videlicet unum ad summum altare ecclesie sue parochialis, et alterum ad summum altare ecclesie de Hychyn post

---

[1] Colston was for more than half a century the registrar of successive bishops of Lincoln. See *Linc. Vis.* (Lincoln Record Soc.), ii, p. i, &c.

[2] The italicized names are interlined in the MS.

peractam penitenciam [offerendo], et quod nuncio predicto pro iniuria sibi illata de nobili satisfaciat; et monitus est quod disponat se et peragat huiusmodi penitenciam, et premunitus per mandatarium incipiat peragere huiusmodi penitenciam aut circa ecclesiam aut circa mercatum infra quatuor dies a die premunicionis huiusmodi numerandos, et inceptam penitenciam diebus dominicis et mercati extunc sequentem continuet et perficiat sub pena excommunicacionis. Qua penitencia sic iniuncta, idem reverendus pater prefatos Ricardum, Thomam, Johannem, Thomam, Henricum, Johannem, Willelmum, Johannem et Ricardum, sicut prefertur citatos, preconizatos et nullo modo comparentes pronunciavit contumaces et in penam contumaciarum suarum ipsos et eorum quemlibet excommunicavit in scriptis. Tenor vero certificatorii de quo supra fit mencio talis est: Reverendo &c. Presentibus magistro Thoma Colstone, Breton, Malyns et Bugg.

8 die Julii, a.d. 1446, in domo registri apud Vetus Templum London. coram Derby comparuerunt Ricardus Burgeys, Ricardus Tydy, Johannes Sam', Henricus Dawng' et Johannes Cateson predicti; et primo Ricardus Burgeys et Henricus Dawng' consencientes in diem et locum, iurati de stando mandatis ecclesie &c. absoluti sunt a sentencia excommunicacionis quam reverendus pater episcopus Lincoln. alias ut prefertur tulit. Et deinde, obiecto sibi articulo, fatentur quod ipsi presentes fuerunt &c. et quod consensum et auxilium et favorem prebuerunt &c.; unde idem Derby commissarius suas confessiones sequens, ipsos Ricardum et Henricum in sentenciam excommunicacionis in constitucione *Accidit novitate perversa* &c. in hoc casu edita latam incidisse declaravit nulla causa in sui excusacionem racionabili per eos proposita seu allegata. Quos sic excommunicatos et pro excommunicatis publice denunciatos et declaratos idem commissarius ad eorum instantem peticionem, prestito primitus per eos et eorum utrumque juramento ad sancta Dei evangelia de peragendo penitenciam occasione premissorum, a sentencia excommunicacionis huiusmodi absolvit et eisdem penitenciam infrascriptam iniunxit pro modo culpe, ut videlicet dictus Ricardus pro offensa apparitori illata solvat eidem apparitori in partem penitencie xl. d.; et habet quinque fustigaciones circa ecclesiam et totidem circa mercatum cum cereo libre cere. Et Henricus Dawng' pro simili offensa solvat xx d.; et habet similes fustigaciones in forma penitencie. Et eisdem 8 die Julii et loco idem commissarius Ricardo Tydy, Johanni Sam' seniori et Johanni Cateson per eundem commissarium a sentencia excommunicacionis occasione contumaciarum suarum predictarum &c. absolutis et de veritate dicenda iuratis, ad purgandum se super premissis per eos negatis cum sex viris honestis in premissis non suspectis de convicinis suis in ecclesia de Lidyngton diem Veneris prox. post festum sancti Jacobi apostoli futurum[1] assignavit et prefixit.

Tandem dictus reverendus pater ex gracia de consensu et ad peticionem instantem dictorum compurgatorum assignavit eisdem dictum terminum apud Woubourn tenendum &c. Quo termino, videlicet 15 die Julii, ut supra.[2]

[1] 29 July.
[2] In the MS. the records of the *acta* of 15 July were entered before those of the 8th, which accounts for the *ut supra*. Subsequently the entry for 8 July was marked in the margin A, and that for 15 July B.

15 die Julii, a.d. 1446, termino utique partibus infrascriptis per dictum reverendum patrem prefixa et assignata [sic], in ecclesia de Wobourne Episcopi coram dicto reverendo patre in infrascripto negocio iudicialiter sedente, pro tribus comparuerunt personaliter predicti Johannes Catteson, Johannes Samme et Ricardus Tydy, afferentes se ad se purgandum super premissis sibi ut prefertur impositis et per eos negatis iuxta assignacionem per eundem reverendum patrem factam, non obstante quod alias alius terminus Lincoln. ad id eis per commissarium domini assignatus erat. Et deinde predictus Ricardus Tydy ad huiusmodi purgacionem suam faciendam produxit dominum Johannem Jercok capellanum, quem vice duorum compurgatorum admisit, ac Thomam Crabbe, Robertum Crabbe, Johannem Haukyn et Thomam Yver, cum quibus idem Ricardus purgavit se et dimissus est. Et iuravit idem Ricardus ad sancta Dei evangelia, corporaliter tacto libro, quod nunquam decetero erit in consilio vel consensu ad talia committenda nec ea committentibus dabit assistenciam vel favorem, ymo quatenus in eo erit ea et eos impediet. Et deinde prefatus Johannes Samme purgavit se de premissis sibi obiectis cum Roberto Crabbe, Thoma Crabbe, Johanne Haukyn, Thoma Iver', Ricardo Tydy et Adam [sic] Tydy; et prestito per eum simili iuramento de non favendo &c. ut supra dimissus est. Postea prefatus Johannes Catteson purgavit se de sibi impositis cum Thoma Crabbe, Ricardo[1] Crabbe, Thoma Yver', Ricardo Tydy, Johanne Haukyn et Adam Tydy; et prestito per eum simili iuramento de non assistendo &c. ut supra dimissus est, presentibus J. Breton, J. Beuues, Thoma Holden, G. Byrkes, Roberto Offord et me Colstone.

30 die Julii, a.d. 1446, in ecclesia de Lidyngton coram ipso domino comparuit personaliter Thomas Every predictus et iuratus in forma consueta absolutus est; et habet pro contumacia et rebellione suis tres fustigaciones circa ecclesiam suam parochialem in forma penitencie cum uno cereo dimidie libre cere, et obiecto sibi articulo, prestito primitus per eum iuramento de fideliter respondendo, negat omnia in ipso articulo contenta. Unde dominus assignavit sibi diem Jovis prox. post festum Exaltacionis sancte Crucis prox. futurum[2] in ecclesia prebendali de Bugden coram domino aut commissario suo ad purgandum se cum viris fidedignis convicinis suis de Peryton premissorum factorum non consciis, et ad cetera facienda et recipienda &c. Eisdem penultimo die Julii, anno et loco, coram domino comparuit personaliter Willelmus Dyx supradictus, et iurato ipso de fideliter respondendo &c., obiecto sibi articulo predicto, negat omnia in eo contenta; unde dominus assignavit sibi dictos diem Jovis et locum &c. ad purgandum se simili forma qua Ever' &c. Tandem peciit se absolvi a dicta sentencia excommunicacionis et iurato ipso forma consueta absolutus est; et pro contumacia et rebellione suis habet tres fustigaciones in forma supradicta. Et deinde dictis die penultimo Julii, anno et loco predictis, coram domino comparuit dictus Adam Tydy, et prestito per eum iuramento de fideliter respondendo obiectoque sibi articulo, negat omnia in eo contenta; unde dominus assignavit sibi dictos diem Jovis et locum ad purgandum se simili forma et ad cetera &c., presentibus Breton, Thorp, Malyns et me Colstone.

---

? Roberto.                                    [2] 15 Sept., as below.

15 die Septembris, a.d. 1446, in ecclesia de Bugden coram Derby comparuerunt dicti Thomas Every et Willelmus Dix ac Adam Tydy et produxerunt compurgatores, videlicet Thomas, Willelmum Ivery, Ricardum Edmund, Johannem Bykley, Thomam Taylour et Robertum Maykyn; et Willelmus Dix produxit Ricardum Tydy, Willelmum Snell, Thomam Crabb, Johannem Tailour et Robertum Dix; ac Adam Tydy produxit Ricardum Tydy, Johannem Taylour, Robertum Maykyn, Robertum Dix et Thomam Crabbe, cum quibus in forma iuris iuratis se purgaverunt et dimissi sunt, presentibus Colston, vicario loci et aliis et Bugg.

3. (Lincoln, fo. 5, no. 36.) Grantham. (Belton.) Willelmus Dale de Belton et Margareta eius uxor in casu a iure non permisso manus violentas in dominum Willelmum Wither, rectorem ecclesie parochialis de Belton, patrem suum˙ spiritualem, in porticu ecclesie ibidem iniecerunt et eorum uterque iniecit primo die Decembris, die videlicet dominico.[1]

8 die Januarii, a.d. 1448 in ecclesia de Sleford decanus loci certificavit dictos virum et mulierem citatos; quos preconizatos et non comparentes Balscot ab ingressu ecclesie suspendidit in scriptis, presentibus Thorp, Johanne Walbrond et me Colstone.

Eisdem die et anno in domo registri apud Sleford comparuerunt ambo et [consencientes in] diem et locum, prestito etiam iuramento de veritate dicenda, absoluti sunt. Et primum articulum negant; unde habent diem Mercurii prox. post festum Purificacionis prox. futurum in ecclesia predicta ad purgandum se cum tribus[2] viris et tribus mulieribus honestis de convicinis suis et ad cetera, presentibus Thorp et Walbrond.

Quo die Mercurii, videlicet 5 die Februarii, in dicta ecclesia de Sleford coram Balscote comparuerunt ambo et purgaverunt se super dicto articulo cum Johanne Foster, Thoma Saunder, Johanne Wilson et Willelmo Aslok, Elizabetha Shirbury, Elizabetha Wilson, Sara Saunder et Johanna Aske de Belton predicta: unde dimissi sunt.

Idem Willelmus et Margareta, quando audiverunt missam dicti rectoris, renuerunt dare osculum pacis vel recipere. Comparuerunt ut supra; et, obiecto eis articulo predicto, allegant se in hiis se habere et facere sicut convicini sui faciunt: unde habent dictos diem et locum ad probandum . . . consueta super premissis . . . observare, presentibus ut supra.

Dicta Margareta prefatum rectorem suum indutum et paratum ad missam celebrandam verbis contumeliosis reprobavit, vexavit et perturbavit, sic quod rector vestimenta sua deponens in defectu dicte Margarete a celebracione misse supersedebat. Mulier comparuit et obiectum sibi articulum negat: unde habet dictos diem et locum ad purgandum se ut supra.

Die assignato purgavit se ut supra.

Eadem[3] Margareta, habens pullum, dicto rectori nomine decime debitum,

---

[1] i.e. A.D. 1448.

[2] *Sic. Quatuor*, as appears from the sequel, should be the number in the cases both of men and of women.

[3] This is added lower down on the leaf, after a memorandum (no. 37) that Robert Northon, vicar of Ulceby in the deanery of Yarborough, owes tenpence to the fabric of the church of Lincoln for violence done to Robert Crosby, vicar of the neighbouring church of Kirmington.

venit ad ecclesiam cum magna festinacione et huiusmodi pullum ad caput
dicti rectoris in medio misse existentis ex magna malicia adiecit, dictum
rectorem perturbando. Mulier comparuit et obiectum sibi articulum negat:
unde habet dictos diem et locum ad purgandum se ut supra. Purgavit se
ut supra.

Idem Willelmus et Margareta diffamant dictum rectorem super crimine
adulterii cum Agnete, uxore Willelmi Osbern de eadem.

(Ibid., no. 38.) Dominus Willelmus Wither, rector de Belton, notatur
cum Agnete Osbern de eadem super crimine incestus.[1]

16 Decembris, a.d. 1448, apud Sleford emanavit commissio directa
magistro Thome Thorp, rectori de Ingoldesby, et decano de Grantham[2]
ad recipiendum purgacionem dicti rectoris cum tribus curatis et sex viris
fidedignis parochie. Tandem decanus postea certificavit quod ipse recepit
purgacionem dicti rectoris in ecclesia de Belton die dominica, videlicet in
vigilia Epiphanie Domini extunc prox. cum dominis Willelmo Tapit, rectore
de Magna Paunton, domino Johanne Crake, rectore de Berkston, domino
Rogero Casterton, vicario de Honyngton, Johanne Fermour, Willelmo
Aylyf, Willelmo Graunt, Willelmo Sotterel, Thoma Owgham et Roberto
Graunt de Berkston[3] in forma iuris iuratis: unde dimissus est.

The three instances which have been quoted are referred to in the
text. Of the remainder two (4 and 5) are closely related, while
another (7) is the record of a piece of barbarity committed by
Huntingdonshire villagers who, finding themselves in the presence
of the ecclesiastical judge, seem to have been ready to throw themselves on his mercy without attempting to explain or palliate their
crime.

4. (Lincoln, fo. 6b, no. 45.) Grafhow. Dodington. Dominus Johannes
Pygot, miles, de Dodington. 16 die Decembris, a.d. 1448, in capella infra castrum de Sleford, Lincoln. dioc. coram reverendo in Christo patre et domino
domino Willelmo, Dei gracia Lincoln. episcopo comparuit dictus miles,
et iuratus absolutus est a sentencia suspensionis, quia ipse in casu a iure non
permisso quosdam servientes suos manus violentas in dominum Willelmum
Dighton, rectorem ecclesie parochialis de Dodington predicta, inicere
mandavit et fecit et eundem cum virgis verberari et fustigari, et huiusmodi
factum ratum habuit pariter et acceptum, sentenciam excommunicacionis

[1] This appears to be a counter-charge brought by Margaret and William against
their rector while the charge against them for assaulting him in the church porch
was still pending. The chronology of the various charges against them is not clear,
but their alleged behaviour in church seems to have been in progress for some
time. *Incestus*, sc. *spiritualis*, as committed with a parishioner by her *pater spiritualis*.

[2] Thorp was the clerk of the bishop whose name appears in the proceedings
above. Ingoldsby was in the deanery of Aswardhurn or Lafford (Sleaford). The
commission was no doubt issued to Thorp and the rural dean of Grantham *conjunctim et divisim*, and Thorp should not be confounded with the dean, whose name,
according to an almost invariable practice, is not given.

[3] *Sic*, but Belton is meant. Great Ponton, Barkston, and Honington were all in
the deanery of Grantham.

maioris contra tales generaliter latam dampnabiliter incurrendo. Fatetur articulum. Fatebatur eciam se retinere et retinuisse decimam silve cedue et agnorum debitam rectori: unde iuravit de mandato domini super sacrosanctis Dei evangeliis tacto libro quod prefatas decimas rectori et ecclesie predicte fideliter solvet, et quod iurisdiccionem ecclesiasticam et officiarios ac ministros domini non impediet. Et hoc facto, idem reverendus pater commisit vices suas magistris Thome Balscot et Johanni Derby commissariis suis ad procedendum et procedi videndum ulterius contra dictum militem in premissis et aliis causis et negociis.

Tandem eodem 16 die Decembris in domo registri de Sleford coram dictis commissariis comparuit dictus miles, et interrogatus super articulo violencie facte rectori predicto fatetur eundem articulum: unde habet diem Martis proximum post festum S. Hillarii extunc proximo sequentem in ecclesia de Sleford ad proponendum causam quare occasione huiusmodi violencie in sentenciam excommunicacionis maioris incidisse non debeat declarari. Et habet diem crastinum post festum S. Hillarii ad solvendum decimas suas vicario S. Marie in Wykford Lincoln., ministro domini in hac parte deputato, videlicet de cilva [sic] cedua, agnorum et aliorum iurium [debitorum].

Dictus eciam miles impetitus super eo quod ipse procuravit et fecit alimenta et victualia capellano parochiali ibidem denegari, negavit articulum: unde habet dictum diem Martis post festum Hillarii episcopi in eadem ecclesia de Sleford ad purgandum se cum sex generosis super huiusmodi negatis.

Quibus termino et loco, videlicet 13 Januarii, a.d. 1448,[1] in ecclesia de Sleford prefatus Balscote iudicialiter sedens fecit et mandavit dictum dominum Johannem preconizari ad proponendum causam ut supra et ad purgandum se super premissis negatis publice et sepius preconizari [sic]. Ipsum sic preconizatum et non comparentem pronunciavit dupliciter contumacem et in penam huiusmodi duplicis sue contumacie in non proponendo &c. declaravit eum incidisse in sentenciam excommunicacionis maioris in ea parte late, ac excommunicatum fuisse, esse et fore, et pro sic excommunicato publice et solempniter denunciari. Et quantum ad aliud declaravit eum defecisse in purgacione, et decrevit eundem fore citandum ad dicendum quare non debeat reputari pro convicto et ad cetera facienda &c., presentibus Johanne Walbronde, Johanne Colstone et me Colstone.

13 die Januarii, a.d. 1448, in domo registri apud Sleford Balscote ad magnas instancias Willelmi Cortyng, servientis dicti domini Johannis, decrevit eundem dominum Johannem fore expectandum, et de gracia sua expectavit eundem usque diem Sabbati proximum post festum Purificacionis, et continuavit negocium istud usque in ipsum diem in ecclesia Lincoln. &c. continuavit [sic].

Quo die 8 Februarii in dicta domo registri idem Balscote ad rogatum dicti Willelmi decrevit dictum dominum Johannem fore expectandum, et expectavit eum usque diem Jovis in prima septimana Quadragesime proximo futurum,[2] et negocium istud usque in ipsum diem in ecclesia Lincoln. &c. continuavit.

---

[1] Sic. Tues. after St. Hilary in 1448/9 fell on 14 Jan.
[2] 6 Mar.: Pygot, however, did not appear till Good Friday, 11 Apr.

11 die Aprilis, a.d. 1449, in ecclesia S. Margarete infra clausam Lincoln. coram Balscot commissario comparuit dictus Johannes Pygot miles et peciit se absolvi &c., unde iuratus de stando mandatis ecclesie et parendo iuri et perficiendo penitenciam in presencia dicti rectoris tunc ibidem constituti, nichil contra huiusmodi absolucionem dicentis vel obicientis, absolutus est a sentencia excommunicacionis in quam ut prefertur incidisse extitit declaratus; et iniunctum est sibi tam pro dicta violencia quam pro eo quod fuit convictus super denegacione alimentorum &c. quod discalciatus per quinque dies dominicos et festivos absque zona cum cereo trium librarum in manu sua stabit ante fontem dicte ecclesie tempore alte misse, a tempore offertorii offeret dictum cereum et illum ultimo die pene ad summum altare dimittet.[1] Et habet diem Lune proximum post dominicam Quasi modo geniti &c.[1] in ecclesia Lincoln. ad reddendum racionem de receptis suis &c.

5. (Ibid., no. 46.) (Grafhow.) Dodington. Willelmus Cortyng de Dodington in festo Natalis Domini, a.d. 1448, tempore alte misse impedivit dominum Johannem Gudwyn, vicarium ecclesie S. Marie in Wykford Lincoln., ad recipiendum fructus et emolumenta ecclesie de Dodyngton et ad faciendum eidem ecclesie deserviri de eisdem fructibus congrue in divinis per dominum deputatum, per comminaciones, contumelias et verba contumeliosa quominus potuit recipere oblaciones ipso die factas, et ulterius idem Willelmus absque auctoritate huiusmodi oblaciones temeritate propria recepit.

13 die Januarii, a.d. 1448, in ecclesia de Sleford decanus loci certificavit dictum Willelmum personaliter peremptorie citatum: quem preconizatum et non comparentem Balscote ab ingressu ecclesie suspendidit in scriptis, presentibus Walbrand, Johanne Colstone et me Colstone.

Ultimo die Februarii, a.d. 1448 in ecclesia Lincoln. coram Tylney comparuit et absolutus est. Impetitus negat articulum: unde habet diem Sabbati in prima septimana Quadragesime in ecclesia de Bugden ad purgandum se cum sex viris.

Quo die, videlicet 8 die Marcii, in ecclesia conventuali prioratus canonicorum Huntingdonie coram magistro Thoma Balscot comparuit dictus Willelmus, et consenciens in locum et iuratus de veritate dicenda fatetur et recognovit quod oblaciones dicto die Natalis Domini factas super altare dimissas de eius mandato ad usum capellani recipi auctoritate sua propria, reclamacione dicti vicarii ad recipiendum huiusmodi oblaciones deputati non obstante: unde dictus Balscot commissarius confessionem dicti Willelmi sequens assignavit eidem Willelmo diem Veneris proximum post dominicam in Passione Domini &c. extunc proximam in ecclesia Lincoln. ad proponendum in forma iuris quare non debet declarari incidisse in sentenciam excommunicacionis in impediendo iurisdiccionem et executorem iurisdiccionis.

Quo die Veneris, videlicet 4 die Aprilis, coram Thornton et Tylney commissariis comparuit, et nichil dicto vel proposito declaratus est incidisse in dictam sentenciam.

11 die Aprilis in ecclesia Lincoln. dictus dominus commissarius Balscot

[1] 21 Apr.: see dates in next entry.

dictum Willelmum iuratum de stando mandatis ecclesie &c. absolvit a sentencia excommunicacionis et monitus est quod satisfaciat de oblacione.

21 die Aprilis in ecclesia Lincoln. coram Balscot comparuit et pro impedimento iurisdiccionis &c. habet in penitencia quinque dies dominicos stando in forma penitencie ad fontem cum cereo unius denarii.

6. (Lincoln, fo. 11, no. 79.) Grafhow. Egle. Johannes Wylkyn de Egle impedit iurisdiccionem ecclesiasticam exequendam; nam clauso ostio ecclesie retinuit claves ecclesie et noluit aperire ostium nec dimittere claves aliis, quominus magister Johannes Sutton commissarius domini iurisdiccionem ecclesiasticam in dicta ecclesia circa correccionem subditorum potuit exercere. Idem adulteratur cum Matilde Swand, iam de Lincolnia.

7. (Huntingdon, fo. 9, no. 52.) Brampton. Ricardus Elger de Brampton 20 die Septembris, a.d. 1447, coram reverendo in Christo patre et domino, domino Willelmo, Dei gracia Lincoln. episcopo, in capella sua infra manerium suum de Bugden situata iudicialiter constitutus et impetitus de modo violencie in castrando dominum Willelmum Orgill presbyterum per eum ut dicebatur commisse, fatebatur et recognovit quod ipse una cum Johanne Bosyate et aliis complicibus suis in dictum dominum Willelmum Orgill presbyterum, in domo ipsius Ricardi apud Brampton predictam hospitatum et in lecto suo de nocte cubantem nichilque mali suspicantem, irruit et manus violentas in casu a iure non permisso temere iniecit in eundem, ipsumque invitum, renitentem et quatenus potuit reluctantem et reclamantem diabolico consilio instigatus inhumaniter castravit et eidem virilia abscidit, in maioris excommunicacionis sentenciam a canone qui incipit Si quis suadente diabolo &c.[1] contra tales generaliter latam dampnabiliter ea occasione incidisse et excommunicatum propterea fuisse et esse excommunicatum, iusticia id poscente; presentibus magistro Michaele Amice curie Romane, Breton, Thorp, Malyns et Bug.

Subsequenter, videlicet post nonam illius 20 diei Septembris in ecclesia de Bugden predicta coram magistro Thoma Balscot, decretorum doctore, commissario &c. comparuit Johanna, uxor dicti Ricardi, ad hos diem et locum auctoritate mandati dicti reverendi patris citata, et iurata de veritate dicenda fatebatur et recognovit quod ipsa, ad huiusmodi violenciam perpetrandam consenciens ac opem et operam prebens ad eandem, pedes et tibias dicti presbyteri tempore violencie huiusmodi, ne de manibus dictorum Ricardi et Johannis Bosyate evaderet, quodam linthiamine insimul fortiterque ligavit: unde dictus dominus commissarius, confessionem dicte Johanne sequens, eandem Johannam in dictam maioris excommunicacionis sentenciam ipso facto incidisse ac excommunicatam fuisse et esse declaravit, necnon dictum Johannem Bosyate, pro eo quod latitat sic quod personali citacione apprehendi non potuit, prout per certificatorium domini Johannis Skynner, vicarii ecclesie de Magna Styvecle, mandatarii liquet evidenter, personaliter

---

[1] The Canon 15 of the Lateran Council of 1139: see *infra* ii, c. 29, C. xvii, qu. iv: 'Si quis suadente diabolo huius sacrilegii vicium incurrerit, quod in clericum vel monachum violentas manus iniecerit, anathematis vinculo subiaceat, et nullus episcoporum illum presumat absolvere, nisi mortis urgente periculo, donec apostolico conspectui presentetur, et eius mandatum suscipiat.'

si valeat apprehendi, alioquin per edictum publicum ac aliis viis et modis citandum fore decrevit; presentibus magistro Johanne Bagot, Thorp, Malyns et Bugg.

Subsequenter vero, videlicet 23 die Septembris, in capella dicti reverendi patris infra manerium suum de Bugden situata coram eodem reverendo patre iudicialiter sedente comparuit et personaliter constitutus fuit in iudicio predictus Ricardus Elger, et peciit humiliter se absolvi a supradicta sentencia excommunicacionis, promittens se satisfacere Deo et ecclesie pro huiusmodi commissis suis quatenus sufficit in persona et facultatibus, affirmans se octogenarium et omnia bona sua mobilia per ballivum domini de Brampton fore arestata [*sic*]. Unde idem reverendus pater interrogavit ab eo quid [movebat] eum ut sic crudeliter tractaret dictum capellanum, amputando sibi virilia, utrum invenit eum turpiter agendo cum uxore sua, vel hoc fecit ad extorquendam pecuniam ab ipso. Dicit quod ex nulla harum causarum, sed solum ex instigacione diabolica. Tandem dictus reverendus pater, miserans senectuti et miserie dicti Ricardi, iniunxit sibi, prestito primitus per eum iuramento corporali de parendo iuri et peragendo sibi in hac parte iniungenda, quod die Sabbati iam prox. futuro ad horam nonam ante meridiem accedat ad ecclesiam parochialem beate Marie ville Huntingdonie, et ibidem nudus capud et pedes, camisia et braccis tantum retentis, coram priore Huntingdonie vel magistro Johanne Leke commissariis suis ante fores illius ecclesie iaceat prostratus et veniam de commissis ac absolucionem a dicta sentencia excommunicacionis ab eorum altero humiliter postulet. Quo prestito iuramento, videlicet quod similia decetero non perpetrabit nec ea facientibus prestabit consilium vel assensum, et absolucione a dicta sentencia iuxta formam ipsis commissariis commissam obtenta, sic nudus circuibit omnia loca mercati ville Huntingdonie ipso eodem die Sabbati tempore publici mercati, cum maior affuerit populi multitudo, decano Huntingdonie stola et superpellicio induto cum virga in manu sua ipsum Ricardum insequente et in locis consuetis disciplinante cum virga huiusmodi, et quod per sex alios dies Sabbati prox. extunc sequentes consimilem penitenciam circa dictum mercatum, et per duodecim dies dominicos seu festivos extunc prox. sequentes circa ecclesiam de Brampton predicta tempore processionis et coram processione eiusdem ecclesie eadem forma consimilem penitenciam nudus capud et pedes, braccis et camisia tantum retentis, ipso decano eum ut prefertur insequente,[1] perficiat; quodque singulis annis durante proximo septennio feria quarta in capite ieiunii ad ecclesiam Lincoln. personaliter accedat ab ecclesie ingressu eiciendus, et in feria quinta videlicet in Cena Domini iterum in sinum ecclesie restituendus, quodque infra octavi anni inmediate sequentis spacium limina apostolorum visitet, mandata apostolica super premissis suscepturus, si ad hoc facultates sufficiant et vires corporis per senium non impediantur; presentibus Derby, Byrkes et multis aliis. Et super hoc scriptum est dictis priori, magistro Johanni Leke et decano ad premissa exequenda, et lapsis diebus Sabbati et dominicis seu festivis certificando de facto suo in premissis.

[1] The rural dean of Huntingdon must have done this under special commission, as the church of Brampton, locally in the deanery of Leightonstone, was a peculiar of the prebendary, and therefore outside the jurisdiction of any rural dean.

Postea, videlicet 9 die Octobris, a.d. 1447, in ecclesia de Bugden coram
Derby commissario comparuit dicta Johanna, et iurata de stando mandatis
ecclesie et parendo iuri ac perficiendo penitenciam occasione violencie
huiusmodi habet similem penitenciam cum Ricardo Elger marito suo, et
quod annuatim durante termino septennii visitet pedester ecclesiam Lincoln.
diebus Cinerum, ibidem cum aliis penitentibus penitenciam subitura.

9 die Octobris, a.d. 1447, in ecclesia de Bugden coram Derby commissario
comparuit dictus Johannes Bosyate coram reverendo patre domino Willelmo,
Dei gracia Lincoln. episcopo, in capella infra manerium suum de Bugden
situata, et iuratus de veritate dicenda fatebatur et recognovit quod ipse
unacum Ricardo Elger in dictum dominum Willelmum Orgull presbyterum,
in domo dicti Ricardi apud Brampton predictam hospitatum et in lecto
cubantem nichilque mali suspicantem irruit et manus violentas in casu a
iure non permisso iniecit ipsumque cum baculo verberavit invitum, renitentem et quatenus potuit reluctantem et reclamantem, ad fundum attrociter
et violenter prostravit, et sic prostratum fortiter tenuit et tenendo inhumaniter castrari et virilia sua abscidi procuravit et fecit. Unde dictus reverendus
pater confessionem dicti Johannis sequens eundem in sentenciam excommunicacionis maioris a canone qui sic incipit Si quis suadente diabolo &c.
in hoc casu latam incidisse declaravit, iniungendo eidem ut infra annum
sedem apostolicam pro absolucione impetranda visitet, penitenciam condi-
gnam ibidem subiturus.

Tandem 18 die Octobris in ecclesia de Bugden coram Balscot commissario
comparuit dictus Johannes Bosyate [qui] iuratus allegavit paupertatem
suam sub nomine iuramenti sui: unde de mandato domini dictus dominus
commissarius dictum Johannem sic iuratum et in testimonium iuramenti
dicti Johannis magistrum Willelmum Wrauby, vicarium de Brampton, et
alios ibidem parochianos producentem, prestito primitus per eum iuramento
de stando mandatis ecclesie et parendo iuri et perficiendo penitenciam
occasione commissi, et quod quam cito in facultatibus suis sufficienter
dotatus et potens in sua persona erit sedem apostolicam pro absolucione
condigna visitet, mandata apostolica humiliter subiturus, a dicta sentencia
excommunicacionis absolvit. Et habet penitenciam similem quam Ricardus
Elger et Johanna eius uxor; presentibus (*cetera desunt*).

8. (Huntingdon, fo. 18*b*, no. 113.) Baldok. Weston. Thomas Chapman
de Weston iuxta Baldok 2 die Junii, a.d. 1449, apud Baldok in domo
Johannis Warner iniecit manus violentas in magistrum Johannem Bagot
presbyterum in casu a iure non permisso, et ipsum presbyterum cum gladio
graviter vulneravit, sentenciam excommunicacionis maioris contra tales
generaliter latam dampnabiliter incurrendo. Dirigatur mandatum decano .
de Baldok, rectoribus ecclesiarum de Baldok et A. . . .¹ et vicario de Weston
ad . . . .

4 die Julii, a.d. 1449, in capella infra Vetus Templum London. situata,
coram magistro Ricardo Dykeham commissario domini in hoc negocio
iudicialiter sedente comparuit personaliter in iudicio dictus Thomas, et
prestito per eum de veritate dicenda iuramento corporali, obiectoque sibi

¹ Probably Aston in the same deanery.

ex officio mero domini articulo predicto, eciam presente ibidem dicto magistro Johanne Bagot, fatebatur quod ipse in eundem magistrum Johannem ut articulatur manus iniecit violentas, non volens ut asseruit corporis sui aliter evadere detrimentum, cum alias idem magister Johannes ipsum Thomam absque sui culpa verberavit et male tractavit; et ideo hoc fecit in sui corporis tutelam et defensionem. Unde idem dominus commissarius assignavit eidem Thome eundem diem ad octo dies prox. futurum in eodem loco coram domino aut eius commissario ad probandum in forma iuris superius per eum allegata et ad cetera facienda et recipienda que iuris sunt, presentibus domino Thoma Holden, Roberto Clyppesby, Johanne Rous clerico et me Colstone.

Quibus die et loco, videlicet 11 die Julii, in dicta capella coram dicto domino commissario in dicto negocio iudicialiter sedente venit dictus Thomas in iudicio ad probandum allegata per eum iuxta previam assignacionem, eciam presente dicto magistro Johanne Bagot. Produxit Willelmum Waryn et Johannem Stanmer; quibus productis, admissis et iuratis, inde datus est iste dies ad octo dies in eadem capella coram domino aut commissario suo quocunque ad ulterius faciendum et recipiendum quid iuris fuerit. Assignatus est dictis testibus terminus ad horam terciam post meridiem istius diei 11 Julii in eadem capella ad subeundum examinacionem &c., presentibus Roberto Percy notario, Gregorio Byrkes, Henrico Lumby, Johanne Walbrond et me Colstone. Quibus quidem termino et loco idem dominus commissarius ad examinacionem unius dictorum testium, videlicet Johannis Stanmer, altero, videlicet Willelmo Waryn, absente nec se ad examinacionem [huiusmodi] offerente, processit et ipsum examinavit; cuius dictorum unacum rubrica eorundem sequente in hec verba facta fuit &c.

Dicto vero octavo die, 18 Julii coram dicto commissario in hoc negocio iudicialiter sedente comparuit personaliter dictus Thomas; et deinde idem dominus commissarius de consensu ipsius Thome continuavit negocium huiusmodi in statu quo tunc erat usque diem tunc crastinum, 19 videlicet diem Julii hora octava ante meridiem in eodem loco et ad idem, presente Beuues.

II. Several instances occur in which executors of wills were called to a conscientious discharge of their duties. The following is an interesting example in which the bishop's commissary appears to have acted upon insufficient information and to have been ignorant of the existence of the last will and testament of a deceased rector.

(Lincoln, fo. 3, no. 28.) Loveden. Brantbroghton.[1] Thomas Gosse de Brantbroghton notatur super alienacione duorum vasorum plumbi, implementorum rectoris de Broghton predicta, et unius magne tabule cum trestellis et unius cathedre bone et unius olle enee et unius acervi fabarum et

---

[1] Brant Broughton in the deanery of Loveden. Another note with regard to this occurs fo. 21 (no. 145): 'Thomas Gosse (or Goffe) de Brent Broghton occupat et administrat nonnulla bona rectorie.'

pisarum et meremii valoris xl s., quod rector ultimo iam defunctus emebat
ad reparacionem rectorie; quod dictus Thomas divertebat ad usum edificiorum tenementorum dicte ville. Et fiat memoria de reparacione iuxta
inquisicionem reperta ad xiiii s. Idem notatur quod ipse administrat et
occupat omnia et [*sic*] huiusmodi bona et fructus domini Roberti Stokworth,
nuper rectoris dicte ecclesie defuncti, absque auctoritate.

22 die Septembris, a.d. 1446, in ecclesia de Bugden comparuit dictus
Thomas coram Leek commissario, et impetitus super premissis fatetur se
administrasse bona huiusmodi ut executor [*sic*] testamenti dicti defuncti:
unde habet diem Martis prox. post¹ festum sancti Luce evangeliste extunc
prox. sequens in eadem ecclesia de Bugden ad exhibendum testamentum
eiusque approbacionem &c., presentibus Colstone, Thoma Lowe et Bugg.

Quibus die et loco, videlicet 11 die Octobris, in ecclesia de Bugden
predicta coram Derby commissario comparuit dictus Thomas et exhibuit
testamentum, in quo dictus defunctus ordinavit dictum Thomam solum et
insolidum suum executorem; cuius testamenti ulteriori execucioni, potestati
et administracioni ulteriori, sibi ut executori in hac parte commisse, ac
iuribus, beneficiis et remediis quibuscunque, racione seu occasione huiusmodi testamenti sibi in hac parte competentibus, totaliter renunciavit. Et
tunc et ibidem idem dominus commissarius commisit administracionem
huiusmodi bonorum dicti defuncti, tanquam intestati, dicto Thome in
forma iuris iurato, et commisit magistrò Johanni Sutton tunc ibidem
presenti potestatem committendi similem administracionem Willelmo
Dalton de eadem: unde emanavit commissio in forma consueta, compoto
reservato. Et dictus Thomas habet citra festum Natalis Domini proximum
ad exhibendum inventarium, presentibus dicto Sutton, Colston, Thoma
Lowe et Bugg.

## III.  *Cases of sorcery.*

1. (Lincoln, fo. 2, no. 10.) Holand. Boston. Isabella Leche de Boston
exercet artem nigromancie et sortilegii.

26 die Aprilis, a.d. 1446 in ecclesia Lincoln. Derby dictam Isabellam citatam &c. suspendidit.

3 die Maii extunc prox. sequente in domo registri ad Nettelham comparuit: iurata de stando mandatis ecclesie absoluta est per Derby. Obiectum
sibi articulum negat; unde, quia mulier est pauper et valetudinaria, Derby
commisit oretenus istud negocium correccionis magistro Johanni Sutton, et
dimissa est.

2. (Ibid., no. 11.) Holand. Boston. Ricardus Fleyn de eadem notatur
super eodem articulo nigromancie.

26 die Aprilis in ecclesia Lincoln. Derby dictum Ricardum citatum &c.
suspendidit. Commissum est negocium commissario quia paraliticus est.

---

¹ *Sic. Ante* is certainly meant, if the day of the month given below is correct.
Tuesday after the feast of St. Luke, which itself fell on a Tuesday, would have
been 25 Oct.

3. (Ibid., no. 12.) Holand. [Boston.] Isabella Baylyfson de eadem notatur super eodem articulo nigromancie.

26 die Aprilis in ecclesia Lincoln. Derby dictam Isabellam citatam &c. suspendidit. Mulier decrepita est.

4. (Ibid., fo. 21, no. 148.) Bullyngbrok. Bullingbrok. Thomas Staynfeld de Bullingbroke utitur sortilegio et incantacionibus. Vocetur . . . super contemptu; nam exercuit huiusmodi artem pro bonis, videlicet pro panno ablato Ricardi Draper de Hagworthingham, asserendo Johannem Ringoth de Hagworthingham abstulisse: cuius contrarium est verum, nam quidam Couper, manens in Lusseby, a Beverlaco, ubi post huiusmodi factum residebat, misit dicto Ricardo Draper quod ipse reus erat. Item idem Thomas Johannem Frenssh, mandatarium, circa execucionem mandatorum laborantem arrestari et incarcerari fecit.

19 die Septembris, a.d. 1447, in ecclesia de Bugden coram Derby comparuit, et iuratus fatetur se exercuisse huiusmodi artem iuxta regulas in quodam libro quem habuit de Willelmo Tetteford iam defuncto. Allegat tamen correccionem per Skaymond &c.: unde habet diem Veneris post festum Luce evangeliste in ecclesia de Bugden ad probandum correccionem.

Quo die Veneris, videlicet 20 die Octobris, anno supra, in dicta ecclesia coram Balscot comparuit et deficit probacione: unde iuratus de peragendo penitenciam habet sex fustigaciones circa ecclesiam et tres fustigaciones circa forum ville de Spillesby in forma penitencie. Peregit penitenciam.

5. (Ibid. fo. 23*b*, no. 170.) Grantham. Berkston. Dominus Johannes Gall, rector de Berkston, notatur super eo quod ipse quendam nigromanticum pro quibusdam bonis Johannis Bluet de Harleston[1] ablatis consuluit.

6. (Huntingdon, fo. 10, no. 55.) Hychyn. Ikelford. Johanna Leper de Ikelford in parochia de Pyriton utitur sortilegio, nigromancia et incantacionibus, et facit quedam ponenda circa colla, ut patet per billam in li . . . . . . et ut dicitur alias abiuravit.

23 die Novembris, a.d. 1447, in ecclesia de Lidyngton Derby commissarius decrevit dictam Johannam latitantem fore citandam per edictum.

19 die Septembris, a.d. 1447, in ecclesia de Bugden comparuit et iurata negavit crimen, unde (*cetera desunt*).

7. (Ibid., fo. 10, no. 57.) S. Neoti. Staunton.[2] Thomas Gamelyn de Staunton utititur (*sic*) sortilegio, incantacionibus et nigromancia, que omnia coram Leek confessata abiuravit.

8. (Ibid., fo. 10, no. 58.) Huntingdon. Huntingdon. Agnes uxor Willelmi Portose de parochia S. Andree Huntingdon. notatur super nigromancia, incantacionibus et sortilegio, inspiciendo flammiola et birreta hominum et mulierum, vulgariter dicendo Thow art thus farr' yn, mensurando zonam vel liripipium hihando et stando in camera sua.

---

[1] Harlaxton.   [2] Fenstanton.

9. (Ibid., fo. 13b, no. 79.) Leghtonston. Stonle. Johannes Dixson, coke de prioratu de Stonle, exercet coniuraciones per invocaciones malignorum spirituum pro rebus furtive ablatis et cum clave posita in libro, videlicet psalterio, cum billa nomen illius qui redditur suspectus continente; idemque operatur huiusmodi artem cum membro defuncti, per quam artem asseruit Elizabetham Bold de Swyneshede defunctam restaurasse xl s. per eam in vita sua a viro suo furtive ablatos.

19 die Septembris, a.d. 1448, in ecclesia de Bugden Derby dictum Johannem citatum et non comparentem suspendidit.

10. (Ibid., fo. 13b, no. 80.) Leghtonston. Stonley. Dominus Thomas Bedill, canonicus de Stonley, notatur super huiusmodi artis exercicio.

## IV. Cases of heresy.

1. (Buckingham, fo. 1, no. 3.) Citacio concernens Johannem Nowers diaconum.

Die Lune, 12 videlicet Februarii, a.d. 1448,[1] in capella infra castrum de Sleford coram reverendo in Christo patre et domino domino Willelmo, Dei gracia Lincoln. episcopo iudicialiter sedente constitutus Johannes Nowers personaliter, quem idem reverendus pater ex certis causis subscriptis de heresi habuit [vehementer] suspectum. Iuratus ad sancta Dei evangelia de veritate dicenda super veritate articulorum subsequencium, et in virtute iuramenti sui interrogatus numquid fuerat ordinatus ab eodem reverendo patre in subdiaconum die Sabbati quatuor temporum in prima septimana Quadragesime, 10 videlicet kalendarum Marcii, a.d. 1444,[2] in ecclesia prebendali de Lydyngton, Lincoln. dioceseos &c.

Negat articulum. Dicit tamen se subiisse examinacionem a magistro Johanne Depyng pro habilitate sua ad huiusmodi ordinem subdiaconatus, ac ipsum magistrum Johannem Depyng eum in ea parte habilitasse, nomenque suum intitulatum fuisse per registrarium ipsius reverendi patris in ea parte inter nomina aliorum ad huiusmodi subdiaconatus ordinem promovendorum ad mandatum dicti magistri Johannis Depyng; et quod in dicto die Sabbati, cum et quando idem reverendus pater adtunc subdiaconos ordinaret et ipse registrarius suus ordinandos adtunc in subdiaconos nominatim singillatimque vocaret, et de navi ipsius ecclesie in chorum eiusdem per ostium ipsius cancelli iuxta cuiuslibet vocacionem singillatim intrare permitteret, ipse sicut ceteri ordinandi tempore vocacionis sue intravit, sed exquisita postmodum per eum causa exeundi, similando se adstatim et incontinenti reversurum, illicenciatus exivit, ut asseruit, nec demum rediit; sicque ipsum reverendum patrem ad huiusmodi ordinacionem subdiaconorum tunc ibidem processisse et eum minime ordinasse. Attamen, ut dicit, litteras ipsius reverendi patris episcopi Lincoln. testimoniales de

---

[1] 1448/9. The heresy involved in this case consisted in the defendant's assertion, as a married deacon, that the marriage of persons in holy orders was lawful, coupled with an attempt to deny his own ordination and an ingenious story that the letters of orders which he had shown were obtained by altering the name in those of another man.

[2] 1444/5.

ordinacione sua adtunc in subdiaconum, et si ac non licet [sic] fuerat sic
ordinatus, sicut ceteri ordinati post missam finitam recepit.

Item interrogatus in virtute iuramenti sui &c. numquid ordinatus erat
in diaconum subsequenter ab eodem reverendo patre episcopo Lincoln. in
ecclesia parochiali de Bekenesfeld dicte Lincoln. dioceseos die Sabbati qua
cantatur in ecclesia Dei Scicientes &c. 3 idus Marcii, a.d. supradicto,

Dicit quod non, et respondet ut in precedenti articulo, hoc excepto quod
non intravit cancellum ipsius ecclesie de Bekenesfeld tempore quo vocatus
erat huiusmodi ordinem diaconatus suscepturus, sed quod se omnino subtraxit &c. De recepcione littere ordinacionis sue in diaconum, et si non
fuerat sic ordinatus, fatetur ut supra in alio articulo.

Interrogatus insuper in virtute iuramenti sui qualiter litteram testimonialem non ordinacionis que sic incipit, Universis &c. ab ipso reverendo
patre obtinuit,

Dicit quod fecit et procuravit quendam cognominatum T . . . ton, apparitorem eiusdem reverendi patris generalem in archidiaconatu Bedfordie,
ipsam litteram testimonialem de non[1] ordinacione Johannis Newton obtinere;
qua sic obtenta, instit. . . . . . ton de secunda littera ipsius cognominis
Newton, E videlicet, fecit O, et abrasit T . . . . litteras T.O.N. dicti cognominis Newton, [ac] has litteras, videlicet E.R.S. loco ipsarum litterarum
inseri fecit per quendam Ybernicum cuius nomen et cognomen, ut asserit,
omnino ignorat et tunc [inseri nomen] suum, videlicet Nowers; quas litteras
sic abrasas secum detulit in quampluribus locis ac scienter eis usus fuit, ut
confessus est palam et notorie.

Item interrogatus numquid huiusmodi monicionibus se parere adtunc
tanquam clericus et sic in sacris subdiaconatus et diaconatus ordinibus constitutus, presentibus adtunc Colston, Bugg, Malyns et aliis, dixerat expresse
et annuebat,

Fatetur, tamen dicit se hoc fecisse metu ac timore fratris sui adtunc
presentis et astantis, qui aliter dicere propter ipsum minime erat ausus.

Item interrogatus an et numquid citra huiusmodi moniciones in incedendo
modo clericali sibi factas &c. vestibus laicalibus absque omni tonsura, ac
si esset merus laicus, dederat[2] et usus fuerat, et cum quadam Elizabeta
Weston, alias dicta Isabella Weston de Hamuldon,[3] dicte Lincoln. dioc.
matrimonium, quinverius effigiem matrimonii, contraxit,

Fatetur.

Item interrogatus numquid asseruit [et] tenuit publice ac predicavit
quemcunque in sacris ordinibus constitutum posse contrahere et uxorem
superducere,

Negat articulum et quamlibet particulam eiusdem.

Quibus sic habitis confessatis, prefatus reverendus pater dixit quo ad confessiones et responsiones suas ad primum et secundum articulos [premi]ssas,
veritati minime fore subnixas pro eo, ut idem reverendus pater asseruit,
quod de suis certis noticia et sciencia nunquam exivit aliquis ordinandus
tempore [dict]o de choro alicuius ecclesie in qua ipsum ordines celebrare
contigerat postquam semel in huiusmodi chorum nominatim fuerat vocatus

[1] *Sic.*                              [2] *Sic.*
[3] Hambleden, Bucks.

pariter et receptus, nisi ipse reverendus pater ab ulteriori ordinacione omnino cessaret donec qui sic exivit reintraret et cum ceteris ordinandis in ordine locaretur,[1] aut alias nomen et cognomen ipsius sic non revertentis de registris eiusdem reverendi patris penitus delerentur, cancellarentur et abraderentur, et ad hoc tam ipse reverendus pater dixit quam singuli officiarii [quod huiusmodi] ordinacionum temporibus maximam dederunt attendenciam. Et quo ad hoc quod dicit se non intrasse chorum tempore vocacionis sue &c., dixit idem reverendus pater quod nunquam fuit aliquis vocatus tempore suo quin adstatim vel intraret vel nomen eius a registris extraheretur in continenti: unde idem reverendus pater iussit registrum suum exhiberi coram eo de ordinatis suo tempore. Quo quidem exhibito et per eum viso, quia in eodem registro continebatur prefatum Johannem Nowers ad subdiaconatus et diaconatus ordines fuisse temporibus supra-scriptis promotum, idem reverendus pater dixit standum esse registro suo in ea parte magis quam responsionibus frivolis eiusdem Johannis, in quibus ut asseruit firmiter credebat eum reatum periurii commisisse et ipsum periurum esse. Unde consuluit eum omnino ut, dimissa omni levitate carnis mundique voluptate protinus abiecta, conscienciam suam, solum Deum habens pre oculis, reformaret et veritatem planius explicaret, asserens se micius velle agere cum eo, si veritatem in ea parte dicere vellet et sic ut melius deliberaretur, et sub spe reformacionis consciencie sue mandavit eum servari sub salva custodia usque crastinum tunc diem sequentem, xiii[um] videlicet diem dicti mensis Februarii, presentibus tunc ibidem magistro Thoma Balscot decretorum doctore, domino Thoma Holden capellano et me Malyns.

Quo quidem crastino superveniente, dicto videlicet xiii[o] die Februarii, in eadem capella coram prefato reverendo patre iudicialiter sedente com-parens, idem Johannes Nowers personaliter ad corque penitencie rediens, ut apparuit, et sua dampnabiliter commissa emendare proponens ut asseruit et intendens, fatebatur lamentabiliter cum lacrimis se de facto memoratis temporibus de quibus supra articulatur in sacros subdiaconatus et diaconatus ordines fuisse promotum, sicque in sacris ordinibus fuisse constitutum tempore quo sic ut premittitur contraxit. Igitur submisit se correccioni et reformacioni graciosis ipsius reverendi patris: unde idem reverendus pater, suis huiusmodi inherendo confessatis, monuit eum primo, secundo et tercio peremptorie ne quovismodo sub pena lapsus in heresim se subtraheret, sed quatinus familiam suam ubicunque fuerit sequeretur ac semper iudicio ipsius reverendi patris se s[ubmitteret donec] idem reverendus pater premissa omnia debite reformaret ac eum recedere permitteret et . . . ciaret. Ac decrevit dictam Isabellam Weston alias dictam Elizabetam Weston citan-[dam iudic]ialiter erga diem Veneris proximam post festum S. Gregorii tunc proxime futurum[2] in ecc[lesia cathedrali] Lincoln. coram eo aut commis-sario suo, super eo quod ipsa cum dicto Johanne Nowers, in sacris subdia-conatus et diaconatus ordinibus notorie constituto et quem ipsa scivit in sacris ordinibus constitutum, matrimonium, quinverius effigiem matrimonii, dampnabiliter presumpsit contrahere, eidem ex officio mero ipsius reverendi

---

[1] *Sic*: for *vocaretur*.                              [2] 14 Mar.

patris episcopi Lincoln. ad anime sue correccionem et ad omnem iuris
effectum qui exinde sequi possit obiciendo responsuram, facturam ulterius
et recepturam quod iuris fuerit. Et super hoc emanarunt littere ipsius
reverendi patris directe commissario suo in archidiaconatibus Oxonie et
Buckinghamie generali in hec verba: Willelmus &c., presentibus in premissis
ut supra.

Subsequenter vero xxii^do die mensis Februarii supradicti anno memorato
idem reverendus pater in capella sua infra manerium suum de Nettelham
iudicialiter sedens pro tribunali prefatum Johannem Nowers fecit coram se
sisti et produci, et in supradictis ei in forma iuris iterato propositis per
eundem reverendum patrem atque ministratis et per eum adtunc denuo
confessatis, hoc excepto quod negavit quod unquam asseruit, tenuit, docuit
aut predicavit quemquam ordinatum posse ad nupcias convolare &c. idem
reverendus pater peciit ab eodem aut [sic] scivit dicere aut proponere
aliquam causam racionabilem pro eo quare non deberet pronunciari,
decerni et declarari in maioris excommunicacionis sentenciam incidisse
latam a canonibus contra omnes generaliter sic aspirantes ad vota [matri-
moni]alia postquam fuerint in sacris ordinibus constituti &c., ac quare eum
interim ex[communicare] minime deberet eo quod monicionibus eiusdem
reverendi patris de utendo tonsura et vestibus clericalibus &c. non parebat
&c. Ad quod idem Johannes nullam causam pro eo reddidit, proposuit
seu allegavit: quapropter idem reverendus pater eundem Johannem sic
minime proponentem in huiusmodi sentenciam excommunicacionis
contra tales generaliter latam incidisse et excommunicatum fuisse et esse
declaravit, et quo ad sentenciam in eum . . . [l]atam eo quod non paruit
mandatis dicti reverendi patris ut supra, idem reverendus pater sub spe
melioracionis vite eiusdem Johannis supersedit: unde idem Johannes
graciam genubus flexis petens et ad gremium sancte matris ecclesie se
revertens absolucionem in forma iuris sibi impendi humiliter postulabat.
Unde prestito per eum ibidem primitus iuramento corporali ad sancta
Dei evangelia de stando mandatis ecclesie et de peragendo penitenciam
canonicam sibi injungendam occasione premissorum a dicta maioris
excommunicacionis sentencia quam incurrebat ut predicitur absolutus
est; et habet in forma penitencie ut per tres dies dominicos seu festivos
more penitentis cum candela accensa in manu sua duarum librarum
ad fontem baptismalem in ecclesia beate Marie universitatis Oxon.
tempore missarum solempniter inibi celebratarum, nudato capite, zona
sua abiecta seu pro tempore adminus dimissa, septem psalmos peni-
tenciales cum letania genuflectendo humiliter dicat, et ultimo dierum
huiusmodi candelam ad summum altare ibidem offerat, et quod similem
penitenciam in ecclesia de Hamulden predicta peragat eciam per tot dies.
Et quia idem reverendus pater ut asseruit eundem Johannem Nowers de
heresi habuit omnino suspectum, licet per prius negaverat se unquam
asseruisse, credidisse, predicasse vel docuisse quemquam in sacris ordinibus
constitutum posse uxorem superducere, eo quod sic post ordinacionem
huiusmodi scienter contraxit ut premittitur, sciens hoc esse ei prohibitum,
nec unquam paruit monicionibus canonice sibi factis de utendo tonsura et
vestibus clericalibus, sed quod tociens disobedivit pertinaciter, infidelem

se in facto et operibus demonstrando, cum plus per factum quam verba demonstratur, monuit adtunc ibidem eundem Johannem Nowers primo, secundo et tercio peremptorie, sub pena declaracionis ipsum in heresim eo ipso incidere et incidisse, ut nullatinus de cetero cum dicta Isabella Weston aut cum quavis alia contraheret aut huiusmodi contractum illicitum cum prefata Isabella initum ratum quovismodo haberet, sed in quantum in eo fuit huiusmodi contractui resisteret et renunciaret et quod tonsura et vestibus clericalibus ordini suo congruentibus uteretur decetero omni tempore, matutinasque ac horas canonicas et vesperas omni die diceret ut tenetur. Quibus monicionibus idem Johannes se parere velle dixit; unde statim et in continenti more clericali rasus [fuit ac] vestibus clericalibus indutus, presentibus magistris Thoma Balscot, Johanne Bugg . . . . Thoma Holden capellano et me Malyns.

Adveniente vero dicto die Veneris [coram rever]endo patre episcopo Lincoln. antedicto, in presencia prefati Johannis Nowers in capella [dicti rever]endi patris infra manerium suum de Nettelham, comparuit magister Willelmus Rath' procurator necnon prefate Isabelle exhibens procuratorium una cum certificatorio prelibati domini commissarii de et super execucione mandati ipsius reverendi patris ad citandum prefatam Isabellam ut premittitur, quem [sic] ipsi reverendo patri episcopo Lincoln. tradidit et liberavit, petens ac supplicans humiliter ut cum dicta Isabella citata erat ad respondendum et in ecclesia Lincoln. ipse magister Willelmus Roth' procuratorio eius nomine ibidem posset respondere, in locum illum consenciens et consenciebat; ad cuius peticionem idem reverendus pater, lectis primitus per me Johannem Malyns de ipsius mandato certificatorio et procuratorio huiusmodi, ipsoque procuratorio per eundem reverendum patrem admisso, articulabatur eidem procuratori nomine ipsius Isabelle procuratorio articulus memoratus in dicto citatorio et certificatorio contentus quatenus eam de facto concernebat; quem idem procurator nomine procuratorio prefate Isabelle, prestito primitus per eum in animam dicte Isabelle ad sancta Dei evangelia de veritate dicenda &c. iuramento corporali, negavit in forma [qua] articulabatur. Unde interrogatus idem procurator numquid dicta domina sua cum prefato Johanne contraxit per verba de presenti &c. fatetur. Interrogatus in virtute iuramenti sui iuxta informacionem sibi factam quando sic contraxit cum eodem, dicit quod mense Augusti vel Septembris ultimo extunc preterito, sed de die vel tempore ignoravit. Interrogatus an unquam per prius ante illud tempus cum ipso Johanne contraxerat, dicit quod non iuxta omnem informacionem sibi in ea parte datam. Interrogatoque prefato Johanne Nowers ibidem personaliter constituto an perprius ipsa Isabella cum eo contraxit, dicit in virtute iuramenti sui per eum prestiti quod non, ymo vel mense Augusti vel Septembris, quo die tamen vel tempore non recolit, secundum quod dictus procurator dicte Isabelle fatebatur, ipse ac dicta Isabella primo ut asseruit contraxerunt. Interrogatus . . . prefatus magister Willelmus procurator supradictus numquid dicta domina sua tempore huiusmodi contractus scivit eundem Johannem Nowers in sacris fuisse ordinibus constitutum, dicit plane quod non; nam ut dicit . . . . (*cetera desunt.*)

2. (Huntingdon, fo. 2, no. 9.) Hychyn. Lynlee.[1] Robertus Long de Lynlee tenet certas opiniones heresim sapientes.

19 die Septembris, a.d. 1448, in ecclesia prebendali de Bugden coram Derby comparuit et iuratus obiectis sibi articulis negavit eosdem: unde Derby commissarius decrevit ... super eis et eorum veritate fore inquirendum, presentibus Balscot, Colston et Bugg.

3. (Huntingdon, fo. 10*b*, no. 60.) Memorandum quod 26 die Oct., a.d. 1447, indiccione xi, pontificatus sanctissimi in Christo patris et domini domini Nicholai divina providencia pape quinti anno primo, in ecclesia prebendali de Bugden coram reverendo in Christo patre et domino domino Willelmo, Dei gracia Lincoln. episcopo, tunc ibidem iudicialiter sedente, venit magister Johannes Leek, dicti reverendi patris in hac parte commissarius, et in presencia Johannis Hore de Esyndon[2] Lincoln. dioc. quandam inquisicionem per ipsum commissarium contra eundem Johannem Hore super certis articulis et opinionibus heresis et errorum detectum et delatum auctoritate dicti reverendi patris captam et factam, clausam et autentice sigillatam eidem patri exhibuit, tradidit et liberavit; quam quidem inquisicionem idem reverendus pater recepit et dicto Johanni Hore ostendit, ac eidem diem tunc crastinum, videlicet 27 diem Octobris in eadem ecclesia ad videndum huiusmodi inquisicionem aperiri et publicari et ad cetera facienda et recipienda que iuris sunt in hac parte prefixit et assignavit, presentibus honorabili viro magistro Thoma Balscot, magistris Johanne Buterwyk, Johanne Malyns et Bugg.

Quo die 27 Octobris in dicta ecclesia de Bugden coram dicto reverendo patre episcopo Lincoln. tunc ibidem iudicialiter sedente comparuit dictus Johannes Hore, et idem reverendus pater interrogavit dictum Johannem Hore an noverit aliquem [sibi] fore inimicum; qui Johannes respondet quod sic, nominando dominum Johannem Kendale, rectorem ecclesie de Esyndon.[3] Et tunc incontinenti idem reverendus pater dictam inquisicionem in presencia dicti Johannis Hore aperuit, publicavit et perlegit; post cuius quidem inquisicionis lecturam idem reverendus pater assignavit eidem Johanni diem Lune proximo tunc futurum in eadem ecclesia de Bugden ad procedendum et procedi videndum ulterius in dicto negocio et ad recipiendum que iuris sunt in hac parte prefixit et assignavit, presentibus magistro Thoma Balscot, Johanne Stonham, generoso, Malyns et Bugg et aliis.

Tandem 13 die Novembris in ecclesia de Bugden predicta reverendus pater episcopus Lincoln. predictus predictum Johannem occasione heresium et errorum per eum tentorum et predicatorum, prout per inquisicionem in hac parte contra eum captam liquebat, contra quam nichilo per eundem Johannem proposito vel allegato, in sentenciam excommunicacionis maioris incidisse pronunciavit, declaravit et [*sic*] sub hac forma In Dei nomine amen; quo facto idem Johannes Hore peciit humiliter absolucionem et ipsum restituendum fore ad ecclesiam tanquam filium ecclesie. Ad cuius peticionem

---

[1] Lilley. Neither in this nor in the next case are there any details of the heretical opinions laid to the defendants' charge.

[2] Essendon, Herts.

[3] No record of Kendale's institution remains. He resigned by 24 Sept. 1449 (Clutterbuck, ii. 133).

idem reverendus pater, abiuratis primitus per eundem Johannem omnibus opinionibus heresis et errorum sub hac forma In the name of God &c., eundem Johannem absolvit in scriptis sub hac forma In Dei nomine amen &c., presente magistro Thoma Balscot.

4. (Lincoln, fo. 1, no. 4.) [Candlesho]we. Waynflete Omnium Sanctorum. Thomas Cosyn alias Flesshewer de parochia Omnium Sanctorum de Waynflete quolibet anno tempore quadragesimali transfert se ad partes Norfolkie et ibidem moratur usque quindenam post Pascha, et tunc redit ad propria; et ignoratur ubi recipit sacramenta penitencie et eukaristie, sicque redditur suspectus de heresi.

26 die Aprilis, a.d. 1446 in ecclesia Lincolniensi Derby decrevit decanum fore citandum super contemptu propter suam contumaciam [in] certificando.

24 die Septembris, a.d. 1448 in ecclesia de Bugden Balscot decanum ab ingressu ecclesie suspendidit propter suam contumaciam.

11 die Decembris, a.d. 1448 in ecclesia prebendali de Sleford coram magistro Thoma Balscot commissario comparuit dictus Thomas et per eundem commissarium est absolutus et negavit articulum sibi obiectum: unde dictus commissarius decrevit fore inquirendum. Et habet diem Jovis proximo post festum Epiphanie ad interessendum et procedi videndum in huiusmodi negocio &c.

9 die Januarii, a.d. 1448 in ecclesia de Sleford coram Balscot comparuit dictus Thomas, et deinde ob testimonium valencium virorum pro dicto Thoma ibidem testancium idem Balscote revocavit decretum suum per eum prius latum; et deinde assignavit dicto Thome diem Jovis proximo post festum Purificacionis Beate Marie in ecclesia eadem et coram eodem vel alio dicti reverendi patris commissario ad purgandum se super premissis cum sex viris fidedignis premissorum noticiam melius obtinentibus &c.

Quo die Jovis, videlicet 6 die Februarii coram Balscot comparuit dictus Thomas et produxit Johannem Gysvel de Waynflete; qui iuratus dixit et deposuit quod presens fuit quando Thomas Cosyn predictus, nauta, circiter quatuor annos elapsos recepit sacramentum penitencie et eukaristie apud Burnham in Northfolkia,[1] et per duos annos apud South Town in Yermouth.[2] Unde dimissus est.

5. (Lincoln, fo. 2b, no. 15.) [Hill.] Sausthorp. Thomas Sarpotson alias Jonson alias Taylour de Sausthorp sacramenta penitencie et eukaristie ultimo tempore quadragesimali et Pasche non recepit, sed se ab huiusmodi sacramentorum recepcione abstinens comedit carnes.

6. (Lincoln, fo. 3, no. 20.) Horncastre. Baumburgh. Dominus Robertus Est capellanus parochialis de Bawmburgh iuxta Horncastre dedit licenciam Ricardo Acton et Olive eius uxori ad confitendum alii; qui sic licenciati confessi fuerunt, videlicet Ricardus vicario de Stretton et Oliva rectori de Wadingworth in principio Quadragesime; et adveniente festo Pasche dicta

[1] One of the Burnhams in the deanery of that name, probably Burnham Deepdale, on an inlet of the Wash.

[2] Southtown, a chapel in the parish of Gorleston, Suffolk, on the south side of the Yare.

Oliva in caritate ex[istens] peciit a dicto domino Roberto capellano se admitti ad sacramentum penitencie. Qui requisitus nolens ministrare illud sacramentum ministravit eidem Olive sacramentum eukaristie, et extunc misit eam ad rectorem de Wadyngworth pro confessione sua huiusmodi audienda; de quibus premissis dictus dominus Robertus non ignarus diffamavit dictam Olivam predicando de illo quod ipsa Oliva erat lollarda, recipiens sacramentum penitencie post sacramentum receptum eukaristie.[1]

14 die Marcii, a.d. 1446 in ecclesia Lincoln. coram Tylney commissario comparuit, et iuratus negat articulum. Unde purgavit se tunc ibidem cum Willelmo Baumburgh, Thoma Taylour, Willelmo Alcok, Johanne Bray et Ricardus Webster; unde dimissus est.

7. (Huntingdon, fo. 10, no. 56.) Leghtonston. Thyrnyng. Ricardus Billing de parochia de Thirnyng absentavit se ab ecclesia sua parochiali per quatuor primos dominicos Quadragesime a.d. 1446, et in dominica in Passione, tempore matutinarum, missarum et vesperarum, ducendo ordeum suum a villa de Rypton Regis ad Thirnyng; idemque consuevit absentare se ab ecclesia sua parochiali per annum continue a matutinis diebus dominicis huiusmodi matutinarum celebracionis tempore, in lecto suo cubando, et vix vult surgere ad missam audiendam, reddendo se suspectum super heresi.

16 die Novembris, a.d. 1447, in ecclesia de Lidygton coram Balscot commissario comparuit dictus Ricardus, et iuratus fatetur se duxisse ordeum a villa de Thirnyng ad villam de Rypton diebus dominicis: dixit tamen se audivisse missas et matutinas ipso die. Unde pro confessatis habet tres fustigaciones circa ecclesiam.

8. (Huntingdon, fo. 13, no. 78.) Leghtonston. Hamerton. Willelmus Burgeys de Hamerton non erat confessus nec communicatus a suo proprio curato, et ignotum est ubi recipit ipsa sacramenta penitencie et eukaristie.

9. (Huntingdon, fo. 12b, no. 70.) Leghtonston. Hamerton. Johannes Cawe de Hamerton est communis blasphemator nominis divini, iurando frequenter per singula eius membra.

16 die Marcii, a.d. 1447, in ecclesia Lincoln. Balscot commissarius decrevit dictum Johannem latitantem fore citandum per edictum.

19 die Septembris, a.d. 1448, in ecclesia de Bugden coram Derby purgavit se sola manu et cum magistro Johanne Elveden.

V. The following cases of clerical misdemeanour are of a miscellaneous kind, including several in which the charges involve neglect of divine service and parochial duties, and dilapidation of churches and rectory houses. With some of them further charges of incontinence are associated. The manuscript contains numerous instances

[1] In this instance the defendant was accused of attempting to fasten the stigma of heresy on another person with the object of covering his own irregularity. Of the places mentioned, Great Sturton, the parish adjoining Baumber on the north, and Waddingworth were both in the deanery of Gartree. The church of Baumber, in which no vicarage was ordained, was appropriated to the prior and convent of Bridlington, Yorks., E.R.

in which clerical incontinence is the single charge, and of these it seems necessary to quote only one in which the vicar of the prebendal church of Buckden was concerned. It may be stated, however, that 37 such cases occur in the Lincoln gathering, 8 in that for Buckingham, and 8 in that for Huntingdon, as compared with 26 in Lincoln, 5 in Buckingham, and 18 in Huntingdon, where the persons charged were lay-folk. In addition to these, there are a few cases in which charges were brought against religious. In none of these are there any noteworthy statements apart from the actual charge itself, nor is the procedure recorded in any way out of the ordinary. It is needless to say that any attempt to obtain definite statistics from such evidence is fruitless. We may no doubt regret that so many as 37 suspect priests should be found in an archdeaconry of some 550 parishes; but, when we remember that the record is spread over some six years and that some of those named in it belonged to the very large class of unbeneficed clergy, the percentage, if any basis could be found for it, of clergy involved in any given year would be insignificant. A similar caution may be given with regard to any of the faults mentioned below: the cases have been selected for the sake of their intrinsic interest rather than as supplying examples upon which the shocked moralist may build untenable theories.

1. (Lincoln, fo. 3*b*, no. 23.) Holand. Gedney. Dominus Robertus Alcok de Gedney, presbiter, absentavit se a celebracione misse a festo Assumpcionis usque festum Pasche, a.d. 1446, et absque sacramentis penitencie et eukaristie comedit carnes.

14 die Marcii, a.d. 1446 apud Lincolniam decanus certificavit quod dictus dominus Robertus fuit mente alienatus.

2. (Lincoln, fo. 6, no. 42.) Grymesby. Grymesby. Dominus Robertus David, vicarius ecclesie sancti Jacobi de Grymesby,[1] exercet communes tabernas usque mediam noctem, per quod inebriatur.

Vir comparuit personaliter in domo registri apud Sleford 11 die Januarii, a.d. 1448, preveniendo diem Lune tunc proximo futurum ad quem fatetur se citatum, et consenciens in diem, locum et iudicem, prestito iuramento de fideliter respondendo, obiectum sibi articulum negat expresse: unde habet diem Jovis proximum post festum Purificacionis proximo futurum[2] in ecclesia de Sleford ad purgandum se de premissis cum duobus capellanis et duobus parochianis suis honestis et ad cetera, presentibus Johanne Walbrond, Johanne Colstone et me Thoma Colstone.

4 die Februarii in dicta domo registri, preveniendo dictum diem Jovis, comparuit dictus vir et de gracia purgavit se de dicto crimine cum domino Ricardo, rectore de Hawardeby,[3] Johanne Warde et Johanne Marshall de

---

[1] The parish church of Great Grimsby.  [2] i.e. 6 Feb. 1448–9.
[3] Hawerby in the deanery of Grimsby.

Grymesby, et dimissus est. Et deinde iniunxit Balscote commissarius dicto vicario quod non frequentet huiusmodi tabernas publicas nec eas exerceat extra casum necessitatis sub pena iuris, presentibus Perch, Bug, Walbrond et me Colstone.

3. (Ibid., no. 43.) [Aveland.] Demelby. Dominus Ricardus Wynter, rector ecclesie de Demelby, celebrat in ecclesia de Ounesby[1] et ibidem moram trahit, ecclesiam suam de Demelby inofficiatam dimittendo, et cancellus ecclesie sue in eius defectu patitur magnos defectus.

20 Decembris, a.d. 1448 in ecclesia de Sleford coram Balscot commissario comparuit dictus rector et iuratus fatetur quod ipse absentavit se ab ecclesia sua a festo S. Andree ultimo preterito: unde pro modo culpe habet peregrinacionem Lincoln. bina vice, offerendo ibidem utraque vice cereum libre cere, et monitus est quod decetero resideat et ecclesie sue deserviat in divinis sub pena excommunicacionis in personam suam in casu quo huiusmodi monicionibus parere non curaverit fulminande. Et fatetur eciam defectum cancelli: unde monitus est iuxta effectum constitucionis Improbam &c. sub pena in dicta constitucione lata.[2]

4. (Lincoln, fo. 11b, no. 83.) Grymesby. Swalowe. Dominus Ricardus Burd, rector de Swalowe, non residet et celebrat annale in ecclesia S. Clementis Wintonie,[3] et non habet litteras ordinum. Idem adulteratur cum Alicia Bucher de Clanfeld.[4]

5. (Lincoln, fo. 15b, no. 109.) Walscroft. Lindewod. Dominus Willelmus Martyn, rector de Lindewod,[5] est communis mercator in granis et aliis animalibus, et non residet et dimittit ecclesiam suam ad firmam.

6. (Ibid., no. 114.) Horncastre. Morby.[6] Dominus Willelmus Knowt, rector de Morby, dimittit rectoriam suam pati ruinam, et vix celebrat semel in septimana, nam frequentat communem tabernam. Et adulteratur cum Alicia uxore Johannis Lang de Wylsby.

7. (Lincoln, fo. 17, no. 122.) Wraghow. [Ludford S. Petri.] Dominus Robertus Smyth, rector ecclesie S. Petri de Longludford[7] non deservit cure sue nec facit deserviri, et vix celebrat semel in septimana: cuius rectoria in ipsius defectu patitur ruinam.

8. (Lincoln, fo. 18b, no. 132.) Grymesby. Barnolby. Dominus Johannes Werkworth, rector de Barnolby, omissis matutinis et aliis horis canonicis, missas celebravit; et expectavit apud Grymesby diebus rogacionum, sic quod ipsis diebus processiones non fuerunt. Et notatur cum Isabella Pawcenermaker infra domum fratrum . . .[8] de Grymesby.

---

[1] Aunsby in the deanery of Lafford. The parish adjoins that of Dembleby.
[2] Tit. 17 of the constitutions of Ottobon. The defaulting rector was charged to make repairs good out of an adequate sum taken from the fruits of the church.
[3] A church in Winchester, now long destroyed.
[4] Clanfield in Hampshire, near Petersfield.
[5] Linwood, the birthplace of the famous canonist.          [6] Moorby.
[7] Ludford Parva.                    [8] Either *minorum* or *Augustinensium.*

9. (Lincoln, fo. 24, no. 174.) Holand. Kirkton. Dominus David Olton, vicarius ecclesie de Kirkton in Holand, capellanum parochialem, quem in dicta ecclesia suis sumptibus et expensis cubantem et levantem invenire et exhibere tenetur, subtraxit et subtrahit.

10 die Januarii, a.d. 1446, in ecclesia de Sleford coram Derby comparuit dictus vicarius, et obiectis sibi articulis infrascriptis, negat eosdem: unde habet diem Martis post festum S. Vincentii in eodem loco ad purgandum se cum sex curatis. Tandem obtinuit commissionem directam magistro Johanni Sutton commissario generali ad recipiendum eius purgacionem, certificando citra festum Annunciacionis unacum nominibus et cognominibus compurgatorum.

Idem (*cetera desunt*).

Idem vicarius subtraxit et subtrahit ac prohibet celebracionem matutinarum et aliarum horarum canonicarum diebus dominicis et festivis in dicta ecclesia cum nota decantari; que matutine diebus huiusmodi cum nota consueverunt honorifice celebrari &c. Obiectum sibi articulum negat ut supra.

Idem in malum et perniciosum exemplum aliorum per tumultus et strepitus divinum officium in eadem ecclesia celebratum perturbavit et perturbat. Istum articulum sibi obiectum negat ut supra.

10. (Buckingham, fo. 5, no. 12.) In decanatu Buckinghamie. Moreton.[1] Dominus Willelmus Sandebach, rector ibidem, non fuit confessus alicui sacerdoti de quo constat hiis septem annis, et tamen missarum celebracioni quotidie se ingerit impudenter et subtrahit ab officio registri nomine iurium suorum spiritualium xx s.

7 die Januarii, a.d. 1448, in ecclesia de Sleford magister Johannes Crosby certificavit dictum dominum Willelmum citatum; quem preconizatum non comparentem Balscote ab ingressu ecclesie suspendidit in scriptis, presentibus T. Thorp et J. Walbrond.

Item idem rector in iure . . . oria diei et locum predictorum ad quos fuit citatus et quibus non comparuit, verisimiliter presumens . . . eisdem die et loco processurum, ista negligencia crassa et supina non obstante, missas et alia divina officia . . . publice et sepius celebravit.[2]

11. (Buckingham, fo. 8.)[3] Berkhamstede. Berkhamstede. Dominus Robertus Sturman, rector ecclesie parochialis de Berkhamstede S. Petri, non residebat per duos [annos], et iam residens nullam tenet hospitalitatem; et notatur cum Johanna Durant, uxore Willelmi Durant.

19 die Februarii, a.d. 1447, in domo registri de Nettelham comparuit dictus rector, consenciens in diem et locum; et interrogatus fatetur se non residenciam [*sic*] per duos annos et quod iam residens nullam tenet hospitalitatem: unde pro confessatis subiit correccionem, comparendo cum officio [*sic*]. Crimen tamen adulterii cum dicta Johanna Durant ab omni tempore

[1] Maids Moreton. Sandebach appears under the form Sandbacke in Lipscomb's list of rectors (*Hist. Bucks*. iii. 43).
[2] This paragraph in the original is nearly illegible.
[3] This entry should have been made among the Huntingdon memoranda. There appears to be no other mention of the rector named here, who is not in Clutterbuck's list (*Hist. Herts*. i. 300); but there is room for him between 1435 and 1462.

constanter negavit; unde ex favore obtinuit commissionem directam magistro Johanni Leek ad recipiendum eius purgacionem cum certo numero et cum clausula certificandi citra festum Luce evangeliste proximum.

12. (Buckingham, fo. 8, no. 21.) Buckingham. Merssh. Dominus Thomas Humfrey, rector de Merssh[1]—refugit et est alius admissus—valoris annui xxiiii li. de patronatu domini Suffol', non residet et deservit in officio capellani parochialis apud Tring, in cuius defectu rectoria sua ad terram est quasi collapsa; cuius procurator per magistrum Johannem Crosby monitus fuit ad faciendum residenciam die Mercurii post festum Epiphanie, a.d. 1447,[2] vigore mandati domini.

13. (Buckingham, fo. 11b, no. 38.) Wendover. Weston Turvile. Dominus Johannes Dudley alias Parker, rector ecclesie de Weston Turvile,[3] subtrahit exhibicionem unius capellani in capella infra manerium de Broghton situata, in parochia dicte ecclesie annexa, ubi huiusmodi capellanus celebrare tenetur ter singulis septimanis, videlicet diebus dominica, Mercurii et Veneris.

Idem rector notatur super dilapidacione mansi rectorie sue.

26 die Aprilis, a.d. 1446, in ecclesia Lincoln. Johannes Derby dictum rectorem die Sabbati post dominicam in Passione Domini[4] apud Eylesbury per Johannem Wyberd personaliter citatum, preconizatum et non comparentem a divinorum celebracione suspendidit.

1 die Junii, anno predicto, coram Leek in ecclesia de Lidyngton comparuit dictus rector et negavit articulum: unde Leek decrevit fore inquirendum.

14. (Buckingham, fo. 11b.)[5] S. Neoti. Offord Deynys.[6] Dominus Robertus Edous, rector ecclesie de Offord Deynys, notatur super eo quod ipse a dicta ecclesia sua a longis retroactis temporibus indebite absentavit se et absentat ut dicitur absque causa, ecclesiam suam inofficiatam ac curam animarum parochianorum eiusdem neglectam miserabiliter dimittendo.

14 die Februarii, a.d. 1446, apud London. reverendus in Christo pater et dominus dominus Willelmus, Dei gracia Lincoln. episcopus, decrevit prefatum rectorem fore evocandum ad residenciam et monendum quod resideret in ecclesia sua predicta infra terminum duorum mensium a die monicionis sue huiusmodi sub pena privacionis, cum clausula quod in casu quo huiusmodi monicionibus non paruerit cum effectu ad ipsius rectoris

[1] Marsh Gibbon.
[2] 10 Jan. 1447–8. This must have been quickly followed, if not anticipated, by Humfrey's resignation. See Lipscomb, op. cit. iii. 54. The patron of the living was William de la Pole, marquess of Suffolk.
[3] Parker, whose alternative name is wrongly given by Lipscomb (ii. 498) as Budley, had been rector of Weston Turville since 1430. He exchanged the living for the church of Buxted, Sussex, in 1455.
[4] 1 Apr. 1447.
[5] Wrongly entered in Buckingham archdeaconry, as noted in Huntingdon, fo. 4, no. 15.
[6] Offord Darcy. Edous is called Richard in Noble's list of the rectors (op. cit. iii. 160). See also Huntingdon, no. 18 below.

privacionem prout iustum fuerit procederetur, ipsius rectoris absencia vel contumacia in aliquo non obstante.

Super quo quidem [decreto] prefato 14 die Februarii emanavit mandatum directum magistro Johanni Leek, in archidiaconatu Huntingdonie commissario generali, ad evocandum et monendum dictum rectorem quod resideat &c.

Postea vero, videlicet 1 die Junii, a.d. supradicto, in ecclesia de Lidyngton dictus magister Johannes Leek commissarius constitutus personaliter liberavit et tradidit dicto reverendo patri tunc ibidem iudicialiter sedenti quoddam certificatorium suum retroscriptum autentice sigillatum de facto suo in premissis; quod idem reverendus pater recipiens illud publice perlegi fecit. Post cuius quidem certificatorii lecturam idem reverendus pater, ulterius in dicto negocio prout iustum fuerit contra dictum rectorem volens procedere, eundem rectorem per dictum magistrum Johannem Leek commissarium, 24 die Februarii, anno predicto, in villa de Brampton,[1] dicte Lincoln. dioc., personaliter apprehensum, iuxta effectum mandati dicti reverendi patris monitum et monicionibus huiusmodi non parentem nec parere curantem, et ipsam ecclesiam inofficiatam ac curam animarum parochianorum eiusdem neglectam miserabiliter dimittentem, ad diem Veneris proximum post festum SS. Medardi et Gildardi episcoporum, videlicet in ebdomada Pentecostes[2] extunc proximo sequente, in ecclesia parochiali de Bekenesfeld, dicte Lincoln. dioc., compariturum ad proponendum causam racionabilem si quam haberet aut dicere sciret, quare dictus reverendus pater eundem rectorem occasione premissa sua ecclesia privare et ab eadem sentencialiter et diffinitive amovere non deberet, citandum fore decrevit, cum clausula comminacionis quod si compareat &c. Certificatorium de quo supra fit mencio talis [sic] est: Reverendo in Christo patri &c. Presentibus magistro Thoma Colstone, Johanne Malyns et Bug et multis aliis.

(Huntingdon, fo. 4b, no. 18.) In decanatu Huntingdon. Brampton. Dominus Ricardus Edous, nuper rector de Offord Daneys, propter ipsius multiplicatas contumacias &c. per magistrum Johannem Leke maioris sentencia excommunicacionis innodatus et pro tali publice denunciatus existit, huiusmodi sentenciam excommunicacionis per xl dies et amplius sustinuit et sustinet animo indurato. Et dominus [Willelmus Wrauby],[3] vicarius ecclesie prebendalis de Brampton, sciens ipsum dominum Ricardum sic excommunicatum et pro excommunicato publice denunciatum et in sentencia ista perseverantem, ipsum ad mutuas communicaciones et ad missas et ad alia divina officia in dicta ecclesia de Brampton scienter admittit

---

[1] It seems from the following paragraph that Edous was living at Brampton, within a few miles of his own church.

[2] Apparently the date given above as 14 Feb. 1446 should be 14 Feb. 1445(-6). The feast of St. Medard and St. Gildard (8 June) fell on Wednesday in Whitsunweek in 1446, whereas in 1447 it came a week later, coinciding with Corpus Christi day.

[3] The name of the vicar is a blank in the original. It is supplied, however, by Huntingdon, fo. 4, no. 17 (see no. 23 below) and fo. 9, no. 52 (see I, no. 7, above) as Mag. William Wraby, rightly given as Wrauby in Noble's list (op. cit. ii. 181).

et secum in huiusmodi excommunicacionis sentencia participat, eandem sentenciam excommunicacionis una cum eodem domino Ricardo incurrendo.

15. (Huntingdon, fo. 5*b*, no. 22.) Baldok. Aspeden. Dominus Rogerus Bill, rector ecclesie de Aspeden, non celebrat missas in ipsa ecclesia sua diebus ferialibus, et diebus S. Clementis et S. Katerine[1] abstinuit se a divinis et nullum divinum servicium inibi fuit celebratum.

Vacant omnes isti articuli, nam commissum fuit magistro Johanni Leek commissario, qui eum super hiis responsurum ad iudicium evocavit.

Item in defectu dicti rectoris obitus Margarete Wales et Roberti Fen' non fuit celebratus, quorum obitus capellanus ad nutum Morley generosi celebravit.

Idem rector non residet, et ecclesia pro tempore absencie sue stat inofficiata.

Idem rector vendidit quoddam vas plumbeum quod erat implementum rectorie pro x s.

Item vendidit domum rectorie Johanni Smyth de Berkeden[2] pro iiii s. et domum Kirkhous Willelmo Archer pro xl s.

Idem rector de Aspeden prosterni fecit arbores pomerii et xiiii fraccinos magnas . . . et quarcus [*sic*] in magna multitudine, et vendidit et alienavit et dilapidavit.

Idem rector totum plumbum cum quo cancellus erat coopertus dilapidavit et vendidit pro xvii marcis vi s. viii d. et illum cancellum recooperuit cum tigulis.

Idem rector nullas dixit horas canonicas nec missas in ipsa ecclesia celebravit ultima Quadragesima, preter in die Veneris in prima septimana Quadragesime.

Item idem noluit solempnizare matrimonium inter Johannem Barbour de Buntyngford et mulierem in die feriali, quousque idem Barbour composuit cum ipso rectore pro xx d. et ita fecit cum Willelmo Bond de Munden.

Idem rector noluit celebrare purificacionem Margarete Darlyng parochiane sue, mulieris paupercule, nisi convicine cum ea oblacionem facerent.

Idem rector, quando aliqui parochiani sui eum offendunt, eos in curia de Arcubus prosequitur in magnum detrimentum parochianorum, et sic eos fatigat laboribus et expensis.

Idem rector, quando parvi de parochia sua obierunt, noluit requisitus ad locum accedere, nec cum ferentibus ipsos ad ecclesiam iuxta ritum ecclesie preces et suffragia ecclesie ministrare.

16. (Huntingdon, fo. 6*b*, no. 24.) Leghtonstone. Hamerton. Dominus Johannes Marshall, rector de Hamerton, notatur super eo quod ipse se a dicta ecclesia sua a longo tempore absque causa absentavit.[3]

4 die Novembris, a.d. 1446, in ecclesia de Bugden coram Leek commissario comparuit et fatetur se absentasse: allegat tamen metum. Unde habet

---

[1] i.e. 23 and 25 Nov.    [2] Berkesdon, near Buntingford.

[3] See p. 207 above, note 2.

crastinum diem, videlicet quintum diem Novembris in eodem loco ad probandum in forma iuris allegata.

Quo die coram Derby comparuit et defecit in probacione; unde monitus
est quod decetero resideat et ibidem personaliter ministret.

17. (Ibid., no. 26.) Dominus Thomas Hevy, rector de Aldebury,[1] auctoritate abbatis et prioris de Sautre et Huntingdonia decimarum collectorum
propter non solucionem decime a divinorum celebracione suspensus et pro
suspenso publice denunciatus, immiscuit se divinis missas celebrando.[2]

14 die Decembris, a.d. 1446, in ecclesia de Lidyngton Derby dictum
rectorem latitantem per edictum fore citandum decrevit.

18. (Huntingdon, fo. 8, no. 44.) Jakesley. Conyngton. Dominus
Egidius Chawcere, rector ecclesie de Conyngton, notatur super ruina mansi
rectorie sue, &c.

19 die Septembris, a.d. 1447, in ecclesia de Bugden Derby commissarius
dictum rectorem citatum &c. et non comparentem a divinorum celebracione suspensit.

1 die Novembris, a.d. 1449, in domo registri de Lidyngton coram Balscot
comparuit, et consenciens in diem et locum absolutus est; et pro contumacia
habet unam fustigacionem Lincolnie, offerendo nobile et cereum citra
dominicam Quasi modo geniti. Et monitus est iuxta effectum Improbam[3]
quod reparet defectus sub pena inibi lata.

19. (Huntingdon, fo. 14b, no. 86.) Jakesley. Conyngton. Dominus
Egidius Chawceres, rector de Conyngton, a divinorum celebracione suspensus [se] immiscuit divinis missas celebrando, cuius rectoria in ipsius
defectu non modicam patitur ruinam, et non tenet hospitalitatem. Alias
monitus est iuxta effectum Improbam, ut patet prius.

19 die Septembris, a.d. 1448, in ecclesia de Bugden Derby decrevit eum
fore citandum per edictum.

20. (Huntingdon, fo. 12, no. 68.) Herteford. Bengeho. Dominus
[Thomas Frytewell], vicarius ecclesie de Bengeho, deservit cure ecclesie
de Munden, absentando se ab ecclesia sua.

19 die Septembris, a.d. 1448, in ecclesia de Bugden comparuit et fatetur:
unde habet diem Martis post festum Luce in ecclesia Lincoln. ad proponen-
dam causam quare non debet puniri.

Quo die, videlicet 23 die Octobris, Balscot suspendidit (cetera desunt).

[1] Albury, Herts., in Berkhampstead deanery.
[2] This is followed by an almost precisely similar entry, relating to Thomas
Copton, vicar of Weston by Baldock, with the words irregularitatem incurrendo after
celebrando.
[3] See p. 231 above, note 2. Several similar cases from the archdeaconry came up
before Derby at Buckden on the same day, 19 Sept. 1447, the places involved being
Sawtry Beaumes and Stilton, also in Yaxley deanery, Offord Darcy in St. Neots
deanery (where John Smyth had succeeded Richard Edous, mentioned above),
Somersham in St. Ives, Hamerton and Molesworth in Leightonstone, and Aston,
Radwell, Rushden and Walkern in Baldock deaneries.

21. (Huntingdon, fo. 14, no. 84.) Herteford. Hertfordingbire. Dominus Gilbertus Haksmale, rector de Hertfordingbury, excommunicatus et pro excommunicato denunciatus scienter missas celebravit. Idem recusavit ministrare sacramenta penitencie et eukaristie Johanni fitz Johannis in articulo mortis tunc existenti.

22. (Huntingdon, fo. 19b, no. 118.) Berkhamstede. Whethamstede. Dominus Robertus Shirley, rector de Segrave in archidiaconatu Leycestrie, occupat hospitale iuxta Derby, et per annum traxit moram apud Whetham-stede, unum annale celebrando.

23. (Huntingdon, fo. 20b, no. 130.) Hertford. Eyot. Dominus Nicholaus Boney, rector ecclesie de Eyot Munfichet, non residebat per quinque annos elapsos. Detectus fuit ipse London. 5 die Novembris a.d. 1444.

24. (Huntingdon, fo. 4, no. 17.) Bugden. Memorandum quod 16 die mensis Septembris, a.d. 1446, indiccione nona, pontificatus domini Eugenii pape quarti anno decimo sexto, in ecclesia de Bugden coram reverendo in Christo patre et domino domino Willelmo, Dei gracia Lincoln. episcopo, ipsis die et loco in infrascripto correccionis negocio iudicialiter sedente com-paruit dominus Robertus Fenton, vicarius dicte ecclesie de Bugden;[1] cui sic comparenti idem reverendus pater apud Lincolniam ex officio suo mero ad meram ipsius vicarii anime correccionem obiecit et articulavit quod ipse, anime sue salutis immemor, citra et postquam confessionem Agnetis uxoris Roberti Lokyngton de Bugden predicta, parochiane et filie sue spiritualis in foro anime, de facto audivit et sacramentum penitencie eidem mini-stravit, gravia crimina adulterii et incestus spiritualis cum eadem Agnete dampnabiliter commisit. Ad que idem vicarius respondens publice fate-batur et recognovit quod ipse confessionem dicte Agnetis omni anno per septennium audivit ac eidem sacramentum penitencie ministravit; sed expresse negavit omne crimen adulterii et incestus cum eadem Agnete ab omni tempore. Unde idem reverendus pater assignavit eidem vicario de eius consensu et peticione diem Mercurii extunc proximo futurum, videlicet festum S. Mathei apostoli et evangeliste in dicta ecclesia de Bugden coram eo aut commissario suo, ad purgandum se de dictis criminibus cum tribus curatis et tribus capellanis noticiam meliorem sue conversacionis habentibus, et ad cetera facienda &c.

Quo die Mercurii in ecclesia de Bugden predicta coram magistro Johanne Leek commissario comparuit dictus vicarius intra missarum solemnia et produxit magistrum Willelmum Alnewyk, prebendarium de Bugden, magi-strum Willelmum Wraby, vicarium de Brampton,[2] dominum Willelmum Adz [sic] vicarium de Gomecestria, Johannem Roger vicarium de Covyngton, Ricardum Pippewell de Brampton, Johannem Foules de eadem, Stephanum Broun de Bugden et Johannem Hosier, capellanos, cum quibus in forma iuris iuratis, preconizacione oppositorum primitus facta, se purgavit et dimissus est.

---

[1] In Noble's list (op. cit. ii. 185) the date of Fenton's institution is not given. He died in 1449.  [2] See p. 234 above, note 3.

25. (Buckingham, fo. 1, no. 2.) Woddesdon. Northmerston. Dominus
Walterus Bird, vicarius de Northmerston,[1] commisit crimen blasphemie,
fodiendo caput unius defuncti a terra et imponendo tres guttas sanguinis
super illud, asserendo illud caput fore caput sancti, videlicet magistri
Johannis Shorn.[2]

Idem vicarius notatur super manuum violentarum inieccione in magistrum Ricardum Farney, officialem domini archidiaconi Buckinghamie.

8 die Septembris, a. d. 1448, in ecclesia de Bugden coram Balscot commissario comparuit et allegavit purgacionem: unde habet diem Mercurii
post festum Luce in ecclesia Lincoln. ad exhibendum . . . et probandum
allegata.

Idem notatur super manuum violentarum [inieccione] in dominum
Willelmum Lyncroft presbiterum. . . .

24 die Septembris, a.d. 1448 in loco supra[3] [sic] comparuit coram Balscot
et fatetur. Allegat absolucionem, et pro violencia confessata habet quatuor
peregrinaciones Lincoln. pedester a vicaria sua, offerendo ibidem qualibet
vice cereum libre cere, certificando citra festum Pentecostes; et iuratus est
quod peragat huiusmodi penitenciam sub pena excommunicacionis, presentibus magistro Willelmo Alnewyk, vicario[4] et Bugg.

(Buckingham, fo. 4b, no. 9.) Woddesdon. Merston. Willelmus Lyncroft
de Oxonia asportavit ab ecclesia de Merston predicta candelas cereas . . .
et alia vicario debita absque licencia vicarii ibidem, sacrilegium committendo.

(Ibid., no. 10.) Thomas Carter de North Merston impedit oblaciones in
purificacionibus mulierum, nam dicit quod maior elemosina esset dare
al[iis] pauperibus huiusmodi oblaciones quam vicario sive curato.

(Buckingham, fo. 12b, no. 40.) [Woddesdon. Merston.] Memorandum
quod Johannes Colyn de Ampthill vendidit unam placeam in Bedfordia
vicario de Northmerston pro xx li. de quibus idem vicarius solvit ix li.
tantum, et idem vicarius extortive adquisivit omnia evidencias et muni-
menta dicte placee et non vult satisfacere de residuo debiti.

## VI. Cases of Simony

1. (Buckingham, fo. 8, no. 20.) Newport. Shenle, Chichele. Magister
Willelmus Clerk, rector de Shenley,[5] simoniace ad suam ecclesiam est

---

[1] Called Walter Budde in Lipscomb's list of vicars of North Marston (Hist.
Bucks. i. 343). His institution to the vicarage is not recorded, but he resigned it by
11 Sept. 1452.

[2] This local saint, famous for 'conjuring a devil into a boot', died in 1314. His
body was translated to St. George's chapel, Windsor, in 1478, and the dean and
canons of Windsor acquired the rectory of North Marston from the prior and
convent of Dunstable in 1480. See Hope, Windsor Castle, ii. 411, and V.C.H.
Bucks. iv. 79.

[3] The summons was actually for 23 Oct. at Lincoln, but the date seems to have
been anticipated on 24 Sept. at Buckden.

[4] i.e. the vicar of Buckden, Robert Fenton, who died in the following year.
Master William Alnewyk was the prebendary and rector of Buckden at this date.

[5] Clerk's institution is not recorded. He died before 8 Aug. 1449 (Lipscomb, iv.

promotus, nam obligavit se Thome G[re]y militi, patrono, in **xx** li. pro presentacione facta de persona sua ad eandem, et solvit pre manibus x li.

2. (Buckingham, fo. 9, no. 24.) Wodesdon. Wodesdon. Dominus Walterus Seale, porcionarius de Woddesdon, iuratus, impetitus alias per magistrum Johannem Kirkeby commissarium, ultimo die Maii, a.d. 1449,[1] [comparuit] in ecclesia de Crendon Superiori super eo quod ipse convenit cum domino Petro Bysshop precessore suo pro resignacione facienda de dicta porcione ad usum dicti domini Walteri facienda [*sic*] ad dandum eidem resignanti annuam pensionem decem marcarum ad terminum vite sue, cuius convencionis occasione dictus dominus Petrus ipsam porcionem resignavit et huiusmodi pensionem a dicto novo porcionario ut dicitur recepit.[2] Negavit huiusmodi articulum &c. et quia ut dicitur huiusmodi pensio fuit multum gravis eidem novo porcionario, sic quod idem porcionarius aretro et multum remissus erat in dicta solucione huiusmodi pensionis, tandem per mutuos tractatus amicorum per partes easdem electorum huiusmodi pensio mitigata fuit ad summam octo marcarum, de qua porcionarius in festo S. Michaelis, a.d. 1445, xl s. per manus domini Thome Wilington eidem resignanti solvebat; de quibus xl s. idem dominus Walterus mutuatus est de Johanne Lamborn xiii s. iii d. et solvebat in festo Pasche extunc proximo sequente eidem resignanti xl s. per manus Johannis Lome, subreceptoris domini de Devenshire,[3] pro qua quidem annua pensione fideliter solvenda dictus dominus Walterus porcionarius et frater eius Willelmus Scathe obligaverunt se dicto resignanti per suum scriptum obligatorium in xl li.

14 die Decembris, a.d. 1446 in ecclesia de Lidyngton coram magistro Johanne Derby comparuit magister Thomas Bysshop nomine procuratorio dicti porcionarii, et iuratus negat articulum: unde decretum est fore inquirendum.

12 die Julii, a.d. 1448 apud Sleford emanavit commissio directa magistro Johanni Crosby per magistrum Willelmum Rathe ad recipiendum purgacionem, certificando citra festum Michaelis.

3. (Buckingham, fo. 9*b*, no. 28.) Muresley. Wyngrave. Dominus Ricardus Ilston,[4] vicarius ecclesie de Wyngrave, notatur super eo quod ipse cum domino Ricardo Stacy precessore suo, dicte ecclesie vicario proximo immediate, convenit quod in casu quo idem precessor suus ipsam vicariam suam ad nutum dicti nunc vicarii dimittendam vellet simpliciter resignare,

---

328, 329). Sir Thomas Grey of Ridgmont, Beds., known later as Lord Richemount Grey, was the second husband of Margaret Ferrers, daughter of William, Lord Ferrers of Groby, and wife of Richard, Lord Grey of Wilton. She died in 1451–2: he was one of the Lancastrians executed in 1461. See *Complete Peerage* and *V.C.H. Bucks.* iv. 447.　　　　　　　　　　　　　[1] ? 1446.

[2] Seale is not in Lipscomb's list (i. 498). Bishop exchanged the church of Headon, Notts., for this portion 19 Apr. 1422. Nothing further is recorded of him. Seale must have resigned between 1445 and 5 May 1447, when Nicholas Buckland was instituted on the death of Richard Hervey.

[3] The patron of the living.

[4] Not in Lipscomb's list of vicars (iii. 536). Stacy was instituted 8 Oct. 1438.

quod extunc dictus nunc vicarius daret dicto resignanti pro instrumento
resignacionis xx marcas; cuius simoniaci contractus occasione dictus dominus
Ricardus Stacy ipsam vicariam resignavit, et instrumento resignacionis dicto
nunc vicario tradito, dictus nunc vicarius solvit huiusmodi xx marcas,
crimen simonie committendo.

3 die Novembris, a.d. 1446, in ecclesia de Bugden coram Leek commissario comparuit dictus nunc vicarius et iuratus obiectum sibi articulum
negat: unde habet diem Veneris proximum post festum S. Hugonis[1] in
ecclesia de Lidyngton ad purgandum se cum xii[a] manu. Tandem obtinuit
commissionem ad recipiendum eius purgacionem directam magistro Johanni
Crosby, cum clausula de certificando circa festum S. Mathee [sic] apostoli.

Postea dictus magister Johannes Crosby certificavit per suas litteras quod
ipse vigore commissionis sibi in hac parte facte, cum dominis Henrico Hall
de Soulbury, Ricardo Offley de Hoggeston, Thoma Alford de Coblynton,
Johanne Mele de Donyngton, Henrico Upton de Drayton Beauchamp,
Petro Rach de Holkot, Roberto Horword de Chedington, Thoma Hull de
Slapton et Thoma Gray de Muresley ecclesiarum parochialium rectoribus,
dominis Thoma Clyf de Stukley, Willelmo Watton de Abbot Aston et
Johanne Coper de Masseworth ecclesiarum vicariis,[2] in forma iuris iuratis,
in ecclesia parochiali de Wyngrave purgacionem dicti domini Ricardi Ilston
vicarii predicti, in forma iuris iurati, penultimo die Februarii, a.d. proximo
&c. recepit &c.; unde dimissus est.

4. (Huntingdon, fo. 1b, no. 6.) Baldok. Clothale. Dominus Johannes
Fill, rector ecclesie de Clothale,[3] notatur super eo quod ipse promisit pre-
cessori suo, dicte ecclesie rectori, xx li. legalis monete, pro quibus solvendis
obligavit se per suum scriptum obligacionis in c li. quod idem precessor
suus dictam ecclesiam suam resignaret ad usum nunc rectoris consequen-
dum; quam de facto resignavit, sicque dictus nunc rector se simoniace promoveri . . . procuravit.

11 die Januarii, a.d. 1444, in ecclesia cathedrali Lincoln. coram Depyng
comparuit dictus rector, et iuratus de veritate dicenda obiectum sibi articulum constanter negavit. Unde idem Depyng decrevit fore inquirendum
super veritate huiusmodi articuli et aliis circumstanciis et ad cetera facienda
et recipienda que iuris sunt, presentibus domino Roberto Colst' rectore
ecclesie de Westmyll, Petro Thornton et Bugg.

[1] 18 Nov. 1446.
[2] All these parochial clergy were beneficed in the rural deanery of Mursley,
except the vicar of Aston Abbots, which, though locally in the same area, was in
the peculiar jurisdiction of St. Albans. The rectors of Soulbury, Cublington,
Dunton, Cheddington (called Roger Horwood), and Slapton are fully accounted
for in Lipscomb's lists in *Hist. Bucks.* iii. Dates of institution or of demise are
wanting in the cases of the rectors of Hogston, Hulcot (called Peter *Rushe*) and
Mursley, and of the three vicars. Like the vicar of Wingrave, the rector of Drayton
Beauchamp is not mentioned by Lipscomb (iii. 334), but there is room for him
between 1441 and 1459. William, vicar of Aston Abbots in 1430 (ibid. iii. 307),
may be William Watton, but details of vicars of this church are very scanty.
[3] Institutions to Clothall appear to be wanting between 1349 and 1453, which
may have been the date of Fill's demise.

Tandem 15 die Junii, a.d. 1446, in domo registri apud Vetus Templum coram Derby comparuit dictus rector et iuratus negat articulum ut prius. Unde ex gracia purgavit se sola manu et dimissus est, presentibus Colstone, Malyns et Bugg.

5. (Huntingdon, fo. 1*b*, no. 7.) Jakesley. Sautre. Dominus Ambrosius Vitell, rector ecclesie parochialis de [*sic*] Omnium Sanctorum de Sautre,[1] dilapidat mansum rectorie sue collabi [*sic*], et alienavit bona et fructus ecclesie sue.

Idem simoniace est promotus, nam dictus rector ante adeptam presentacionem dedit uxori Thome Claryvaunce, illius ecclesie patroni, pro huiusmodi presentacione eidem facta decem marcas.[2]

Idem non vult celebrare missas in ebdomada, si aliqui alterius parochie intersint.

Idem notatur cum quadam Alicia serviente sua que manet apud Jakesley.

VII. *Assignation of pension to retiring incumbent*

23. (Huntingdon, fo. 5, no. 20.) S. Ivonis. Rypton Abbatis. 11 die Septembris, a.d. 1446, indiccione nona, pontificatus &c. sexto decimo, in ecclesia prebendali de Bugden coram venerabili viro magistro Johanne Derby legum doctore, reverendi in Christo patris domini Willelmi, Dei gracia Lincoln. episcopi, commissario generali iudicialiter sedente, venit quidam Radulphus Osborn literatus mandatarius infrascriptus, et exhibuit eidem domino commissario quoddam certificatorium de facto suo. Quod quidem certificatorium dictus dominus commissarius recepit et illud michi Johanni Bugg, scribe suo, tradidit et liberavit, mandans michi ut illud legerem publice. Quo certificatorio ad mandatum dicti domini commissarii per me Johannem Bugg perlecto, cuius tenor talis est, Reverendo &c., preconizatoque magistro Thoma Waren, rectore dicte ecclesie de Rypton Abbatis,[3] venit quidam magister Thomas Berford notarius publicus, procurator et nomine procuratorio ut asseruit dicti rectoris, et protestatus est primo et ante omnia de non consenciendo in dictum dominum commissarium tanquam iudicem in hac parte competentem, et extunc salva sua huiusmodi protestacione exhibuit idem procurator quoddam procuratorium

[1] Sawtry Moyne. Vitell's institution is not recorded.

[2] The family of Clarevaux for some time held a third of the advowson, which had been divided into three parts in consequence of the death in 1411 of Mary, widow of Sir William le Moyne (*V.C.H. Huntingdon*, iii. 392).

[3] Waren, according to Noble's list of the rectors of Abbots Ripton, was instituted in 1445, on the resignation of Thomas My (op. cit. iii. 172). It would appear that My was identical with Thomas Pulter, instituted to the same church in 1424, who seems to have held with it the church of Hemingford Abbots, at any rate till 1444 (ibid. iii. 120); for, on 21 Nov. 1447, the rectors of Coppingford and Wood Walton appeared before the bishop at Buckden as *pretensi executores* of the last will of Thomas My, deceased, late rector of Hemingford Abbots, which had been proved by them before the abbot of Sawtry. The bishop sequestrated the goods of the deceased in their hands until further proof was found of the abbot's authority in the premises (Huntingdon, fo. 11, no. 62). The abbot and convent of Ramsey were the patrons of both churches.

generale eidem domino commissario; quod quidem procuratorium idem dominus commissarius de manibus dicti procuratoris recipiens, illud michi Johanni Bugg scribe suo tradidit et liberavit et illud per me perlegi mandavit. Quo procuratorio ad mandatum dicti domini commissarii per me perlecto, idem dominus commissarius peciit a dicto magistro Thoma procuratore an vellet aliquid proponere quare, attenta dicti[1] domini Thome My veneranda canicie, aliquam porcionem competentem de fructibus dicte ecclesie de Rypton eidem domino Thome ad terminum vite sue ex qua valeat sustentari assignare minime debeat. Et tunc dictus procurator peciit copias commissionis dicti domini commissarii, citacionis et certificatorii predictorum sibi decerni, et terminum competentem ad dicendum contra; ad cuius peticionem dictus dominus commissarius decrevit huiusmodi copias eidem procuratori fieri, et peciit iterato a dicto procuratore an aliquid vellet proponere quare non debeat assignare aliquam porcionem de fructibus dicte ecclesie eidem domino Thome My. Et dictus procurator ut prius peciit copias antedictas sibi decerni, et iterato idem commissarius ut prius decrevit; et tandem ex gracia idem dominus commissarius assignavit procuratori diem Sabbati proximum post festum S. Michaelis proximo iam futurum[2] in eadem ecclesia de Bugden ad proponendum causam racionabilem &c. ut prius, cuius termini assignacioni idem procurator dissenciit, presentibus Colston, Malyns et Bugg.

Quibus die et loco, videlicet primo die Octobris, a.d. 1446, in ecclesia de Bugden predicta coram magistro Johanne Derby legum doctore, dicti reverendi patris episcopi Lincoln. commissario comparuerunt personaliter magister Thomas Waryn, dicte ecclesie rector modernus, et prefatus dominus Thomas My; et habito tractatu per personas indifferentes inter partes easdem pro pensione annua eidem domino Thome My ad terminum vite sue concedenda, tandem eedem partes ordinacioni, decreto et assignacioni pensionis annue huiusmodi eidem domino Thome My limitande reverendo patri episcopo Lincoln. in alto et in basso se humiliter submiserunt. Quibus submissionibus sic factis habitoque tunc ibidem consensu patronorum dicte ecclesie in hac parte, idem dominus commissarius de mandato et auctoritate dicti reverendi patris suum decretum in hac parte in scriptis legit; per cuius decretum assignavit dicto domino Thome My pensionem annuam sexaginta solidorum legalis monete Anglie solvendorum eidem de fructibus illius ecclesie ad terminum vite sue ad duos anni terminos, videlicet ad festa Pasche et S. Michaelis extunc proximo sequens per equales porciones &c., presentibus domino Roberto Fenton vicario de Bugden,[3] magistro Waltero Roch, Roberto Dersy, Johanne Malyns et Bugg, notariis publicis.

## VIII. *Illiterate presentee to benefice*

(Huntingdon, fo. 2*b*, no. 12.) Jakesley. Fletton. Dominus Thomas Dale, ante admissionem suam ad dictam ecclesiam examinatus in litterarum

---

[1] *Sic.*                                     [2] 1 Oct. 1446.

[3] Between these two dates Fenton himself had been a defendant in a case of defamation in the same court. See p. 237.

sciencia, paciebatur defectum, sic quod ad curam animarum gerendam inhabilis reddebatur, tamen ad instanciam in predictam [ecclesiam] admissus fuit sub condicione et moderamine, videlicet quod per biennium extunc proximum litterarum studium excerceret; et in fine triennii se domino episcopo representet in litterarum sciencia examinandum; et in casu quo invenietur habilis, gaudere suo beneficio censeatur: alioquin noverit se eidem renunciaturum et debeat removeri.

14 die Octobris, a.d. 1446, in ecclesia prebendali de Bugden coram Derby comparuit dictus rector et submisit se examinacioni huiusmodi; quem sic in litteratura et construccione et aliis ad curam animarum gerendam, et presertim in sacramentis et eorum circumstanciis et pertinenciis diligenter per dictum Derby commissarium examinatum idem dominus commissarius ad huiusmodi curam exercendam habilem et idoneum reputavit, et quo ad articulum predictum ab officio dimisit, presentibus magistris Willemo Alnewyk prebendario de Bugden et Ricardo Dycolon' et aliis.[1]

## IX. *Cases concerning Letters of Orders*

1. (Huntingdon, fo. 9*b*, no. 54.) Baldok. Baldok. Dominus Johannes Selby, rector de Baldok, citetur litteras ordinum suorum exhibiturus.[2]

20 die Novembris, a.d. 1447, in ecclesia de Lidyngton coram Balscot commissario [comparuit] et exhibuit litteras ordinum, per quas compertum fuit dictum dominum Johannem, Cantuariensis diocesis, a suo diocesano sufficienter dimissum, fore ordinatum in subdiaconum apud [*sic*] et in die Sabbati qua cantatur officium Sicientes 20 die Marcii, a.d. 1427, per episcopum Londoniensem,[3] et die Sabbati in vigilia Pasche, 3 die April. a.d. 1428, in ecclesia S. Laurencii Pulteney London. per Johannem Dromorensem, suffraganeum episcopi Londoniensis,[4] in diaconum, et in vigilia sancte Trinitatis, a.d. 1428, in capella de Trottesclyf in presbyterum per episcopum Roffensem[5] ad titulum prioratus beate Marie de Bysshopes-

---

[1] Dale resigned in 1470 (Noble, op. cit. iii. 51). The register of Thomas Bekynton, bishop of Bath and Wells 1443–65, contains a large number of examples of insufficiency in letters on the part of presentees to livings. Such persons were admitted provisionally to their benefices, with the obligation of coming up after an interval for further examination. Thus Thomas Smyth, priest, was admitted to the vicarage of Portbury, Somerset, on 16 July 1448, 'in view of his youth and the liveliness and aptness of his mind', but was required 'to apply himself with diligence for two years to increasing his knowledge of the rules of grammar and obtaining a better knowledge of letters and at least a grammatical understanding of the Scriptures, and to offer himself for examination within a month after Michaelmas 1450, on condition that, in the event of his being found not to have made sufficient progress by then, he should resign his vicarage' (*R. Bek.* i. 98).

[2] Selby was instituted to Baldock 4 Feb. 1440–1: his successor was instituted 12 Mar. 1447–8 (Clutterbuck, ii. 270).

[3] William Gray.

[4] John Curlew, who appears to have resigned his Irish see in 1418. He died in 1433.

[5] John Langdon. The chapel of Trottiscliffe was the bishop's chapel in his manor house there.

gate London. ad omnes ordines concessum; et dicit quod quidam capellanus cuius nomen et cognomen ignorat, in comitiva sua aliquamdiu existens ad . . . litteras huiusmodi clanculo abstulit et cum eis recessit xiiii annis elapsis, ipso rectore invito, et quod Ricardus Selby frater suus sumptibus et expensis suis easdem litteras perquisivit. Creditque ipsum capellanum fore apostatam et nescit ubi moratur; et super istis per eum depositis iuravit ad sancta Dei evangelia quod fuerunt vera.

2. (Huntingdon, fo. 11*b*, no. 63.) S. Neoti. Hemmyngford Abbatis. Robertus Glover de Hemmyngford Abbatis et Henricus Drewell de eadem notantur super eo quod ipsi sigillum reverendi patris episcopi Lincoln. falso et dolose et litteras tam institucionis et ordinum quam alias diversarum formarum fabricarunt et registrarunt, ac eas cum sigillo sic falso fabricato sigillarunt, et eis usi fuerunt; sicque nonnullos per huiusmodi litteras falso fabricatas et sigillatas deceperunt et decipiunt, pecunias ab eis racione feodi extorquendo.

10 die Novembris, a.d. 1447, in ecclesia de Lidyngton Balscot commissarius dictum Robertum citatum et non comparentem ab ingressu ecclesie suspensit in scriptis.

## X. *A doubtful abbot and two apostate religious*

(Huntingdon, fo. 11*b*, no. 65.) Leghtonston. Saltreia. Memorandum quod 3 die Januarii, a.d. 1447, in aula infra castrum de Sleford, [diocesis] Lincoln. coram reverendo in Christo patre et domino, domino Willelmo, Dei gracia Lincoln. episcopo, ipsis die et loco in infrascripto negocio in mei notarii et testium infrascriptorum presencia iudicialiter sedente ut apparuit, venit quidam monachus de ordine ut apparuit Cisterciensi, asserens se abbatem monasterii de Saltreia predicta,[1] et exhibuit dicto reverendo patri quoddam transumptum sub nomine magistri Thome Bekyngton, tunc officialis curie Cantuariensis, cum sigillo officii officialitatis sue huiusmodi ac signo et subscripcione magistri Johannis Counde notarii publici de data in ecclesia beate Marie de Arcubus London. 24 die Novembris, a.d. 1431, in quo continebatur quoddam privilegium per dominum papam Alexandrum quartum[2] dicto ordini ut pretenditur concessum, petens a dicto reverendo patre ut dicto privilegio absque dicti reverendi patris vel suo impedimento libere uti possit et gaudere. Quod quidem transumptum idem reverendus pater de manu dicti abbatis recepit et inspexit, et ipso inspecto illud michi notario et scribe suo tradidit, mandans ut unam copiam de transumpto facerem de substancialibus privilegii huiusmodi pretensi, sumerem et originale dicto abbati retraderem. Et deinde idem reverendus pater assignavit dicto abbati diem Martis prox. post festum sancte Scolastice prox. futurum[3] in ecclesia cathedrali beate Marie Lincoln. coram ipso reverendo patre aut commissariis suis pluribus vel uno ad faciendum, audiendum et recipiendum que iuris sunt super huiusmodi exhibitis; presentibus magistro Thoma Balscote, magistro

---

[1] The list of abbots of Sawtry is at this date very imperfect.
[2] 1254–61.
[3] 13 Feb. 1447–8.

Johanne Derby legum doctoribus et me Thoma Colstone notario et scriba.

2. (Huntingdon, fo. 14, no. 83.) Leghtonston. Catworth. Frater Robertus Cosnet alias Cornewayle, monachus de Spaldyng, abiectis vestibus monachalibus utitur secularibus, qui deservit in officio capellani parochialis in ecclesia de Catworth.

Idem frater Robertus iniecit manus violentas in fratrem Ricardum Spaldyng alias Mathewe, nuper monachum dicti prioratus de Spaldyng, quem apud Snargate in partibus Cancie interfecit; et interfectus sepultus erat apud Fairford,[1] a quo sic interfecto surripuit xv li.

Idem predicat heresim, asserendo quod nulli nisi fures et meritrices peregrinaciones peragunt, et quod universalis pestilencia fit per misericordiam Dei et non per vindictam.

Idem recepit nonnullos parochianos ville de Kymbolton absque licencia curati sui ad sacramenta penitencie et eukaristie.

3. (Huntingdon, fo. 14b, no. 85.) Berkhamstede. Treng. Dominus Johannes Bentbowe, canonicus de Landa,[2] dimisso habitu canonicali utitur seculari, et deservit in officio capellani parochialis apud Treng: post cessit ad London.

## XI. *Proposed appropriation of a Nunnery to a College at Cambridge*

(Huntingdon, fo. 16b, no. 100.) Hynchynbroke. Die Veneris, videlicet 20 die Septembris, a.d. 1448, in ecclesia de Bugden, Lincoln. diocesis, coram magistro Thoma Balscot, decretorum doctore, commissario domini ibidem iudicialiter sedente comparuit magister Walterus [*sic*] Byngham et exhibuit certificatorium inquisicionis facte super suggestis pro unione, annexione, incorporacione, consolidacione et subieccione prioratus monialium de Hynchyngbroke, eiusdem Lincoln. diocesis, cuidam collegio de Goddeshous in Cantabrigia ut dicitur erecto.[3] Post cuius quidem certificatorii exhibicionem et inspeccionem prefatus dominus commissarius prefixit et assignavit dicto magistro Willelmo Byngham diem Mercurii prox. post festum sancti Luce evangeliste[4] in ecclesia Lincoln. ad docendum et probandum idem collegium fore erectum et ordinatum et stabilitum et ad cetera facienda et recipienda que iuris sunt. Et ibidem, videlicet dicto die Veneris coram eodem domino commissario venit quidam magister Johannes Walbrond, clericus, notarius publicus, procurator abbatis et conventus monasterii de Thorney, et exhibuit suum procuratorium et, ipso recepto et inspecto, allegavit dominos suos fore patronos ipsius prioratus: unde

[1] *Sic.* Evidently Fairfield, the parish adjoining Snargate in Romney Marsh, is meant. Why the two monks should have been in that neighbourhood is not explained: possibly they were on pilgrimage to Canterbury and were seeing the neighbourhood, and the incident may have deepened, if it was not responsible for, Cosnet's heterodox opinion of pilgrimages.

[2] Laund in Leicestershire.

[3] God's House, the predecessor of Christ's College at Cambridge. The founder, William Byngham, was rector of St. John Zachary in the city of London, 1426–51.

[4] 23 Oct. 1448.

habet dictum diem Mercurii post festum Luce in eadem ecclesia Lincoln. ad probandum allegata. Et ibidem apud acta dictus magister Willelmus Byngham constituit magistrum Johannem Derby, legum doctorem, suum procuratorem, etc.[1]

# APPENDIX IV

## PLURALISM IN 1366

AMONG the returns of pluralists in R. Langham is a most interesting statement, given at length probably as a specimen of others similar, by master Roger Otery, LL.B., priest, *clericus commensalis* of Lewis (Charlton), bishop of Hereford (fo. 26.):

'In hiis scriptis dico allego et propono quod fui a diu et adhuc sum bone vite et conversacionis honeste nulloque crimine irretitus seu de aliquo notabiliter diffamatus nullaque suspensionis excommunicacionis seu interdicti sentencia iuris vel hominis innodatus industriosus in temporalibus et spiritualibus et potissime circa correccionem et reformacionem morum subditorum episcoporum iuxta morem ecclesie Anglicane et Wallie prout experiencia docet et docuit iam multis annis. Sitque sacris canonibus cautum quod persona bona et industriis [*sic*] et literata posset melius et sciret regere duas ecclesias vel decem quam alius unam et altari servire intelligitur tam qui residet quam qui non residet dummodo bene vivat et bene expendat quod inde percipit. Et dico eciam quod de consuetudine ecclesie Anglicane fuit et est consuetum usitatum et approbatum a tempore cuius contrarii memoria hominum non existit et ab ecclesia Romana tolleratum quod episcopi et alii patroni dicti regni Anglie possent clericis bene meritis de beneficiis maxime sine cura in numero quocumque providere sine contradiccione seu offensa sedis apostolice aliquali. Unde premissis et aliis consideratis coram vobis exhibeo et insinuo in hiis scriptis clare particulariter et distincte nomina et qualitates necnon taxaciones beneficiorum meorum ecclesiasticorum.'

The list of benefices includes preb. 'atte Crosse' in the church of Crediton, provided 'in forma quam sedes apostolica pro pauperibus clericis beneficiandis scribere consuevit'; the church of Bledlow, co. Buckingham, to which he had been presented by the Crown; a preb. in the church of Ottery St. Mary which he owed to Bishop Grandisson's wish 'ipsi collegiate ecclesie providere de me non propter me set propter ecclesiam ad onus meum et non honorem'; the subdeacon preb. of Weston St. Laurence in the church of Westbury-on-Trym, conferred on him *proprio motu* by Bishop Brien, in a church 'destituta consilio et ministris, ipsius collegii utilitate et necessitate consideratis';

---

[1] Byngham's petition did not succeed. It is not clear how far the abbot and convent of Thorney were justified in claiming the advowson of the priory, as documents relating to Hinchingbrooke are few and far between.

a prebendal portion in the church of Holdgate, Salop, 'que nullam requirit residenciam'; and preb. Hunderton in the church of Hereford. The last two had been given him by Bishop Charlton, but the second was disputed at law. The six benefices, of which five were sinecures, were assessed at a total of £47. 1s. 4d. The statement concludes:

'Et protestor me velle quatenus mandatum domini nostri Urbani pape quinti si quod sit seu quod emanavit me ad ista seu plura artaverit eidem mandato in omnibus parere et ex habundanti eligo duo prima compassibilia salvo semper iure meo in hiis electis et aliis beneficiis meis michi adquisito subiciens me nichilominus statum personam et beneficia quecumque defensioni tuicioni et proteccioni domini nostri summi pontificis sedis apostolice et ecclesie Romane que est semper de consilio consimili si quem leserit satisfacere et reformare parata.'

There is a note that a similar protestation *in materia et quasi forma* accompanied other returns; but Otery's is the only one given in full. Apart from its bold defence of the pluralist *litteratus* as a desirable feature in ecclesiastical affairs, it has value as introducing us to a *litteratus* who owed promotion to his work in the service of bishops who were all of the *sublimis* class.

## APPENDIX V
## COLLEGES OF CHANTRY PRIESTS

No more typical illustrations of the origin and development of these foundations can be found than in a group which owed its existence to clerks occupied in the royal service during the first half of the fourteenth century. The earliest of these, the chapel of St. Peter at Kirkby-on-Wreak in Leicestershire, was founded in 1319 by Roger Beler or Bellers. In 1327 Gilbert Middleton, archdeacon of Northampton, founded a chantry of a warden and seven chaplains in the church of Wappenham in his own archdeaconry. Before this Thomas Sibthorp, rector of Beckingham in Lincolnshire, on the road from Newark to Sleaford, had taken the first step towards the establishment of a college in the parish church of his native place, Sibthorpe, on the other side of Newark in the rural district east of the Fosseway. Here the college reached its full development in 1342, and almost contemporary with it was the college of Cotterstock in Northamptonshire, in the valley of the Nene near Oundle, founded by John Giffard, a canon of York in the service of the dowager queen Isabel.

Of these the most interesting is Sibthorpe. Thanks to the

archiepiscopal registers at York and a large number of entries in the
patent rolls, we can trace its growth and are provided with a number
of details with regard to the medieval arrangements of a church which
still exists, though shorn of the aisles that play so large a part in the
history of the college. Sibthorpe, who at the close of the reign of
Edward II and the beginning of that of Edward III was keeper of
the hanaper in Chancery, was a wealthy man who, in addition to
his chantry at Sibthorpe, founded a chantry of St. Mary in the north
aisle of his church of Beckingham[1] and had probably paid for the
rebuilding of both aisles, still excellent examples of the architectural
work of the period. In December 1323 he was concluding purchases
of land in the neighbourhood of Sibthorpe for the endowment of a
chantry which he proposed to found in the chapel of Our Lady in
the north aisle of Sibthorpe church, built at his expense. At the
same time he was making further purchases which the warden of
the chantry was to regrant to him for his life with reversion to the
chantry after his death. The principal documents relating to these
two blocks of property are included in the ordination of the chantry
issued by Archbishop Melton, 26 May 1326,[2] and with them are the
two royal licences for the alienation of the premises in mortmain to
the chaplain, dated at Cippenham near Slough on 23 October in
the previous year. The first of these provides for the grant of 2
messuages with a toft, 60 acres of land and 10 acres of meadow in
Hawksworth and Aslockton to the chaplain, with remainder after
the death of the present tenant of a messuage, 12 acres of land and
3 of meadow in Sibthorpe and Syerston of which Thomas Sibthorpe
had the reversion.[3] The second concerns 3 messuages, 3 bovates, 50
acres of land, 20 acres of meadow and 10 shillings rent in Sibthorpe,
Syerston, Aslockton, Elston, and Thoroton, which constituted the
second block aforesaid. From this, upon its reversion to him, the
chaplain, whose name at this date is given as John Notebroun, was
expected to find a 'secondary' chaplain, preferably a native of
Sibthorpe, to celebrate at the same altar or, if this were not convenient, at the altar either of St. Katherine or of St. Nicholas.

---

[1] The first licence for the chantry at Beckingham bears date 6 Dec. 1332 (*C.P.R.*
1330–4, p. 376). A further licence, 16 July 1338, accompanied a charter, exemplified with one relating to the foundation at Sibthorpe, 9 Apr. 1340 (ibid. 1334–8,
p. 301; 1338–40, p. 522). A number of pleas relating to the chantry at Beckingham
followed those concerning Sibthorpe exemplified 16 May 1343 (ibid. 1343–5,
pp. 63–5). On 5 Dec. 1345 Edward III took the wardens of both chapels under
his protection (ibid. 1345–8, p. 17). See also the exemplification of a record
relating to the lands of both, 20 Mar. 1350–1 (ibid. 1350–4, p. 77).

[2] The earliest document of acquisition of property recorded bears date 1 Dec.
1323 (R. Melton, fo. 356*b*).

[3] *C.P.R.* 1324–7, p. 182; R. Melton, ff. 356*b*, 357.

Sibthorpe's grant of the premises to his chaplain was confirmed by letters patent, dated 28 November following.[1]

The chapel thus founded and endowed was dedicated to Our Lady, St. John Baptist, and St. Thomas the Martyr. The object of its services, as stated in the letters patent, was continual intercession for the founder himself in his lifetime and for his soul after death, and for the souls of William his father, Maud his mother, his brothers and sisters, Simon Sibthorpe and his sons William and Reynold, Geoffrey le Clerc, Alice his wife and their children William, Henry, Thomas, and Margery. The archbishop's ordination also prescribed that, while on Sundays mass was to be of the day and on Saturdays of Our Lady, on other week-days not festivals it was normally to be a mass for the dead, with a special collect for the good estate of the founder, the king, Hugh le Despenser the younger, and the well-known Chancery clerk Robert Bardelby, and for their souls after death. While the chaplain, as warden, had full control of the chapel and its services, the rights of the rector of the church had to be safe-guarded, and mass might not be said or sung in the chapel on any high day before the offertory at the parochial high mass, without leave of the rector or his deputy, the parish chaplain.

This ordination was followed by the documents relating to the second block of property granted, as already stated, in reversion and by a supplementary series of statutes with regard to the secondary chaplain and his duties. But neither these nor the main body of ordinances were permanent and in Melton's register were vacated in favour of a new endowment and ordination nine years later, bearing date 10 June 1335. The ordination, printed here, is a thorough revision of the earlier one, and now provides for a warden of the chapel, whose name is given as John Cosyn,[2] two assistant chaplains and a clerk, and for twenty-six wax tapers, the directions for which are explicit and elaborate. It is not definitely stated that at this time the reconstruction of the whole church at Sibthorpe's expense was in progress, but we hear for the first time of the chapel of St. Anne in the south aisle of the nave, which appears to have borne the additional dedications to St. Katherine, St. Margaret, and St. Mary Magdalene. Here we need note only two points. First, it is interesting to see that the name of Hugh le Despenser is kept among the names of those for whose benefit the chantries were founded, indicating the direction in which Sibthorpe's political sympathies had lain at the close of the late reign. Secondly, the directions for the use of the wax tapers on special occasions give us a complete view of the

---

[1] *C.P.R.* 1324–7, u.s.; R. Melton, fo. 358.
[2] Otherwise known as John of Edwalton, who had succeeded Notebroun.

arrangement of the altars in the church west of the chancel, the altar of Our Lady in the north aisle, the rood-screen with the crucifix and attendant figures across the chancel arch, with the altar of St. Andrew and St. Nicholas on the north and that of St. Stephen and St. Laurence on the south side of the entrance, and the altar of St. Anne in the south aisle.

This meant a considerable increase in endowments, and the letters patent by which Sibthorpe's resettlement of his foundation was authorized show that the original endowment had been augmented by 10 messuages and 60 or 70 acres of land.[1] During the next few years, however, he continued his work with great energy, and in 1342 it was possible for Archbishop Zouche to say that he had caused both chapels and the nave and chancel of the church to be constructed at his own expense. Further, the foundation had enjoyed prosperity and Sibthorpe himself was a wealthy man, so that he was well able 'to make some recompense for the grievous sins which he had contracted' in the course of his busy life. He set about acquiring the advowson of the church from the patrons, the prior and convent of St. John of Jerusalem in England, with the intention of appropriating it to the uses of a body of seven chaplains with the warden at their head, four chaplains being added to the three already existing. On 20 January 1340-1 the prior and convent had licence to alienate the advowson to him for a grant to the warden of the chapel.[2] On 12 February, at their preceptory of Shingay in Cambridgeshire, an indenture was drawn up between the prior and Sibthorpe, and at Easter (8 Apr.) the whole property previously acquired with the advowson of the church formed the subject of an indenture, concluded at Sibthorpe, between Sibthorpe and the warden Cosyn.[3] The final act in the completion of the foundation lay with the archbishop as diocesan. On 16 January 1342-3 Zouche, Melton's successor at York, ordered the official of the archdeacon of Nottingham to hold an inquiry into the petition presented by Sibthorpe. The official sent in his certificate from Newark on 22 January.[4] It seems probable that he was the rural dean of Newark, Hugh, rector of Barnby-le-Willows, whose seal was appended to each of the three letters, dated at Newark 2 January, in which Cosyn, Sibthorpe, and the rector of Sibthorpe submitted

---

[1] *C.P.R.* 1334–8, p. 340; R. Zouche, fo. 93.

[2] *C.P.R.* 1340–3, p. 81; R. Zouche, ff. 93*b*, 94.

[3] R. Zouche, ff. 94, 95.

[4] Ibid., ff. 96, 97. The commission is on fo. 92. The three submissions and that of the prior and convent of Thurgarton are on ff. 97–8*b*. The statutes, printed here, follow, ff. 98*b*–103. They are followed by the decree of appropriation of the church, 6 Feb. 1342–3 (fo. 103) and this by the rector's deed of resignation, 8 Feb. (fo. 103*b*).

themselves to the archbishop's decree. The rector in the early days of the chantry had been William Aslacby, who since then had been succeeded by John Sibthorpe, evidently a kinsman of the founder. Finally the submission of the prior and convent of Thurgarton, as one of the parties interested in the patronage of the establishment, was obtained on 25 January, and on 4 February the archbishop issued his ordination of the college of priests from Cawood Castle.

The text of that ordinance is printed here, and no further comment need be made upon it, save to call attention to its elaborate and detailed character, of special value for its liturgical and ritual directions. In this respect no document of the kind within the present writer's experience represents the mind of the founder better, for it is unnecessary to say that the archbishop's part in such a decree was in the main a work of revision of a document previously submitted to him by the founder for inspection, correction, and confirmation.

The documents cited in the registers include several private charters in addition to licences by letters patent and a certain number of records of pleas. Such licences and records are greatly augmented by licences and exemplifications of pleas entered on the patent rolls in great number. From these Sibthorpe's arrangements for the gradual enlargement of his college are clear, but they come to an end with his tragic death, which seems to have taken place between 6 July and 26 October 1351, to which allusions without detail are abundant after the later of these dates.[1]

---

[1] Licences for alienation in mortmain of divers pieces of property by the founder will be found *C.P.R.* 1324–7, pp. 38, 182; 1327–30, p. 246; 1334–8, p. 113 (first mention of the chapel of St. Anne in this series, 28 May 1335), 340; 1338–40, pp. 24–5 (first mention of 30 wax tapers and lamp, 8 Feb. 1337–8); 1340–3, p. 81 (assignation of advowson to warden and chaplains, to find four more chaplains and two clerks, 20 Jan. 1340–1); 1343–5, p. 518 (total number of chaplains increased to warden and eight, of clerks from two to three, 1 June 1345); 1345–8, pp. 157–8, repeated p. 332; 1348–50, pp. 228–9, 341, 357. The repeated licence noted, which is very comprehensive, appears to have entailed the vacation of licences relating to the manor of Sibthorpe (ibid. 1343–5, p. 17; 1345–8, p. 78): the warden had an exemplification of this, as in the repeated version, 5 Feb. 1347–8. Licences for alienations, &c., to Sibthorpe or the warden by various persons occur *C.P.R.* 1321–4, p. 326; 1324–7, pp. 334, 335; 1327–30, p. 334; 1334–8, p. 335; 1338–40, pp. 206–7, 543 (transfer of advowson by the Hospitallers, with first mention of enlargement of staff by four chaplains, 7 June 1340); 1343–5, pp. 383–4. Exemplifications of pleas are as follows: (1) A set of six, from quindene of Michaelmas 19 Edward II, to the like date, 14 Edward III (*C.P.R.* 1340–3, pp. 131–6); (2) nine, all 15 Edward III, relating to advowson (ibid., pp. 399–402), with six and eight, also 15 Edward III (ibid., pp. 402–8); (3) six, 15–17 Edward III (ibid. 1343–5, pp. 62–3); (4) six, from Michaelmas, 19, to Martinmas, 20 Edward III, with four, octave of Michaelmas, anno 19 (ibid. 1345–8, pp. 324–6); (5) four, for Michaelmas and Hilary, anno 20 (ibid., pp. 326–7); (6) five, from quindene of Martinmas, anno 20, to quindene of Trinity, anno 21 (ibid., pp. 327–8); (7) five,

The method of composition and revision of statutes is well illustrated by the series of documents relating to the foundation of the
chantry college at Cotterstock. Of its endowment by John Giffard
nothing need be said here, but references to various entries in the
patent rolls and Bishop Bek's register may be given. The actual
scheme appears to be later than that which Thomas Sibthorpe
matured very gradually from 1323 onwards and the number of
chaplains was in this case fixed from the beginning, for the founder's
set of statutes, composed in the first person, was dated at Cotterstock 5 December 1339 and confirmed by Bishop Burghersh's vicar-
general, Simon Islip, the future archbishop of Canterbury, at Lincoln
a month later, 7 January 1339–40.[1] Burghersh himself died before
the end of 1340 and his successor Thomas Bek did not enter upon
the see until more than eighteen months later. Bek's short episcopate
(1342–7) was active and he seems to have taken the matter of Cotterstock vigorously in hand. His revision of Giffard's statutes was
issued at Buckden 16 January 1343–4, with considerable rearrange-
ment and rephrasing and some enlargement by additions, making
for clearness and definiteness. It should be noticed that Giffard's
phraseology is in many places identical with that used by Sibthorpe

from quindene of Hilary, anno 20, to like date, anno 21 (ibid. 1348–50, pp. 54–5);
(8) seven, all 21 and 22 Edward III (ibid., p. 180); (9) seven, all anno 22 (ibid.,
pp. 230–4); ten, all anno 22 (ibid., pp. 380–2). These pleas, it need hardly be
said, were for the settlement of the property in the hands of the warden and
chaplains by record of court obtained by formal litigation. Exemplifications of
other charters and records appear at intervals. Much of the property alienated
by the founder was in part satisfaction of licences obtained by Notebroun and
Cosyn for property to the value of £10. The first of these seems to have been lost,
but was exemplified for Cosyn, 9 Mar. 1336–7 (C.P.R. 1334–8, pp. 390–1), who
obtained a licence to the value of 100s. 4 July 1338 (ibid. 1338–40, p. 109) and the
licence for £10 above mentioned 28 May 1345 (ibid. 1343–5, p. 473).
  [1] R. Burg., ff. 227b–229b. The appropriation of the church to the college, also
in the name of Islip, 14 Jan., with the consent of the chapter of Lincoln, 15 Jan.,
follows on fo. 232. The entries on the patent rolls are few compared with those
referring to Sibthorpe. On 2 Sept. 1337, at the request of Queen Isabel, Giffard
had licence to alienate property in mortmain to the future provost and twelve
chaplains (C.P.R. 1334–8, p. 515), and on 9 May 1338, a further licence for land
acquired at an earlier date, together with a licence for the foundation of the
college. This and other licences were exemplified 12 Apr. 1340, and on 21 Apr.
came an inspeximus and confirmation of Giffard's ordinances as confirmed by
Islip. Also on 21 Apr. the provost and chaplains had licence to acquire property
in mortmain to the value of 20 marks. On 8 June 1340 they had a further licence
to alienate rent to meet the demands of the bishop and dean and chapter of
Lincoln in compensation for loss sustained by the appropriation of the church;
and on 12 June the charter granted to Giffard on 24 Jan. 1338–9 received exemplification (ibid. 1338–40, pp. 61–2, 82, 463–4, 472, 478–9, 539: see also pp. 122,
160–1). Letters patent, 3 Feb. 1341–2 and 20 Oct. 1347, refer to tithes from recent
and future assarts in Rockingham forest (ibid. 1340–3, p. 374; 1345–8, p. 419).

in his statutes, and it is obvious that both must have worked upon the same common form, or that possibly Sibthorpe may have borrowed from Giffard, whose statutes as we have them are the earlier. At the same time, no very lively sympathy can have existed between two men whose political interest lay on opposite sides, for Giffard owed his career to the queen dowager, whom he duly remembered as an object of intercession at Cotterstock, while, as we have seen, Sibthorpe cherished the memory of the younger Despenser, whom her partisans had pursued with implacable hatred.[1]

Bek, however, seems to have been dissatisfied with the Cotterstock statutes as they stood, even after careful revision. On 2 March 1343–4, six to seven weeks after they had been sealed at Buckden, he was at Wappenham in Northamptonshire. Here Gilbert Middleton, archdeacon of Northampton, had founded a chantry of a warden and six chaplains in 1327,[2] and it is possible that Bek was curious to see how the scheme worked nearly fourteen years after the founder's death. The ordinances for the Wappenham chantry are considerably more brief than the Cotterstock statutes and have no obvious influence upon their arrangement or wording. Nevertheless, it was at Wappenham that Bek issued a new and final set of statutes for Cotterstock which is printed here and will be seen to be notably distinct in form from its predecessors.[3]

Two points remain to be noticed. The archiepiscopal registers at York supplement the story of the foundation of Cotterstock with an account of the acquisition of the advowson of the church of Barnby-upon-Don near Doncaster in 1345 by John Giffard and its appropriation to his chantry college. The details of this are given elsewhere, but the preamble is worth quoting as expressing the pious objects of the foundation.

'Ad relevandum inopiam devotorum christi multum in agro suo laboran-

[1] For Bek's first statutes see R. Bek, ff. 60–3.

[2] The founder's statutes, confirmed by the bishop, are in R. Burg., ff. 198–201b. Their date 9 Apr. 1327.

[3] R. Bek, ff. 74–77b. Other documents in the same register are as follows: (1) ff. 53b–55. *Inspeximus* and confirmation by Bek, Buckden, 12 Feb. 1343–4, of appropriation of the church of Cotterstock to the provost and chaplains, 13 Feb. 1339–40, by Islip, vicar-general, acting under commission from Burghersh dated Antwerp, 21 Dec. 1339. Bek assigns the cure of souls to the provost without ordaining a vicarage. Another version of this decree is given on fo. 64 and b; (2) fo. 63b. Ratification by Bek, Buckden, 15 Feb. 1343–4, of royal licence granting tithes of assarts and wastes in Rockingham forest; (3) fo. 73b. Another version of the decree of appropriation, dated as before, with power to the provost to depute the cure of souls to one of the *fratres capellani*; (4) fo. 77b. Submission of the provost and chaplains, Cotterstock, 29 Jan. 1343–4, to the bishop's ordination, sealed with their common seal, followed by the founder's submission, sealed with the seal of the rural dean of Oundle.

cium tunc potissime sacerdotum per quorum ministerium verum et sacratis-
simum corpus christi conficitur in altari domini ut . . . sufficienter habeant
unde vivant et divinis obsequiis liberius et quiescius [sic] insistere valeant
et vacare cure pastoralis nobis incumbentis officio provocamur ac divina
pietas nos admonet et inducit.'[1]

Secondly, of the history of both foundations little is recorded, and
we do not know how far the number of chaplains was maintained
in either church. Sibthorpe, as we have seen, certainly had a larger
number of priests in mind, and some provision was made for bringing
up the number from seven to nine. In both churches the office of
warden or provost continued until the dissolution of chantries in the
sixteenth century, and the last warden of Sibthorpe was that noted
pluralist, a native and benefactor of the neighbouring town of
Newark, Thomas Magnus. If at Sibthorpe the church has lost much,
the beautiful chancel which was part of Thomas Sibthorpe's rebuilding remains with its interesting Easter Sepulchre, while the chancel
which John Giffard very probably rebuilt at his own expense at
Cotterstock on a large scale survives, and in the middle of the floor
is the fine brass of an early fifteenth-century provost, Robert
Wintringham, who was prebendary of Liddington in the church
of Lincoln and died in 1420.

## I. Ordinacio Cantariarvm in Capella de Sibthorp

(R. Melton, fo. 387b, a revision of a similar document, fo. 356b)

Universis sancte matris ecclesie filiis hanc presentem ordinacionem
visuris vel audituris Willelmus *permissione divina archiepiscopus Anglie primas*[2]
salutem in amplexibus salvatoris. Inspirat divinitus consilii spiritus in pia
corda cultorum dei bone intencionis oblectamina ex quorum affluencia
salubria insecuntur opera pietatis. Quid enim tam dulce memoria quid
suavius in mente pura aut quid sonorius in aure divina seu perfeccius in
anima quam corpus christi filii dei in ara crucis pro peccatoribus extensum
ad nominis sui gloriam in spiritu mundicie patri suo diebus singulis immo-
lare: profecto nichil in corde revolvi poterit quod tam celebre tamque
sanctum opus excelleret in hac vita. Et iccirco meditantes dona dei in
huiusmodi operis execucione ad sui laudem in ejus ecclesia dilatare *haut
longe a christi sequacibus recedit*[3] dum vivis et defunctis pro quibus oratur
propensius *extendit*[4] viscera caritatis. Sane exhibita nobis dilecti filii domini
Thome de Sibthorp persone ecclesie de Bekyngham peticio continebat quod
cum ipse quasdam capellam in honore dei et beate marie matris sue ex

[1] R. Zouche, fo. 10b: for the licence for appropriation 1 July 1344 see *C.P.R.*
1343–5, p. 323. See *Fasti Paroch.* i (Y.A.S. Record ser., vol. lxxxv), 29, 30.

[2] So fo. 356b: *&c.*, fo. 387b.

[3] So fo. 356b: *merito sunt gracius prosequendi*, fo. 387b, apparently the beginning of
an alteration which was not completed, as neither reading continues the construction.                                          [4] So fo. 356b: *extendunt*, fo. 387b.

parte boriali ecclesie de Sibthorp nostre diocesis suis construi sumptibus
fecerit et parari cui quendam capellanum custodem perpetuum prefici
desiderat qui duos alios capellanos ydoneos et unum clericum secum ibidem
habeat et illuc viginti et sex cereos ardentes perpetuis temporibus inveniat
et sustentet pro quorum custodis capellanorum et clerici sustentacione ac
cereorum predictorum invencione certas dedit possessiones et redditus prout
per cartas et scripta ejusdem domini Thome inde confecta plenius poterit
apparere dictusque dominus Thomas se ac dominus Willelmus de Aslakby
se ac dominus Johannes Cosyn capellanus cui prefatus dominus Thomas
prefatos possessiones et redditus ex causis contulit supradictis se et prefatos
possessiones et redditus nostris ordinacioni voluntati arbitrio consilio et
decreto pure sponte submiserint et devote velimus submissiones hujusmodi
clementer admittere et super premissis ordinare salubriter intuitu caritatis.
Nos igitur Willelmus archiepiscopus memoratus pium et laudabile propositum dicti domini Thome contemplantes qui grata consideracione
prefatam ecclesiam de Sibthorp in qua fuit sacri baptismatis unda lotus
honorare disposuit et divina servicia in eadem dilatare ac volentes votis
suis tanta devocione subnixis condescendere graciose quia per quandam
inquisicionem auctoritate nostra rite captam nobis constat quod dicti
possessiones et redditus ad congruam sustentacionem dictorum custodis
duorum capellanorum et clerici ac invencionem et sustentacionem cereorum
predictorum et supportacionem onerum infrascriptorum et aliorum
incumbencium comode se extendunt dictas submissiones nobis ut premittitur rite factas de assistencium nobis peritorum consilio admittimus et ad
ordinaciones super premissis faciendas de consensu omnium et singulorum
quorum interest ex causis premissis et aliis legittimis procedimus in hunc
modum.

In dei nomine amen. In primis ordinamus statuimus et decernimus
in hiis scriptis quod in dicta ecclesia de Sibthorp sint tres cantarie perpetue
due videlicet in dicta capella beate marie et tercia in capella beate Anne
ibidem quas in ipsis capellis creamus et erigimus per decretum et quod
dictus dominus Johannes Cosyn sit custos perpetuus dicte capelle beate
marie ad totam vitam suam. Et post mortem ejus in singulis vacacionibus
dicte capelle beate marie unus capellanus ydoneus et discretus nobis et
successoribus nostris Eboracensibus archiepiscopis ecclesie nostre sede plena
et ipsa vacante reverendis viris decano et capitulo Eboracensibus per dictum
dominum Thomam quociens dictam custodiam in vita ipsius domini Thome
vacare contigerit et post mortem eius per capitulum ecclesie nostre beate
marie Suwellensis vel presidentem eidem infra tres septimanas a tempore
vacacionis huiusmodi continue numerandas et ipsis infra dictum tempus
non presentantibus tunc per religiosos viros priorem et conventum de
Thurgerton nostre diocesis infra alias tres septimanas continuas extunc
immediate sequentes ad perpetuam dicte capelle custodiam presentetur per
nos et successores nostros sede plena ac dictos decanum et capitulum sede
vacante instituendus custos perpetuus in eadem. Quem custodem capelle
illius nominamus et nominari volumus perpetuo in futurum. Et si dictum
capitulum Suwellense vel presidens eidem per tres septimanas et postea
dicti prior et conventus per alias tres septimanas a tempore vacacionis

huiusmodi capellanum ydoneum modo quo premittitur presentare distulerint vel distulerit sit nobis et successoribus nostris sede plena et prefatis decano et capitulo Eboracensibus sede vacante dicte capelle seu custodie collacio devoluta salvo iure dicto domino Thome et prefatis capitulo Suwellensi et presidenti eidem ac priori et conventui ad dictam capellam alias cum vacaverit iuxta formam ordinacionis predicte libere presentandi. Qui quidem custos sic institutus liberam et legittimam habeat administracionem terrarum tenementorum rerum et bonorum omnium ad dictam capellam et custodiam eiusdem pertinencium seu spectancium presencium et futurorum.

Et teneat idem custos et successores sui custodes capelle predicte secum continue in domo et in mensa duos capellanos providos honestos scientes valentes et volentes in ecclesia et capellis predictis cantare et legere competenter quos in esculentis et poculentis teneantur sufficienter procurare et ultra id utrique eorum pro aliis minutis necessariis viginti et quinque solidos solvere annuatim qui dicto custodi et successoribus suis subsint et in admissione sua corporaliter sibi iurent fidelitatem et obedienciam ac sibi in mandatis canonicis pareant et intendant. Teneant eciam iidem custos et successores sui continue unum clericum sciolum et honestum qui sibi et dictis capellanis in divinis ministret obsequiis et cereos predictos illuminet et custodiat iuxta ordinacionem infrascriptam et singulis noctibus iaceat in dicta ecclesia pro salva custodia eiusdem cereorum ornamentorum ac aliorum in eadem ecclesia et capellis predictis existencium et pulset diebus singulis campanam in aurora diei et in vesperis hora cubandi consueta et ad missam de beata virgine statim post matutinas dictas seu cantatas ibidem et in diebus cum vacare poterit parvulos parochie illius qui addiscere litteras voluerint in hiis instruat et informet cui dictus custos et successores sui victum inveniant in communi et ultra id sibi solvant singulis annis decem solidos. Proviso quod tociens quociens dicti capellani vel clericus seu eorum aliquis notabiliter criminosi vel culpabiles aut alias insufficientes seu negligentes fuerint notorie vel remissi prefatus custos illos vel illum absque more dispendio ammoveat et infra quindecim dies continuos quociens aliquem ex dicta causa vel alia ammoveri vel eciam mori contigerit alium vel alios in locis eorum assumat ydoneos sub pena privacionis a capella seu custodia capelle predicte quam ipsum custodem si hoc non fecerit incurrere volumus ipso facto precipientes ut extunc alius capellanus ydoneus in forma prescripta ad dictam custodiam capelle predicte illico presentetur et instituatur in eadem. Et ne per magnum tempus missarum celebracio differatur volumus ut statim post lapsum dictorum quindecim dierum infra quos dictus custos de capellano vel capellanis seu clerico ydoneis non providit liceat presidenti dicto capitulo Suthwellensi vel eius locum tunc tenenti in loco capellani vel capellanorum amoti vel amotorum seu mortuorum alium vel alios ydoneos (fo. 388) subrogare qui procurentur et recipiant in omnibus ut est superius ordinatum salvo alias iure dicto custodi predicte capelle cum opus fuerit de capellanis ydoneis et clerico providere.

Inveniant eciam iidem custos et successores sui viginti et sex cereos perpetuo annis singulis ad festum concepcionis beate marie virginis si opus fuerit innovandos quorum quilibet ponderet duas libras in ecclesia predicta

stantes ex transverso videlicet decem in dicta capella beate marie quorum
quinque precipua gaudia dicte virginis et sextum [sic] specialiter annuncia-
cionem dominicam et quatuor residui honorem et memoriam beatorum
Johannis Baptiste Petri et Pauli apostolorum et Thome martiris. In navi
vero ipsius ecclesie et capella beate Anne matris virginis Marie ex parte
australi ipsius ecclesie per ipsum dominum Thomam de novo constructe
sint sexdecim cerei duo videlicet in honore beatorum Andree apostoli et
Nicholai confessoris coram altari eorum et septem coram ymaginibus crucifixi beate marie et sancti Johannis Evangeliste in commemoracione passionis
dominice et doloris matris et discipuli predictorum et duo coram altari
sanctorum Stephani et Laurencii in laudem eorundem et quinque coram
altari predicte Anne et beatarum Katerine Margarete et Marie Magdalene
ad ipsarum gloriam et honorem arsuros perpetuo subscriptis temporibus
et cum minutis candelis cum opus fuerit sustentando videlicet omnibus
majoribus dupplicibus festis et in quinque festis beate marie virginis et in
festis omnium predictorum sanctorum et sanctarum in primis et secundis
vesperis matutinis et missa de die. Quas vesperas matutinas et missas in
festis predictis ob devocionem quam idem dominus Thomas erga dictos
sanctos et sanctas habet iubemus et volumus cum nota in dictis capellis et
ecclesia coram dictis altaribus eorundem sanctorum per rectorem capellanum parochialem et diaconum dicte ecclesie ac prefatos custodem capellanos
et clericum suum solempniter celebrari. Diebus vero dominicis et aliis
festivis ardeant cerei predicti ad missam de die tantum. Et quod septem de
cereis predictis quolibet die imperpetuum ardeant cum suplemento minu-
tarum candelarum ad missam de beata virgine cum nota in dicta capella ut
infra scribitur celebranda.

Item ordinamus decernimus et iubemus quod prefatus custos et successores sui vestibus dumtaxat utantur de blueto non nimis albo nec nimis
nigro cum supertunica clausa et talari sicut decet et faciat pro viribus ut
alii duo capellani sibi in huiusmodi habitu sint conformes. Sint eciam
custos et capellani predicti honeste mutuo conversantes prout sacerdotalem
condecet gravitatem et de una mensa vescantur et in una camera iaceant
nisi aliquis eorum per infirmitatem vel aliud impedimentum canonicum
fuerit impeditus quem tunc iuxta humanitatis delictum prout sua requirit
necessitas volumus in necessariis micius procurari. Diebus eciam singulis
in predicta ecclesia conveniant predicti custos et capellani horis debitis
superpelliceis induti tam diebus ferialibus quam festivis et in diebus
dominicis festis duplicibus et aliis diebus festivis una cum clerico predicto
imperpetuum dicant matutinas vesperas et completorium cum nota et
omnes alias horas canonicas cum nota vel sine nota pro voluntate sua in
cancello eiusdem ecclesie tractim et devote cum rectore vel capellano
parochiali et diacono eiusdem ecclesie si interesse voluerint et personaliter
in eadem ecclesia intersint temporibus debitis et consuetis secundum usum
in dicta ecclesia usitatum ab antiquo. Alioquin ipsas dicant matutinas
vesperas et alias horas per se sine nota secundum eundem usum distincte
et devote in dicta capella beate marie superpelliciis induti dictorum rectoris
seu capellani parochialis aut diaconi presencia minime expectata. Quibus
diebus ferialibus et festis trium leccionum et aliis minoribus diebus festivis

ante horam vesperarum cessante impedimento legittimo simul dicant dicti custos et capellani in dicta capella beate marie imperpetuum pro anima predicti domini Thome et animabus subscriptis et aliorum pro quibus exorare tenentur ac omnium fidelium defunctorum plenum servicium mortuorum sicut pro corpore presenti et in crastino in dicta capella beate marie ante incepcionem matutinarum commendacionem pro animabus predictis. In maioribus vero festis duplicibus diebus dominicis et aliis festis maioribus in quibus vespere matutine et missa solempniter cum nota in dictis ecclesia seu capellis cantari contigerint dictum dicant officium mortuorum et commendacionem in eadem capella beate marie vel alibi ubi magis sibi placitum fuerit et devotum. Item diebus singulis missam celebrent eorum singuli tam custos quam alii duo capellani videlicet unus eorum de beata virgine in dicta capella beate marie solempniter et cum nota statim post matutinas et horas dictas seu cantatas in ecclesia seu capella beate marie predictis. In qua missa tam custos quam capellani una cum dicto clerico interesse et continue psallere dum missa cum nota celebratur teneantur. Et in eodem altari postea dicatur alia missa sine nota pro salubri statu dicti domini Thome domini Thome de Baunburgh clerici et Simonis de Sibthorp dum vixerint et cum ab hac luce migraverint pro animabus eorundem et Willelmi patris ipsius domini Thome de Sibthorpe et Matilde matris sue dominorum Henrici avunculi et Johannis consanguinei suorum Willelmi filii predicti Simonis et nostra ac inclite memorie domini Edwardi filii regis Edwardi secundi Hugonis le Spenser junioris domini Roberti de Bardelby clerici Galfridi le Clerc et Alicie uxoris eius et Johannis Campion et omnium liberorum et heredum eorundem ac animabus fratrum sororum avunculorum antecessorum parentum et heredum et omnium benefactorum eiusdem domini Thome de Sibthorp ac animabus custodum capelle predicte capellanorum et clerici predictorum et omnium parochianorum eiusdem ecclesie ac omnium fidelium defunctorum. Set et tercia missa pro salute predictorum dominorum Thome Thome et Simonis dum vixerint et cum de medio sublatus fuerit vel sublati fuerint pro animabus eorundem et predicti Willelmi filii Simonis Margarete matris eiusdem Willelmi Willelmi le Lord patris et Hugonis avunculi eiusdem Simonis et omnium aliorum antecessorum et parentum suorum quorum ossa infra eandem capellam beate Anne sunt tumulata necnon animabus omnium liberorum et heredum eiusdem Simonis et omnium parochianorum eiusdem ecclesie et omnium fidelium defunctorum singulis diebus dicatur sine nota in dicta capella beate Anne matris marie ex parte australi ipsius ecclesie de Sibthorp ut est dictum constructe [*sic*]. Diebus vero dominicis et in maioribus dupplicibus festis celebrent dicti duo capellani de eisdem festis vel pro defunctis pro voluntate sua. Proviso quod premissa fiant quatenus comodius fieri poterunt absque impedimento misse parochialis eiusdem ecclesie cum eam cum nota contigerit celebrari.

Qui quidem custos capellani et clericus et eorum successores liberum habeant ingressum et egressum in prefatam ecclesiam et capellam beate marie et ostii eiusdem penes se habeant unam clavem.

Et quia salubriter a sanctis patribus est statutum ut nullus sacerdos feminas de quibus suspicio esse possit retineat set nec illas quas canones concedunt ut matrem ami(fo. 388b)tam et sororem quia instigante diabolo eciam in illis scelus perpetratum reperitur aut in pedisecis earundem firmiter inhibemus ne dicti custos seu capellani aliquam mulierem infra mansum suum morantem et de nocte cubantem retineant quovis modo. Nostre tamen intencionis non existit quin consanguinee dictorum custodis et capellanorum in infirmitatibus suis et alias pro brevi recreacione mutuo optinenda visitare valeant et cum ipsis prout necessitas exegerit per tempus modicum honeste morari.

Ad hec quia grata consideracione merito ipsius domini Thome et patris ac matris suorum memoria est ipsa capella beate marie quam idem dominus Thomas sic extulit et ditavit piis placacionum officiis perpetuis temporibus recolenda statuimus et iubemus ut predicti custos et capellani et clericus qui nunc sunt vel pro tempore erunt exnunc diem anniversarium predictorum Willelmi patris ipsius domini Thome et Matillis matris sue Willelmi filii Simonis de Sibthorp ac eciam predictorum domini Thome et Simonis cum ab hac luce subtracti fuerint vel subtractus fuerit cum solempni pulsacione campanarum perpetuo annis singulis festive celebrent et devote dicendo cum nota in vesperis dierum precedencium placebo et dirige et plenum officium mortuorum sicut pro corpore presenti et in ipsis quinque diebus anniversariis pro animabus predictis et omnium prenominatorum et omnium fidelium defunctorum missam solempniter in dicta capella beate marie decantent et statim post missam sic cantatam custos dicte capelle qui nunc est vel qui pro tempore fuerit tresdecim de pauperioribus de dicta parochia in dicta ecclesia in fine misse predicte repertis tresdecim denarios videlicet cuilibet eorum unum denarium pro animabus predictis annis singulis perpetuo distribuant intuitu caritatis.

Ordinamus eciam et statuimus quod quilibet custos dicte capelle qui pro tempore fuerit statim post institucionem suam in presencia rectoris ecclesie predicte vel capellani parochialis ibidem si idem rector residens non fuerit et duorum proborum hominum parochie illius fidele faciat iuramentum de calicibus libris vestimentis ornamentis et rebus aliis pro divinis obsequiis ibidem ordinatis ac eciam de omnibus et singulis vasis argenteis stagneis ereis et aliis utensilibus domorum pro ipsis assignatis vel in posterum assignandis que per aliquem custodem seu capellanos aut alium quemcunque alienari elongare vel ammovere prohibemus sub pena excommunicacionis maioris et de quibus vel melioribus aut saltim equivalentibus teneantur iidem custos et successores sui integraliter respondere. Ad quod omnia bona ipsius custodis sint tacite obligata et maneant sub sequestro. Qui tamen de bonis seu catallis provenientibus de terris et possessionibus dicte capelle et omnibus predictis assignatis non faciat testamentum set ea omnia necnon quicquid tempore vacacionis predicte custodie ex ipsis pervenire [sic] contigerit futuro custodi integraliter reserventur per alterum capellanorum predictorum seniorem et in talibus plus expertum per consilium et testimonium rectoris ipsius ecclesie qui pro tempore fuerit interim fideliter conservanda et dicto futuro custodi per eosdem rectorem et capellanum integre liberanda. Prohibemus expresse ne sequestrator seu quicumque minister noster vel successorum nostrorum de bonis prefatis racione vacacionis huiusmodi se aliqualiter intromittant.

Teneantur eciam iidem custos et successores sui cum ipsos cedere vel decedere contigerit futuro custodi specialiter dimittere que sequntur videlicet terram bene cultam et seminatam vel granum pro semine earundem terrarum prout anni temperies id exposcit ac frumentum braseum et aliud granum necessarium tam pro expensis domus quam liberacionibus famulorum una cum instauro et aliis sufficientibus tam pro sustentacione futuri custodis et dictorum capellanorum et clerici ac servientum suorum quam pro omnibus aliis oneribus supradictis usque ad novum granum in orreo reconditum supportandis carectas eciam et carucas pro terris suis excolendis bene munitas cum equis bobus et affris sufficientibus et attilio competenti pro eisdem. Proviso quod tociens quociens dicta vasa vel utensilia vel eciam libri calices vel vestimenta fuerint vetustate corupta vel alias enormiter deteriorata teneantur dictus custos et successores sui qui pro tempore fuerint de novis et sufficientibus tempore oportuno providere.

Si vero aliquis custos ipsius capelle pro tempore in senium vel in infirmitatem incederit [*sic*] vel languorem ita quod personaliter non valeat ministrare provideat sibi de coadiutore ydoneo infra duos menses proxime sequentes qui omnia ad ipsam custodiam spectancia faciat et exerceat in forma superius annotata quod si infra dictos duos menses non fecerit liceat extunc presidenti predicto capitulo Suthwellensi vel ipsius locum tunc tenenti de coadiutore ydoneo sumptibus dicti custodis racionabilibus providere ita tamen quod dicto custodi infirmo vel impotenti ad totam vitam suam ministrentur necessaria competenter cuius coadiutoris officium cessare volumus cum dictus custos ad ministrandum fuerit potens factus.

Volumus eciam et ordinamus quod quilibet capellanus ad custodiam dicte capelle decetero presentandus in admissione sua tactis sacrosanctis evangeliis sacramentum prestet corporale quod omnia et singula predicta et subscripta quatenus ipsum contingunt iuxta formam presentis ordinacionis nostre plene et fideliter faciet et complebit et quod nullam alienacionem faciet de terris vel tenementis seu bonis immobilibus ad dictam capellam et cantarias qualitercumque pertinentibus seu spectantibus nisi evidens utilitas id exposcat. Proviso quod si custos qui nunc est vel qui pro tempore fuerit vastum vendicionem seu destruccionem de terris domibus gardinis aut tenementis predictis seu eciam dilapidacionem rerum et bonorum mobilium de terris et possessionibus eidem custodie assignatis vel assignandis proveniencium fecerit ita quod de residuo dicti custos capellani et clericus et successores sui iuxta formam presentis ordinacionis nostre non possint sufficienter vivere et onera predicta ac alia onera incumbencia supportare vel alias inventus fuerit inhabilis vel indignus statim per nos vel successores nostros qui pro tempore fuerint sede plena et decanum et capitulum Eboracenses ipsa vacante per processum summarium ex officio sine instancia partis simpliciter et de plano et sine strepitu iudiciali ammoveatur perpetuo a dicta custodia et alius sufficiens et ydoneus instituatur in eadem in forma qua premittitur canonice loco sui.

Jurent eciam tam custos quam capellani et clericus sepedicti quod non usurpabunt sibi nec occupabunt decimas oblaciones seu obvenciones aliquas ad rectorem dicte ecclesie de Sibthorp pertinentes nec in aliis iuribus ipsius ecclesie parochialis et rectoris eiusdem quomodolibet derogabunt nec aliqua bona res seu catalla dictam custodiam spectancia vel qualitercumque pertinencia ipsa custodia plena vel vacante aliqualiter ammovebunt vel suis privatis aut alienis usibus applicabunt sub pena excommunicacionis maioris.

Ad hec rectori ipsius ecclesie et capellano parochiali diacono eiusdem ecclesie clerico aquam benedictam in parochia illa deferenti et parochianis dicte ecclesie in virtute obediencie et sub pena excommunicacionis maioris firmiter inhibemus ne libros calices vestimenta ornamenta cereos seu quascumque res alias ad dictos custodem capellanos et clericum vel capellas predictas pertinentes seu pro ipsis et eorum usibus deputatas vel inposterum deputandas contra voluntatem eorundem occupare vel ammovere presumant vel presumat seu alias de ipsis disponere quoquo modo.

Premissa vero omnia et singula secundum eorum vim formam et effectum invocato dei nomine auctoritate nostra pontificali modo quo premittitur ordinamus et ea in suo robore perpetuo duratura statuimus dicimus laudamus pronunciamus diffinimus et ea semper subsistere inviolabiliter observanda decernimus iubemus et imponimus per decretum. Et ad omnia premissa facienda tenenda observanda et fideliter exequenda consciencias predicti domini Johannis custodis et successorum suorum predictorum (fo. 389) custodum ac predictorum capellanorum et clerici successorum suorum penes altissimum oneramus qui per presentes successive onerati perpetuo remaneant in futurum salvo nobis iure presentem ordinacionem nostram corrigendi declarandi et suplendi et ipsam de assensu predicti domini Thome prout expedire viderimus innovandi. Set omnem ordinacionem seu ordinaciones per nos super hoc prius factas ex certa sciencia revocamus annullamus et eam ac eas omnino carere volumus viri· bus et effectu. Et ut presentes littere nostre et statutum dictum laudum pronunciacio diffinicio et decretum subscripta vim perpetuitatis optineant easdem litteras sub sigillo nostro fieri fecimus communiri et ad maiorem securitatem et perpetuam rei memoriam presentes litteras nostras sub sigillo nostro fieri fecimus quadruplicari quarum una penes dictum dominum Johannem custodem et successores suos custodes alia vero penes dictum capitulum ecclesie nostre beate marie Suwellensis et tercia penes prenominatos priorem et conventum et quarta penes nos et successores nostros remaneant in futurum fideliter observanda. Data apud Thorp iuxta Eboracum x^{mo} die Junii anno domini m° ccc^{mo} tricesimo quinto et pontificatus nostri xviii^{mo}.

## II. STATUTES OF THE CHANTRY AND COLLEGE OF SIBTHORPE[1]

### 4 February 1342–3

### (York R. Zouche, ff. 98b–103.)

Universis sancte matris ecclesie filiis hanc presentem ordinacionem visuris vel audituris Willelmus permissione divina Eboracensis archi-

---

[1] Words, phrases, &c., which these statutes have in common with the text of John Giffard's statutes for Cotterstock, as in Bishop Bek's first recension (16 Jan. 1343–4), are printed in italics. There is some difference between the order of the statutes in the two documents, and, where the text of both is identical, occasionally one omits one or two words which are to be found in the other.

episcopus Anglie primas et apostolice sedis legatus salutem in domino sempiternam. Nostre consideracionis judicium animum nostrum movet ut ea que aliquando juxta qualitatem temporis tunc currentis verisimiliter credebantur bene et utiliter ordinasse [sic], quibusdam novis emergentibus expost facto immutacionem poscentibus, quantum poterimus cum dei adjutorio in melius cupimus reformare; nec debet reprehensibile judicari juxta canonicas sancciones si ·secundum varietatem temporum statuta quandoque varientur humana, ipse namque deus ex hiis que in veteri testamento construxerat nonnulla mutavit in novo. Dudum siquidem dilectus filius dominus Thomas de Sibthorp, rector ecclesie de Bekyngham Lincolniensis diocesis, duas capellas, unam videlicet in honore dei et gloriosissime virginis Marie matris ejus ex parte boriali ecclesie parochialis beati Petri de Sibethorp nostre diocesis in qua per regeneracionem christiano nomini est ascriptus, et alteram in honore beate Anne matris ejusdem virginis Marie ex parte australi ejusdem ecclesie, una cum corpore et cancello ejusdem ecclesie, in recompensacionem saltem aliqualem pro peccatis gravibus que contraxit, de assensu omnium quorum intererat de propriis bonis suis de novo construi fecerit [sic], ac pro sustentacione unius capellani custodis dicte capelle beate Marie et duorum aliorum capellanorum et duorum clericorum ac triginta cereorum in ecclesia et capellis predictis ex transverso earundem ac unius lampadis coram ymagine crucifixi certis temporibus prout subscribitur arsurorum, de consensu tunc archiepiscopi Eboracensis predecessoris nostri et ejusdem loci capituli et aliorum quorum intererat dotari. Qui quidem predecessor noster tunc statuit et ordinavit quod dicta capella in honore dicte virginis Marie constructa et parata capella beate Marie de Sibethorp extunc nuncuparetur et pro capella per se tanquam unum grossum perpetuo haberetur, et quod in eadem capella et dicta capella beate Anne essent tres cantarie perpetue, quas capellas et cantarias in eisdem creavit et erexit per decretum, quodque [sic] dominum Johannem Cosyn capellanum custodem dicte capelle beate Marie admisit et ipsum custodem instituit in eadem, quem custodem ejusdem capelle beate Marie nominavit et nominari decrevit perpetuo in futurum et omnem ordinacionem sive ordinaciones precedentes ex certa sciencia revocavit et anullavit. Cum itaque diviciarum domino largiente in tantum dicte capelle beate Marie excreverint facultates quod ultra dictum numerum prius statutum quatuor capellanis et eorum ministris possint sufficere competenter, si dicto custodi dicte capelle beate Marie et sacerdotibus ejusdem eadem ecclesia de Sibethorp cum omnibus suis juribus in Sibethorp et Shelton per nos de consensu dicti capituli nostri approprietur canonice et in usus proprios assignetur; et in dicta ordinacione quam dictus predecessor noster in dicte capelle beate Marie fundacione fecit potestatem sibi et successoribus suis reservavit [sic] specialem hiis que tunc statuit et ordinavit addendi et ea eciam corrigendi, mutandi et minuendi prout eis melius videbitur expedire; et quamplura in ipsa ordinacione videantur esse statuta que difficultatem aliaque obscuritatem inducunt quedamque emendacione et nonnulla que mutacione indigent et suplecione, receptis primitus per nos submissionibus tam predicti domini Thome fundatoris quam predicti custodis, patroni dicte ecclesie, domini Johannis de Sibethorp rectoris ipsius ecclesie et prioris et conventus de Thurgarton nostre diocesis nobis in hac parte recte factis, necnon inquisicione auctoritate nostra rite capta per quam nobis constat quod dicta appropriacio nullatenus in dampnum seu prejudicium nostrum vel ecclesie nostre predicte aut aliquorum aliorum set in augmentum cultus divini tendere dinoscitur manifeste, habitaque super premissis deliberacione pleniori, cum peritis, vocatis vocandis, communi tractatu diligenti ac solempni cum capitulo ecclesie nostre predicte invicem ac cause cognicione et aliis que in hac parte requiruntur sufficienter prehabitis, de consensu et assensu ejusdem capituli nostri expressis necnon dicti fundatoris et omnium quorum interest, de ministris ipsarum ecclesie, capellarum et capellanorum ibidem degencium numerum augmentando necnon de cereis et lampade predictis, ut cultus divinus in dictis ecclesia et capellis augeatur ad laudem et gloriam et honorem dei et beatissime virginis Marie et omnium sanctorum et ad procurandum vivis merita et suffragia pro defunctis auctoritate nostra pontificali Christi nomine invocato procedimus in hunc modum:

(1) In primis *statuimus et ordinamus quod ex presenti ordinacione nostra* in universo *sint* septem *sacerdotes* in dictis ecclesia et capellis *divina celebrantes domino nostro imperpetuum servituri, viri* itaque[1] *litterati et bone fame, casti, sobrii et quieti, a commesacionibus, ebrietatibus, luxuriis, rixis et contencionibus ac ceteris que devocionem tanti* misterii[2] *minuunt et eciam confundunt totaliter abstinentes. Dictorum vero sacerdotum unus in spiritualibus et temporalibus circumspectus sit superior et magister qui* custos dicte capelle beate Marie de Sibethorp ut est dictum nuncupetur.[3] *Ceteri vero capellani* [fo. 99.] dicte *cantarie* vocentur. Et ne abjecta mendicitas ipsos in divinis efficiat segniores set metant pocius temporalia qui duce gracia spiritualia seminabunt, eidem custodi et successoribus suis in predictis ecclesia et capellis ut predicitur perpetuo servituris ad usus et fundacionem earundem capelle et cantarie et sustentacionem suam et dictorum sex capellanorum et duorum clericorum congruam ac invencionem et sustentacionem triginta et unius cereorum ac unius lampadis necnon certorum elemosinarum et anniversariorum ac supportacionem incumbencium onerum, de licencia et assensu serenissimi principis domini Edwardi regis Anglie illustris et ceterorum omnium quorum interest, idem fundator dedit, concessit et assignavit certa mesuagia, tofta, terras, prata, pasturas, redditus et tenementa cum pertinenciis in Sibethorp, Hokesworth, Sireston, Eyleston, Aslacton et Thurverton, tam ea videlicet que fuerunt de hereditate sua, quam ea que nuper perquisivit de heredibus Galfridi le Clerk, Johannis Campion, Nicholai de Orston, Roberti le Smyth et Willelmi le Clerk de Hokesworth ac de Simone de Sibethorp, Johanne de Aslacton, Johanne Colier, Johanne de Cougham, Johanne le Loverd de Eyleston, priore et conventu de Thurgarton, priore et fratribus hospitalis sancti Johannis Jerosolimitani in Anglia ac aliis diversis hominibus in eisdem villis et alibi, nec non advocacionem ecclesie ejusdem ville de Sibethorp cum suis juribus et pertinenciis quibuscunque in Sibethorp et Shelton auctoritate qua decet in proprios usus possidenda et tenenda sibi et successoribus suis in liberam, puram et perpetuam elemosinam imperpetuum, prout per cartas regis et scripta

[1] *Sic*: for *utique*.    [2] *Sic*: for *ministerii*.
[3] A hand and the word *custos* in margin.

dicti fundatoris inde facta et fines inter ipsum et dictum custodem de tenementis predictis in curia regis levatos et postmodum per cartam regis in
perpetuam elemosinam confirmata ac per alios fines eorundem tenementorum similiter levatos et postmodum per diversa brevia regis de recto
terminata et per judicia inde reddita et recorda et processus inde per cartas
regis exemplificata evidenter apparet.

(2) *Quociens*[1] autem *et quandocunque dicta* custodia *per mortem, cessionem vel alias
quandocunque*[2] *vacaverit,* dicti *capellani* unum de seipsis, quem in debito
juramenti sui senserint meliorem et apciorem eciam ad regendum infra decem
dies a tempore vacacionis sibi note continue numerandos, absque juris
vel forme canonice solempnitate debita nominent in communi, quem sic
nominatum ab omnibus vel saltim majoris partis numero *nobis* seu *successoribus nostris* vel vicario nostro generali sede plena, ipsa vero vacante dicto
capitulo nostro ecclesie nostre Eboracensis custodi spiritualitatis ejusdem,
quamcicius presentent, per nos et successores nostros vel vicarium nostrum
generalem sede plena vel dictum capitulum custodem spiritualitatis sede
vacante sine difficultate qualibet admittendum, sub nomine custodis instituendum in eadem. Si[3] autem in hujusmodi nominacione infra dictum tempus
ut predicitur, quod absit, predicti capellani vel major pars consentire
nequeant, liceat tunc dicto priori de Thurgarton vel vacante prioratu illo
suppriori ejusdem loci, unum capellanorum predictorum qui magis idoneus
et sufficiens fuerit eciam ad regendum juxta eorum arbitrium, prout coram
summo deo respondere voluerint, et nullum alium quam de dicto collegio,
infra quindecim dies tunc proxime sequentes a tempore noticie sue numerandos illa vice nobis et successoribus nostris aut vicario nostro generali sede
plena vel dicto capitulo custodi spiritualitatis sede vacante presentare modo
quo premittitur admittendum et custodem instituendum in eadem. Et si
predictus prior vel vacante prioratu predicto supprior ejusdem unum
capellanorum de collegio predicto infra dictos quindecim dies nobis et successoribus nostris aut vicario nostro generali sede plena seu eciam dicto
capitulo custodi spiritualitatis sede vacante presentare neglexerit, liceat tunc
nobis et successoribus nostris vel vicario nostro generali sede plena aut dicto
capitulo custodi spiritualitatis sede vacante meliorem et idoniorem capellanum collegii predicti infra quindecim dies tunc proxime sequentes a
tempore noticie numerandos illa vice in custodem eligere et preficere jure
nostro; alioquin ob defectum vel negligenciam nostri aut successorum
nostrorum vel vicarii nostri generalis sede plena preficere non curancium
eleccio et prefeccio custodis illa vice modo simili et infra tempus simile
facienda ad dictum capitulum nostrum Eboracense devolvatur jure suo, ne
ex diuturna vacacione dictarum capelle et cantarie debito regimine destituta
in rebus vel personis diminucionem sustineat aut jacturam: *salvo semper dictis
capellanis in aliis vacacionibus quibuscumque jure nominandi* custodem et ipsum
presentandi in forma predicta.

(3) Admittendus[4] vero et proficiendus hujusmodi tam in admissione sua
quam in induccione sua *juramentum prestet et faciat corporale quod in dicta cantaria*

[1] A hand and the word *nominacio* in margin.
[2] *Sic:* for *qualitercumque.*          [3] *Presentacio prioris* in margin.
[4] *Juramentum custodis* in margin.

*personaliter et continue residebit* nisi ipsum pro negociis dicte domus necessario oportebit abesse et utilitatem ejusdem faciat et in quantum poterit procurabit, quodque presentem ordinacionem nostram pro viribus conservabit et faciet quatenus in eo est ab aliis observari et jura dicte capelle beate Marie et cantarie manutenebit et defendet pro posse. Alias *autem* de ipso facto admissio *seu prefeccio absque prestacione dicti juramenti nullius penitus sit momenti nec ceteri sacerdotes* ut custodi *sibi obedire* seu intendere *teneantur.* Qui quidem custos sic institutus, inductus et juratus liberam et legitimam habeat administracionem et disposicionem *omnium* rerum *spiritualium et temporalium ac tenementorum ad dictam* capellam et custodiam ejusdem *ubique pertinencium* seu *spectancium presencium et futurorum.*

(4) *Et licet* idem custos *sic inductus fuerit, bonis* dictarum capelle et *cantarie nullatenus se immisceat antequam de calicibus, libris, vestimentis et aliis ornamentis ecclesie ac aliis* [fo. 99b] *rebus quibuscumque et utensilibus domorum et quocumque instauro* ac *bonis et catallis omnibus et singulis in specie una cum quantitatibus separatis et divisis* ibidem et apud Hokesworth et alibi existentibus *ac de nominibus debitorum et creditorum sub* sociorum *suorum legali testimonio inventarium fecerit dupplicatum, cujus altera pars sub communi custodia in una cista ad hoc specialiter ordinata* reponatur *et alteram sibi ipsi retineat ut sciatur in quo statu ipse predictam* recepit *cantariam.*

(5) *Et ut de statu* dicte *cantarie et administracione dicti* custodis *certa semper noticia habeatur, singulis annis bona et catalla omnia una cum quocumque* instauro dictarum capelle et *cantarie per ipsum* custodem *et tres vel quatuor capellanos ad hoc ·communiter eligendos semel saltem cum idem scilicet* custos *compotum reddiderit de receptis et expensis, quod semel ad minus reddere teneatur quolibet anno et per ipsum reddi volumus et ordinamus coram ceteris capellanis vel majori parte eorundem, infra mensem post festum sancti Michaelis clarius videantur, et eciam in inicio kalendarum Maii exprimat et recitet singula nomina debitorum et creditorum, ut sic sciri semper poterit si in administracione fuerit utilis dispensator et fidelis. Et rotuli compotorum hujusmodi post dictum mensem Michaelis ponantur* in thesauraria domus *in predicta cista* tribus *seruris firmata ad perpetuam rei memoriam* custodiendi, quarum serurarum nulla aliam valeat aperire et quarum unam clavem penes predictum custodem et alteram penes subcustodem et terciam penes illum qui diucius fuerit in dicto collegio volumus in custodia remanere. *Et illis duobus temporibus anni ordinent ipsi de stauro domus meliorando et de providenciis faciendis.* Et volumus et ordinamus quod si que bona supersint cedant in augmentum restauracionis terrarum et tenementorum dictarum capelle et cantarie et non in alios usus sub pena excommunicacionis majoris. Ita tamen quod aliqua pars sufficiens in thesauro pro defensione juris earundem capelle et cantarie reponatur.

(6) *Ceteri*[1] *vero capellani in gradu dumtaxat sacerdocii* per ipsum custodem *in socios admittantur. Qui sic admissi maneant* quamdiu voluerint, dummodo absque morbo contagioso videlicet lepra fuerint ad celebracionem divinorum potentes et bene, laudabiliter ac fideliter se gesserint infamie macula non contracta nullumque crimen notorium commiserint detestandum quod superioris dispensacionem exigat aut requirat, quibus casibus ac eciam tociens quociens dicti capellani seu clericus vel eorum aliquis notabiliter incesti, adulteri, criminosi aut alias insufficientes, communiter contrariantes

---

[1] *Admissio capellanorum* in margin.

seu negligentes inventi fuerint notorie vel remissi, prefatus custos illos vel illum absque more dispendio amoveat libere juxta sue beneplacitum voluntatis et alios sacerdotes et clericum idoneos vel idoneum sciencia, moribus atque cantu loco ipsorum vel ipsius subrogare et preficere teneatur ad celebrandum divina in ecclesia et capellis supradictis, quibus eciam subrogatis et subrogandis de esculentis et poculentis et salario suo debeat ministrari. Idem in criminibus minoribus statuimus firmiter observari dum tamen post trinam correccionem vel correpcionem sui custodis criminosus hujusmodi se corrigere non curaverit ex contemptu. Proviso semper quod dictus custos nullum de predictis capellanis amoveat antequam de alio sacerdote et clerico ut premittitur idoneis fuerit sibi provisum. Et in predictis casibus et in casu quo cesserit vel decesserit aliquis eorundem predictus custos statim infra tres, quatuor, quinque vel sex menses proxime tunc sequentes ad tardius eligere et assumere sacerdotem idoneum seu clericum teneatur modo simili amovendum sub pena privacionis a capella et cantaria predictis quam ipsum custodem si hoc non fecerit incurrere volumus ipso facto. Precipientes ac statuentes ut extunc alius capellanus de collegio predicto idoneus et sufficiens ut premittitur ad dictam capellam et custodiam ejusdem illico presentetur et instituatur in eadem absque aliquali contradiccione seu obstaculo alicujus appellacionis per ipsum custodem interponendis nulloque appellacionis aut alterius beneficii remedio sibi contra hoc aliqualiter valituro. Et quia dicti capellani et singuli eorum si bene se gesserint et fideles, habiles, sobrii, honesti fuerint et casti, erunt ut perpetui, si contingat ipsorum aliquem debilem fore, cecum vel senio confractum seu alias morbo perpetuo vel continuo non contagioso videlicet lepra impeditum quominus missam suam et aliud sibi incumbens officium peragere valeat et proprium non habeat unde competenter sustentari, volumus et ordinamus quod, hujusmodi casu perpetuo non obstante, de bonis communibus quamdiu in eodem collegio moram facere voluerit sustentetur. De salario vero suo et aliis bonis dicte capelle loco ipsius et eciam aliorum sic infirmorum vel impeditorum alii capellani idonei quamcicius poterit bono modo per predictum custodem subrogentur qui hujusmodi infirmorum vel impeditorum vices in omnibus valeant adimplere.

(7) Custodis *vero destitucio sicuti et admissio ad* nos *pertineat suo casu, proviso quod* si custos qui pro tempore erit vendicionem, vastum seu destruccionem aliquorum tenementorum seu eciam dilapidacionem rerum et bonorum mobilium de terris et possessionibus eidem custodie assignatis vel assignandis proveniencium fecerit vel in quantum poterit fieri permiserit aut alias inventus fuerit luxuriosus, incestus, adulter, inhabilis seu indignus, vel alia *evidens causa et probabilis* ipsum custodem *urgeat amoveri*, statim per nos vel successores nostros aut commissarios nostros vel vicarium (fo. 100) nostrum generalem sede plena et dictos decanum et capitulum ipsa vacante per processum summarium sive ex officio sive instancia partis habitum solempnitate ordinis judiciarii non servata simpliciter et de plano et sine strepitu et figura judicii totaliter amoveatur perpetuo a dicta custodia nec ulterius bona dictarum capelle et cantarie aliqualiter valeat dispensare, et alius sufficiens et idoneus capellanus de collegio predicto et non alius instituatur custos in forma qua premittitur canonice loco sui, appellacione, in integrum

restitucione, querela et omni alio juris remedio ex hac ordinacione eidem omnino interdictis.

(8) *Quilibet capellanus in admissione sua coram suo* custode *et ceteris capellanis presentibus simile sicut de* custode *dicitur prestet juramentum et nichilominus dicto* custodi fidelitatem et *obedienciam juret canonicam et promittat. Singuli vero capellani in omnibus tam morum* correpcionem et *correccionem quam* bonorum dicte cantarie *administracionem* et custodiam pro utilitate cantarie et domus *concernentibus* custodi *pareant et intendant* et injuncciones subeant salutares.

(9) *Habeant insuper dicti* custos et capellani unum clericum per dictum custodem eligendum et pro voluntate sua amovendum in lectura et cantu sufficienter instructum qui dicto custodi et domui in admissione sua coram prefatis capellanis juret fidelitatem ac sibi in mandatis licitis pareat et intendat, et quod sibi et dictis capellanis in divinis humiliter ministret obsequiis et cereos et lampadem illuminet vel faciat illuminari et eos et omnia in dictis capellis, cancello et ecclesia salvo custodiat, quodque eisdem custodi et capellanis tam in mensa quam in ecclesia et alibi in omnibus deserviat ut tenetur, et quod singulis noctibus jaceat in dicta ecclesia pro salva custodia ejusdem, librorum, vestimentorum et omnium aliorum in dicta ecclesia existencium et pulset diebus singulis campanam in aurora diei et in vesperis hora cubandi consueta et ad missam de beata virgine et ad alias missas, matutinas et vesperas horis debitis et ei injunctis, et ad premissa fideliter facienda omnia bona et tenementa dicti clerici si que habeat obligentur, ac nichilominus securitatem eis inveniat sufficientem. Et volumus, ordinamus et precipimus quod idem clericus diebus singulis quibus convenit et vacare poterit parvulos parochie illius et alios qui addiscere litteras voluerint in hiis instruat et informet pro salario suo racionabiliter de pueris predictis vel eorum amicis capiendo. Cui dictus custos et successores sui victum inveniant in communi et ultra id sibi solvant singulis annis pro indumentis et aliis necessariis suis terminis infrascriptis unam marcam.

(10) Inveniant eciam quendam pauperem clericum de parochia predicta in puerili voce bene cantantem et eis in ecclesia predicta deservientem et eum dum in puerili voce bene cantaverit et se bene gesserit sustentent in victu et vestitu prout pauperi clerico decet; ita tamen quod post vocem suam puerilem mutatam semper alium pauperem puerum modo predicto de parochia predicta et non aliunde eligendum dum in ea aliquis fuerit in hujusmodi voce puerili bene cantantem et eis deservientem in victu et vestitu sustentent de elemosinis capelle supradicte.

(11) Item statuimus et ordinamus quod predictus custos et successores sui inter pauperiores dicte parochie de Sibethorp singulis septimanis per dies lune, mercurii et veneris quolibet die septem panes de frumento, quolibet pane ponderis quinquaginta solidorum, preter elemosinas suas proprias pro anima predicti fundatoris et animabus subscriptorum imperpetuum distribuant intuitu caritatis.

(12) Statuimus eciam et ordinamus quod dictus custos et successores sui imperpetuum inveniant predictos triginta et unum cereos perpetuo annis singulis ad festum Concepcionis beate Marie virginis si opus fuerit innovandos, quorum quilibet viginti et octo cereorum de predictis triginta et uno

cereis ponderet duas libras cere, in ecclesia, capellis et cancello predictis
stantes ex transverso, videlicet novem cereos in eodem cancello supra altare,
quorum duo tantummodo erunt pro processionibus, et decem et septem
cereos stantes ex transverso ecclesie et capellarum predictarum, videlicet
septem cereos in dicta capella beate Marie et quinque in dicta ecclesia
coram ymagine crucifixi et quinque in dicta capella beate Anne, ad gloriam
et honorem domini nostri ihesu christi et memoriam passionis ejusdem ac
honorem predictarum virginis Marie et beate Anne matris ejus et omnium
sanctorum ardentes perpetuo subscriptis temporibus et cum minutis candelis
cum opus fuerit sustentandos, videlicet in omnibus majoribus dupplicibus
festis et in quinque festis beate Marie et in festo predicte Anne. In primis
vesperis et missa de die omnes ardeant cerei predicti. In secundis vesperis
et matutinis eorundem festorum quilibet alter eorundem cereorum ardeat
in dictis ecclesia et capellis una cum quinque cereis in dicto cancello in
medio stantibus. In omnibus aliis minoribus dupplicibus festis et dominicis
diebus omnes ardeant cerei predicti una cum eisdem quinque cereis in
cancello ad missam de die tantum. In primis vero et secundis vesperis et
matutinis eorundem festorum ardeant aliqui dictorum cereorum in ecclesia
et capellis prout custodi placuerit et preceperit una cum duobus dictorum
cereorum in cancello. Aliis vero simplicibus diebus festivis ardeant dicti
duo cerei in cancello (fo. 100b) et quilibet alter dictorum cereorum in
ecclesia et capellis predictis ad missam de die tantum una cum aliquibus
dictorum cereorum in cancello in primis et secundis vesperis et matutinis
de festo predicto prout antea in eodem cancello fieri consuevit. In ferialibus
vero diebus ardeant dicti duo cerei in cancello tantum ad missam de die
cum nota celebrandam, et quod dicti septem cerei in dicta capella beate
Marie quolibet die imperpetuum ardeant ad missam de eadem virgine cum
nota in eadem capella. Et tres de predictis triginta et uno cereis sint magni
cerei ponderis cujuslibet sex librarum et duo ex ipsis ardeant singulis diebus dominicis et festivis ad levacionem corporis christi in magno altari ad
missam de die cum nota et alter eorundem cereorum singulis profestis diebus et ferialibus ad levacionem dicti corporis christi in eodem altari ad
eandem missam de die tantum et tercius eorundem ad levacionem dicti
corporis christi in missa beate Marie in capella predicta cum nota celebranda.
Et residui duo cerei ardeant singulis annis continue in cancello predicto
juxta sepulcrum domini ibidem ab hora nona diei Parasceves usque post
complecionem servicii Resurreccionis domini in die Pasche ibidem facte [sic].

(13) Inveniant eciam predictam lampadem in cancello predicto et non
alibi singulis diebus et noctibus quibus convenit et necesse fuerit juxta pre-
ceptum dicti custodis et voluntatem suam ardentem.

(14) Et volumus, statuimus et eciam ordinamus quod nec dictus custos
nec successores sui de pluribus cereis vel lampadibus in dictis ecclesia,
capellis seu cancello aut alibi inveniendis vel sustentandis racione aliquorum
tenementorum suorum seu rerum aut aliqua de causa quacunque aliqualiter
onerentur, nec ad dictas ecclesiam seu capellas per ipsum dominum Thomam
ex mera voluntate sua de propriis bonis in exoneracionem parochianorum
predictorum communi assensu suo ut prescribitur de novo factas aut ad
aliquam partem earundem reparandam, cooperiendam, emendandam vel

sustentandam seu de novo faciendam aliquibus de causis emergentibus per nos vel successores nostros aut alios quoscunque quocunque colore quesito compellantur vel teneantur temporibus successivis.

(15) Custos vero et omnes sacerdotes *vivant in communi*, et idem custos eisdem capellanis et clericis exhibicionem in victualibus tribuat competentem, videlicet panem de frumento per medium stricti cribri cribratum ponderis quinquaginta solidorum et cervisiam bonam videlicet septem lagenas de uno bussello Londoniensi de meliori et de uno tantum ferculo sufficienti tamen et ad minus de duobus generibus piscium vel carnium diebus simplicibus dupplicato sint contenti, ita tamen quod major pars ferculi sit de carnibus salsis et in stauro domus predicte et alia pars de carnibus recentibus vel parum salsis maxime tempore estivali. Diebus vero dominicis et festivis pitanciam habeant non nimis exilem nec eciam excessivam.

(16) Prefatus eciam custos singulis annis pro indumentis et omnibus aliis necessariis suis et pro honore suo et utilitate dictarum capelle et cantarie expendendos quadraginta solidos dumtaxat percipiat et cuilibet sacerdotum predictorum pro indumentis et omnibus necessariis suis duas marcas ad festa Annunciacionis beate Marie et beati Petri ad vincula per equales porciones distribuat annuatim. Presbitero tamen quem ad regimen cure parochie predicte si curam illius per annum continuum gesserit triginta solidos tribuat terminis supradictis; alioquin eidem pro rata temporis satisfaciat dicto salario suo duarum marcarum in eadem summa triginta solidorum computato. Inveniat eciam dictis capellanis superpellicia honesta et almicias nigras nigris fururis furratas quibus semper uti debent in choro ecclesie et capellis predictis dum divinis insistunt, et ipsas almicias et superpellicia predicta statim cum amoti fuerint, cesserint, vel eorum executores si decesserint dicto custodi vel eo absente subcustodi retradi teneantur et penes eum dimitti. Residuum vero omnium et singulorum bonorum dictarum capelle et cantarie ubicunque existencium presencium et futurorum sub debito juramenti prestiti absque aliquali elongacione, consumpcione, destruccione, alienacione vel amocione aliquorum capellanorum aut aliorum quorumcunque, deductis expensis necessariis domus et familie sue quam habeant necessariam et non onerosam, dictus custos et successores sui convertant in utilitatem cantarie predicte et non in aliquos alios usus sub pena excommunicacionis majoris et sicut coram deo in extremo examine voluerint respondere et de quo suam volumus conscienciam onerari, nec testetur aliqualiter de eisdem. Ceteri vero presbiteri qui se ut deberent fraudem ut premittitur facientibus non opponunt pro tempore quo premissa sine debita contradiccione permiserint nichil percipiant de stipendiis sibi constitutis. Et si dante domino excrescentibus facultatibus dictarum capelle et cantarie multiplicari contigerit ibidem numerum sacerdotum, volumus eandem constitucionem quo ad eorum stipendia et omnia alia prescripta et infrascripta firmius observari.

(17) *In aula omnes simul comedant, in qua nichil loquantur penitus quod sit turpe quodve rixe seu dissensionis aut inhonestatis alicujus materiam administret, set dum in mensa steterint* alter clericorum predictorum cum custodi placuerit et ad hoc vacare poterunt *de biblia vel vita alicujus sancti* vel alia scriptura sancta *legat aliquid in communi ceteris interim cum silencio audientibus reverenter.*

(18) *In communi autem dormitorio nulla facta divisione* simul *dormiant omnes* capellani dum sani fuerint seu impedimento (fo. 101) racionabili non detenti, *set* custos *pro occupacionibus variis cameram habeat* cum voluerit *separatam.* *Infirmi cum fuerint in alia camera separata et cibis cum necesse fuerit laucioribus vel aliis* cibis *congruis secundum bonorum saltim exigenciam humaniter reficiantur.*

(19) Item statuimus et ordinamus quod custos qui pro tempore fuerit unum de capellanis predictis quem ad hoc sciencia et moribus idoneum judicaverit in subsidium regiminis cure parochialis predicte deputet ipsumque amoveat et alium idoneum deputet pro sue libito voluntatis *qui* subcustos *collegii vocitetur* et *qui in absencia* custodis *defectus tam in ecclesia quam extra corrigat et emendet et libros ornamenta ac luminaria ecclesie* custodire faciat et sumptibus domus reficere faciat et emendare. *Et de* omnibus et *singulis libris* tam in ecclesia quam in mansura sua existentibus, *vestimentis* et ornamentis ecclesie et singulis utensilibus domorum ac de instauro quocunque et ceteris bonis et catallis omnibus ubicunque fuerint quolibet anno post dictum compotum per dictum custodem post festum sancti Michaelis ut predicitur redditum *faciat duos rotulos* speciales et eos sociis suis demonstret in communi, *quorum* rotulorum *uno sibi* et sociis suis *retento alter remaneat communibus in archivis.* Prohibentes, statuentes et precipientes expresse ne libri predicti vel aliqui eorum vendantur seu invadientur vel alicui extra dictam ecclesiam vel mansuram cantarie aliqua de causa seu colore acomodentur seu ad inspiciendum tradantur quovismodo, nec aliqui pueri quicunque sint super dictos libros vel aliquem eorum decetero addiscant sub pena excommunicacionis majoris et privacionis contrafaciencium a custodia et cantaria predictis.

(20) *Vacante vero* custodia *predicta per mortem, cessionem aut alio quovis modo, statuimus et* eciam *ordinamus quod omnes fructus redditus et proventus ad prefatas* capellam et *cantariam durante vacacione illa qualitercumque* pertinentes vel spectantes aut ex possessionibus suis *provenientes in usus cantarie predicte et non in alios usus sub pena excommunicacionis majoris integre convertantur, et legitima administracio omnium bonorum* dictarum capelle et *cantarie durante hujusmodi vacacione ad* dictum subcustodem *collegii integraliter pertineat. Ipse tamen* subcustos collegii *futuro* custodi *infra mensem post* induccionem ejusdem custodis *de receptis* quibuscumque *et expensis per eundem tempore dicte vacacionis* factis *compotum seu racionem plene reddet, juramento corporali prius prestito ab eodem de fideli compoto inde reddendo. Si vero* custodia et subcustodia collegii *simul vacent, durantibus hujusmodi vacacionibus custodia et administracio bonorum omnium* dictarum capelle et *cantarie ad illum de dicto collegio sacerdotem qui diucius* deservivit[1] *ac laudabiliter se gesserit et honeste corporeque fuerit satis potens pertineat,* eodem et *eisdem oneribus sicut ad* subcustodem *collegii si viveret* ipsa *vacante* custodia *pertineret.* Statuentes, ordinantes et precipientes pro nobis et successoribus nostris ne sequestrator noster nec quivis alius minister noster vel successorum nostrorum aut alterius cujuscunque de bonis seu rebus capelle et cantarie predictarum vel aliqua parte eorundem racione alicujus vacacionis vel alia de causa quacunque quocunque colore quesito se aliqualiter intromittat.

(21) *Nullus vero sacerdotum* mercandisas aliquas seu *tabernas excerceat nec*

---

[1] *Sic*: for *deservierit.*

aliqua animalia, firmas seu catalla infra quinque leucas habeat aut ferias *seu mercata domosve alienas ex consuetudine visitet aut subintret nec in locis exteris devagetur, set cum magna occasio fuerit sine* custodis *licencia non recedat. Semel* tamen bis vel ter *in anno de licencia* custodis *poterit eorum quilibet dum tamen vicibus separatis amicos proprios visitare, set tunc missam suam nisi graviter impeditus celebret omni die et* de negociis suis expeditus *redeat festinanter.*

(22) Nullus sacerdotum sine licencia speciali custodis aut ejus vices gerentis in hoc casu et nisi sit pro communi utilitate domus et cantarie ad mensam invitet extraneos seu inducat, et si quis contrarium fecerit vel ad introducendum licencia petita assuetus, introducens pro prandio sui hospitis tres denarios sterlingorum et pro qualibet alia refeccione duos denarios custodi si presens fuerit vel subcustodi solvere teneatur, quam pecuniam de stipendiis taliter hospitem introducentis deduci volumus et eciam retineri ac in utilitates communes expendi.

(23) *Campanellam quandam habeant ad cujus sonitum omnes ad prandium seu cenam* convocent, *ita quod omnes sint in* ipsa *domo de clara luce diei et non exeant illa nocte nisi forsitan ad* visitandum infirmos, *et tunc exeant illi dumtaxat qui ad hoc per* custodem *fuerint deputati.*

(24) Nullus insuper administrator bonorum ecclesie, capelle et cantarie earundem de aliquibus bonis ipsarum ecclesie, capelle et cantarie testari valeat ullo modo.

(25) *Et quia dictus fundator assignavit, dedit et concessit eisdem* custodi *et capellanis in subsidium uberioris sustentacionis sue* predicte duodecim boves, octo equos, quatuor jumenta pro carectis et carucis suis ibidem, et apud Hokesworth duodecim vaccas, unum taurum, quadraginta oves matrices et quaterviginti multones, tres sues cum quadraginta porcis et porciculis quorum medietas est fere etatis unius anni et amplius et alia medietas est etatis duorum annorum et amplius et unus [*sic*] aper bonus; volentes, ordinantes ac statuentes *quod ipsi et eorum successores tot* sufficientes et *congruos boves seu bovectos, equos, jumenta, vaccas, oves matrices, multones vel hoggastros, sues cum earum* (fo. 101*b*) *exitu unius anni, aprum, porcos* fere *etatis unius anni* seu *amplius* et porciculos *vel plures semper habeant, et precipue in festo Invencionis sancte crucis et in festo sancti Michaelis vel cito post* ac eciam in dicto festo sancti Michaelis vel cito post tot porcos duorum annorum et amplius vel plures *quolibet anno ad instaurum* vel *lardarium suum inde nutriendos et faciendos ut sic possint onera* ipsarum capelle et *cantarie futuris temporibus commodius et facilius supportare. Et eciam cum ipsum* custodem *cedere vel decedere contigerit futuro* custodi *specialiter instaurum et animalia predicta dimittere et similiter ea que secuntur, videlicet omnes terras suas ubique bene cultas, compostatas et seminatas vel granum pro semine earundem prout anni temperies id* exposcit, *ac frumentum, brasium et quodcunque aliud granum necessarium, tam pro expensis domus quam liberacionibus famulorum, una cum instauro et aliis sufficientibus tam pro sustentacione futuri* custodis, *dictorum capellanorum, clericorum et omnium serviencium suorum quam pro omnibus aliis oneribus* incumbentibus *usque ad novum granum in orrio* reconditum supportandis. *Carectas eciam et carucas pro omnibus terris suis ubique excolendis necessarias bene munitas cum* equis, bobus, jumentis sufficientibus et *attilio* competenti *pro eisdem.* Et quousque premissa effectualiter compleantur et fiant omnia propria bona dicti custodis mortui sint obligata ad premissa

facienda et maneant sub sequestro illius penes quem episcopalis jurisdiccio remanebit.

(26) Statuentes eciam, decernentes et precipientes ne alique mulieres infra mansum dictorum custodis et capellanorum immorentur vel hospitentur, vel eisdem infra hospicium aut aliquis de parentela dicti custodis vel successorum suorum eis ibidem vel alibi deserviant in futurum.

(27) Custos *autem dictas* capellam aut *cantariam* vel *bona ejusdem* mobilia vel *immobilia* nullatenus *obliget, dissipet, distrahat aut consumat nec* per se seu cum capellanis *pensionem,* liberacionem *seu corrodium alicui* statuat, vendat, donet *vel concedat* perpetuo nec ad tempus, neque eciam terras, prata vel tenementa ad terminum vite vel annorum alicui concedat seu dimittat, domibus reddituialibus tantummodo exceptis quas liceat ei ad terminum annorum pro commodo domus dimittere; *set ab omni alienacionis specie quam eis et eorum cuilibet sub debito juramenti sui specialiter interdicimus penitus se abstineant, nisi per aliquam earum major procuraretur utilitas* capelle et *cantarie* predictarum, et super hoc prius habeatur loci diocesani super hoc plenarie consulti vel predicti fundatoris in vita sua licencia specialis. *Faciens autem contrarium seu* concedens aut auxilium vel consensum prebens eo ipso a statu quem in dicta capella et cantaria habuit eciam si custodia *fuerit* ipso jure *decidat et privetur.* Et ut talia attemptandi facultas eisdem totaliter auferatur usum sigilli communis quo semper careant et quod nunquam habere valeant eis penitus interdicimus per presentes.

(28) Singuli vero sacerdotes et custos in colore habitus et apparatu exteriori quantum fieri poterit conformentur. Supertunicas talares de nigro vel russeto clausas habeant quibus sive mantellis aut clothis nigris communis precii desuper induantur. Coronas largas habeant, tonsuram congruam et aures patulas canonibus diffinitam [*sic*] uniformiter deferentes, ad quarum observanciam per custodem compellantur.

(29) *Ceterum quia parvi libelli facilius quam magni* possint *subtrahi et variis modis occultari, statuimus et ordinamus quod quecumque inventaria supradicta et quecumque indenture et scripture predicte in unum librum qui Registrum domus dicatur in substanciali et aperta littera secundum ordinem redigantur, qui liber in prefata cista remaneat sub custodia memorata, ipsique registro plenam volumus fidem contra* predicte capelle custodem *et singulos* presbiteros *adhiberi.*

(30) Item circa officium divinum in ecclesia et capellis predictis digne et laudabiliter exequendum hec in predicta cantaria statuimus et ordinamus perpetuis temporibus observari, quod cessante impedimento legitimo non ficto officium illud ebdomadario dicatur, et quod custos et omnes capellani et clerici dicte cantarie singulis diebus tempore hiemali tempestive saltem ad tardius circa auroram diei et tempore estivali ad tardius circa ortum solis consurgant et convenientes in ecclesia predicta superpelliciis et almuciis nigris induti matitunale[1] et prime officium una *cum missa* de die et [de] dicta virgine Maria et vesperis ac completorio *secundum* ordinale et *usum* dicte ecclesie nostre Eboracensis et in quantum poterunt secundum regimen ecclesie nostre Suthwellensis singulis diebus *cum nota solempniter* decantent. Horas vero de die dupplicibus festis et dominicis diebus et festivis cum nota

---

[1] *Sic:* for *matutinale.*

et diebus ferialibus cum nota si eis vacaverit vel sine nota pro disposicione custodis vel subcustodis simul in choro dicant, *et hoc distincte et* aperta[1] *in bona psalmodia et pausacione in medio versus congrua. Matutine* vero et hore ac vespere de domina secundum dictum usum ante incepcionem vesperarum et matutinarum (fo. 102) diei et completorium de ea post completorium diei dicantur eciam *diebus singulis* in communi in choro ecclesie predicte.

(31) Item zelo pie devocionis quam dictus fundator erga matrem gracie gloriosam virginem Mariam et ipsius virginis intuitu erga dictam beatissimam Annam ejusdem virginis genitricem habet, volumus et ordinamus ut post officium matutinarum et ante incepcionem singularum horarum et vesperarum dicte virginis Marie dicat sacerdos et executor officii eadem voce qua officium compleverit vel incepit salutacionem angelicam et recomendacionem genitricis ejusdem temporibus inperpetuum futuris hoc modo AVE MARIA GRACIA PLENA DOMINVS TECVM BENEDICTA TV IN MVLIERIBVS ET BENEDICTVS FRVCTVS VENTRIS TVI IHESVS AMEN. *Chorus.* Et benedicta sit venerabilis mater tua Anna ex qua tua caro virginea immaculata processit amen. *Post primam* tamen *dictam immediate* dicatur *psalmus* DE PROFVNDIS *pro defunctis in ordinacione contentis et ceteris benefactoribus* dictorum cantarie et collegii et defensoribus jurium eorundem *cum versiculis et oracionibus* competentibus, videlicet ante mortem predicti fundatoris OMNIPOTENS SEMPITERNE DEVS QVI VIVORVM etc. et DEVS QVI INTER APOSTOLICOS SACERDOTES FAMVLOS TVOS SACERDOTALI etc., post mortem vero ejus prima oracio DEVS QVI INTER APOSTOLICOS SACERDOTES etc. Hiisque *sic finitis* dicat idem sacerdos: Anima Thome de Sibethorp fundatoris nostri et omnium parentum et benefactorum suorum et nostrorum omniumque fidelium defunctorum per dei misericordiam requiescant in pace. Et idem faciant singulis diebus post magnam missam in cancello celebratam et eciam post gracias in mensa deo redditas et prandium eorundem. Quibus expletis ebdomadarius celebret subsequenter singulis diebus missam de beata virgine Maria cum nota in dicta capella ejusdem pro predicto fundatore et parentibus suis et benefactoribus cantarie et collegii predictorum et defensoribus jurium eorundem tam vivis quam defunctis. Et ut devocius ac solempnius celebretur, volumus et ordinamus quod in ipsa missa intersint omnes vel ad minus quinque de sacerdotibus antedictis quos custos si presens fuerit vel eo absente subcustos ad id voluerit ordinare una cum duobus clericis supradictis. Diebus vero dominicis et majoribus dupplicibus festis volumus dictam missam beate Marie cum nota vel sine nota pro voluntate custodis post missam parochialem in dicta capella celebrari. Et prohibemus ne aliquis capellanorum predictorum vel alius dominicis diebus vel majoribus festis predictis aliquam missam sine legitima causa celebret ante incepcionem evangelii misse parochialis supradicte. Quociens tamen de eadem virgine plenum servicium fit in choro, tunc loco ejusdem misse celebrande ad altare dicte virginis celebretur cum nota a sacerdotibus et clericis memoratis vel majori parte eorundem missa pro benefactoribus cantarie et collegii et defensoribus jurium eorundem et ceteris subscriptis, videlicet SALVS POPVLI EGO SVM etc. *et post missam ipsam ad chorum redeant* et reliquas horas ut est dictum decantent vel dicant in communi.

[1] *Sic:* for *aperte.*

(32) Et quod unus sacerdos secundum disposicionem custodis vicissim esse debeat ebdomadarius et in officio divino preesse tam in ecclesia quam capellis memoratis, qui suis vicibus magnam missam parochialem cum nota celebrare in choro diebus singulis teneatur cum oracionibus secundum usum ecclesie nostre Eboracensis communiter usitatis. Quam missam parochialem majoribus dupplicibus festis per dictum custodem si voluerit vel alium pro disposicione sua et cum diacono et subdiacono et duobus rectoribus chori in capis sericis ad hoc ordinatis, ac eciam singulis diebus dominicis et minoribus festis dupplicibus ac festivis cum diacono et subdiacono in sacris vestibus ipsis competentibus statuimus devote et honeste fieri ac eciam celebrari una cum aliis sacerdotibus et clericis antedictis vel saltim majori parte eorundem.

(33) Alius autem dictorum sacerdotum ebdomadarius missam SALVS POPVLI etc. cum quinque oracionibus subscriptis ad minus celebret omni die pro dictis benefactoribus cantarie et collegii ac defensoribus jurium eorundem et pro omnibus parochianis dicte ecclesie tam vivis quam defunctis, et specialiter pro domino Edwardo a conquestu tercio nunc illustri rege Anglie ac dominis regibus Anglie et archiepiscopo Eboracensis ecclesie et canonicorum[1] ejusdem qui nunc sunt et qui pro tempore erunt et pro dicto domino Thoma fundatore et domino Johanne de Sibethorp dudum rectore ecclesie predicte consanguineo et herede ejus Simone de Sibethorp et magistro Adam de Heselbech ac dicto custode et ceteris capellanis collegii predicti qui nunc sunt et qui pro tempore erunt fideliter in eadem cantaria ut infrascribitur deservientes dum vixerint, necnon pro animabus Willelmi patris et Matillis matris dicti fundatoris et omnium parentum suorum ac animabus domini Edwardi regis Anglie secundi, dominorum Thome de Baumburgh, Radulphi de Gunthorp et Roberti de Bardelby clericorum, Hugonis le Despenser junioris, Godekini de Reule, Willelmi Durant et Isabelle uxoris ejus ac eciam dominorum de Byngham, Staunton, Cotum, Shelton, Flyntham et Sireston qui pro tempore erunt et heredum et antecessorum suorum, ut ipsi domini protectores et defensores dicti collegii et jurium suorum specialiter assistant (fo. 102b) et existant, ac animabus omnium illorum de quibus terras vel tenementa habent vel ipsos habere continget in futurum tam vivis quam defunctis et omnium fidelium defunctorum, necnon pro animabus dictorum dominorum regis [Edwardi] tercii et archiepiscopi et successorum suorum regum Anglie et pontificum Eboracensis ecclesie et canonicorum ejusdem et dictorum fundatoris, Johannis, Simonis, Ade ac custodis et capellanorum cum migraverint ab hac vita cum hac oracione sive collecta principali OMNIPOTENS SEMPITERNE DEVS QVI VIVORVM etc. et quatuor oracionibus subsequentibus prout vivis conveniunt et defunctis, videlicet secunda oracio pro predictis archiepiscopo, canonicis, fundatore, Johanne, Adam, Thoma, Radulpho, custode et capellanis DEVS QVI INTER APOSTOLICOS SACERDOTES ut supra; tercia oracio pro rege et regina et eorum liberis etc. DEVS IN CVJVS MANV CORDA SVNT REGVM etc.; quarta oracio pro patre et matre ipsius fundatoris et parentibus suis, dictis parochianis et omnibus prescriptis et omnibus fidelibus defunctis INCLINA DOMINE etc. VT ANIMAM FAMVLI TVI ET ANIMAM FAMVLE TVE ET ANIMAS FAMVLORVM,

---

[1] Sic: for canonicis.

FAMVLARVM etc.; quinta vero pro pace DEVS A QVO SANCTA DESIDERIA etc. Istum ordinem oracionum conservent singuli capellani qui missam celebrent specialem excepto quod in aliis missis specialibus loco oracionis que fit pro pace dicatur predicta oracio OMNIPOTENS SEMPITERNE DEVS ut supra. Et volumus, precipimus et eciam ordinamus quod qualitercumque et de quocumque celebrant capellani predicti semper pro predicto fundatore et omnibus suprascriptis et animabus eorum in singulis missis suis memoriam faciant specialem.

(34) Alii vero capellani qui missam celebrant generalem pro dicto fundatore et ceteris defunctis primam dicant oracionem DEVS QUI INTER APOSTOLICOS SACERDOTES et ceteras oraciones ita quod quinta oracio sit pro benefactoribus, videlicet OMNIPOTENS SEMPITERNE DEVS ut supra.

(35) Item statuimus et ordinamus quod unus dictorum capellanorum, ille videlicet qui ebdomadarius fuerit dictam missam celebrando [sic] cum nota in dicta capella beate Marie nisi modo legitimo fuerit impeditus, et tunc alius capellanus loco sui in proxima septimana sequenti ebdomadarius sit ad missam singulis diebus celebrandam in dicta capella beate Anne principaliter et nominatim pro animabus predicti Simonis et Roberti de Stridelyngton ac Willelmi patris et Hugonis avunculi ipsius Simonis, necnon Willelmi et Reginaldi filiorum ejus et Margarete matris eorundem et omnium heredum ac liberorum eorundem Simonis et Willelmi filii ejus et antecessorum suorum necnon pro animabus predictorum fundatoris et parentum suorum et benefactorum predictorum imperpetuum cum oracione principali OMNIPOTENS etc. CVI NVNQVAM SINE SPE MISERICORDIE etc. et quatuor collectis prescriptis.

(36) Item in recompensacionem saltem plurimorum beneficiorum et expensarum que tam predictus Willelmus Durant in vita sua prefato fundatori in maxima necessitate sua fecit quam predicta Isabella uxor ejus post mortem ejusdem mariti sui in fundacione cantarie et collegii predictorum pro salute animarum suarum multipliciter et graciose impendit, de consensu et assensu dicti fundatoris expressis statuimus et ordinamus quod ille videlicet capellanus qui ebdomadarius fuerit missam de die in choro dicte ecclesie celebrandam in proxima septimana sequente nisi modo legitimo fuerit impeditus et tunc alius capellanus loco sui ebdomadarius sit ad missam singulis diebus imperpetuum celebrandam in dicta capella beate Marie ad altare ejusdem principaliter et nominatim pro animabus dictorum Willelmi Durant et Isabelle, patrum, matrum, parentum et benefactorum suorum ac predictorum fundatoris, patrum, matrum et parentum suorum et omnium fidelium defunctorum cum hac collecta principali DEVS VENIE LARGITOR etc. VT ANIMAM FAMVLI TVI ET ANIMAM FAMVLE TVE etc. et quatuor oracionibus suprascriptis. Ceteri vero capellani pro defunctis communiter celebrent cum dicta oracione principali DEVS QVI INTER APOSTOLICOS SACERDOTES ut supra, alias de die aut de sancto spiritu vel alio sancto secundum devocionem celebrantis vel votum alicujus devoti audientis seu alias secundum disposicionem dicti custodis vel successorum suorum. Et quod custos, subcustos et ceteri capellani *celebrent omni die nisi infirmitas aut alia causa racionabilis* adversetur *de qua fidem* custodi *facere teneantur.*

(37) Item statuimus et ordinamus quod *ante vesperas* dicant sacerdotes

omnes *singulis diebus in ecclesia secundum usum* et dictum ordinale Eboracensis
ecclesie *Placebo et Dirige in communi* et in crastino ante incepcionem matutinarum diei commendacionem mortuorum pro animabus prescriptis. Completorio vero diei et de beata Maria expletis, ut cursus diei fine laudabili
concludatur, volumus quod *singulis diebus* post hoc majori *campana ter tinniente*
solempniter *cantetur ab omnibus in* dicta capella beate Marie *genuflexis hec
antiphona* MATER ORA FILIVM. *Postea premisso* dicto *versiculo de beata Maria* et
beata Anna, videlicet AVE MARIA ut supra *dicatur hec oracio per ebdomadarium
se superius erigentem: Deus qui sine materno dolore de matre tua dulcissima in lucem
prodiens castitatis ejus illesa signacula custodisti da nobis famulis tuis per interces-
sionem matris tue gloriose mundiciam mentis et corporis et hujus loci devocionem amplio-
rem, ut ad laudem matris crescat hic filii gloria et nos agnum sequentes sine macula te
filium cum matre tua leti videamus in patria* per christum dominum nostrum amen.

(38) Item statuimus et ordinamus quod dictus custos et omnes capellani
et clerici convenientes in dicta capella beate Anne singulis annis in vigilia
Anunciacionis beate Marie et nocte precedente anniversarium predictorum
Simonis, Willelmi et Reginaldi filiorum ejus, heredum et antecessorum
suorum predictorum sicut pro corpore presenti cum solempni pulsacione
campanarum faciant imperpetuum. Et eciam in eadem vigilia beate Marie
(fo. 103) et dicto die Anunciacionis sequente omnes predicti capellani et
clerici convenientes in dicta capella beate Marie anniversarium predictorum fundatoris, Johannis consanguinei sui, patrum, matrum et omnium
parentum suorum et predictorum Willelmi Durant et Isabelle et omnium
benefactorum predictorum et parochianorum simili modo cum solempni
pulsacione faciant imperpetuum, quodque eodem die Anunciacionis statim
post missam custos qui pro tempore fuerit inter pauperiores parochie predicte in fine misse ibidem repertos sexaginta quadrantes vel panem ad
valorem annuatim in cimiterio dicte ecclesie distribuat pro animabus supradictis. Et si custos vel aliquis capellanorum predictorum seu clericus qui
pro tempore fuerit transgressor istius ordinacionis scienter, nequiter vel
maliciose in aliquo sui articulo inventus fuerit, tanquam perjurus puniatur
et a capella et cantaria predictis eo ipso imperpetuum amoveatur nullo sibi
remedio in hac parte valituro.

(39) *Et ne fundacio predicta et ea que presentibus sunt inserta oblivioni tradantur*
statuimus et ordinamus quod dicta fundacio predicti domini Thome de Sibethorp et
hec presens nostra ordinacio *et decretum singulis annis imperpetuum* certis
terminis, videlicet *in singulis* quinque vigiliis beate Marie virginis et in
vigilia Nativitatis sancti Johannis Baptiste in presencia custodis et omnium
capellanorum per aliquem eorundem capellanorum distincte perlegantur et
*recitentur ut sic nullus contrafaciens de ignorancia probabili* poterit *se excusare.*

(40) *Premissa vero omnia et singula secundum eorum vim, formam et effectum*
invocato dei nomine *auctoritate nostra pontificali modo quo premittitur ordinamus
et ea in suo robore duratura statuimus, dicimus, laudamus, pronunciamus, diffinimus
et ea semper subsistere inviolabiliter observanda decernimus, jubemus et imponimus per
decretum. Et ad premissa omnia et singula prout cuilibet eorum attinet impedimento
legitimo ut est dictum cessante facienda tenenda observanda et fideliter exequenda consciencias tam predicti* custodis *et successorum suorum* custodum *quam predictorum
capellanorum* et clerici *et successorum suorum penes altissimum oneramus qui per pre-*

*sentes successive onerati perpetuo remaneant in futurum.* Salvo nobis jure presentem ordinacionem nostram corrigendi mutandi declarandi suplendi et hiis addendi et eam de assensu dicti fundatoris tociens quociens expedire viderimus innovandi. Salva eciam prefato domino Thome fundatori quam diu vixerit potestate in singulis premissorum prout sibi placuerit dispensando [*sic*]. *Et omnem ordinacionem sive ordinaciones* per aliquem predecessorum nostrorum super premissis vel *aliquo* premissorum *prius factas, quatenus istam presentem ordinacionem non compaciuntur seu eidem contrariantur* vel ab eadem alterantur, *de consensu dicti* capituli nostri *et omnium aliorum quorum interest ex certa sciencia revocamus anullamus et eam ac eas omnino carere volumus* [viribus] *et effectu.*

(41) *Et ut presentes littere nostre statutum ordinacio dictum pronunciacio et decretum suprascripta vim perpetuitatis optineant easdem litteras sigilli nostri impressione fecimus communiri.* Et ad majorem securitatem et perpetuam rei memoriam presentes litteras nostras sub sigillo nostro fecimus quadruplicari; quarum unam penes dictum custodem et successores suos, aliam vero penes dictos priorem et conventum de Thurgarton et terciam penes dictos decanum et capitulum et quartam penes nos et successores nostros remanere volumus in futurum fideliter conservandas, jure, jurisdiccione, privilegiis, statu, honore et dignitate nostris et successorum nostrorum et ecclesie nostre Eboracensis in omnibus semper salvis.

In quorum omnium testimonium sigillum nostrum presentibus est appensum. Dat. apud Cawode quarto die mensis Februarii anno domini millesimo trecentesimo quadragesimo secundo et pontificatus nostri anno primo.

## III. Statutes of the Chantry and College of Cotterstock[1]

### (Lincoln Reg. vi, ff. 74–7*b*)

Bishop Bek's recension (2 March 1343/4) of the founder's statutes dated at Cotterstock 5 December 1339 and confirmed by Simon Islip, vicar-general of Bishop Burghersh, at Lincoln 7 January 1339/40, as in Lincoln Reg. IV, ff. 227*d*–229.

Ad rei memoriam sempiternam. *Universis sancte matris ecclesie filiis ad quorum noticiam pervenerit hec scriptura Thomas permissione divina Lincolniensis episcopus salutem in domino sempiternam cum gracia et benediccione salvatoris.* Acceptum utique deo hominibusque laudabile censeri debet si ea que precatis devocionisque optentu meritorie inchoata et gesta sunt ac eciam sufficienti auctoritate ordinata et stabilita diligenciori postea recensita studio approbacionem et confirmacionem omni declaracione et addicione ac mutacione in melius recipiant eciam auctoritate eadem recto in omnibus observato libramine racionis. Sane exposito nobis seriose et diligenter pro parte domini Johanne Gyffard de Cotherstok clerici ac prepositi et fratrum capellanorum cantarie de Cotherstok nostre Lincolniensis diocesis quod idem dominus Johannes zelo pie devocionis accensus pro divini cultus augmento eciam prehabita licencia regia sicut moris est *cantariam seu collegium tresdecim sacerdotum quorum unus prepositus ceteri vero fratres capellani vocitarentur perpetuo servi-*

[1] Words and phrases taken from Bek's first recension (ibid., ff. 60–3) are printed in italics.

*turorum in honore sanctissime trinitatis et gloriose et beatissime virginis marie matris*
*dilectissime dei et domini nostri ihesu christi ac beatorum apostolorum et specialiter*
*beati Andree et omnium sanctorum in ecclesia sancti Andree de Cotherstok nostre*
*Lincolniensis diocesis predicte in qua per regeneracionem christiano nomini est ascriptus*
et pro *statu celebri serenissimi principis domini Edwardi regis Anglie* illustris *et*
*dominarum Isabelle* et *Philippe reginarum Anglie et liberorum suorum ac salubri statu*
*ipsius domini Johannis* fundatoris *et domini Willelmi fratris sui necnon pro ipsorum*
singulorum antecessorum dicti fundatoris *et aliorum benefactorum suorum et*
dicti *collegii* sacerdotum *ac animabus omnium fidelium defunctorum* eciam de
licencia consensu et assensu rectoris ecclesie qui tunc erat necnon *de consensu*
*et assensu* bone memorie *Henrici Lincolniensis episcopi predecessoris nostri immediati*
*sub certa forma* fundavit et *instituit ipsumque collegium dotavit* competenter de
manerio suo de Cotherstok cum pertinenciis in comitatu Northamptoniensi
ac eciam certis terris et tenementis in quodam loco qui vocatur le South-
side de Totenhowe existentibus ac communa pasture cum pertinenciis in
foresta de Rokyngham in eodem comitatu necnon de advocacione ecclesie
de Cotherstok predicta sub intencione pia et spe devota quod eadem
ecclesia cum suis iuribus et pertinenciis universis in usus cedent proprios
et perpetuos prepositi et fratrum capellanorum predictorum ad uberiorem
sustentacionem eorundem qui eidem ecclesie habenti prius solum rectorem
in numero tresdecim sacerdotum melius laudabilius et devocius solito
habeant in divinis presencialiter et continue deservire. Quodque ordinaciones quedam cum reservacione potestatis *mutandi* declarandi et inter-
pretandi eas et addendi ad easdem (fo. 74*b*) per dominum Johannem
fundatorem predictum bonum ipsius collegii statum ac prepositi et fratrum
eiusdem conversacionem regularem honestamque et moralem vitam con-
cernentes facte fuerint ac eciam auctoritate dicti predecessoris nostri
in omnibus capitulis suis approbate et confirmate. Et quod consequenter dicta ecclesia de Cotherstok cuius patronatus ad predictos prepositum
et fratres capellanos ut premittitur pertinebat auctoritate prefati predecessoris nostri predictis preposito et capellanis et eorum successoribus ad
sustentacionem ipsorum uberiorem interveniente eciam consensu capituli
ecclesie Lincolniensis in proprios usus concessa fuerit et eciam assignata ita
quod cedente vel decedente rectore dicte ecclesie qui tunc erat ipsius ecclesie
possessionem in omnibus suis iuribus et pertinenciis universis dicti tamen
predecessoris nostri vel eius successoris auctoritate precedente libere apprehendere possent et nancisci ac fructus eiusdem convertere in proprios suos
usus congrua tamen porcione de fructibus et proventibus eiusdem ecclesie
vicario vel ei saltim qui curam ipsius regere deberet necnon potestate plenaria
ipsam porcionem taxandi et qualiter et per quem ipsa cura geri vel fieri
deberet ordinandi dicto predecessori nostro seu ipsius successori specialiter
reservata. Et quod nos postmodum eidem predecessori nostro immediate
succedentes et in consideracionem deducentes quod dicti prepositus et
fratres capellani non potuerunt onera iuxta formam ordinacionis predicte
cantarie eis incumbencia comode supportare si porcio et cota notabilis
fructuum et proventuum eiusdem ecclesie in usus alicuius alterius quam
prepositi et fratrum capellanorum predictorum aliqualiter assignaretur
aliisque causis legitimis veris et iustis nobis cognitis nos ad id moventibus

volumus concessimus ordinamus ac auctoritate pontificali diffinimus quod cedente vel decedente rectore dicte ecclesie de Cotherstok qui tunc erat extunc liceret predictis preposito et fratribus capellanis libere propria auctoritate possessionem eiusdem ecclesie cum suis iuribus et pertinenciis universis ingredi nancisci apprehendere et adeptam pacifice plene continuare possidere et tenere fructus et proventus eiusdem ecclesie percipere et habere et in proprios usus suos licite convertere nostra vel successorum nostrorum seu cuiusvis alterius licencia alia generali aut speciali minime petita vel optenta quodque regimen ecclesie et cura animarum parochianorum eiusdem per prepositum predictum et successores suos qui pro tempore fuerint singulos singulariter pro suis temporibus singularibus successivis regantur laudabiliter et debite gubernentur ita quod dicta ecclesia debitis non fraudetur obsequiis et eidem incumbencia onera in spiritualibus et temporalibus per prepositum predictum et successores suos sicuti per rectores dicte ecclesie dum erant agnosci solebant extunc in futurum fideliter agnoscantur. Ad que quod animarum curam et regimen prepositus qui tunc fuit vel qui esset infra mensem post nactam et adeptam possessionem pacificam ecclesie memorate cum suis iuribus et pertinenciis universis ut premittitur ac extunc singuli futuri preposti in singulis prefeccionibus suis et admissionibus ad officium prepositure predicte per nos et successores nostros forma et modo similibus quibus perpetui vicarii ad vicarias suas admittendi sunt et per officialem Lincolniensem sede episcopali vacante admitterentur et proficerentur pro temporibus tunc futuris. Volumus tamen et concessimus quod liceret preposito predicto unum de predictis fratribus capellanis quem ad hoc sciencia et moribus idoneum iudicaverit in subsidium exercicii cure et regiminis parochie predicte deputare ipsumque amovere et alium idoneum ad hoc assignare pro sue libito voluntatis quociens viderit expedire.

Et eciam quod nos subsequenter predicta ecclesia de Cotherstok de iure et de facto vacante per resignacionem Willelmi de Stok ultimi rectoris eiusdem in manus nostras pure sponte et simpliciter factam ac per nos acceptatam et admissam ut predicti prepositus et fratres capellani possessionem dicte ecclesie de Cotherstok sic vacantis corporaliter libere apprehendere possent et tenere fructusque ipsius in usus suos proprios convertere iuxta dictarum appropriacionis et concessionis ac ordinacionis nostrarum exigenciam et tenorem liberam eisdem preposito et fratribus capellanis concessimus facultatem ; et quod curam animarum predicte ecclesie iuxta omnem vim formam et effectum in concessione et ordinacione nostris huiusmodi contentam preposito plene commisimus supradicto prout hec omnia et singula per litteras autenticas sigillo dicti predecessoris nostri et discreti viri magistri Simonis de Islep tunc vicarii ac commissarii sui generalis necnon per diversas scripturas sigillis domini regis ac domini Johannis fundatoris et eciam rectoris predictorum consignatas ac insuper per diversas litteras nostras super ordinacione et concessione nostris predictis ac commissione nostra proxime supratacta factas asserebant manifeste apparere quodque tandem virtute concessionis et ordinacionis nostrarum predictarum prefati prepositus et fratres capellani possessionem pacificam ecclesie de Cotherstok predicta sunt adepti et assecuti ; et quod prefatus prepositus infra mensem a tempore vacacionis ecclesie predicte auctoritate commissionis nostre antedicte curam animarum parochianorum eiusdem ecclesie canonice optinuit et exercuit ac optinet et exercet in presenti peticio humilis et devota eorundem domini Johannis fundatoris ac prepositi et fratrum capellanorum post premissa nobis seriosius exposita ex ordine submissa continebat ut nos premissa omnia et singula debite consideracionis examine mediante recenseremus eademque secundum nostre moderacionis arbitrium in corrigendo et mutando et addendo et declarando prout iustum et pium ac canonicis et regularibus institutis conveniens visum fuerit approbacionis nostre robore muniremus et confirmaremus expresse submiseruntque nobis ac promiserunt dominus Johannes fundator ac prepositus et fratres capellani supradicti per suas patentes litteras pro se ipsis et cantaria seu collegio supradictis firmum et stabile perpetuis temporibus se habituros quicquid duxerimus faciendum et ordinandum in ea parte, nos igitur domini Johannis fundatoris ac prepositi et fratrum capellanorum predictorum peticioni favorabiliter annuentes fundacionem et institucionem ac dotacionem dicte cantarie seu collegii necnon concessionem et assignacionem ecclesie parochialis predicte ac eciam omnia et singula concurrencia ad ipsam fundacionem seu concernencia eandem de quibus exposicio seriosa suprascripta facit mencionem solicite examinacioni et discussioni subiecimus diligenti ac super premissis cum peritis deliberacionem habuimus pleniorem. Et quia per scripturas veras et auctenticas de quibus premittitur ac alias legitime et sufficienter comperimus et nobis constat fundacionem et institucionem ac dotacionem dicte cantarie seu collegii fratrum capellanorum predicti ac eciam concessionem et assignacionem ecclesie parochialis predictas canonice et rite factas extitisse et esse et ad sufficienciam personarum dicti collegii racionabilem et competentem predictas fundacionem ac dotacionem et eciam concessionem et assignacionem ecclesie parochialis predicte necnon et ipsam cantariam seu ipsum collegium auctoritate ordinaria ex certa sciencia approbamus et ratificamus expresse. Concessiones vero et ordinaciones nostras specialiter factas circa apprehensionem possessionis et exercicium cure parochialis ecclesie predicte de quibus superius est premissum et de quibus nobis satis constat tenore presencium approbando innovamus. Quantum vero ad ordinaciones in novitate fundacionis premisse per dictum dominum Johannem fundatorem factas eius devotam intencionem in ea parte sicut et in ipsa fundacione cantarie seu collegii predictorum in domino commendamus. Et quia in eisdem ordinacionibus aliqua videntur contineri que difficultatem alia que obscuritatem inducunt ac quedam que emendacione et melioracione ac suplecione nostro et aliorum super hoc diligencius consultorum iudicio reputantur indigere hoc moderamine subsequenti duximus providendum eciam predictorum fundatoris ac prepositi et fratrum capellanorum interveniente peticione et consensu in hac parte videlicet quod eas et earum quamlibet valere volumus et ut validas et validam approbamus quatenus ordinacionibus presentibus ordinacionibus in ea parte sub nostro nomine et nostra auctoritate immediata ex predictis et aliis certis causis nos moventibus conceptis et descriptis non contradicunt set eisdem noscuntur convenire et in eo casu ordinaciones domini Johannis fundatoris predicti tanquam nostras ex approbacione speciali predicta effectum suum habere volumus et ligare. Quarum quidem ordinacionum nostrarum subinfertur tenor qui talis est:

(fo. 75) (1) *In primis* quidem volumus *et ordinamus quod ex presenti ordinacione nostra* episcopali et ordinaria secundum tenorem precedentis ordinacionis dicti domini Johannis fundatoris *sint tresdecim sacerdotes in dicta ecclesia de Cotherstok divina celebrantes* virtutum *domino inperpetuum* ministraturi et *servituri viri* silicet honeste et bone fame gramaticam suam saltim competenter intelligentes et in officio ecclesiastico regulando legendo et cantando bene instructi.

Quos omnes et singulos in ihesu christo omnium salvatore attencius exhortamur quod a comessacionibus ebrietatibus luxuriis rixis et contencionibus ac vagacionibus exteris et conventiculis inhonestis ac ceteris enormitatibus et insolenciis diligenti cautela se curent prout ipsis cum dei adiutorio possibile est abstinere. *Dictorum* quorum *sacerdotum unus in spiritualibus et temporalibus circumspectus* per viam deliberate nominacionis et institucionis inferius descriptarum *sit superior et magister qui prepositus ceteri vero fratres capellani cantarie* seu collegii *de Cotherstok perpetuo nomine vocitentur.* Qui fratres capellani et eorum quilibet sub cura in foro anime et obediencia vivant prepositi eorum supradicti.

(2) Item quia dei servitores sacerdotes simplices predictos in simplicitate cordis altaris ministerio iugiter insistentes quietos esse volumus occasione quacumque prout possibile est amputata inquietudine et distractus [*sic*] contingencium propter traditas a iure subtiles eleccionum formas non servatas quam frequenter et eo periculosius quo simpliciores ipsi electores exsistere noscuntur volumus et ordinamus hac compendiosa subsequenti forma prefeccionem prepositi in qualibet exnunc secutura vacacione debere expediri videlicet quod octavo die continue numerando a tempore publice note vacacionis prepositure in loco cantarie seu collegii predictorum per mortem prepositi vel alias die vacacionis note minime computata hora matutinali missa primitus decantata solenniter de spiritu sancto ieiuni et sobrii fratres capellani cantarie seu collegii predictorum qui iurati fuerint ut subsequitur tunc presentes absentibus extunc ulterius non expectatis cum competenti maturitate conveniant in loco capitulari solito et communiter inter se ipsos tractatum habeant diligentem super nominanda persona quam habiliorem reputaverint de se ipsis pro officio prepositure predicte que persona communiter vice et nomine omnium et singulorum episcopo Lincolniensi loci ordinario qui pro tempore fuerit vel protunc iure episcopali in ipsa diocesi principaliter et actualiter presidenti in prepositum canonice instituenda et preficienda valeat presentari. Et quod persona illa de predictis fratribus capellanis in quam omnes vel saltim eorum maior pars secundum numerum de presentando ad preponituram vacantem consenserint vel consenserit sine mora dicto episcopo seu iure episcopali ut prefertur presidenti vice et nomine omnium presentetur per litteras patentes communi sigillo cantarie seu collegii predictorum communitas. Dilacionem vero octo dierum supradictam duximus faciendam tam propter absenciam si que fuerit cuiuscunque fratris expectandi quam propter maturiorem deliberacionem seorsum et separatim habendam in quam personam de dicto collegio utilius et deo placabilius dirigere possit unusquisque votum suum et illud expedicius expromere cum contigerit eos propter hoc capitulariter convenire sicut est premissum. Monemus autem attencius et in domino ihesu christo exortamur quod fratres omnes et singuli cantarie seu collegii predictorum postposita omni affeccione inordinata oculos mentis habentes ad solum deum et

utilitatem regiminis cantarie seu collegii predictorum illam personam presen-
tandam nominare solicite studeant et procurent quam pro officio dicte
prepositure meliorem et utiliorem fore verisimiliter crediderint de quo
ipsorum singulorum consciencias oneramus. Quam quidem per fratres
capellanos sic presentatam personam admittendam habeat absque difficultate dominus episcopus seu episcopali [sic] ut premittur presidens nisi
evidentissimis et promptissimis probacionibus constiterit pro regimine dicti
collegii moribus vel sciencia vel industria convenientem habilitatem sic
presentatam personam non habere. Admissionem vero sic presentate habilis
persone fieri volumus per expressionem canonice et perpetue institucionis
in prepositura cantarie seu collegii de Cotherstok et in cura parochianorum
ecclesie eiusdem. Et si infra dictos octo dies omnes vel maior saltim pars
numero fratrum capellanorum predictorum in nominando ut prefertur non
poterunt consentire quod absit extunc omni quarta et sexta feria reliqui
temporis mensis tunc currentis computando mense a die noticie vacacionis
predicte ieiunet ipsorum quilibet in pane et aqua donec in nominando unum
de confratribus presentandum ut prefertur contingat omnes concordare vel
saltim ipsorum maiorem partem numero ut est dictum. Et si durante ipso
mense predicti fratres capellani inimico homine discordiam inter eos pro-
curante quod advertat [sic] deus auctor et amator pacis de huiusmodi
nominacionis negocio se non expediverint extunc episcopus Lincolniensis
qui pro tempore fuerit seu predictus presidens unum de dictis fratribus
capellanis in prepositum preficiat prout sibi secundum deum videbitur
expedire. *Salvo semper iure dictis* fratribus capellanis in aliis vacacionibus cum
*occurrerint quibuscunque nominandi* et presentandi ac ipsas nominacionem et
presentacionem *prosequendi ut premittur prout possent si negligentes vel remissi
aliqualiter* prius *non fuissent.*

(3) Admissus vero et institutus *seu prefectus* ut premittitur *in prepositum
cantarie predicte* statim post huiusmodi admissionem et institucionem seu
prefeccionem de se factam coram sic admittente et instituente seu preficiente
eundem in prepositum obedienciam episcopo Lincolniensi loci diocesano
seu iure episcopali ut prefertur presidenti in diocesi Lincolniensi si per eum
admissus et institutus seu prefectus prestet canonicam et eciam *iuramentum
prestet et faciat corporale quod in dicta cantaria* seu collegio *residebit* perpetuo *et
continue* alioquin nisi ut predictum est huiusmodi prestiterit iuramentum
ipsius admissio et institucio sive prefeccio nullius penitus sit momenti. Quod
quidem iuramentum (fo. 75*b*) in omni sui parte civiliter et absque capcione
et artacione scripulosa [sic] iurantis intelligi volumus et quod utilem vel
necessariam absenciam dicti prepositi ultra diem artificialem per omnes
confratres presentes vel maiorem partem eorundem antequam se absentaverit
prepositus ipse approbatum huiusmodi iuramentum non impediat vel
excludat. Quantum vero ad absenciam breviorem quam est dictum ipsius
prepositi conscienciam solummodo oneramus precipientes tamen quod
causam seu colorem cause ultra quam crediderit expedire non queret se
absentandi. Qui sic iuratus litteras habeat ab admittente et instituente seu
preficiente eundem de admissione et institucione seu prefeccione necnon et
prestacione iuramenti predictis specialem et expressam mencionem facientes.
Quas quidem litteras cicius quo comode ad confratres suos in primo adventu

suo per eum propter hoc congregandos redire poterit legi faciat in communi. Post premissa vero sic ex ordine adimpleta et non ante induccio ipsius prepositi in corporalem possessionem prepositure predicte immediate subsequatur de mandato admittentis et instituentis seu preficientis eundem facienda per illum ad quem induccio ipsa de iure vel consuetudine pro tempore pertinebit.

(4) Post induccionem vero huiusmodi administracionem omnium bonorum cantarie seu collegii predictorum habeat prepositus supradictus. Cuius tamen administracionis actualem execucionem suspendi volumus donec *de calicibus libris vestimentis et aliis ornamentis* ecclesiasticis ceterisque bonis et rebus *et* tam *utensilibus domorum* quam aliorum ac instauro quocunque videlicet singulis *in specie una cum* valore eorum in quantitate *separatis et divisis ad ipsam cantariam* seu collegium *spectantibus tempore induccionis sue predicte ac de nominibus debitorum et creditorum eiusdem cantarie et* collegii ac quantitatibus eorum que tunc sibi debebuntur et que ipsi debebunt de quibus tunc eidem clare constare poterit *sub fratrum suorum eiusdem collegii legali testimonio inventarium* faciat *duplicatum* et indentatum *cuius altera pars* remaneat *sub communi custodia* collegii *in* communi *cista* de qua inferius subicietur *et alteram partem eiusdem inventarii sibi ipsi retineat ut sciatur in quo statu ipse predictam receperit cantariam.* Quod si aliquid de rebus seu bonis aut quantitatibus predictis de quibus tunc eidem clare constare non poterit extra dictum inventarium omissum fuerit extunc quamcicius eidem preposito inde constabit utrique parti dicti inventarii ponatur et addatur.

(5) *Prepositi vero destitucio sicuti et ipsius admissio* et institucio *ad episcopum loci vel sede vacante ad ipsum qui loco eiusdem in similibus succedit pertineat suo casu proviso quod ubi evidens et probabilis causa dictum prepositum* exegerit *amoveri circa id eciam fiat quod sancciones canonice dictaverint in hac parte.*

(6) Circa vero admissionem fratrum capellanorum cantarie seu collegii predictorum volumus et ordinamus quod admittendus quilibet in eisdem cantaria seu collegio tempore admissionis sue sit in sacerdotali ordine constitutus. Liceatque sibi infra annum a tempore admissionis sue computandum libere recedere quandocunque ac eciam dictis fratribus capellanis liceat infra idem tempus sic receptum licenciare et amovere si eisdem vel maiori parti eorundem displicuerint conversacio et mores sui. Quod si ultra predictum annum integrum in ipsa cantaria seu collegio permanserit extunc quamdiu obedientem ac disciplinabilem et corrigibilem in casu quo excesserit seipsum prebuerit dictum collegium et fratres ipsum sic ut premittitur ultra annum commorantem pro confratre et persona dicti collegii tenere et habere et eidem in necessariis sicut uni de confratribus salva regulari disciplina providere teneantur. Indisciplinabilem vero et incorrigibilem episcopo Lincolniensi vel iure episcopali in ipsa diocesi presidenti liceat amovere summario super hoc observato processu. Teneaturque ipse per annum manens ultimo die ipsius anni bona si que protunc habuerit preposito et fratribus capellanis predictis expresse indicare et ea ad communem utilitatem dicte cantarie seu collegii conferre et possessionem eorundem bonorum in quantum sibi possibile est in ipsum collegium et fratres supradictos perpetualiter transferre. Corporale eciam prestet iuramentum sic ut premittitur per annum manens quod fidelis erit preposito et fratribus

capellanis cantarie seu collegii predictorum ac eciam presentes ordinaciones nostras et iura eiusdem collegii in quantum eum concernunt et sibi possibile est cum dei adiutorio curabit observare ita videlicet quod occasionem ex proposito non queret contra eas veniendi et eciam quod preposito seu eius vices gerenti scilicet custodi collegii de quo subicietur obedienciam iuret canonicam et promittat. In locum vero deficientis fratris per mortem vel alias assumatur alius ex communi consensu prepositi et fratrum capellanorum predictorum vel maioris partis eorundem preposito existente. Si vero pro-tunc prepositus non fuerit pro assumpcione confratris huiusmodi sufficiat consensus tocius collegii vel maioris partis eiusdem. Dictam vero assump-cionem confratris huiusmodi legitimo semper impedimento cessante fieri volumus infra mensem a tempore quo dicto collegio notum fuerit deficere fratrem suum per mortem vel alias sicut est premissum. Pro singulis vero septimanis in quibus post mensem proximum supradictum ex eorum negli-gencia vel culpa caruerint noviter assumendo in loco deficientis ut est dictum quilibet de dicto collegio sexta feria in pane et aqua ieiunet. Ante vero predicti anni lapsum et iuramenti prestacionem de quibus est predic-tum ad tractatus communes cum fratribus capellanis noviter admissi non conveniant nec administracionem vel officium aliquod habeant vel gerant qualicunque modo preterquam in serviendo in divinis dumtamen curam predicte ecclesie de Cotherstok non exerceant infra dictum primum annum quoquomodo. Curam vero dicte parochialis ecclesie et parochianorum eiusdem exerciciumque eiusdem cure ad eum seu ad eos pertineat et per eundem modum committatur prout in aliis nostris super hoc specialiter confectis litteris de quibus superius fit mencio seriosius continetur.

(7) Item volumus et ordinamus quod predicti *prepositus et fratres* capellani *habeant duos clericos* in lectura et cantu sufficienter instructos *quibus provideatur de bonis communibus* cantarie seu collegii predictorum ad plenam sus-tentacionem prout eorum statui simplici videbitur convenire. Quorum quidem clericorum admissio et occupacio ac ipsorum mora et recessus predictorum preposito et fratrum capellanorum regimini et arbitrio com-mittantur.

(8) Item circa ea que in divinis officiis in dicta ecclesia de Cotherstok fieri debent et perpetuis futuris temporibus exerceri hoc *volumus et ordinamus* fide-liter observari videlicet *quod diebus singulis* matutinis horis et vesperis dicendis et phallendis [*sic*] ac eciam missis decantandis in predicta ecclesia in com-muni ut clare inferius est distinctum tam prepositus cum sibi vacaverit quam singuli fratres capellani domi commorantes conveniant et intersint nisi infirmitas aut alia causa racionabilis non conficta eos reddiderit excusa-tos de qua singuli ipsorum sacerdotum fidem in assercione debita obediencie preposito facere teneantur si de huiusmodi absencia sua se voluerint excusare. Absentes vero sine causa puniat prepositus et castiget. Prepositum autem consciencie sue proprie quam super hoc oneramus dimitti volumus in hac parte. Convenientes vero persone de collegio supradicto ad officium (fo. 76) matutinale persolvendum in predicta ecclesia secundum usum et con-suetudinem in eadem ecclesia et aliis ecclesiis parochialibus parcium earun-dem usitatos et in diebus in quibus idem usus hoc exigit seu permittit dicant in communi ante incepcionem matutinarum de die matutinas vero [*sic*] de

beata virgine maria sine nota et hoc quando in choro non fiet plenum et solenne servicium de eadem beata virgine illo die. *Matutine* vero *de die secundum usum* predictum ac modum et regimen eiusdem diebus singulis iuxta dierum et festorum exigenciam in choro ecclesie predicte *solenniter decantentur et hoc distincte et aperte in bona psalmodia et pausacione congrua in medio cuiuslibet versus.* Hoc eciam in psallendis singulis aliis horis canonicis de die precipimus observari. Post matutinas vero de die immediate dicatur cum nota prima de die qua dicta legatur martilogium in domo capitulari *cum facta fuerit et interim in choro.* Deinde dicatur tunc ibidem PRECIOSA *et ipsa dicta immediate post psalmus AD TE LEVAVI pro pace et vivis benefactoribus cum versiculis et oracionibus competentibus videlicet DEVS QVI CARITATIS DONA et DEVS A QVO et post psalmus DE PROFVNDIS pro defunctis in* presentibus ordinacionibus nostris contentis *et ceteris benefactoribus* eiusdem collegii *cum oracionibus que sequntur OMNIPOTENS SEMPITERNE DEVS QVI VIVORVM, etc. MISERERE QVESVMVS DOMINE et FIDELIVM DEVS. Quibus sic finitis* cantetur subsequenter cum nota in choro predicto donec capellam beate marie decentem habuerint et extunc in ipsa capella per aliquem de predictis fratribus capellanis missa de beata virgine maria singulis diebus preterquam in maioribus festis duplicibus et tribus diebus ante Pascha ac in diebus in quibus fiet de ea in choro plenum servicium. Et omni die qua de ea plenum fiet servicium in choro si eadem die simplex festum sancti contigerit tunc loco illius misse beate virginis alias de ea post dictam oracionem FIDELIVM DEVS decantande ut predicitur missa de eodem sancto sinautem missa tunc DE ANGELIS decantetur hoc salvo quod de maioribus festis duplicibus superius est expressum. Et postea poscente hora diei tercia et sexta de die dicantur cum nota in communi et hiis dictis celebretur cum nota maior missa de die in choro ecclesie antedicte. Et per totum annum dicatur nona post maiorem missam nisi in quadragesima et tunc precedat et vespere statim post missam ita quod pulsetur ad vesperas post SANCTVS ut dies et festa requirant. Unus eciam fratrum capellanorum predictorum gerat officium ebdomadarii qui pro ipsa ebdomada in officiis divinis in ecclesia habeat preesse et dictam maiorem missam celebrare.

(9) Valeat tamen prepositus si voluerit diebus dominicis seu in aliis festis duplicibus seu solemnibus huiusmodi officia divina in parte vel in toto exequi et excercere vel alium fratrem capellanum qui melius sciverit aut poterit quandocumque voluerit idem prepositus ad hoc assignare. Exhortamur autem in domino ihesu christo quod ebdomadarius vel alius horas psallens diurnas ante incepcionem cuiuslibet earundem oracionem premittat dominicam cum angelica salutacione predicte virginis gloriose in corde suo meditans studiose quod per devocionem earum que non ab homine set divinitus processerunt graciam uberiorem reperiet in psallendis. Proviso semper quod in predicta maiori missa diebus dominicis et festivis *diaconus et subdiaconus induti dalmatica et tunica celebranti serviant et assistant.* Alius vero fratrum capellanorum predictorum *pro domino rege Anglie ac progenitoribus et successoribus suis et aliis superius nominatis et benefactoribus* dicte cantarie seu collegii *missam SALVS POPVLI celebret omni die et non incipiat eandem* missam *quousque maior missa fuerit in dicendo.* Ita quod *in casu quo celebrantem ipsam maiorem missam infirmitas aut alia causa racionabilis impediret alter sic expectans defectum suplere poterit non valentis et a dicta missa SALVS POPVLI per hoc illa die*

*totaliter excusetur.* Et tercius eorum dicat singulis diebus specialiter pro dicta *domina Isabella regina* unam missam DE ANGELIS *dum rebus fuerit in humanis et ipsa mortua de defunctis.* Et quartus eorum *missam celebret pro anima domini Willelmi* filii domini Willelmi *de Bereford et animabus omnium fidelium defunctorum. Omni vero die dominica una missa de Trinitate omni vero die lune una missa de beato Andrea omni vero die martis alia de sancto Thoma martire quolibet die mercurii alia de sancto Johanne Baptista quolibet die iovis alia de corpore christi omni vero die veneris una de sancta Cruce et quolibet die Sabbati alia de sancto Martino per eorum aliquem celebretur.* Ceteri vero fratres *capellani qui dictas missas non celebraverint* celebrent *communiter pro defunctis aut de die aut de sancto spiritu vel* aliquo *sancto secundum devocionem celebrantis vel* votum *alicuius devoti audientis pro* predicto *fundatore et parentibus ceterisque benefactoribus ipsius ac dicte cantarie* seu collegii *et quorum existunt debitores animabusque omnium fidelium defunctorum.* Et tam prepositus quam singuli fratres capellani predicti salva honestate sua et debita devocione cotidie celebrare teneantur nisi corporis infirmitate fuerint impediti. Quilibet vero sacerdotum predictorum celebrans in missis suis pro salubri statu domini Edwardi regis dominarum Isabelle et Philippe reginarum ac *liberorum suorum* supradictorum ac pro salubri statu nostro et successorum nostrorum necnon *canonicorum ecclesie nostre Lincolniensis predicte* et dictorum dominorum Johannis fundatoris et Willelmi fratris sui ac *aliorum* parentum et *benefactorum ipsius fundatoris et cantarie* seu collegii predictorum ac eciam *Ricardi Knyvet Johanne uxoris eius Walteri de Houby heredum et liberorum ipsorum* quoad vixerimus et animabus nostris cum ab hac luce subtracti fuerimus ac pro animabus patris dicti domini regis et aliorum progenitorum et heredum suorum et bone memorie *Henrici Lincolniensis episcopi* predecessoris nostri predicti *domini Willelmi de Kyrkeby Cristine uxoris eius Johannis de Houby* Johannis Knyvet Johanne uxoris eius et omnium fidelium defunctorum orare teneatur *et specialiter pro dicto fundatore dum superstes fuerit dicat hanc collectam que sic incipit* OMNIPOTENS SEMPITERNE DEVS MISERERE FAMVLO TVO *etc. et post mortem suam* collectam *que sic incipit* DEVS QVI INTER APOSTOLICOS SACERDOTES FAMVLVM TVVM SACERDOTALI FECISTI vel OMNIPOTENS SEMPITERNE DEVS CVI NVNQVAM SINE SPE *etc. preterquam in missis in quibus necessario secundum dictum usum unica tantum* vel certe et determinate alie collecte fuerint dicende. Presentes autem persone de collegio supradicto vesperas et complectorium de die extra quadragesimam simul dicant cum nota singulis diebus temporibus congruis in communi. Proviso utique quod ante vesperas de die vespere de beata virgine maria et completorium eiusdem post completorium diei dicantur in communi sine nota diebus singulis quibus hoc permittit usus supradictus. Et statim postea ad devocionis uberioris excitacionem tinniat ter campana et *cantetur ab ipsis omnibus in choro genuflexis* (fo. 76b) *hec antiphona* MATER HORA FILIVM *preterquam in pascali tempore. Tunc enim* loco illius antiphone *cantetur antiphona* REGINA CELI LETARE. Deinde post versiculum *de beata maria dicatur* aliqua *oracio de ipsa conveniens per ebdomadarium se superius erigentem.*

(10) Volumus eciam et ordinamus quod prepositus et fratres capellani predicti singulis diebus in quibus usus exigit supradictus salvo tamen eo quod in ordinacione de anniversariis est subscriptum officium complete dicant mortuorum et hoc in ipsa ecclesia et illo ordine pro diebus illis in quibus usus supradictus obligat ad dicendum. In aliis vero diebus dictum

officium mortuorum dici ab eis permittimus quando ipsorum singulis separatim vel alias melius et competencius vacare videbitur ad dicendum.

(11) *Item volumus et ordinamus quod prepositus si presens fuerit alioquin custos collegii* de quo inferius subicietur *ac omnes et singuli* fratres *capellani predicti* qui presentes fuerint *anniversarium dicte domine Isabelle regine ac eciam patris et matris* dicti *fundatoris anniversarium* post uniuscuiusque mortem *annis singulis* extunc eo *die* quo ipsorum quilibet migraverit ab hac luce *nisi duplex festum fuerit quo casu in diem transferatur proximo subsequentem extra duplex festum in ecclesia predicta solenniter facere teneantur ita* videlicet *quod die anniversarium huiusmodi proximo precedente* ante vesperas pulsato primitus de more classico dicant cum nota *PLACEBO et DIRIGE in communi* in choro ecclesie antedicte. Pro illo vero die non astringantur amplius ad officium mortuorum preterquam ad commendaciones secrecius et separatim vel in communi eodem die vel in crastino dicendas hora que ad hoc videbitur oportuna. *In crastino* autem *videlicet die anniversarii* dicatur immediate ante missam maiorem *missa* de anniversario *cum nota in communi. Et in diebus* singulis *anniversariorum* predictorum *habeant* predicti *prepositus et* fratres *capellani unam pittanciam* competentem et moderatam *in prandio suo ultra modum solitum de communibus bonis cantarie* seu collegii predicti.

(12) *Singuli* eciam *sacerdotes* predicti videlicet *tam prepositus quam alii in colore habitus et apparatu exteriori* et potissime dum domi incedunt in *quantum* commode *poterit* se curent conformari. *Supertunicas de nigro vel russeto clausas desuper habeant sine birro vel anteriori apertura quacumque cum manicis* competenter largis et *longis ultra medium brachiorum* ipsorum cubitus complectentibus *ac rotundis* nullatenus pendentibus una cum capuciis et aliis indumentis *prout* graves et honestos *capellanos habere decet. Et dum in ecclesia divinis officiis interfuerint capis nigris cum almuciis nigro furratis vel linitis et superpelliceis vel* regetis[1] *ad modum vicariorum ecclesie Lincolniensis* desuper *induantur. Liceat tamen eis in vigilia Pasche quando incipitur GLORIA IN EXCELSIS DEO* deponere capas suas et deinde usque post finitum totum divinum officium in festo *Exaltacionis sancte crucis superpelliceis albis indui et vestiri. Coronas largas aures* patulas *et* tonsuram *congruam* a *canonibus diffinitam uniformiter* habeant *ad* quod *per prepositum vel eius locum tenentem diligencius compellantur.* Exhortamurque eosdem et singulariter ipsorum quemlibet in domino ihesu christo quod captare studeant horas competentes in quibus valeant corditer repetere ecclesiasticum officium cui mancipantur ac litterarum studio secundum ipsorum capacitatem valeant indulgere horam ab occupacione fructuosa quantum eis cum dei adiutorio possibile est nequaquam dimittentes.

(13) Habeant eciam dicti prepositus et fratres capellani ordinatam eis competentem domum pro refectorio suo communi et inibi pendentem campanellam ad cuius sonitum omnes ipsi domi commorantes ad prandium seu ad cenam curent convenire ac ibidem commedant *in communi. Et uno tantum ferculo sufficienti tamen et ad minus de duobus generibus piscium vel carnium diebus simplicibus sint contenti. Diebus vero dominicis ac feriatis pittanciam habeant non nimis exilem nec eciam excessivam.* Monemus autem attencius et exortamur in domino ihesu christo ne quis predictorum prepositi et fratrum capellanorum in refectorio predicto quicquam loquatur *penitus quod sit turpe quodve rixe seu*

---

[1] *Sic*: for *rochetis*.

*dissensionis aut inhonestatis alicuius materiam administret set dum in* maiori refeccione fuerint *unus eorum* de textu biblie vel de vita sanctorum seu aliqua scriptura sancta *legat aliquid in communi* ceteri autem hiis que legantur indulgeant *reverenter* et devote. *Benedicciones eciam et gracias ante prandium sive cenam et post dicendas dicant stando in refectorio quibus graciis* post maiorem refeccionem completis transeuntes simul versus ecclesiam incipiant *psalmum* MISERERE vel alium prout preposito seu custodi collegii visum fuerit magis tempori et diei convenire. Sicque psalmodizantes chorum intrent et in medium eius se ordinatim collocent finem psalmodie et laudis huiusmodi faciendo cum KIRYELEYSON PATER NOSTER et AVE MARIA et collectis competentibus tam pro vivis quam pro defunctis.

(14) *In communi autem dormitorio* in quo quilibet eorum se habeat honeste pacifice et quiete patenter habeant singuli fratrum capellanorum singulariter pro quiete lectos suos pro quiete eorum corporali oportuna hoc salvo quod *prepositus habeat cameram separatam* eidem dormitorio coniunctam seu contiguam pro se et aliquo de confratribus suis predictis per se eligendo qui in lecto separato quiescat in eadem. Infirmi[1] *cum* eorum aliqui *fuerint de alia camera* et *separata et cibis cum necesse fuerit laucioribus vel aliis sibi congruis secundum saltim exigenciam bonorum* predicte cantarie seu collegii precipimus *humaniter* refoveri. Ordinamus eciam et volumus quod singulis diebus preterquam in cena domini et die parasceves pro cubiculari hora et ignitegio sonora pulsetur campana *ad cuius sonitum* tam absentes fratres de vicino quam presentes valeant convenire ad intrandum dormitorium commune predictum a quo post ingressum huiusmodi nullus eorum exeat illa nocte *nisi forsan* ad visitandum *infirmos vel pro alia utilitate cantarie* seu collegii predictorum.

(15) Volumus eciam et ordinamus quod pro reponendis et secure conservandis preciosis si que fuerint et notabilioribus rebus dicti collegii habeatur communis cista situata in loco securo *quatuor seruris diversis quarum serurarum nulla clavis alteri conveniat* firmata. In qua eciam cista *commune sigillum* predicte cantarie seu collegii ac prepositi et fratrum capellanorum predictorum quod eosdem habere volumus secure custodie eciam committatur. *Unam vero clavem habeat prepositus et tres alias claves habeant tres capellani ad hoc a toto collegio specialiter electi* quos *in principio recepcionis clavium* earundem (fo. 77) precipimus *se de dicto sigillo nunquam aliquid consignare aliter quam et sub forma* qua *fuerit saltim per maiorem partem* eiusdem *collegii communiter concordatum. Ceterum quia parvi libelli facilius quam magni possunt subtrahi et variis modis occultari* volumus *et ordinamus quod quecumque* inventura ac indentura *et scripture predicte* seu subscripte ac transcripta quarumcunque cartarum scriptarum et litterarum patencium sigillo suo predicto qualitercumque consignandarum *in unum librum qui registrum domus dicatur in substanciali et aperta littera secundum ordinem redigantur qui liber in prefata cista remaneat sub custodia memorata ipsique registro plenam fidem* per fratres predictos *volumus adhiberi.*

(16) *Bona vero* dicte cantarie seu collegii *sint communia nec prepositus* nec *quivis alius ipsa vel eorum* aliquid *vendicet vel* retineat ut appropriatum *sibi soli.* Proviso quod de eisdem bonis communibus prepositus ipse *duas marcas* quilibet eciam *fratrum capellanorum* ut predicitur iuratorum *viginti solidos*

---

[1] *Sic*: should have been altered to *infirmos.*

sterlingorum pro *emendis et providendis* hiis quibus indiguerint annis singulis *ad festa annunciacionis beate marie et beati Petri advincula per equales porciones* percipiant *annuatim.* Ad hec eciam volumus et ordinamus quod tam prepositus quam singuli fratres capellani predicti qui circa curam parochie et iura ac alia utilia negocia dicte cantarie seu collegii supportanda exercenda promovenda vel exequenda pro tempore ex nominacione commissione vel deputacione per eum seu eos ad quem vel ad quos pertinet fuerint occupati habeant quod eis sufficiet competenter pro se et negociis illis secundum exigenciam negociorum ac status cantarie seu collegii predictorum. *Et cum domino* omnium bonorum largitore *concedente bona et possessiones eorum* in tantum *augeri contigerit* quod eorundem bonorum communis et verus valor in tantum excreverit quod ultra *omnia onera* predicte *cantarie* seu collegii *supportanda ac iura et libertates eiusdem defendenda* instaurum *predictum manutenendum et utiliter augmentandum ac providencias* necessarias cantarie seu collegii predictorum *congruis locis et temporibus faciendas* superesse de claro apparuerit secundum iudicium omnium et singulorum confratrum dicti collegii iuratorum septem marcas sterlingorum in valore extunc *ultra id quod dicti prepositus et fratres capellani* iurati *sunt percepturi ut predicitur prefatus prepositus unam marcam quilibet vero fratrum capellanorum* iuratorum *dimidiam marcam percipiant* pro singulis annis in quibus ut premittitur eorundem bonorum valor excreverit antedictus. Exhortamurque predictos prepositum et fratres capellanos ac ipsorum quemlibet in ihesu christo quod huiusmodi uberior superveniens pecuniaria recepcio arrogancie et insolencie occasionem non prebeat set pocius ad honorem dei et ad honestiorem sustentacionem ipsorum deo serviencium cedat et ad utilitatem cantarie seu collegii predictorum. Quod si aliquis fratrum capellanorum predictorum culpabilis in abusu recepte pecunie ut premittitur eis assignate repertus fuerit per predictum prepositum arguatur et arbitrio puniatur. Proviso quod si iudicio dicti prepositi et maioris saltim partis collegii per duos annos successive vel interpellatim circa premissa se culpabilem reddiderit aliquis de fratribus capellanis supradictis extunc pro sequentibus annis retenta pecunia alias per eum ut premittitur recipienda et provisionem predictam dummodo alias habilis fuerit sibi faciat prepositus supradictus. *Residuum vero* omnium bonorum dicte cantarie seu collegii in thesauraria communi reponatur in virtute sancte obediencie *in communem utilitatem* dicte *cantarie* seu collegii committendum. Alienaciones autem et obligaciones quascumque immobilium vel reddituum ecclesie aut cantarie seu collegii predictorum aut decimarum eiusdem ecclesie ad firmam ultra unum annum dimissiones seu tradiciones librorum eciam et ornamentorum ecclesie et cantarie seu collegii eorundem distraccionem vel inpignoracionem necnon cuiuscumque pensionis corrodii vel liberacionis concessionem ac bosci distraccionem vel destruccionem fieri inhibemus sub pena excommunicacionis maioris quam incurrant ipso facto contrarium facientes vel contrarium facientibus consencientes sine causa utili et necessaria ab episcopo Lincolniensi qui fuerit pro tempore approbata.

(17) Ardua vero negocia utpote cum de aliquo facto seu negocio perpetuo vel alio temporali et magno fuerit disponendum prepositus solus non expediat set consensum et consilium exigat singulorum et exequatur quod fuerit tunc communiter concordatum. Levissima tamen et minora negocia cotidianam

seu frequentem ac colorem¹ expedicionem exigencia secundum communem morem perficere prout expediens fuerit valeat ipse solus nec in hiis fratrum consilium necesse habeat expectare. Si tamen frequencius quo commode poterit super expediendis eciam huiusmodi levibus negociis fratres consuluerit et eos audierit eo magis ipsum reputamus commendandum.

(18) Et ut de statu predicte cantarie seu collegii et administracione dicti prepositi semper certa noticia habeatur volumus et ordinamus quod idem prepositus singulis annis de receptis et expensis per ipsum factis compotum reddere teneatur coram ceteris confratribus capellanis iuratis vel maiori parte eorundem infra mensem post festum sancti Michaelis. Post cuius quidem compoti reddicionem ac eciam in inicio kalendarum Maii quodcumque instaurum et quecumque alia bona et catalla dicte cantarie seu collegii per ipsum prepositum et aliquem de confratribus ad hoc a toto collegio vel maiori parte eiusdem deputatum clarius videantur. Et in illis duobus anni temporibus in scriptis exprimat et recitet idem prepositus singula nomina debitorum et creditorum predicte cantarie seu collegii ut sic tam per reddicionem huiusmodi compoti quam per visum et consideracionem dictorum bonorum semper sciri poterit si in administracione fuerit dispensator utilis et fidelis. Et rotuli compotorum huiusmodi post dictum mensem sancti Michaelis ponantur in predicta communi cista vel in alia modo consimili sub seruris firmata ad perpetuam rei memoriam reservandi. Quibus quidem duobus anni temporibus ordinent prefati prepositus et fratres capellani de instauro domus meliorando et de providenciis faciendis.

(19) Item volumus et ordinamus quod *per* predictos *prepositum et confratres suos* iuratos in communi *vel* prepositura vacante *per ipsos confratres quociens necesse fuerit et sibi viderint expedire* assumatur *unus de eisdem qui custos collegii vocitetur* et *qui in absencia prepositi* et eciam prepositura vacante sit gerens vices eiusdem preterquam in exercicio cure parochialis predicte de quo dispositum est per litteras nostras de quibus superius est expressum. Idemque custos *defectus diurnos tam in ecclesia quam extra corrigat et emendet. Et alius eciam eorum* quem prefatus prepositus in subsidium exercicii cure parochialis predicte deputaverit sacrista nominetur *qui libros ornamenta ac luminaria ecclesie custodiat reficiat et emendet et de singulis libris vestimentis iocalibus vasisque* [fo. 77b] *argenteis* dicte cantarie seu collegii ad ornatum ecclesie seu altaris pertinentibus *faciat duos rotulos quorum uno sibi retento alter remaneat communibus in archivis. Tercius eciam* pari *modo* assumatur sicut de custode dicitur *qui receptor vocitetur et qui sub preposito vel* custode *omnia recepta* vel *expensas diurna dictam cantariam* seu collegium *intrinsecus contingencia singulis diebus redigat in scripturam qui de receptis et expensis huiusmodi dicto preposito vel* custodi assistentibus eis aliis aliquibus de collegio *compotum reddat fidelem* in fine septimane. *Quartus vero pari modo* assumatur *qui celerarius vocitetur qui sub preposito et eciam prepositura vacante omnes possessiones et alia bona extrinseca* predicte *cantarie* seu collegii *supervideat quod bene et utiliter custodiantur et ad commodum* eiusdem *cantarie* seu collegii *convertantur. Et super hoc informet prepositum et confratres suos* predictos *quociens viderit expedire et prout* melius *fuerit faciendum.*

(20) *Vacante vero prepositura predicta per mortem cessionem aut alio quovis modo*

---

¹ *Sic*: for *celerem.*

volumus *et ordinamus quod omnes fructus redditus et proventus ad prefatam cantariam* seu collegium *durante vacacione illa qualitercumque provenientes vel spectantes in usus* eiusdem *cantarie* seu collegii *et non in alios usus integre convertantur. Et legitima administracio omnium bonorum dicte cantarie* seu collegii *durante huiusmodi vacacione ad dictum custodem collegii integraliter pertineat prout ad dictum prepositum pertineret si ipsa prepositura nequaquam vacaret.* Idemque *custos de receptis et expensis per* ipsum factis *tempore vacacionis* predicte prepositure coram preposito tunc futuro et ceteris fratribus capellanis iuratis vel maiori parte eorundem infra mensem a tempore actualis exercicii administracionis eidem preposito competentis prout superius est expressum *compotum seu racionem plene reddat iuramento corporali prius prestito ab eodem de fideli compoto inde reddendo.* Et nichilominus durante vacacione prepositure predicte de omnibus et singulis officium suum contingentibus informet collegium predictum quociens super hoc ab eodem fuerit debite requisitus.

(21) Et ne pretextu ignorancie presencium ordinacionum nostrarum excusacio forsan aliquando allegetur vel fingatur volumus et ordinamus quod eedem ordinaciones nostre plene et plane distincte et intelligibiliter in singulis quarteriis cuiuslibet anni saltim semel legantur publice in communi et quod ad lecturam earundem singuli de collegio tunc presentes sedulum auditum prebeant pariter et attentum.

(22) Ordinamus insuper quod prepositus qui pro tempore fuerit presens alioquin custos collegii supradictus quociens necesse seu expediens visum fuerit omnes confratres convocet in loco capitulari consueto et venientes contra dictas ordinaciones vel aliquas earundem seu alias minus bene se habentes corripiat corrigat et puniat canonice secundum demerita et qualitatem excessus eorundem.

(23) Presentes siquidem ordinaciones nostro nomine et nostra auctoritate ut premittitur conceptas et scriptas necnon precepta et monita atque exhortaciones pro eisdem ordinacionibus inviolabiliter observandis a tempore publicacionis earundem ordinacionum volumus et decernimus habere plenum effectum suum. Quantum vero ad prefeccionem prepositi et assumpcionem fratrum capellanorum cantarie seu collegii predictorum qui nunc sunt nichil penitus innovamus set eos volumus in solito statu permanere hoc salvo quod dictas ordinaciones nostras precepta et monita nostra ad eosdem et eorum quemlibet referri volumus quatenus in eis amplius est vel aliter quam in prius [*sic*] ordinacionibus predicti fundatoris quoad agenda et exercenda per eos et eorum quemlibet in futurum. Et si dante domino excrescentibus facultatibus cantarie seu collegii predictorum multiplicari contigerit dictorum numerum sacerdotum volumus et ordinamus quod singuli sacerdotes numero excedentes sub ordinacionibus presentibus preceptis et exhortacionibus nostris sicut et sacerdotes presentes effectualiter sint complexi.

In quorum omnium testimonium et perpetuam memoriam sigillum nostrum fecimus hiis apponi. Data apud Wappenham vi non. Marcii anno domini millesimo ccc$^{mo}$ quadragesimo tercio et consecracionis nostre secundo.

# APPENDIX VI
# WILLIAM OF CLOWN, ABBOT OF LEICESTER

Knighton, *Chron.* (Rolls Ser.), ii. 125–7:

Xi° kalendarum Februarii Willelmus de Clowne abbas mortuus est qui monasterium b. M. de pratis Leycestrie luculenter circiter per xxxiii annos cum laude virtutum et incremento temporalium bonorum tramite inviolabili gubernavit. Hic quante pietatis et patientie quanteque discretionis et moderaminis erga subditos suos suoque auxilio et consilio indigentes seu eius subsidium in causa verisimili petentes lingua tabescit evolvere mens hebet advertere manus pigrescit scribendo memorie commendare voluntas tepescit excogitare timens relationis veritatem apud audientium aures sub adulationis obumbrasse velamine me forte posse. Hic pacis et tranquillitatis amator erat hic discordiarum et injuriarum in patria sua et ubique reformator fuit quas suis temporibus ubique motas pro suo posse pro labore vel expensis non omittens reformare et pacificare totis viribus elaborare stud·iit sanguinis semper abhorrens et pertimescens effusionem. Hic bonorum operum sector incessabilis subditis et minoribus mitis et affabilis majoribus et magnatibus regni inedicibiliter amabilis vultus eius et presentia divitibus et pauperibus omnibus inenarrabiliter desiderabilis. Hic pie memorie piissimus abbas in evidentiam et signum quod totus dei servus fuerit et pacis atque quietis amator pacis tempore et hora quietis scilicet media nocte diei dominice inter brachia et manus confratrum suorum eius decessum plangentium et animam eius deo commendantium ab hac luce migravit ad dominum qui ut verisimile erat in omnibus operibus eius dilexit eum. Quid plura? In temporibus illius de eiusdem laudabili collegio talem pastorem commendabilem imitante duo postulati sunt in abbates scilicet ad abbathia de Myssyndena et Wellowe juxta Grymmysby et duo in priores scilicet apud Tortyngton et Motsfonde. Duo convolarunt ad anachoriticam vitam scilicet apud Cestriam et Leycestriam in ecclesia sancti Michaelis et duo migraverunt ad beneficia ecclesiastica curata. Eius etiam temporibus due ecclesie sunt appropriate . . . duoque maneria adquisita . . . similiter quoque redditus et possessiones in Hertyshorne [etc.]. Cartam quoque de non veniendo ad parliamentum pro se et successoribus suis de rege adquisivit. Vacationem quoque abbathie post mortem cuiuscunque abbatis eiusdem similiter adquisivit ita ut cum contigerit aliquem abbatem ab hac luce discedere escaetor domini regis solum in abbathiam intrabit et ibi simplicem seysinam pro omnibus possessionibus abbathie capiet nomine regis sicque ibidem moram faciet per unum diem et noctem tantum non tamen intra vel extra in aliquo gravando vel se intromittendo et tunc exibit et si noluerit bene licebit eum inde expellere licet invitum per cartam regis Edwardi III que quidem carta fuit ratificata per regem Ricardum proximo sequentem sic quod nullus escaetor regis in aliquo manerio vel loco dicte abbathie se intromittet nisi solum in abbathia tantum. Isti benigno abbati Willelmo deus tantam gratiam in oculis omnium tam dominorum quam aliorum contulit quod vix erat aliquis qui ei quod petebat negaret. In tantum enim erat affabilis domino regi quod burdando petebat a rege nundinas sibi concedi pro leporariis et aliis canibus cuiuscunque conditionis essent emendis et vendendis. Rex vero credens ipsum nundinas affectuose petisse ei concessit quod petebat abbas vero noluit instare circa negotium. In venatione leporum inter omnes regni dominos famosissimus et nominatissimus habebatur ita ut ipse rex et princeps filius eius Edwardus et plures domini de regno cum eo retenti erant sub annua pensione leporare. Ipse tamen sepius voluit asserere in secretis se non delectasse in huiusmodi frivolis venationibus nisi solum pro obsequiis dominis regni prestandis et affabilitate eorum captanda et gratia in suis negotiis adipiscenda.

## APPENDIX VII

# PROGRAMME OF INQUIRIES AT THE VISITATION OF A MONASTERY

An exhaustive list of the questions asked at visitations of monasteries by a diocesan bishop is given in R. Langley, ff. 20*b*–21*b*, in connexion with his visitation of the cathedral priory of Durham on 23 July 1408. The bishop's summons, issued from Stockton-on-Tees 11 June, was answered by the prior, John Hemyngburgh, on 30 June, in a letter to which was attached a schedule with the names of the monks (ff. 19, 20). Following the prescription of the constitution of Boniface VIII *Debent superioribus*,[1] and having received the formal protest made by John Wessyngton on behalf of the priory, that the prior and convent would rely in the act of visitation upon their rights, liberties, and customs, Langley introduced his assessors, John Henton, a monk of St. Mary's, York, Richard Holme, canon of York and rector of Bishop Wearmouth, Alan Newerk, canon of Lanchester, and Thomas Lyes, notary public. In the certificate of the visitation the notice of the oath of obedience taken by the prior and safeguarded by the bishop's assurance that it would constitute a precedent for the future is followed thus:

Et subsequenter quasdam moniciones nostras proferri et publicari fecimus sub hac forma: Quia plerumque contingit quod episcopi in locis sibi subiectis tam in capite quam in membris habeant visitacionis officium exercere quidam proprie salutis immemores coniuraciones colligaciones et confederaciones faciunt ac tractatus ineunt ne veritas eorum que ipso[2] visitanti et deputantis[3] ab eodem in quibus correccio canonica ipsius episcopi foret utilis necessaria vel honesta aliquatenus reveletur et sic visitacionis officium scienter impediunt et eciam fraudulenter Nos Thomas permissione divina Dunelmensis episcopus deliberacione prehabita omnes coniuratores colligatores et confederatores huiusmodi ac si qui fuerint huiusmodi tractatus monemus primo secundo tercio peremptorie in virtute sancte obediencie et in

---

[1] *Extrav. comm.* i. vii. 1.      [2] *Sic*: for *ipsi*.      [3] *Sic*: for *deputatis*.

periculo animarum suarum cum tempus non paciatur ulterius deliberandi consilium quatinus a talibus coniuracionibus colligacionibus et confederacionibus que in preiudicium seu impedimentum instantis visitacionis nostre vergere vel extendi possent totaliter desistentes omnia et singula que sciunt tam in personis quam in rebus huiusmodi conventus nostri Dunolmensis esse corrigenda vel reformanda nobis aliisve ad hoc deputandis a nobis distincte et aperte revelent nichil omnino occasione coniuracionum colligacionum et confederacionum tractatuumque predictorum aut alias favore odio gracia timore vel amore seu alio quesito colore occultantes quas quidem coniuraciones colligaciones confederaciones et tractatus et iuramenta si que secuta sint super eisdem cassamus annullamus et irritamus ac cassa nulla et irrita pronunciamus. Et quia quandoque evenit quod mutuo queritur inter aliquos quid quesiverit episcopus in articulis visitacionum et que responsio ad interrogata sibi facta fuerit et ex hoc suscitantur odia inter fratres scandala generentur[1] et eciam pericula subsecuntur monemus eciam vos priorem et singulos monachos huius nostre ecclesie Dunolmensis in virtute obediencie qua nobis estis astricti ne clam vel palam dicto vel facto seu quocumque quesito colore hanc visitacionem nostram presumatis aliqualiter impedire.

Quibus monicionibus lectis amotis omnibus de dicto capitulo monachis nos cum dicto fratre Johanne Henton et aliis tribus clericis nostris predictis in capitulo predicto remanentibus ad -visitacionem nostram nobiscum exercendam assumptis ipsam visitacionem in dei nomine actualiter inchoantes fratrem Johannem Hemyngburgh priorem predictum super statu domus sive prioratus prelibati in personis et rebus eiusdem examinavimus et visitavimus diligenter secreto et singillatim ipsum de veritate omnium et singulorum articulorum quorum tenores hic inseruntur solicite inquirentes videlicet:

(1) An aliqua sentencia a priore seu capitulo lata fuerit quominus monachi statum ecclesie personarum vel rerum suo episcopo audeant manifestare vel aliud quicquam attemptatum fuerit quod possit visitacionem nostram liberam impedire.

(2) Item utrum ministretur ecclesie in divinis solenniter et horis congruis ut decet ecclesiam cathedralem secundum statuta et observancias ordinis sancti Benedicti.

(3) Item utrum ornamenta ecclesie vasa utensilia vel aliqua alia necessaria in spiritualibus fuerint subtracta vel alienata. Et si sic per quos et cuius tempore et qualiter ad usus prophanos transferuntur et ad quos et cuius manus devenerunt seu ad aliqua minus utilia in gravamen conventus sunt irracionabiliter instituta et si sic per quos et qualiter.

(4) Item que et quot officia sunt in monasterio et quot monachi quot eciam conversi. Et an statutus numerus et solitus tam in monasterio quam in cellis observetur.

(5) Item an regula sua in communi legatur ut debet et quociens in anno.

(6) Item an bona assignata sacristie vel aliis officiis seu piis usibus monasterii per predecessores nostros et alios devotos integraliter conserventur et

---

[1] Sic: for generantur.

circa fabricam ecclesie et alia secundum assignancium voluntates fideliter expendantur et si subtrahantur vel ad alios usus transferantur et quid quantum per quos et qualiter tam pium opus immutatur.

(7) Item an omnes monachi sint professi regulam et ordinem sancti Benedicti secundum instituta regule et formam composicionis CONVENIT[1] et in cuius manibus.

(8) Item an monachi servaverint et servent veram obedienciam suis superioribus et debitam reverenciam prout debent et qui non.

(9) Item an aliquis fratrum habuerit vel habeat equos canes pecora vel alia bona separata seu iocalia cistas carolas secretas et serratas garcionem vel aliud compendium temporale et qui quid quantum et qualiter.

(10) Item an prior vel supprior permiserit quemquam fratrum aliquid habere proprium. Et si sic quo et quomodo et quantum.

(11) Item an aliqui sint vel fuerint incontinenter viventes vel de incontinencia notati (fo. 21). Et si sic qui et quales et quomodo.

(12) Item an prior secum habeat monachos honestos testes vite sue in camera et alibi ubicumque fuerit vel merito suspectos.

(13) Item an hactenus servatum fuerit et adhuc servetur silencium in claustro choro dormitorio refectorio et ceteris locis ac temporibus ad hoc deputatis. Et qui et quales in hoc deliquerunt vel delinqunt.

(14) Item an sint vel fuerint aliqui obstinati scismatici conspiratores conventiculas illicitas facientes aut rebelles vel suo superiori inobedientes. Et si sic qui et quales.

(15) Item an observent ieiunia per ecclesiam et sanctam suam regulam instituta et qui et quales in hoc deliquerunt et delinqunt.

(16) Item an sint vel fuerint aliqui secularibus negociis preterquam obedienciarii quibus incumbit ex officio se inmiscentes.

(17) Item an aliqui negocientur vel hactenus fuerint negociati in mercimoniis causa lucri. Et si sic qui et in quos usus illud convertitur.

(18 Item an aliqui fratrum in morte vel in vita fuerint proprietarii. Et si sic qui et in quanto et an secundum regulam debite fuerint puniti.

(19) Item an aliqui sint vacabundi et qui.

(20) Item an aliqui in domo commorantes ad cellas vel de cellis ad domum vel alibi declinaverint sine licencia superioris. Et si sic qui et quales et qualiter ob hoc fuerint castigati.

(21) Item an aliqui sint vel fuerint suis superioribus vel fratribus conviciis nequiter blasphemantes et pacem fratrum perturbantes. Et si sic qui et quales et qualiter ob hoc fuerint castigati.

(22) Item an inter fratres sint vel fuerint aliqui conspiratores per fraudulentam et maliciosam machinacionem in suos superiores coniurantes vel eorum fame detrahentes. Et si sic qui et quales et qualiter.

(23) Item an aliqui conspiraverint inter se quod nullus in monachum huius domus recipiatur qui natus fuerit ultra Trentam vel alios limites quoscumque. Et si sic qui et quales.

(24) Item an aliquis frater superior vel inferior suo fratri crimen con-

[1] The composition between Bishop Poore and the prior and convent, see *Script. tres*, App., pp. lxx–lxxii.

spiracionis vel aliud grave crimen falso imposuerit contra statutum capituli generalis. Et si sic quis et cui.

(25) Item an interventu pecunie vel precum seu alia carnali affeccione aliqui in monachos hactenus fuerint recepti.

(26) Item an aliqui fratrum sint excommunicati a iure vel ab homine et si ex post facto non habita absolucione congrua in divinis ministraverint. Et si sic qui et qualiter.

(27) Item an aliqui monachi in suos commonachos manus iniecerint temere violentas et atroces vel in carcere seu in vinculis detinuerint. Si qui huiusmodi manus inici incarcerari vel detineri alios qualitercumque procurarunt. Et si sic qui et in quos et si mors vel mutilacio membri aut alia deformitas inde fuerit subsecuta.

(28) Item an aliqui monachi traxerint aliquas ecclesiasticas personas ad forum seculare seu vetitum examen causas sanguinis vel alias secularia iudicia prosequendo contra clericos vel alios laicos quoscumque. Et si sic qui et quales et contra quos.

(29) Item an presentandi ad vicarias vel alia beneficia per priorem et capitulum iurent solvere pensiones quas dicunt sibi debitas antequam presententur.

(30) Item an aliqua beneficia simoniace sint collata vel aliqui ad ea presentati. Et si sic qui et quales que per quos et quibus.

(31) Item an libertates ecclesie conserventur indempnes in episcopatu vel extra ut in diocesi Eboracensi et alibi in cellis capitulo subiectis et que non et si que violentur. Et si sic per quos et qualiter et cuius tempore.

(32) Item an per priorem regulariter et debite corrigantur excessus et ex caritate.

(33) Item an celebrentur frequenter capitula et quid in eis agatur et discrete fiant ibidem correcciones et que et qualiter.

(34) Item an fratres in capitulo maiores et sanior pars capituli liberas voces habeant in maioribus ecclesie negociis pertractandis.

(35) Item an hospitalitas secundum antiquam consuetudinem in maioribus et minoribus honerifice conserventur[1] et si non in quem[2] sit defectus. Et an elemosina fideliter et congrue colligatur et debite dispensetur.

(36) Item an redditus et alia bona pro cantariis certis elemosinis refeccione poncium et aliis piis operibus supportandis priori et conventui per predecessores nostros et alios christi fideles data et assignata fuerint et sint in huiusmodi usus plenarie et fideliter erogata. Et si non quantum fuerit subtractum et per quod tempus et in cuius defectu.

(37 Item an bona assignata in testamentis predecessorum nostrorum et aliorum devotorum secundum piam ordinacionem decedencium in anniversariis expendantur. Et si non in quem[3] et per quem sit defectus et in quos usus seu quorum convertantur.

(38) Item [an] priorum statuta bona et sancta sint et fuerint servata et que non et per quos.

(39) Item an monachi ponantur ad custodiendum parrochiales ecclesias ut in Jaruwe Wermouth et qualiter ibi preficiuntur et quomodo ecclesie

---

[1] Sic: for honorifice conservetur.    [2] Sic: for quo.    [3] Sic: for quo.

conserventur. Et qua auctoritate monachi ibidem ponuntur in talibus ecclesiis et qualiter ipsi monachi se gesserint et habuerint ibidem.

(40) Item qua dispensacione retinent pluralitatem beneficiorum et qua auctoritate.

(41) Item an penitenciarii ex monachis deputati audiant confessiones libere sine exaccione pecunie et an in absolvendo excedant potestatem sibi limitatam.

(42) Item an aliquis exeat sine licencia vel visitet amicos sine socio seu discurrat per villam mercatum vel agrum vel domos vineas[1] inordinate et an aliqui vescantur in villa vel alibi nisi distet a monasterio secundum quod congruit statutis regularibus.

(43) Item an aliquis habuerit vel habeat arma in dormitorio vel alibi seu ea portaverit aut eis usus fuerit aliter quam decet secundum regularem disciplinam.

(44) Item quot et que vicarie eis sunt (fo. 21b) pensionarie et in quantum et qua auctoritate.

(45) Item an aliqui per commune sigillum se et capitulum obligaverint sub propriis et expressis nominibus in absencia prioris vel sine consensu omnium seu maioris partis de capitulo. Et si sic qui quales quibus et in quantum et sub quibus penis et utrum in Romana curia vel alibi et ubi et ex qua causa.

(46) Item an sub sigillo capituli potestas data fuerit hactenus vel sit alicui vel aliquibus contrahendi mutuum ad dampnum monasterii. Et si sic quibus qualiter et per quos quot littere et ad quam summam. Et si carte albe fuissent consignate sigillo capituli quot qualiter et per quos et quibus tradite.

(47) Item an prior suo tempore bona temporalia bene dispensaverit et in quo statu ipse recepit ecclesiam oneratam vel exoneratam et queratur de modo et de causa et de quantitate et per quem et cuius tempore.

(48) Item an bona monasterii mobilia et immobilia sint pignori obligata. Et si sic que et qualiter quibus et per quantum tempus.

(49) Item an monasterium sit oneratum ere alieno. Et si sic in quantum quibus et ex qua causa per quem et cuius tempore.

(50) Item an alique infeudaciones illicite in preiudicium ecclesie fuerint facte. Et si sic per quos et quibus.

(51) Item si aliqui servi manumittantur qui et per quem. Et an nemora sint extirpata vel excisa in dampnum domus et per quos.

(52) Item quot sunt ministri seculares in domo et quot esse debent.

(53) Item ad quantum se extendunt proventus monasterii per annum communiter.

(54) Item an omnes proventus monasterii et cellarum convertantur in usibus et necessitatibus monachorum et in utilitate monasterii et qui non.

(55) Item an in monasterio et cellis sint in infirmaria competencia. Et si omnes fratres ibidem secundum ordinis exigenciam visitentur et secundum qualitatem sue infirmitatis a celario et aliunde debite procurentur.

(56) Item an omnes obedienciarii monasterii et custodes cellarum et alii

[1] *Sic*: probably for *vicinas*.

administratores de suis officiis [et] administracionibus reddant et reddide-
rint raciones claras et distinctas et quibus quociens qualiter et quando.

(57) Item an prior singulis annis senioribus et sanioribus fratribus de
capitulo illa raciocinia ostenderit et illa examinaverit prout debet.

(58) Item [an] a singulis queratur an aliqua alia in premissis non expressa
in spiritualibus et temporalibus circa personam prioris supprioris precentoris
sacristie[1] celerarii camerarii hostilarii terrarii bursarii elemosinarii infirmarii
coquinarii vel alterius obedienciarii seu inferioris cuiuscumque aut circa
eorum administracionem vel officium noverit vel crediderit reformanda seu
eciam inmutanda. Et si sic que et circa quas seu circa personas quorumcumque fratrum et hoc sub pena prius lata.

(59) Item an quicquam aliud sit corrigendum circa quoscumque alios
monachos vel conversos aut circa statum monasterii personarum seu rerum
eidem pertinencium. Et si sic quid in quibus et circa quos.

(60) Item an aliqui monachi eiusdem monasterii audeant[2] leges vel
phisicam.

(61) Item an due partes conventus ad minus comedant singulis diebus in
refectorio.

(62) Item an aliqui monachi comedant carnes temporibus eis a iure vel
per regulas sui ordinis prohibitis.

(63) Item an infra cepta monasterii excerceantur taberne mercimonia
ludus alearum aut alius quiscumque ludus inhonestus.

(64) Item an nimis iuvenis[3] et minus provecti ponantur in officiis absque
consensu maioris [partis] de capitulo.

(65) Item an claves claustri bene custodiantur in nocte et in cuius custodia
remanent.

(66) Item an alienaciones rerum inmobilium aut mobilium vel corrodio-
rum alieve alienaciones bonorum temporales vel perpetue seu manumissiones
servorum huius ecclesie facta sint aut fuerint sine consensu et auctoritate
nostra et predecessorum nostrorum seu alias absque debita iuris forma. Et
si sic per quem vel quos quociens et quomodo.

Quo quidem priore examinato et ipsius dictis de precepto nostro in
scriptis redactis fratres Robertum Rypon suppriorem Thomam Lythe
tercium priorem et ceteros eiusdem monasterii monachos in dignitatibus et
officiis constitutos et omnes alios de dicto conventu monachos claustrales
tunc in dicto monasterio existentes secreto et singillatim examinavimus et
per predictos fratrem Johannem Henton et ceteros clericos nostros examinari
fecimus ac eciam visitavimus super articulis supradictis et aliis de quibus
nobis et ipsis clericis nostris videlicet prefatos monachos fore requirendos et
examinandos et eorum dicta in scriptis redigi fecimus per nostros clericos
memoratos monachis predictis omnibus et singulis tunc ibidem existentibus
et dictam nostram visitacionem subeuntibus humiliter et devote.

[1] *Sic*: for *sacriste*.     [2] *Sic*: for *audiant*.     [3] *Sic*: for *iuvenes*.

# SUPPLEMENTARY NOTES

*p.* 13, *note* 2. *Add:* It should be noted, however, that this exchange included, as appears from other sources, the prebend of Brampton in Lincoln, taxed at £35. 6s. 8d., so that Langham actually gained by it.

*p.* 169. Of the canons of Leicester mentioned in this passage as preferred to the headship of religious houses three can be identified, viz. William Bradele, abbot of Missenden 1348–56, John Thorpe, abbot of Wellow 1374–1410, and Ralph Thurleston, prior of Mottisfont 1352–6. The identity of the prior of the small house of Tortington in Sussex is uncertain.

*p.* 205. In connexion with the employment of suffragans for ordinations, the evidence of Wolsey's register at York may be recorded as follows:

1514, 22 Dec., to 1515/16, 22 Mar.: 10 ordinations by John [Hatton], bishop of Negropont, of which in the Lady Chapel of York Minster, 2; in Holy Trinity priory, 2; in the Austin Friars, 3; in the Grey Friars, 2; in the Black Friars, 1.

1516, 17 May: 1 ordination by John 'Ariensis', in the Black Friars.

1516, 20 Sept., to 1523, 4 Apr.: 41 ordinations by Richard [Wilson], bishop of Negropont, of which in the Lady Chapel, 9; in Holy Trinity, 4; in the Austin Friars, 7; in the Grey Friars, 8; in the Black Friars, 7; in the White Friars, 5; in Bishopthorpe church, 1.

1523, 30 May, to 1524, 21 May: 6 ordinations by the same Richard, now bishop of Meath, of which in the Lady Chapel, Holy Trinity, and the four Friars' churches, 1 each. He also held an ordination in the Austin Friars, 1525, 23 Dec.

1524, 24 Sept., to 1528, 11 Apr.: 19 ordinations by Matthew [Makarell], bishop of Chalcedon, of which in the Lady Chapel, 4; in Holy Trinity, 4; in the Austin Friars, 2; in the Grey Friars, 2; in the Black Friars, 3; in the White Friars, 4.

No further ordinations remain on record, and it is probable that the names were never copied into the register.

With these may be compared the complete list from R. Oldham at Exeter. 71 ordinations are on record between 1504/5, 15 Feb., and 1518, 18 Sept., of which 17 were held by the bishop in person, all between 1505, 20 Sept., and 1508/9, 3 Mar.: viz. in the Cathedral, 4, and in the Lady Chapel, 2; in the Palace chapel, 5; at

Bishop's Clyst, 3; and at Bodmin, Crediton, and Paignton, 1 each. In 1504/5, 15 Feb. and 22 Mar., ordinations in the Cathedral were held by Thomas [Cornish], bishop of Tenos. In 1506, 6 Apr., the bishop of Sebaste (name unknown) ordained at St. German's priory. Ordinations by Thomas [Chard], bishop of Solubria, begin with one in 1508, 23 Sept., in the Palace chapel. From 1508/9, 24 Mar., to 1518, 3 Apr., there is an unbroken series of 48 by the same prelate, of which only one (1517/18, 27 Feb.) was at the high altar of the Cathedral. Of the rest 36 were held in the Lady Chapel, described as in the Cathedral, but from 1510 to 1514 as *infra cimiterium*, 4 in the Palace chapel; 2 in the Black Friars; 2 at Ottery St. Mary; and at Cullompton, Glasney (Penryn), and Paignton, 1 each. The last two ordinations of the episcopate (1518, 29 May and 18 Sept.) were held by Thomas [Vivian], bishop of Megara, 1 in the Cathedral and the other in the Lady Chapel.

# INDEX

Abbot's Ripton, Rypton Abbatis, Hants, 241; rector, *see* My, Pulter, Waren.
Abergwili, Carmarthen, collegiate church, 80–1, 155.
Acaster Malbis, Yorks. W.R., church, 121.
Acciajuoli, Angelo, cardinal, dean of Salisbury, 12.
Achonry, co. Sligo, bishop of, *see* Blakedon, Richard.
Acton, Richard and Olive, 238–9.
Adbrighton Hussey, Salop, 152.
Adderbury, Oxon., church, 129.
Adz, William, vicar of Godmanchester, 237.
Ainsty, Yorks. W.R., rural deanery, 120; dean, *see* Paulinus.
Akeld, Northumb., chapel, 133; Robert of, 133.
Akeley, Leices., rural deanery, 124.
Alan, dean of Burhscyr, 66.
Albemarle, earl of, *see* Fors.
Alberbury, Salop, alien priory, 184.
Albury, Aldebury, Herts., 235; rector, *see* Hevy.
Alcock, John, bishop of Rochester, Worcester, and Ely, 148, 156.
Alcok, Robert, 230; William, 229.
Aldbrough, Yorks. E.R., church, 117.
Alexander VI, pope, 26.
Alexander, bishop of Lincoln, 85.
Alford, Thomas, rector of Cublington, 210.
Algarkirk, Lincs., chantry, 136.
Alice, serving maid, 241.
Alien priories, 182–5.
Allerton Mauleverer, Yorks. W.R., alien priory, 184.
Allertonshire, Yorks. N.R., 3, 116.
Alnwick, Northumberland, abbot and convent, 114; castle, 154.
— Alnewyk, William, bishop of Norwich and Lincoln, 5, 41, 43, 45, 55, 57, 70, 72, 91, 93–8, 121, 137, 167, 177–9, 205–6; court-book, 46, 206–46.
— — prebendary of·Buckden, 238, 243.
Amice, Michael, 216.
Ampleforth, Yorks. N.R., prebend (York), 88.
Ampthill, Beds., 238.
Andover, Hants, alien priory, 184 n.
Andrew, Richard, dean of York, 24, 89, 156.
Andwell, Hants, alien priory, 184.
Ankerwyke priory, Bucks., 172.

Annaghdown, co. Mayo, bishop of, 49; *and see* John.
Annandale, dean of, 66.
Annuities, 174–5.
Antwerp, 253.
Apostasy of religious, 245.
Appilton, William, vicar of Huntington, 122.
Appleby, John, canon of Lincoln and Southwell, canon and dean of St. Paul's, 76.
Archdeacons, 5, 57–63, 70; monastic, 68; officials of, 69, 70.
Archer, William, 235.
Arches, dean and court of, 52, 68.
*Archidiaconus major*, 58.
Archpriest, 67; *and see* Dean, rural.
Ariensis episcopus, *see* John.
Arksey, Yorks. W.R., church, 115.
Arras, Congress of, 21.
Arundel, John, bishop of Chichester, 25; Sir John, 177; Thomas, bishop of Ely, archbishop of York and Canterbury, 5, 6, 14, 15, 38, 42.
Ascalon, bishop of, *see* Ralph.
Ashtaroth, 167.
Aske, Joan, 212.
Aslacby, Aslakby, William, rector of Sibthorpe, 251, 255.
Aslacton, John, 263.
Aslockton, Aslacton, Notts., 248, 263.
Aslok, William, 212.
Aspeden, Herts., 235; Kirkhouse at, 235; rector, *see* Bill.
Assheburn, Robert, dean of Chester-le-Street, vicar of St. Oswald's, Durham, 108.
Assheby, John, 52.
Assheton, Richard, abbot of Peterborough, 46.
Aston, Herts., vicar, 218 n, 236 n.
Aston Abbots, Bucks., vicar, *see* Watton.
Asty, Thomas, canon of Leicester Abbey, 171–2.
Aswardhurn, Lafford, Lincs., rural deanery of, 213, 231.
Athelney, Som., abbey, 74.
Atwater, William, bishop of Lincoln, 178.
Auckland, co. Durham, St. Andrew, collegiate church, 80; dean of, *see* Lyes.
Audley, Edmund, bishop of Rochester, Hereford, and Salisbury, 35–6, 89; lady, 172.

Prebends' bridge, 77; St. Oswald's, vicars, *see* Assheburn, Bosum.

Dycolon, Richard, 243.

Dykeham, Richard, 218–19.

Dylew, John, commissary-general dio. Heref., 52.

Eagle, Egle, Lincs., 214.

Easby, St. Agatha's abbey, abbey and convent, 111.

Easington, Yorks. E.R., 102.

East Riding, archdeaconry, 59, 64; archdeacon, *see* Magnus, Poteman, Skirlaw; vice-archdeacon, 65, 66; peculiar of archdeacon, 60; rural deaneries, 65.

Eastnor, Heref., rector, *see* Richard.

Easton, prior and convent, 143.

Ecclesfield, Eclesfeld, Yorks. W.R., decanus, *see* Robert; alien priory, 55, 184; vicarage, 55.

Eden river, 154.

Edgar the Peaceful, king, 81, 86.

Edington, Wilts., rector and convent, 42; William, rector of Cottingham, bishop of Winchester, 17, 105.

Edmund of Langley, duke of York, 150; Richard, 212.

Edous, Richard or Robert, rector of Offord Darcy, 233–4, 236.

Edwalton, Notts., 249; *and see* Cosyn.

Edward the Confessor, king, 82; I, king, 3, 10, 133; II, king, 248, 258, 272; III, king, 13, 81, 82, 84, 150, 163–4, 169, 248, 258, 272, 278, 286; IV, king, 35, 139; VI, king, 134, 137; prince of Wales, 169–70; duke of York, 85.

Edwinstowe, Notts., church, 126–7.

Eggleston, Yorks. N.R., abbot and convent, 111.

Egremont, William, bishop of Dromore, 204.

Elger, Richard, 214–15, 218; Joan, 216, 218.

Elland, Yorks. W.R., chapel, 127.

Ellesmere, Salop, chantry, 140.

Ellys, Anthony, 139.

Elmley Castle, Worces., 148.

Elphin, co. Roscommon, bishop, *see* Foston.

Elsham, Lincs., priory, 179.

Elston, Eyleston, Notts., 248, 263.

Elton, Thomas, 122.

Elveden, Elvedon, John, 207–8, 229.

Elvet, John, archdeacon of Leicester.

Ely, diocese, 40, 58; bishops, *see* Alcock, Arundel, Bourchier, [Fitzhugh], Fordham, Gray, Langham, Louis, Morgan, Morton, [Rudborne], Stanley; monastery, 40; prior and convent, 21.

Epworth, Lincs., Charterhouse, *see* Axholme.

Erghum, Ralph, bishop of Salisbury and Bath and Wells, 14.

Escrick, Yorks., rural deanery, 64.

Essendon, Esyndon, Herts., 227; rector, *see* Kendale.

Est, Robert, chaplain of Baumber, 228.

Ethelfleda, 81.

Eton, Bucks., college, 154–5, 183–4.

Eugenius IV, pope, 19–23, 94.

Everdon, Northants, alien priory, 183; John, 109.

Every, Thomas, 209, 211–12.

Evesham, Worces., abbey, 17; vale, dean of, 68.

Ewelme, Oxon., bedehouse and school, 144, 153.

Exchanges of benefices, 107–9.

*Execrabilis*, papal constitution, 105.

Exemptions, bishops and, 17, 56–7.

Exeter, Devon, 79; diocese, 81, 87; bishops, 87, *and see* Booth, Bronescombe, Fox, Grandisson, King, Lacy, Leofric, Neville, Oldham, Quivil; episcopal registers, 150; cathedral church, 299, 300; prebends, 86; rural deanery of Christianity, 64; Black Friars, 299, 300; castle chapel, 87; palace chapel, 299, 300.

Expectations in cathedral churches, 77.

Eylesbury, *see* Aylesbury.

Eyleston, *see* Elston.

Eynsham, Oxon., abbot, 85.

Eyot, *see* Ayot.

Fabric fund, 130–1.

Fairfield, Fairford, Kent, 245.

Fairford, Glouces., 139.

Falmouth, Cornwall, 81.

Fal river, 153.

*Familia*, episcopal, 58.

Farnacres, co. Durham, chapel, 145.

Farndon, Notts., preb. (Lincoln), 106.

Farney, Richard, 238.

Farnham, Surrey, 33.

Farrer, William, 55, 60.

Felle, William, vicar of Newcastle, 122.

Felter, William, dean of York, 89.

Fenstanton, Hunts., 221.

Fenton, Robert, vicar of Buckden, 237, 242.

Fentongollan, Cornwall, 153.

Fermour, John, 213.

Ferrers of Groby, Henry, 104; William, Lord, and Margaret his daughter, 239.

Field Dalling, Norf., alien priory, 183.

Figheldean, Wilts., 142.

Fill, John, rector of Clothall, 140.

**London** (*cont.*)
chapter, 143; dean, *see* Appleby, Booth, Say; canons, *see* Appleby, Withers; prebends, 107, *and see* Chamberlainwood; minor canons, college, 78; statutes, 97; Blackfriars, 21; Charterhouse, 181, 183; churches, 128; St. John Zachary, rector, *see* Byngham; St. Mary-le-Bow, 52, 244; St. Laurence Pountney, 114, 245; St. Mary, Bishopgate, priory, 243–4; St. Mary Graces, abbey, 163; abbot, *see* Langton; St. Martin-le-Grand, 82–3; archbishop's jurisdiction, 52; bishops' lodgings in, 56; Old Temple, 56, 218–19; registry at, 241; chapel of St. Mary in the Palace, 76.
Long, Robert, 227.
Long Bennington, Lincs., alien priory, 183.
Long Crendon, Crendon Superior, Bucks., 239.
Long Preston, Yorks. W.R., church, 112, 118.
Longland, John, bishop of Lincoln, 178.
Loniciensis episcopus, *see* Nicholas.
Louis of Luxemburg, archbishop of Rouen, bishop of Ely, 22.
Loundres (de), Henry, archbishop of Dublin, 83.
Loveden, Lincs., rural deanery, 219.
Loverd (le), John, of Elston, 263.
Low, John, bishop of Rochester, 35.
Lowe, Thomas, 220.
Lucca, archpriest of, *see* Gigli.
Luddenden, Yorks. W.R., chapel, 127.
Ludford Parva, Longludford, Lincs., 231; rector, *see* Smyth.
Ludgershall, Bucks., rectory, 101, 103; rector, *see* Wycliffe.
Ludlow, Salop, church, 136.
Lumby, Henry, 219.
Lumley, Marmaduke, bishop of Carlisle and Lincoln, 23.
Lusby, Lincs., 221.
Lutterworth, Leices., 103; rectory, 101; rector, *see* Wycliffe.
Lyes, Leys, Thomas, dean of Auckland, 47, 293.
Lyncroft, William, 238.
Lyndwood, William, dean of Arches, bishop of St. David's, 52–3, 68–9, 77, 208.
Lynlee, *see* Lilley.
Lynn, William, bishop of Chichester and Worcester, 15.
Lyre (Eure), abbey, 74, 184.
Lyse (Norway), abbey, 166.
Lythe, Yorks. N.R., church, 115; Thomas, monk of Durham, 298.

McCall, H. B., 131.
McCann, Dom Justin, 161.
Macworth, John, rector of Tredington, dean of Lincoln, archdeacon of Dorset and Norfolk, canon of Wells, 1, 90–9, 103, 159.
Maddison, A. R., canon of Lincoln, 91.
Magnus, Thomas, archdeacon of East Riding, &c., 122, 134, 254.
Maiden Bradley, Wilts., prior and convent, 143.
Maid's Moreton, Bucks., 232, rector, *see* Sandebach.
Maidstone, Kent, college, 158.
Maitland, F. W., 10.
Major pars altaris, prebend (Salisbury), 74.
Makarell, Matthew, abbot of Barlings, bishop of Chalcedon, 204, 299.
Malmesbury, Wilts., abbey, 142.
Malton, Yorks. N.R., priory, 115.
Malyns, John, 210–11, 216–17, 223–4, 226–7, 234, 241–2.
Manchester, Lancs., collegiate church, 158; rector, *see* Warre; Chetham's hospital, 158.
Manfield, Yorks. N.R., church, 111.
Mansel, John, 12.
Manvers, Lord, 131.
Mappleton, Yorks. E.R., church, 55, 60, 65–6.
Marchall, Marshall, John, canon of Lincoln, 94; canon of York, 192; rector of Hamerton, 207.
Margaret of Anjou, queen, 25.
Markby, Lincs., prior, 177; canon, *see* Dryby.
Market Harborough, Leices., 124, 171.
Marlborough, Wilts., prior and convent, 143.
Marmoûtier-lès-Tours (Indre-et-Loire), abbey, 184.
Marsh Gibbon, Merssh, Bucks., rector, *see* Humfrey.
Marshall, *see* Marchall.
Marske, Yorks. N.R., vicar, *see* Whitby.
Marsworth, Masseworth, Bucks., vicar, *see* Coper.
Martin V, pope, 19, 20, 23, 27–9, 33–4.
Martival, Roger, dean of Lincoln, bishop of Salisbury, 76, 125, 148.
Martyn, William, rector of Linwood, 231.
Marwell, Hants, collegiate chapel, 147.
Mascall, Robert, bishop of Hereford, 33, 39, 52.
Masseworth, *see* Marsworth.
Mathewe, *see* Spaldyng.
*Matriculus*, Leicester, 123.
Matthew, bishop of Hebron, 48.

Rudby-in-Cleveland, Yorks. N.R., rector, see Conyers.
Rudestein, decanus de, see Walter.
Rufford, Notts., abbot and convent, 138.
Ruislip, Middlesex, alien priory, 184.
Rushden, Herts., 236.
Rushford (Rushworth), Norf., college, 153.
Rushook, Thomas, bishop of Chichester and Kilmore, 14.
Russell, John, bishop of Rochester and Lincoln, 98.
Ruthall, Thomas, bishop of Durham, 283.
Ruyhall, Edmund, official of Hereford, 52.
Ryedale, Ridale, rural dean, see Helias, Helmsley.
Ryngsted, Thomas, bishop's commissary, 96.
Rypon, Robert, subprior of Durham, 298.
Rypton Abbatis, see Abbot's Ripton.

Sacheverell, Sir Francis, 98.
Sadyngton, William, abbot of Leicester, 170–1.
St. Albans, Herts., abbey, 17, 57, 177; abbot, see Wheathampstead; archdeacon, 68.
St. Allen, Cornwall, church, 147.
St. Andrews, Fife, see of, 14, 15; archbishop, see Betoun.
St. Anselm, archbishop of Canterbury, 41.
St. Asaph, Flints., cathedral church, canon, see Trefnant.
St. Benedict, Rule of, 161, 164; of Aniane, 161.
St. Bernard, 168.
St. Budock, Cornwall, church, 117.
St. Buryan, Cornwall, collegiate church, 82.
St. Chrodegang, bishop of Metz, 185.
St. Crantock, collegiate church, 87.
St. Cross, I.W., alien priory, 184.
St. Cuthbert, 132.
St. David's, Pemb., bishops of, see Bek, Brien, Chichele, Delabere, Gilbert, Gower, Langton, Lyndwood, Nicolls, Patrington, Rudborne, Thoresby; chapter, 80.
St. Dominic, 71.
St. Endellion, Cornwall, collegiate church, 87.
St.-Évroult (Orne), abbey, 184.
St.-Fromond (Manche), abbey, 184.
St.-Georges-de-Boscherville(Seine-Inf.), abbey, 184.
St. German's, Cornwall, priory, 300.

St. Gluvias, Cornwall, church, 117.
St. Hugh, bishop of Lincoln, 41, 181.
St. Ives, Hunts., 171; rural deanery, 236, 241.
St. John of Jerusalem, prior and convent, 250–1, 263.
St. Michael Penkivel, Cornwall, collegiate church, 153.
St. Neots, Hunts., alien priory, 183; rural deanery, 221, 233.
St. Oswald's (Nostell), Yorks. W.R., priory, 74, 116.
St. Peter's, archdeaconry, see York.
St. Probus, Cornwall, church, 87.
St. Richard, bishop of Chichester, 119.
St.-Valéry-sur-Somme, 184.
St.-Wandrille (Seine-Inf.), abbey, 74, 184.
Salisbury, 106; bishops, see Audley, Ayscough, Beauchamp, [Bekynton], Bubwith, Campeggio, Chaundeler, Dean, Erghum, Hallum, Martival, Metford, Neville, Poore, Waltham; archdeacon, see Holes; cathedral church, chapter, 142; dean, see Acciajuoli, Braybroke, Brown, Mountagu, Orsini, Sydenham; canons, see Chitterne, Pittes, Withers; prebends, bishop, 39, 73–4; monastic, 74, and see Bedminster, Bitton, Brixworth, Calne, Grantham, Horton, Major pars altaris, Ogbourne, Potterne, Shipton, Upavon, Writhlington; college of vicars choral, 78; psalter at, 74.
Salisbury Plain, 140.
Salter, H. E., 168.
Salton, Yorks. N.R., prebend (York), 74.
Salzman, L. F., 185.
Sam', Thomas, 208.
Samme, John, 208–11.
Sandale, John, bishop of Winchester, 103.
Sandebach, William, rector of Maid's Moreton, 232.
Sandwell, Staffs., priory, 185.
Sarpotson, Jonson, Taylour, Thomas, 228.
Saumur (Maine-et-Loire), abbey of St.-Florent, 184–5.
Saunder, Sara, 212; Thomas, 212.
Sausemer, William and Maud, 138.
Sausthorpe, Lincs., 228.
Savage, H. E., dean of Lichfield, 85; Maud, see Booth; Thomas, bishop of London, archbishop of York, 46, 194–5, 197.
Sawley, co. Derby, church, 25; preb. (Lichfield), 25.

Smyth, John, rector of Offord Darcy, 236; John, vicar of Portbury, 242; Robert, 263; Robert, rector of Ludford Parva, 231.
Snape, Suff., priory, 185.
Snargate, Kent, 245.
Snell, William, 212.
Sodor and Man, Isles, bishop, see John.
Soltoniensis episcopus, see John.
Solubria, bishop, see Chard.
Somerset, 181; churches of, 128; chantries, 140.
Somersham, Hunts., 236; rector, see Langham.
Sorcery, sortlege, cases of, 220–2.
Sorgues (Vaucluse), 164.
Sotterel, William, 213.
Soulbury, Oxon., rector, see Hall.
Southam, John, archdeacon of Oxford, 47.
Southampton Water, 166.
South Malling, Sussex, dean, 68.
South Newton, Wilts., 142.
South Scarle, Notts., prebend (Lincoln), 106.
South Stoke, Oxon., vicar, see Sperhauke.
Southwell, Notts., church, 73, 114, 139, 203–4, 268, 272; chapter, 4, 78–80, 114, 255–6, 260–1; canon, see Appleby, Haxey; chancellor, 79; chantries, 25; jurisdiction, 73; vicars choral, 145, and see Thurgarton.
Sowerby, Yorks. W.R., 127.
Soyland, Yorks. W.R., 127.
Spalding, Lincs., priory, 177; monk of, see Cosnet, Spaldyng.
Spaldyng, Matthew, Richard, 245.
Sparham, Norf., rural dean, 67–8.
Spenser, Henry, bishop of Norwich, 173.
Sperhauke, John, vicar of South Stoke, 70.
Spilsby, Lincs., 221.
Spofford, Thomas, abbot of St. Mary's, York, bishop of [Rochester] and Hereford, 34–5, 39, 52.
Sponne, William, rector of Towcester, archdeacon of Norfolk, 151.
Stacy, Richard, vicar of Wingrave, 239–40.
Stadhampton, Oxon., church, 116, 121.
Stafford, archdeacon, 81; St. Mary's collegiate church, 81.
Stafford, John, bishop of Bath and Wells, archbishop of Canterbury, 23, 35, 38, 42, 187–8, 204.
Staffordshire, 125.
Stamford, Lincs., St. Michael's, 173.
Stanbury, John, bishop of Bangor and Hereford, 35, 39, 52, 138.

Stanesgate priory, Essex, 185.
Stanley abbey, Wilts., 142; James, bishop of Ely, 148.
Stanmer, John, 219.
Stanwick, Yorks. N.R., prebend (Ripon), 79; vicar, 79.
Staunton, Notts., lord of, 274; and see Fenstanton.
Staynfeld, Thomas, 221.
Steeple Ashton, Wilts., church, 140.
Stephen, 146.
Stevenson, Joseph, 132.
Steventon, Hants, 142.
Stewkley, Stukley, Bucks., vicar, see Clyf.
Stillington, Robert, bishop of Bath and Wells, 205.
Stilton, Hunts., 236.
Stixwould, Lincs., priory, 165.
Stockton-on-Tees, co. Durham, 293.
Stok, William, rector of Cotterstock, 279.
Stoke, Notts., prebend (Lincoln), 106.
Stoke Albany, Northants, rector, see Langton.
Stoke Giffard, Glouces., church, 120.
Stoke-sub-Hamdon, Som., chantry, 148.
Stokworth, Robert, rector of Brant Broughton, 220.
Stoneley, Hunts., priory, canon, see Bedill; cook, see Dixson.
Stow, Lincs., collegiate church, 85.
Stower Provost, Dorset, alien priory, 184.
Stratford, John, bishop of Winchester, archbishop of Canterbury, 32, 208.
Strelley, Robert, 126.
Strickland, William, bishop of Carlisle, 30.
Stridelyngton, Robert, 275.
Stubbs, William, bishop of Chester and Oxford, 49.
Stukeley, Styvecle, Magna, Hunts., vicar, see Skynner.
Sturman, Robert, rector of Berkhampstead St. Peter, 232.
Styles, Mrs., 81.
Subiaco, abbot and convent, 76.
Sublimes, 72.
Sudbury, Suff., archdeaconry, 61.
Suffolk, duke of, 23, 44; earl of, see Pole; county, churches of, 128.
Suffragan bishops, 48, 70, 200–6.
Sugar, Hugh, treasurer of Wells, 156.
Suppression of small religious houses, 184–5.
Surrey, earl of, see Warenne.
Surtees Society, 132.
Sussex, sheriff of, 83.